SAP PRESS Books: Always on hand

Print or e-book, Kindle or iPad, workplace or airplane: Choose where and how to read your SAP PRESS books! You can now get all our titles as e-books, too:

▸ By download and online access
▸ For all popular devices
▸ And, of course, DRM-free

Convinced? Then go to **www.sap-press.com** and get your e-book today.

Getting Started with SAP® BusinessObjects™ Design Studio

 **PRESS**

SAP PRESS is a joint initiative of SAP and Galileo Press. The know-how offered by SAP specialists combined with the expertise of the Galileo Press publishing house offers the reader expert books in the field. SAP PRESS features first-hand information and expert advice, and provides useful skills for professional decision-making.

SAP PRESS offers a variety of books on technical and business-related topics for the SAP user. For further information, please visit our website: *www.sap-press.com*.

John MacGregor
Predictive Analysis with SAP
2014, approx. 500 pp., hardcover
ISBN 978-1-59229-915-7

Christian Ah-Soon, Didier Mazoué, and Pierpaolo Vezzosi
Universe Design with SAP BusinessObjects
2014, approx. 700 pp., hardcover
ISBN 978-1-59229-901-0

Amol Palekar, Bharat Patel, and Shreekant Shiralkar
SAP NetWeaver BW 7.3—Practical Guide (2nd Edition)
2013, 789 pp., hardcover
ISBN 978-1-59229-444-2

Jonathan Haun, Chris Hickman, Don Loden, and Roy Wells
Implementing SAP HANA
2013, 838 pp., hardcover
ISBN 978-1-59229-856-3

Xavier Hacking and Jeroen van der A

Getting Started with
SAP® BusinessObjects™ Design Studio

Galileo Press

Bonn • Boston

Galileo Press is named after the Italian physicist, mathematician, and philosopher Galileo Galilei (1564–1642). He is known as one of the founders of modern science and an advocate of our contemporary, heliocentric worldview. His words *Eppur si muove* (And yet it moves) have become legendary. The Galileo Press logo depicts Jupiter orbited by the four Galilean moons, which were discovered by Galileo in 1610.

Editor Kelly Grace Weaver
Copyeditor Ruth Saavedra
Cover Design Graham Geary
Photo Credit iStockphoto.com/11682470/© pengpeng
Layout Design Vera Brauner
Production Graham Geary
Typesetting SatzPro, Krefeld (Germany)
Printed and bound in the United States of America, on paper from sustainable sources

ISBN 978-1-59229-895-2

© 2014 by Galileo Press Inc., Boston (MA)
1st edition 2014

Library of Congress Cataloging-in-Publication Data
Hacking, Xavier.
Getting started with SAP BusinessObjects design studio / Xavier Hacking and Jeroen van der A. -- 1st edition.
pages cm
ISBN-13: 978-1-59229-895-2 (print)
ISBN-10: 1-59229-895-8 (print)
ISBN-13: 978-1-59229-896-9 (e-book)
ISBN-13: 978-1-59229-897-6 (print and e-book) 1. BusinessObjects. 2. Business intelligence--Data processing.
3. Dashboards (Management information systems) 4. SAP ERP. I. Van der A, Jeroen. II. Title.
HD38.7.H33 2013
658.4'038028553--dc23
2013033422

Contents at a Glance

Dear Reader,

If you think developing a Design Studio application is a challenge, you should try writing a book about developing a Design Studio application. From building the structure, to choosing the components, to making sure all the pieces and parts work together the way they should—a lot goes into both. However, if you're up to the task, you're left with something that people are going to use again and again.

Dear reader, I'm happy to tell you: Xavier Hacking and Jeroen van der A were up to the task. And after months of arduous writing, weeks of detailed editing, and days of follow-up questions from their [okay, I admit it, kind of picky] editor—their work is ready for user testing. Give it a whirl. I think you'll find that these pages have exactly the information you were looking for.

Of course, we at SAP PRESS would be interested to hear whether this book passed your test. What did you think about *Getting Started with SAP BusinessObjects Design Studio*? How could it be improved? As your comments and suggestions are the most useful tools to help us make our books the best they can be, we encourage you to visit our website at *www.sap-press.com* and share your feedback.

Thank you for purchasing a book from SAP PRESS!

Kelly Grace Weaver
Editor, SAP PRESS

Galileo Press
Boston, MA

kelly.weaver@galileo-press.com
www.sap-press.com

Contents

10   Building a DuPont Analysis Application 349

11   Building a Sales Dashboard Application 381

Foreword

Back in April 2012, SAP released a statement of direction on dashboarding that named SAP BusinessObjects Design Studio as a new technology solution for providing rich, professionally authored HTML5 applications and dashboards. The first version of Design Studio was released in November 2012 and allows users to build interactive analytical application and dashboards on top of SAP NetWeaver BW and SAP HANA sources.

As SAP continues to invest heavily in building out functionality in SAP BusinessObjects Design Studio, it's time for developers to add the tool to their skillset. This book is a step-by-step guide that will accomplish exactly this goal—it teaches how to build Design Studio applications via hands-on training. The book is appropriate for a beginner, but also covers more advanced topics. By reading and following along with the steps, you'll finish with an overview of the functionality in Design Studio, as well as some good tips for making your applications both mobile and interactive. In addition, the book covers strategic frequently asked questions (such as the difference between SAP BusinessObjects Design Studio, SAP BusinessObjects Dashboards, and SAP BEx Web Application Designer) and also provides use cases for Design Studio.

Moreover, who better to write this book? I was delighted to hear that Jeroen van der A and Xavier Hacking, who are two of the most passionate and experienced BI consultants I know, were undertaking the task. Both are active bloggers in the BI community, which is how I first got to know them. I still remember, in one of my first days in my new role as director of product marketing in the business intelligence team, being told that I simply must read the "bible"—which was Xavier Hacking's *SAP BusinessObjects Dashboards 4.0 Cookbook*. From there I discovered his blog, *www.hackingsap.com*. In addition to authoring the cookbook, he is also a writer for *SAP BusinessObjects Expert* and part of the Dutch BI Podcast.

I first got to know Jeroen through Twitter and his regular blogs on *sdn.sap.com* and *www.interdobs.nl*, and I first met him at an SAP Insider conference, where we had a lively discussion about the future of dashboards and applications. He had some great experience with Design Studio, being one of the first people to come in early on the beta program and utilize his broad BI experience to pick it up quickly.

So read the book and get started with Design Studio. Don't forget to utilize SCN (*http://scn.sap.com/community/businessobjects-design-studio*) as a resource for any additional questions and to stay abreast of the latest news. If you have ideas that you'd like to share with us at SAP for future releases, you can submit them and vote on others ideas here: *https://ideas.sap.com/ct/s.bix?c={6055F3C4-E8DA-454F-9C49-85D5A5070BCE}*. I'd love to hear about the Design Studio applications you create, so don't hesitate to reach out to me either via Twitter (*@AnitaGibbings*) or SCN.

Anita Gibbings

Director Product Marketing, Business Intelligence at SAP, with global responsibility for SAP BusinessObjects Design Studio

Introduction

SAP BusinessObjects Design Studio (hereafter, Design Studio) was released in November 2012 and has been placed in the SAP business intelligence product portfolio as a primary tool for creating interactive analytical applications for the web and mobile devices. Based on strategy and direction statements from SAP, it is clear that Design Studio will play a central role in the BI portfolio, and we expect that more and more development will take place using Design Studio in the near future.

Given these circumstances, it is time to learn more about this new tool.

Target Group and Prerequisites

This book is intended for anyone who wants to learn more about Design Studio. It can be used by developers who are familiar with dashboard or application development with BEx Web Application Designer or SAP BusinessObjects Dashboards, but readers who are new to these tools will also find the book very helpful. No pre-existing knowledge is required, as the book will explain every aspect of Design Studio in a step-by-step way, building up from easy-to-understand overview chapters to chapters that are dedicated to creating complex applications.

Structure of the Book

As the goal of this book is to help you get started with Design Studio, we begin with a broad overview of the tool. In the first chapters, we introduce you to the product, compare it with other SAP products, and show several use case scenarios.

We follow this by going through every detail of the application. First we walk you step-by-step through the installation procedure. Then we describe the application environment and the general process of building an application. Next we describe every available component and its properties in detail.

Once you have mastered the basics, we go into more depth about how you can enhance an application. We describe how you add interactivity and give you a set of guidelines for creating applications. We then walk you through the creation of two complex applications.

▶ **Chapter 1: Introduction to SAP BusinessObjects Design Studio**
We start the book with a general introduction to Design Studio. We give a high-level overview of what the tool is, what the application developers are able to do and build with the tool, and explain how it is positioned within the range of tools in the SAP BusinessObjects Business Intelligence platform.

▶ **Chapter 2: SAP BusinessObjects Design Studio vs. SAP Business-Objects Dashboards vs. BEx Web Application Designer**
This chapter offers a discussion of how Design Studio is different from SAP BusinessObjects Dashboards and BEx Web Application Designer.

▶ **Chapter 3: Usage Scenarios**
In this chapter, we walk through a variety of examples to show you how applications developed in Design Studio can be used in different business scenarios. Each scenario tells a story of an end user who is using an application designed for his particular role or task. The scenarios show that Design Studio is able to deliver process support in very different situations, varying from real-time operational support to in-depth strategic analysis.

▶ **Chapter 4: Installation and Configuration**
After the broad overview chapters, we focus more on Design Studio itself. In order to get started with Design Studio, we take you through the steps to install and set up Design Studio within your SAP BI environment. We also give an overview of the Design Studio architecture, discuss system requirements, and explain how to gather all the installation material. The chapter ends with your first login with the Design Studio client tool.

▶ **Chapter 5: The Integrated Development Environment**
Once you've installed the Design Studio components and opened the Design Studio client tool for the first time, you will notice a whole lot of elements. This chapter explains the Design Studio integrated development environment, including the menus, toolbar, the Layout Editor,

and the the several views for its components. After reading this chapter, you will be ready to dive into building applications.

▶ **Chapter 6: The Application Design Process**

This chapter introduces you to the general process of building a Design Studio application. It serves as a tutorial to guide you through the steps in creating a simple Design Studio application, and serves as a basis for the more detailed chapters that follow.

▶ **Chapter 7: Components and Properties**

In this chapter, we look at all the components and properties of Design Studio. Components are the building blocks of Design Studio, and an essential part of developing effective applications.

▶ **Chapter 8: Scripting for Interactivity**

In this chapter, we take it to the next level and introduce you to the scripting language you use to create advanced interactive applications in Design Studio. We take a close look at the script language, and show examples of how to use these scripts in your applications.

▶ **Chapter 9: Design Guidelines and Visualization Methods**

Before diving into the development of complex applications, we devote a chapter to the importance of the user experience. In this chapter, we provide some general principles that will help you build applications that have a greater chance of actually being used by the user base. We also describe each Design Studio visualization method, and give tips for when these methods may or may not be appropriate.

▶ **Chapter 10: Building a DuPont Analysis Application**

In this chapter, we use the techniques we showed in the previous chapters to build a more advanced application with Design Studio: a DuPont analysis model. A DuPont analysis is an in-depth look at the return on equity of a company.

▶ **Chapter 11: Building a Sales Dashboard Application**

In this chapter, we show a sales dashboard application that reports on worldwide sales. In this worldwide sales scenario, we track the sales data of seven global companies and their local markets.

▶ **Chapter 12: Outlook for SAP BusinessObjects Design Studio**

In this last chapter of the book, we give you a preview of what you can expect from the future of Design Studio.

Once you are through Chapter 12, you will have a firm grasp of what Design Studio is capable of. You'll know how to install it, how to use it to build interactive applications, and you will have gotten some real-world experience with the tool. Finally, you will also be aware of where Design Studio is headed in the near future.

Downloads

In addition to the content in the book itself, we also offer some helpful downloads. You can use these files to review the applications that we build in the book, or use them to skip parts of the step-by-step tutorials we provide in the book. In the files, you'll find both full applications and CSS files. For the applications, you'll find:

▶ **Calculator application**
This is an application example that we give in Chapter 8. Use this to try the calculator and understand how it has been built. You do not need any data source connections.

▶ **DuPont analysis application**
This is the application we build in Chapter 10. To be able to use the general ledger input, you have to define your own data source connections.

▶ **Sales dashboard application**
This is the application we build in Chapter 11. Again, keep in mind that you have to rebuild the data source connections for your own system.

In addition to the full applications, we also offer bare bone versions of the above. That way you don't have to follow the steps to build the layout, but can move forward to the part where the interactivity is added to the application.

Finally, we also provide CSS files that you can use for the applications. Downloading these and adding them to the applications will save you some time, because you won't have to manually type all the CSS code we give in the examples.

Acknowledgments

Writing this book on SAP BusinessObjects Design Studio has been quite the journey. As Design Studio is a brand new tool, the past 12 months have not only been about writing the book, but maybe even more about figuring out how the tool actually works and what its capabilities are.

First, I want to thank co-author Jeroen van der A for joining me in this adventure. I still remember how it took Jeroen not even a second before saying "Yeah, sure," when I asked him about writing this book as a co-author. Thanks for your unlimited enthusiasm, all those creative ideas, and your dedication. I also want to thank Kelly Weaver from SAP PRESS for the great discussions on the content and the very pleasant teamwork during this project.

Being able to write a book such as this also requires an environment that offers support and the necessary resources. A special word of thanks to Rob Huisman and Leon Huijsmans of Interdobs for doing absolutely everything possible to help us succeed in this project. René van Es also earns a mention here for helping me with the backend platform installation and configuration of Design Studio. Of course, the SAP BI community on Twitter and the SAP Community Network shouldn't be forgotten. They come up with new ideas and solutions on a daily basis (so join us!).

Finally, I want to thank my girlfriend, Marieke, for her support and patience during all those evenings and weekends I was busy working on this book.

Xavier Hacking

Writing a book is a journey that you cannot take alone, without the help of many others. Over the last months, I have learned a lot about the process of writing a book, and how important it is that people in your environment support you.

I want to thank co-author Xavier Hacking for undertaking this journey with me. Thanks for the dedication you showed in writing and reviewing; I greatly appreciated your determination to get each chapter out with the best quality possible.

I also want to thank my colleagues at Interdobs—especially Rob Huisman and Leon Huijsmans, who did everything they could to support us. We were also very fortunate that we could rely on René van Es and Sjoerd van Leersum; they seemed to be on call fulltime, and every time we needed something, they immediately responded.

Finally, I want to thank my family, Susanne, Michael, and Tobias, who were all very supportive, even when I disappeared every weekend to continue writing the book. I owe Michael and Tobias a special thanks, because it was their idea to build a calculator application. Thanks, guys.

Jeroen van der A

Design Studio is a data visualization tool that allows you to create interactive applications, with content ranging from high-level dashboards to very detailed OLAP analysis that can be run on any device.

1 Introduction to SAP Business-Objects Design Studio

In this chapter we provide a general introduction to Design Studio. We will give a high-level overview of what the tool is, what the application developers are able to do and build with the tool, and how it should be positioned within the ever-growing range of tools in the SAP Business-Objects Business Intelligence (BI) portfolio.

As you will notice, in this chapter and throughout this book, we refer to *applications* as the output from Design Studio. We don't use terms like *reports* or *dashboards*. The reason for using this terminology is that the products or output you can create with Design Studio go far beyond the classic, quite standardized reports you are used to and which make up the majority of the documents in a business intelligence environment. These traditional reports are executed within reporting tools like SAP Crystal Reports or SAP BusinessObjects Web Intelligence. In these tools the report user has to know how to use the particular reporting tool to be able to use the reports.

Applications versus reports or dashboards

With Design Studio you can create our own user experience by completely developing the user interface of your applications yourself. This means that you can keep the application as simple as you want to by including only those interactivity elements (for example, buttons or filters) that you really need in the user interface. In addition, you can adjust the applications exactly to the devices with which the end user is working. An application interface should look different on an iPhone than on a desktop computer browser; for example, the iPhone application may need relatively bigger buttons to tap with your fingers, while the desktop computer browser version can be more detailed since you are using a mouse cursor to navigate. On the other hand, you can add as many features (and as much complexity) as you want to! It's possible to create applications that consist of multiple tabs, pages, and/or layers that in turn are filled with multiple charts, tables, filters, and buttons that can trigger all sorts of interactive functionality. You can even include your own images to create an exact interface.

But, what about dashboards? Yes, all these points are also true for dashboards, especially those created with SAP BusinessObjects Dashboards. But, the dashboards you create with this tool are only good at working with highly aggregated data. If you want to display or even process large amounts of data you will probably run into all kinds of performance problems. Design Studio doesn't have these limitations.

Shifting from reports to applications means that the work of a business intelligence developer is changing. It's moving away from creating reports that run within standard business intelligence tools, and moving towards designing applications with completely independent, and user- and /purpose -specific interfaces. The developer should be well aware of how a user will deal with such an application interface when working with Design Studio.

Without further ado, let's get started. In this first chapter, we'll discuss two main topics: first, we'll explain what Design Studio is (Section 1.1), and, second, we'll talk about how Design Studio relates to the other products in the SAP BusinessObjects BI portfolio (Section 1.2). All the topics that are mentioned in this chapter will be discussed in more detail later in the book.

1.1   What Is Design Studio?

Design Studio is one of the latest applications SAP has released in its BI/analytics portfolio. It provides a complete toolset for SAP Business-Objects BI developers to create analytical applications that run on top of SAP NetWeaver BW and SAP HANA data sources. These applications are fully integrated in the SAP BusinessObjects BI platform and can be rolled out on a corporate-wide scale.

Following SAP's *mobility first* approach, Design Studio applications, which are created in an Eclipse-based application design environment, are fully HTML5-compatible and therefore can be executed on any device, whether it is a personal computer with a browser or a mobile device like the iPad or iPhone (Figure 1.1).

Mobility first

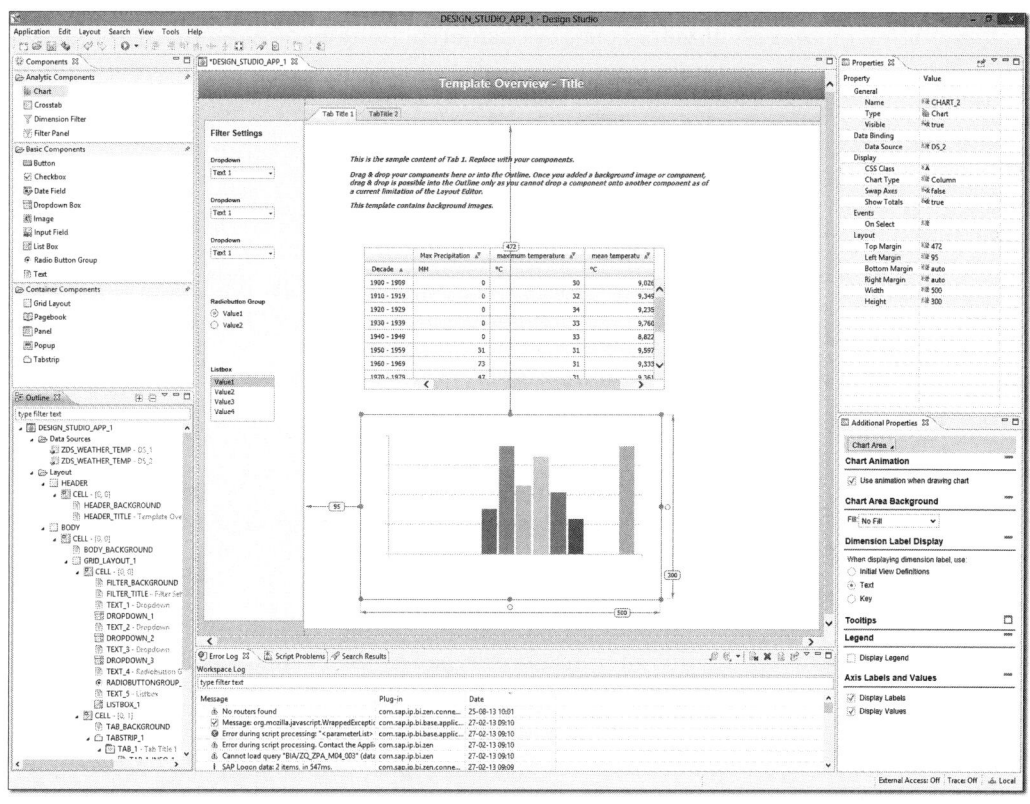

Figure 1.1 Design Studio Overview

In addition to allowing users to design analytic content that is centrally governable and that ranges in complexity from simple templates to feature-heavy applications, Design Studio also enables the building of applications that have built-in iPad support and are immediately compatible with standard web browsers and mobile devices (using HTML5). It also offers native support for SAP HANA and SAP NetWeaver BW.

HTML5

1.1.1 Development Environment

The Design Studio development environment provides a WYSIWYG (*what you see is what you get*) toolset in which you can drag and drop the components that you want to use in an application and edit the layout with pixel-precise detail. This kind of toolset allows you to have a constant understanding of how the application is going to look, without having to execute and test the application in a browser or on a mobile device every time you make a change to it. We'll discuss the Design Studio IDE in more detail in Chapter 5.

1.1.2 Components

A wide set of design components is predelivered with Design Studio. These components are the building blocks of your applications. Design Studio offers analytical components like charts and tables to display and visualize data from data sources. Additionally, a number of filter, text, image, and button components can be used to add interactive features to the application. A set of container components is also available to group other components and to create applications with multiple pages. We'll discuss these components in more detail in Chapter 7.

In addition to these standard components, third-party developers are able to create their own components with the Design Studio SDK.

1.1.3 Data Sources and Platforms

InfoProviders, BEx queries, analytic and calculation views

Design Studio can be used with the SAP BusinessObjects BI platform and with the SAP NetWeaver BW platform. When connected to an SAP NetWeaver BW environment, Design Studio can connect to SAP NetWeaver BW InfoProviders, BEx queries, and BEx query views. Applications can be saved to the SAP NetWeaver BW system and be executed on the SAP NetWeaver BW Java stack.

When connected to an SAP BusinessObjects BI platform, Design Studio can use SAP NetWeaver BW data sources, as well as SAP HANA analytic and calculation views. These are defined on the platform in the OLAP CONNECTIONS screen. As of this writing, Design Studio does not currently support universes; however, this functionality is planned for

2014. Created applications can be saved to the SAP BusinessObjects BI platform and executed from there.

Local Scenarios

Design Studio can also be used locally, without a connection to a platform. Applications can then be run locally on the developer's computer for testing purposes. However, if you want to show data in those locally run apps, you still need a source system (SAP HANA or SAP NetWeaver BW) connected. Design Studio in local mode will use the connections that are defined on your PC (either in SAP Logon for NetWeaver BW or in the ODBC Data Source Administrator for SAP HANA).

Once connected to a data source, the application developer has the option to change and format the output from within Design Studio. We'll discuss data sources in more detail in Chapter 5 and Chapter 6.

1.1.4   Scripting

Adding user interactivity functionality to an application requires some scripting. Whenever the user performs a certain action, a script can be triggered to execute a specific task. For example, if the user clicks a button, a popup screen should appear on the application. With a little script in the button component, this functionality can be realized. As a scripting language, Design Studio uses a subset of JavaScript called the *BI Action Language* (BIAL). A wizard is included to help developers to write these scripts in Design Studio. We'll discuss scripting in more detail in Chapter 8.

1.1.5   CSS

If you want to change the specific look of the components, custom Cascading Style Sheets (CSS) can be used to set, for example, the color and font size of a component. Such a CSS setup can even be used throughout the application for multiple components, where the definition of the CSS class is maintained in a single place. These CSS files can be stored in a central location and be reused by multiple applications. We'll further discuss the usage of CSS in Chapter 8, as well as in Appendix A.

1.1.6 Templates and Themes

Predefined content
for desktops and
iPads

Design Studio comes with a set of predefined templates and themes for desktop, iPhone, and iPad applications; the goal here is to ease and quicken the development process. The *themes* influence the way components—and thus the application—look. For example, in the iPad-specific theme, the components are designed to be pressed by fingers instead of by a computer mouse.

Templates are preformatted Design Studio applications in which a layout is already defined and a number of components are included. These templates can be used as a starting point to develop a custom application. Figure 1.2 shows one of the iPhone templates in Design Studio.

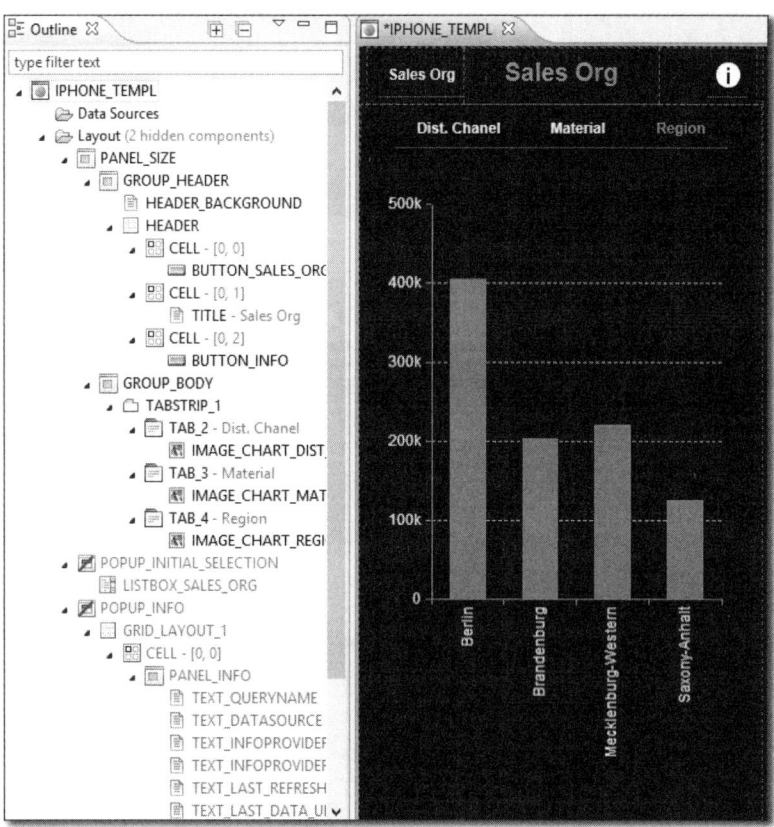

Figure 1.2 Design Studio iPhone Template

1.1.7 Application Execution

As mentioned at the beginning of this section, in line with SAP's *mobility first* strategy, Design Studio applications are fully supported to run on mobile devices. You can run applications in a mobile web browser by entering the URL of the application, or open them within the SAP BusinessObjects Mobile application (Figure 1.3 and Figure 1.4). We'll discuss the SAP BusinessObjects Mobile application in Appendix C.

SAP BusinessObjects Mobile

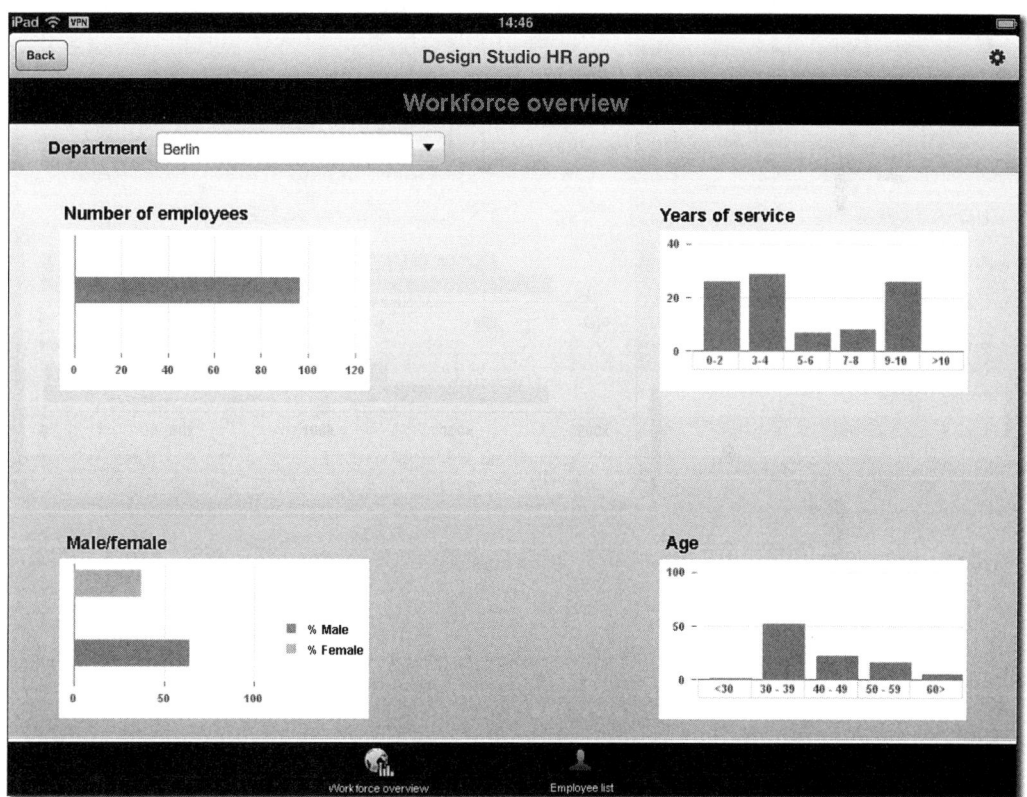

Figure 1.3 Design Studio Application Running in SAP BusinessObjects Mobile: Part 1

Using the Design Studio applications on a desktop computer is, of course, also possible. Applications can be started using the direct URL of the application, or from within the SAP BusinessObjects BI Launch Pad portal environment.

Figure 1.4 Design Studio Application Running in SAP BusinessObjects Mobile: Part 2

1.2 Design Studio and Existing SAP BusinessObjects BI Environments

BEx WAD and BEx
Web Analyzer

Since the acquisition of Business Objects by SAP in 2007, the SAP BI frontend portfolio has changed dramatically. Before the acquisition, there were only a few options in the SAP NetWeaver BW toolset to present data from the SAP NetWeaver BW system to the end user. With BEx Analyzer you could create workbooks in MS Excel, and with BEx Web Analyzer you were able to run BEx queries in a web-based environment. BEx Web Application Designer allowed you to develop interactive web applications based on SAP NetWeaver BW InfoProviders and BEx queries.

The SAP BusinessObjects BI portfolio added a set of new tools and brought in a complete BI enterprise environment. This web-based platform integrates the SAP BusinessObjects BI tools and, with the SAP BusinessObjects BI Launch Pad, offers a single place for end users to create, store, and execute their reports. The new tools included are SAP Crystal Reports, SAP BusinessObjects Web Intelligence, SAP BusinessObjects Dashboards (formerly known as Xcelsius), SAP BusinessObjects Analysis (edition for Microsoft Office and edition for OLAP), and SAP BusinessObjects Explorer.

However, SAP didn't stop with the Business Objects acquisition—it continues to broaden its analytical product suite. Since the introduction of SAP HANA, new tools like SAP Lumira (formerly known as SAP Visual Intelligence) and SAP Predictive Analysis, which are able to use the power of SAP HANA, were presented. And now, last but not least, there is also the product that is the focus of this book: Design Studio.

New SAP BI tools

Design Studio is being positioned as the premium successor to BEx Web Application Designer and BEx Web Analyzer. As you will see in Chapter 2, it also has considerable overlap with SAP BusinessObjects Dashboards.

> **Note**
>
> SAP customers that currently have a license for SAP BusinessObjects Dashboards automatically have a license to use Design Studio as well.

SAP customers using SAP BusinessObjects Dashboards on top of non-SAP data sources should continue to use SAP BusinessObjects Dashboards for their dashboard development, since Design Studio currently only supports SAP NetWeaver BW and SAP HANA data sources. (Again, as we mentioned, the future direction of the tool has it directly supporting universes, a feature that is currently planned for 2014.) For SAP BusinessObjects Dashboards customers concerned about mobility, the more recent versions of the product (version 4.0, Service Pack 05 and higher) even allow dashboards to be used on mobile devices.

SAP BusinessObjects Dashboards

SAP customers that are currently using the BEx Web Application Designer should start thinking about moving to Design Studio as their primary tool for creating BI applications and dashboards.

In this section, we'll take the opportunity to put Design Studio in context with the rest of the SAP BI portfolio. Specifically, we'll briefly discuss the purposes of the different SAP BI tools and then talk about how these tools fulfill different content creation and consumption needs.

1.2.1 SAP BI Tool Categories

The SAP BusinessObjects BI portfolio can be divided into three categories of tools:

- Reporting
- Dashboarding and applications
- Discovery and analysis

Reporting Tools

The purpose of reporting is to share information. This includes distributing information across an organization, giving users the ability to ask and answer questions, and building printable reports.

The reporting tools in the SAP BusinessObjects BI portfolio are SAP BusinessObjects Web Intelligence and SAP Crystal Reports. With these two tools, standard, highly formatted, pixel-perfect reports can be created. End users can refresh and distribute these reports from the SAP BusinessObjects BI Launch Pad platform, or schedule them to do this automatically. Using SAP BusinessObjects Web Intelligence, users can create their own reports based on universes or BEx queries to which they have access.

Whereas SAP Crystal Reports is more focused on delivering predefined, highly formatted reports that are able to present very detailed information,

SAP BusinessObjects Web Intelligence offers a more self-service–like approach and allows the end user to create and edit reports in an ad hoc way. Figure 1.5 shows an example of a highly standardized report created with SAP Crystal Reports. Figure 1.6 shows an example of an SAP BusinessObjects Web Intelligence report.

Employee list

Department:	4200	Alberta					Period: 200301	
Employee		Gender	Country	Age	Years of service	Job		FTE
Mr. Craig Khan	70003	Male	CA	31	4	Journeyperson (CA)	50029148	1
Mr. George Webber	70015	Male	CA	46	5	Superintendent (CA)	50029137	1
Mr. Peter Thompson	70017	Male	CA	43	5	Superintendent (CA)	50029034	1
Mr. Michael Hibbs	70018	Male	CA	55	5	Director (CA)	50029135	1
Mr. Edward Downey	70036	Male	CA	53	4	Advisor (CA)	50025111	1
Mrs Louise O'Dell	70037	Female	CA	43	3	Apprentice (CA)	50029150	1
Mr. Dean Melnyk	70044	Male	CA	45	3	Supervisor (CA)	50029138	1
Mrs Judy Murin	70045	Female	CA	48	3	Assistant (CA)	50029145	1
Mrs Kim McLean	70047	Female	CA	33	3	Journeyperson (CA)	50029148	1
Mr. Earl Burns	70048	Male	CA	31	3	Journeyperson (CA)	50029148	1
M. Claude Carrier	70049	Male	CA	33	3	Journeyperson (CA)	50029148	1
M. George Bourgeois	70050	Male	CA	35	3	Journeyperson (CA)	50029148	1
Mr. Tom Sanders	70051	Male	CA	28	3	Journeyperson (CA)	50029148	1
Mrs Jeannie Maloney	70052	Female	CA	29	3	Journeyperson (CA)	50029148	1
Mr. John Quon	70056	Male	CA	30	3	Journeyperson (CA)	50029148	1
Mr. Alan Williams	70062	Male	CA	33	3	Vice-President (CA)	50029134	1
Mrs Betty Connors	70072	Female	CA	27	3	Advisor (CA)	50029140	1
Mrs Susan Ramsay	70078	Female	CA	31	3	Advisor (CA)	50029140	1
Mr. Bernard Jones	70080	Male	CA	46	2	Niet toegewezen	#	1
Mrs Sharron Russell	70081	Female	CA	32	2	Consultant (CA)	50029139	1
Mrs Connie Tsang	70082	Female	CA	34	2	Consultant (CA)	50029139	1
Mr. John Smith	70089	Male	CA	33	2	Manager (CA)	50029136	1
Mrs Bobbi Keith	70090	Female	CA	30	2	Manager (CA)	50029136	1
Mr. Evan Thomas	70091	Male	CA	31	2	Analyst (CA)	50029141	1
Mrs Diane Lewis	70092	Female	CA	31	2	Supervisor (CA)	50029138	1
Mrs Laurie Dawson	70093	Female	CA	31	2	Analyst (CA)	50029141	1
Mrs Stacey Powell	70099	Female	CA	28	1	Journeyperson (CA)	50029148	1
Mrs Charlene Becker	70101	Female	CA	33	1	Advisor (CA)	50029140	1
Mr. Jerry Harris	70102	Male	CA	35	1	Advisor (CA)	50029140	1
Mr. Jason Clark	70103	Male	CA	32	1	Supervisor (CA)	50029138	1
Mr. Travis Cameron	70119	Male	CA	35	2	Representative (CA)	50029142	1
Mr. Geoff Nagle	70123	Male	CA	30	1	Advisor (CA)	50029140	1
Mr. Dave Roach	70133	Male	CA	27	1	Apprentice (CA)	50029150	1
Mr. Owen Kelly	70181	Male	CA	50	5	Mechanic (CA) (JM)	50012541	1
Mrs Paula Jackson	70182	Female	CA	48	5	Mechanic (CA) (JM)	50012541	1
Mr. David Parsons	70183	Male	CA	43	5	Electrician (CA) (JM)	50012542	1
Mr. Simon Anaviapik	70184	Male	CA	44	5	Electrician (CA) (JM)	50012542	1
Mr. Allan MacDonald	70185	Male	CA	52	5	Welder (CA)	50000723	1
Mr. Simon Ookpik	70186	Male	CA	43	5	Welder (CA)	50000723	1
Mrs Mary Delaney	70187	Female	CA	38	5	Machinist (CA) (JM)	50012543	1
Mr. Glenn Harrison	70200	Male	CA	47	5	Electrician (CA) (JM)	50012542	1
Mrs Tamy Penny	70201	Female	CA	33	5	Electrician (CA) (JM)	50012542	1
Mr. Bob Carson	70202	Male	CA	47	5	Welder (CA)	50000723	1
Mrs Colleen MacDonald	70203	Female	CA	33	4	Mechanic (CA) (JM)	50012541	1
M. Marc Goodwin	70204	Male	CA	32	3	Apprentice (CA)	50012552	1
Mrs Sandra Daku	70205	Female	CA	29	3	Welder (CA)	50000723	1
Mrs Nicole Kidmann	70224	Female	CA	23	1	Clerk	50010817	1
Len Harms MBA	70232	Male	CA	33	0	Director (CA)	50029135	1
Mr. Roger Wheaton	70233	Male	CA	28	0	Journeyperson (CA)	50029148	1
Mrs Jeanette Bradley M	70238	Female	CA	33	0	Manager (CA)	50029136	1
Mary MacLeod	70240	Female	CA	37	0	Manager (CA)	50029136	1
Christa Walsh	70243	Female	CA	43	0	Manager (CA)	50029136	1

Page 1 of 129

Figure 1.5 SAP Crystal Reports Report

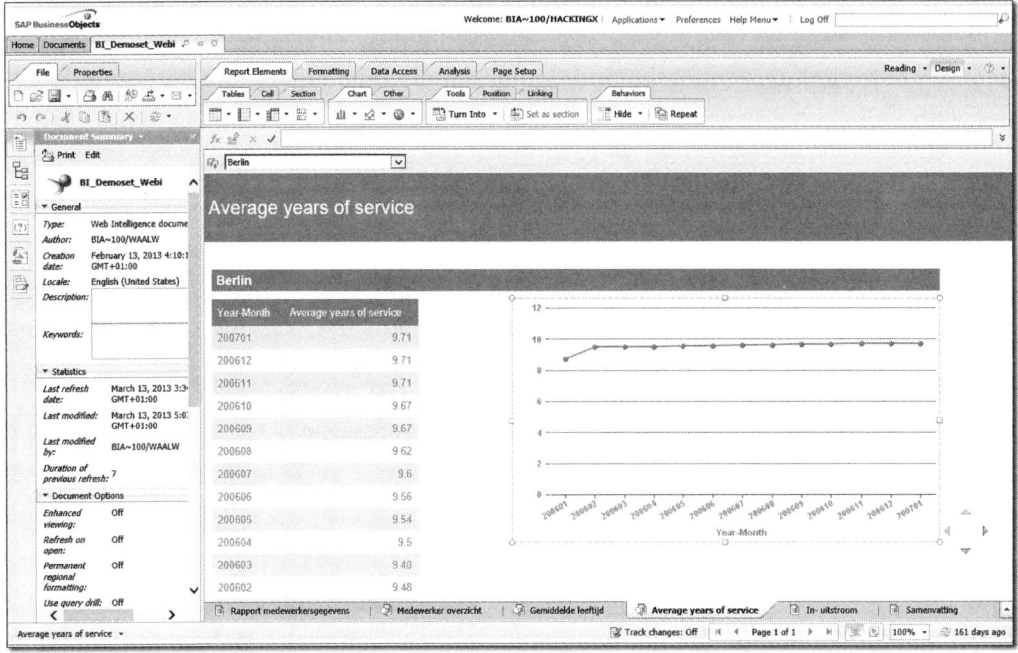

Figure 1.6 SAP BusinessObjects Web Intelligence Report

Dashboarding and Application-Creation Tools

The purpose of dashboarding and applications is to build engaging experiences. This includes delivering the right information to users, tracking key performance indicators (KPIs) and summary data, and building custom experiences that suit users' needs.

The dashboarding and application category includes Design Studio and SAP BusinessObjects Dashboards. With SAP BusinessObjects Dashboards, you can create highly visualized dashboards, showing data with a high level of aggregation. Such a dashboard could, for example, display the company's or department's KPIs. Dashboards created with SAP BusinessObjects Dashboards have a fixed layout and can't be edited by the end user. Just as with Design Studio, the complete interface has to be designed by the dashboard developer. Figure 1.7 shows an example of a dashboard created with SAP BusinessObjects Dashboards. (In Chapter 2, we will discuss SAP BusinessObjects Dashboards in more depth and compare it to the functionality that is available in Design Studio.)

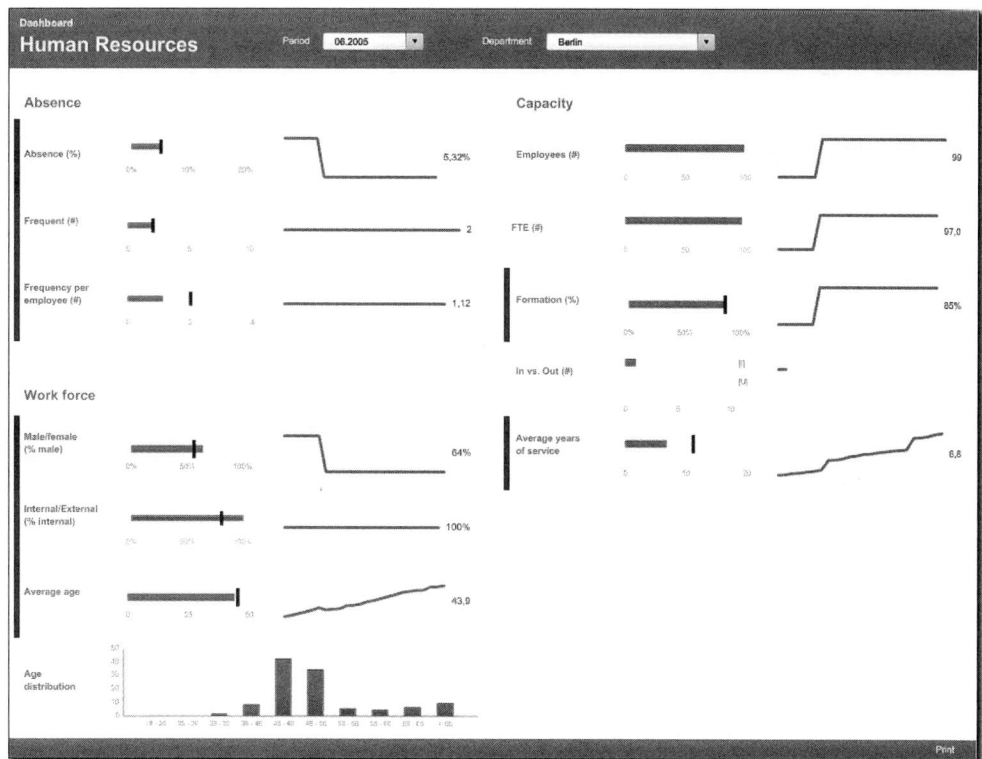

Figure 1.7 SAP BusinessObjects Dashboards Dashboard

Discovery and Analysis

Finally, the purpose of discovery and analysis is to discover, predict, and create. The discovery and analysis category in the SAP BusinessObjects BI portfolio consists of four tools: SAP Lumira, SAP BusinessObjects Explorer, SAP BusinessObjects Analysis (edition for Microsoft Office, edition for OLAP), and SAP Predictive Analysis. These are all tools that give end users the freedom to perform their own analysis. The user starts with a set of data and some questions about that data and uses the tool to find and eventually present the answers.

SAP Lumira (Figure 1.8) is a locally installed tool that can connect to several types of data sources, such as SAP HANA and CSV files. It offers an interface to select, clean, combine, manipulate, and enrich data from multiple data sources and finally visualize it with tables and charts.

35

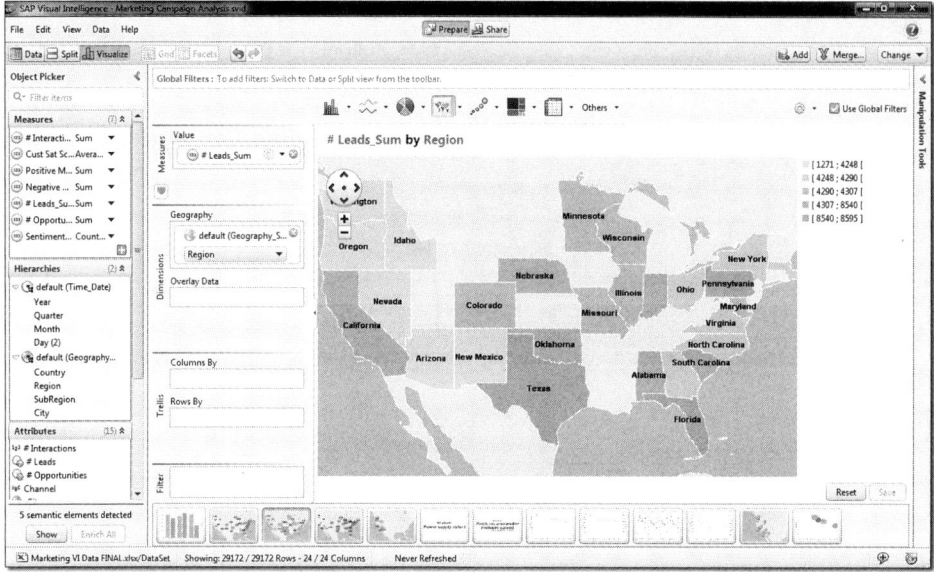

Figure 1.8 SAP Lumira

With SAP BusinessObjects Explorer, you get a very easy-to-use, web-based environment to ask questions about a data set in a Google-like way (Figure 1.9).

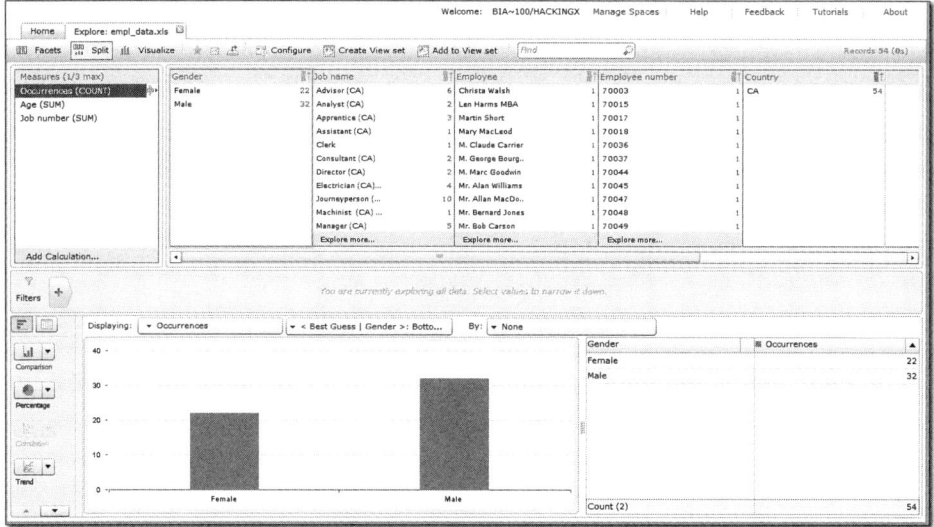

Figure 1.9 SAP BusinessObjects Explorer

SAP BusinessObjects Analysis is the successor to BEx Analyzer and is the tool used to perform OLAP analyses on multidimensional data sources like SAP NetWeaver BW InfoCubes (Figure 1.10). The product is delivered in an MS Office and a web-based variant. The MS Office version integrates this reporting tool in MS Excel and MS PowerPoint; the web-based variant is integrated in the SAP BusinessObjects BI Launch Pad.

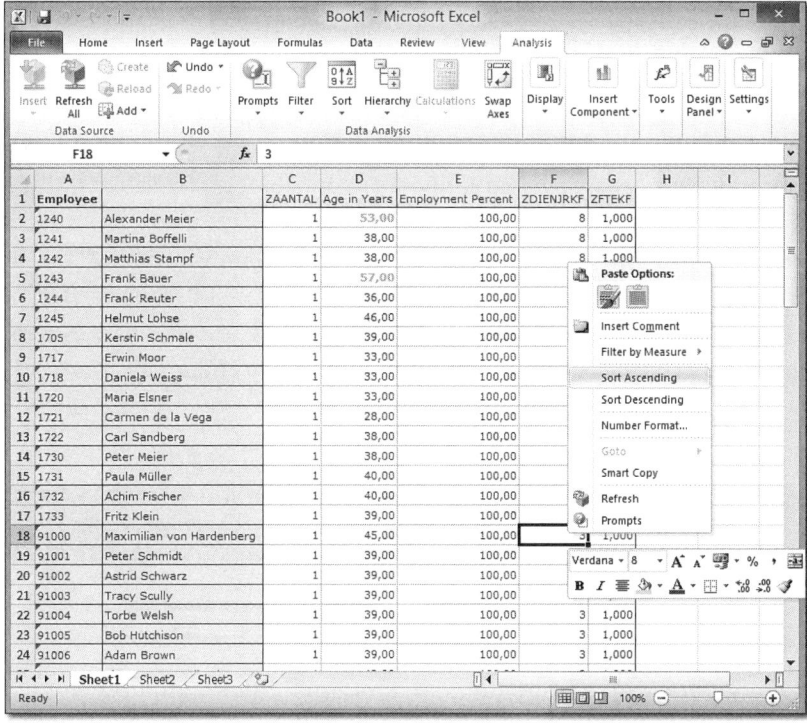

Figure 1.10 SAP BusinessObjects Analysis, Edition for MS Office

1.2.2 Content Creation and Consumption

As you may already have noticed in the previous section, not all tools are used by end users. Table 1.1 shows this clear distinction, where the very fixed reporting outputs (like the SAP Crystal Reports documents, the dashboards from SAP BusinessObjects Dashboards, and the Design Studio applications) are completely created by developers from the IT department. The business users work with the other tools to create their own reports and make custom analyses on their own.

	Reporting	Dashboarding and Applications	Discovery and Analysis
IT	▶ SAP Crystal Reports	▶ Design Studio ▶ Dashboards	▶ Design Studio
Business Users	▶ Web Intelligence	▶ Exploration Views	▶ Analysis ▶ Explorer ▶ SAP Lumira

Table 1.1 Content Creators by Category

Four levels of business users

SAP determines four levels of business users: executive, senior management, business analysis, and individual contributors. In Table 1.2, the products that present more aggregated data in a fixed way are toward the top of the table, and the products that provide more detailed and ad hoc reporting solutions are on the bottom. The broad scope of Design Studio is clearly highlighted here—as you can see, the solution is mentioned for all the user groups in the dashboarding and applications segment, as well as the top two user groups in the discovery and analysis segment.

	Reporting	Dashboarding and Applications	Discovery and Analysis
Executives	None	▶ Design Studio ▶ Dashboards ▶ Exploration Views	▶ Design Studio ▶ Explorer
Senior Management	▶ Web Intelligence	▶ Design Studio ▶ Dashboards ▶ Exploration Views	▶ Design Studio ▶ Explorer ▶ Analysis
Business Analysts	None	▶ Design Studio	▶ Explorer ▶ Analysis ▶ SAP Lumira

Table 1.2 Content Consumption by Category

	Reporting	Dashboarding and Applications	Discovery and Analysis
Individual Contributors	► SAP Crystal Reports ► Web Intelligence	► Design Studio	► Analysis (edition for Microsoft Office)

Table 1.2 Content Consumption by Category (Cont.)

Table 1.3 shows the various options for content consumption environment and the SAP BusinessObjects BI tools. The options are a desktop computer with a local installation of the tool, a web-based version of the report through the SAP BusinessObjects BI Launch Pad, and a mobile device. As you can see, almost all the solutions offer reports that are accessible through mobile devices with SAP BusinessObjects Mobile, which is available for iOS and Android devices.

	Reporting	Dashboarding and Applications	Discovery and Analysis
Desktop	► SAP Crystal Reports ► Web Intelligence	► Dashboards	► Analysis (edition for Microsoft Office) ► SAP Lumira
Web-Based	► SAP Crystal Reports ► Web Intelligence	► Design Studio ► Dashboards ► Exploration Views	► Design Studio ► Explorer ► Analysis (edition for OLAP)
Mobile	► SAP Crystal Reports ► Web Intelligence	► Design Studio ► Dashboards ► Exploration Views	► Design Studio ► Explorer

Table 1.3 Content Consumption Environment by Category

1.3 Summary

In this chapter we gave a high-level introduction to Design Studio. We went through the most important features of the tool, and we discussed its position within the SAP BusinessObjects BI portfolio.

Since Design Studio has such a great overlap with SAP BusinessObjects Dashboards and BEx Web Application Designer, the next chapter is dedicated to comparing these three applications.

Design Studio is not the only option in the SAP BI portfolio to create interactive BI apps. In fact, there are three! It's time to introduce them to you and make some comparisons.

2   SAP BusinessObjects Design Studio vs. SAP BusinessObjects Dashboards vs. BEx Web Application Designer

The number of tools in the SAP BI portfolio increased significantly over the past five years, and, inevitably, some tools contain features that are also included in other tools. Because the objective of SAP Business-Objects Design Studio overlaps with two of SAP's existing products, it is important to identify the differences among the three.

This chapter offers a discussion of how Design Studio is different from SAP BusinessObjects Dashboards and BEx Web Application Designer. If you're already familiar with the basic functionality of SAP Business-Objects Dashboards and BEx Web Application Designer, you'll want to skip down to Section 2.3 for an understanding of how they differ from Design Studio. If you're new to the toolset, or would like a quick refresher, you can read Section 2.1 and Section 2.2 for a quick overview of their functionalities.

2.1   SAP BusinessObjects Dashboards

SAP BusinessObjects Dashboards is SAP's current premier dashboarding solution. Since the acquisition of Business Objects by SAP in 2007, it has been a core part of the SAP BusinessObjects BI portfolio. With SAP BusinessObjects Dashboards, you can create dashboards with great-looking data visualizations and design interactive scenarios without much programming knowledge.

Dashboards are visual displays of information that are able to support the user of the dashboard in making decisions (Figure 2.1).

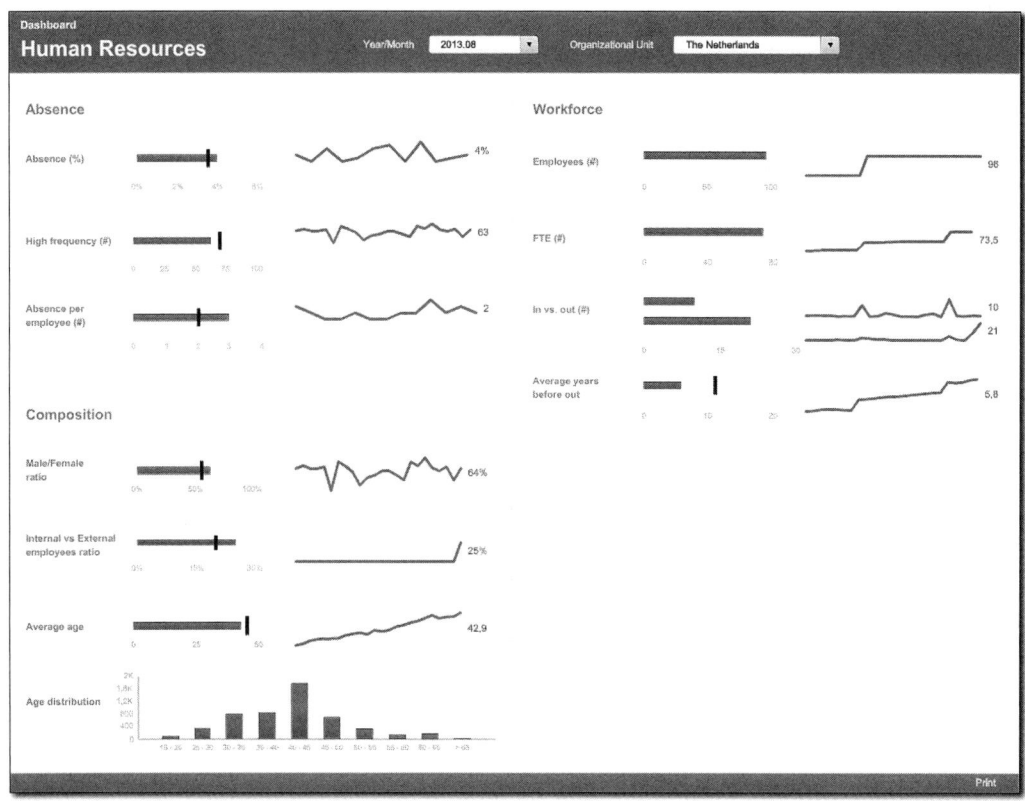

Figure 2.1 Example of a Dashboard Created with SAP BusinessObjects Dashboards

The user should be able to see this information at a glance, without having to perform a lot of manual activities (clicks) before he can find the information he is looking for. Therefore, a dashboard should focus on only those performance indicators that are really relevant for the user to make a certain decision. A dashboard can be used, for example, to provide a sales manager with a high-level overview of the sales performance over time for all the sales regions. He can compare regions with each other, discover the high and low performers, see trends over time, and so on. Such a dashboard could, for example, trigger the sales manager to take action in a specific region if sales went in the wrong direction.

A dashboard shows the course of a dataset over a certain time period in a series of performance indicators. To visualize the data, components like charts, tables, gauges, and maps can be used. Colors can be used to separate data series from each other or highlight a certain result (alerting). Some basic level of drilling down and filtering data can be provided in a dashboard; however, a lot of the information is quite fixed. Other reporting tools are often more suited for highly detailed reporting, data analysis, and data exploration.

Purpose of dashboards

Interactive scenarios—often referred to as *what-if scenarios*—let the user interact with the dashboard by adjusting one or more variables to see how the output changes. A simple example is a dashboard that can calculate the monthly interest payments on a mortgage loan. There are three variables in the formula to calculate the monthly payment: the loan amount, the interest rate, and the repayment period. The dashboard can, for example, consist of three input controls—let's say some sliders—to input the values for these variables. The monthly payment amount can be displayed in a gauge. When the user moves any of the sliders, the payment amount changes too, based on the underlying data model (formula). Increasing the interest rate will also increase the monthly payment amount.

What-if scenarios

In this section, we'll give you a brief overview of SAP BusinessObjects Dashboards by walking you through some of the most important things you should know about the tool. Again, if you're already familiar with the SAP BusinessObjects Dashboards tool, skip on ahead.

2.1.1 Setting Up a Dashboard

Developing a basic dashboard with SAP BusinessObjects Dashboards is pretty straightforward and doesn't require much knowledge or training to get started. It is all about dragging and dropping the components—like charts or maps—in the right place, tweaking the look and feel of the components, and using some Microsoft Excel magic to connect the data to these components. Yes, you read that right: Microsoft Excel. Before SAP changed the product name to SAP BusinessObjects Dashboards, the

Microsoft Excel

tool was called Xcelsius, which—you may notice—sounds a lot like Excel. In fact, SAP BusinessObjects Dashboards was originally developed to turn Excel spreadsheets into interactive dashboards with visualizations that couldn't be provided with standard Excel charts. Even in the current version of SAP BusinessObjects Dashboards, the Excel spreadsheet still has a very important position.

Design environment
Figure 2.2 shows the SAP BusinessObjects Dashboards design environment, including the Excel spreadsheet. Not only can this spreadsheet be used to fill cells with data, but a wide range of Excel formulas are also usable. This means you can make calculations, use if/then statements, and look up values (i.e., with the VLOOKUP formula). These formulas stay active when you run the dashboard. So if a value in a certain spreadsheet cell changes, it will have a direct effect on the outcome of any formula that uses this cell.

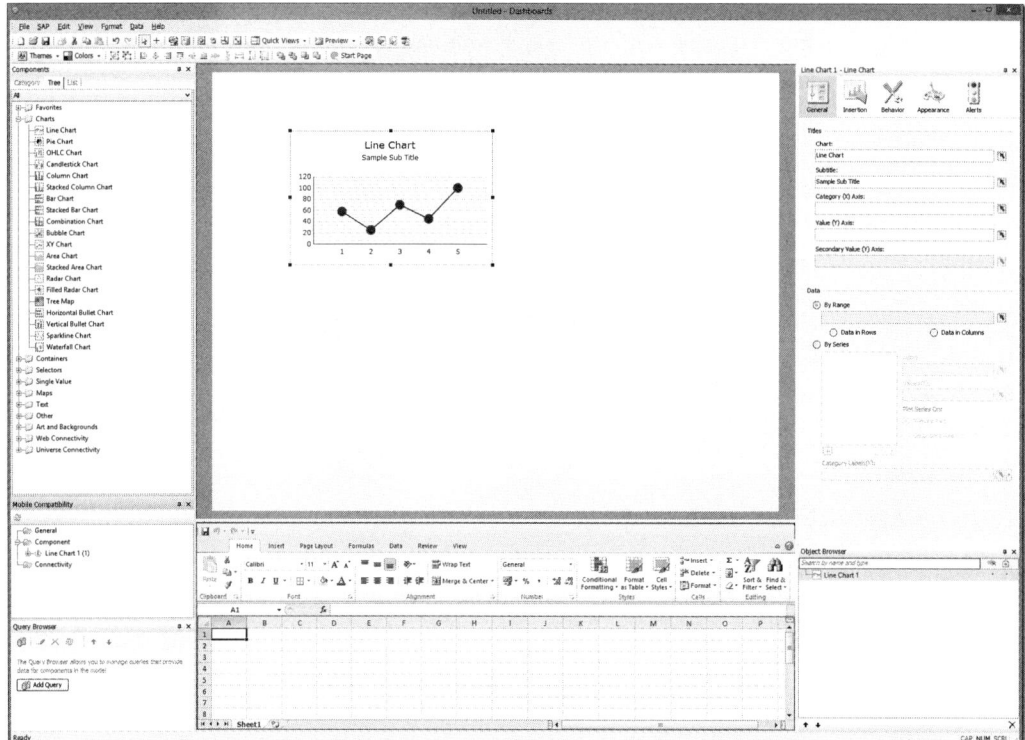

Figure 2.2 The SAP BusinessObjects Dashboards Design Environment

Handy features such as formatting and multiple spreadsheet tabs are also available, just as in the actual Excel software.

The left side of the screen shows a list of all available components. To use a component, you can simply drag it to the canvas in the middle of the screen and use the mouse to adjust the size and the position of the component.

On the right side of the screen are the properties of the selected component. Here the developer can connect the component to the data that is put into the spreadsheet. After executing this *data binding*, the component—in the case of Figure 2.2, a LINE CHART component—will visualize the data set. The trick is that you can change the values of the bound cells to make the dashboard really interactive. In the PROPERTY tabs, there are a legion of settings and tweaks you can use on the component, such as adding labels and titles and setting up the formatting and positioning for these text items. Furthermore, the look and feel of the component in terms of color and size (i.e., thickness of lines and markers) can be completely adjusted. Even alerts can be activated on a certain group of components. With these alerts, the color of a country on a map or a bar in a bar chart can change based on the value it represents; for example, good results could be shown as green, while bad results could be shown in red.

2.1.2 Components

SAP BusinessObjects Dashboards comes with a very large set of standard components. Let's go through them so you get an understanding of the visualization and interactivity possibilities this tool offers.

Charts

The following standard chart types are available. These charts work more or less in the same way and have the same properties overall.

▶ Line chart

▶ Pie chart

▶ Column chart

- Stacked column chart
- Bar chart
- Stacked bar chart
- Area chart
- Stacked area chart
- Combination chart (both lines and columns are possible)

In addition to these charts, a number of more advanced charts are available to choose from. These charts are more unique in their purpose and setup.

- OHLC chart
- Candlestick chart
- Bubble chart
- XY chart
- Radar chart
- Filled radar chart
- Tree map
- Horizontal bullet chart
- Vertical bullet chart
- Sparkline chart
- Waterfall chart

Selectors

Selectors are used for interactivity options: to set filters on data, make selections, push a certain value to a spreadsheet cell, or create menus in the dashboard user interface. The following selector components are available for these purposes:

- Accordion menu
- Checkbox
- Combo box
- Filter
- Fisheye picture menu

- Sliding picture menu
- Icon
- Label-based menu
- List box
- List view
- List builder
- Radio button
- Hierarchical table
- Scorecard
- Ticker
- Toggle button
- Push button
- Spreadsheet table
- Play selector

Single Value

Single value components are used to display or input single values of data. For this purpose, SAP BusinessObjects Dashboards delivers a set of dials, gauges, horizontal and vertical progress bars, and single and dual sliders.

Maps

One of the most interesting categories of components is the maps category. Around 100 maps of countries and continents can be used in a dashboard. Each map is subdivided into regions, and for each region a mouse-over value can be shown. When activating alerts, you can color the regions based on their performance.

Containers, Text, Art, and Background

Container components can contain multiple other components. When you move the container, all components in this container will be moved as well. SAP BusinessObjects Dashboards has three containers: the panel container, which is a panel with a title on top, the tab set container, which has multiple tabs with panels, and the canvas container, which is invisible when the dashboard is running but can be handy during development.

Text labels can be put anywhere in the dashboard. In addition, a number of art components are included to draw lines, rectangles, and circles, as well as create backgrounds. There is also a component to load an image or an SWF file into the dashboard.

Other Components

Besides all the categories of components mentioned above, a set of more specific components is included. Examples are the PRINT button, the URL button, a TREND icon, and a CALENDAR component.

After going through this list of components, it should be clear that SAP BusinessObjects Dashboards offers a very wide range data visualization and interactivity features to tackle most dashboarding challenges.

2.1.3 Data Connectivity

We already talked a bit about the role of the Excel spreadsheet in SAP BusinessObjects Dashboards. But in a business environment, we want a dashboard or report to show fresh or even live data directly loaded from a business system or a data warehouse like SAP NetWeaver BW — and, of course, without having to perform repetitive manual activities every time the dashboard needs updated data. Using Excel to store the data and to upload it into a dashboard therefore is not a workable solution.

Data sources   SAP BusinessObjects Dashboards comes with a number of connectivity options to load data from a data source into the dashboard. In the Data Manager, the following connection types can be set up with data sources:

- ▶ SAP NetWeaver BW connection (BICS): A connection to a BEx query or BEx query view can be made with this connection type.
- ▶ Web Service Query (Query as a Web Service): An SAP Business-Objects universe can be published as a QAAWS, which can be read from this connection type.

▸ Web service connection.

▸ XML data and Excel XML maps.

▸ Live Office connections.

These connections can read values for variables from spreadsheet cells and return the output of the data request to a range of cells in the spreadsheet. From there the data can be further processed and eventually be bound to the components.

In addition to these connectivity options, SAP BusinessObjects Dashboards also supports the creation and usage of SAP BusinessObjects BI 4.0 queries. These queries correspond with the SAP BusinessObjects BI 4.0 queries that can be created in the other SAP BusinessObjects BI tools like SAP BusinessObjects Web Intelligence and SAP Crystal Reports for Enterprise. They also use the same workflow. SAP BusinessObjects UNX universes and SAP NetWeaver BW BEx queries can be used as data sources.

Universes and queries

The big advantage here is that the query results can be bound directly to the components, without having to use the spreadsheet. In the SAP BusinessObjects BI 4.0 query, one or more filters with prompts can be created. With the QUERY PROMPT SELECTOR component, the dashboard user can change the input value for such a prompt.

2.1.4 Publishing

When the dashboard is finished, it should be published so the users can start using it from their own computers. To do this, you have to export the dashboard from the design environment. This export results in an SWF (Flash) file. If the dashboard developer exports the dashboard locally (on his own computer hard drive), the file can also be embedded into a PDF, MS PowerPoint, MS Word or MS Outlook file; an HTML website; or an Adobe Air application. A nonembedded SWF file can be run with a browser that has Adobe Flash Player installed.

Exporting and distributing

Besides exporting locally and distributing the exported file, you can publish the dashboard to the SAP NetWeaver BW environment and the

SAP BusinessObjects BI 4.0 platform. When published to the SAP NetWeaver BW environment, the dashboard becomes an object that can be run from the SAP NetWeaver BW Java portal, in the same way that you can execute BEx queries as web queries. The dashboard can be run from a web URL address. When published to the SAP BusinessObjects BI platform, the dashboard will be available in the BI Launch Pad.

Adobe Flash and HTML5

Adobe Flash has become a huge barrier to running dashboards on mobile platforms and devices like the Apple iPad, since they don't support Flash and there are no signs that they will in the near future. With the release of SAP BusinessObjects BI 4.0 service pack 05, it is now possible to export a dashboard into HTML5 format. This HTML5 dashboard can be run from SAP BusinessObjects Mobile, which is available for Apple iOS and Android. In SAP BusinessObjects Dashboards 4.0 service pack 05, not all components can be exported into the HTML5 format yet; only the SAP BusinessObjects BI 4.0 query connections are supported.

2.1.5   Software Development Kit (SDK)

Add-ons

The SAP BusinessObjects Dashboards Software Development Kit (SDK) provides Adobe Flex developers with the possibility to create components for SAP BusinessObjects Dashboards. These *add-ons* can provide additional functionality to SAP BusinessObjects Dashboards on top of the default set of components and connectivity options.

Google Maps integration

In previous years, a number of interesting add-ons have been developed by a small number of third parties. There are add-ons available that achieve additional connectivity options, for example to load data from CSV files, SAP BusinessObjects Web Intelligence reports, or Salesforce.com accounts. Other add-ons provide more advanced data visualization possibilities, such as adding more specific charts to the list of components, and adding a Google Maps integration component (see Figure 2.3). There is even a specific add-on available with advanced dashboard printing features.

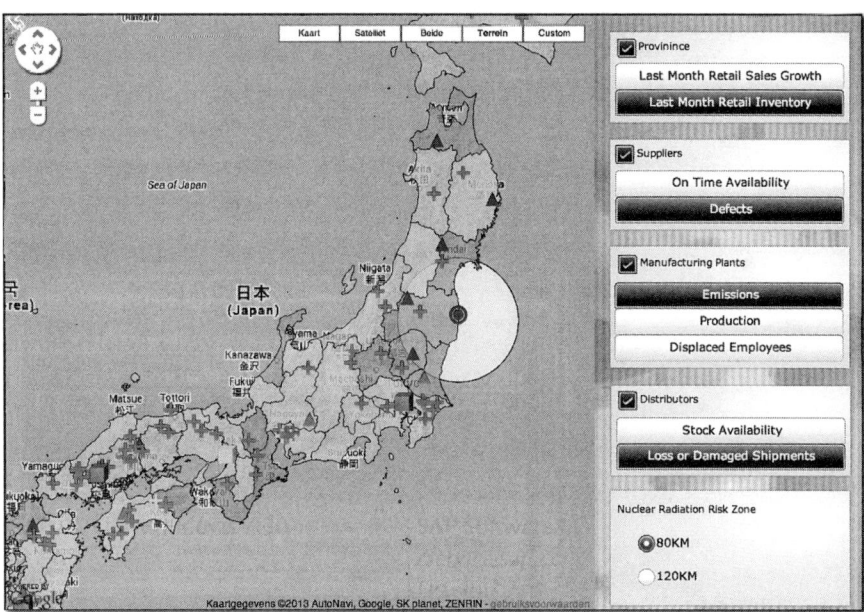

Figure 2.3 Dashboard Created with SAP BusinessObjects Dashboards and the Google Maps Plugin Add-On

2.2   BEX Web Application Designer

BEx Web Application Designer is part of the SAP NetWeaver BW Business Explorer (BEx) toolset, and is used to create web applications. Figure 2.4 shows an example of such an application. You can compare these web applications to the BEx Web Analyzer workbooks that can be created with BEx Web Analyzer. This tool is based on the same principles, only now the report/application runs not as a Microsoft Excel workbook, but as an HTML web application in a web browser.

Web application

A web application can contain objects like analysis tables, charts, or maps to present data. Buttons can be used to create a navigation menu to control which objects should be shown or hidden. With the help of filter and navigation panes, the data can be filtered and the layout can be adjusted.

An example of a web application is the standard template that is used when executing a BEx query in BEx Web Analyzer (Figure 2.4). BEx Web

0ANALYSIS_
PATTERN

Analyzer is in fact a BEx Web Application Designer template (0ANALYSIS_PATTERN) offering an analysis table, a navigation pane, a series of buttons with functionalities like exporting to MS Excel and opening another report, and a dropdown box to switch between an analysis table and a chart.

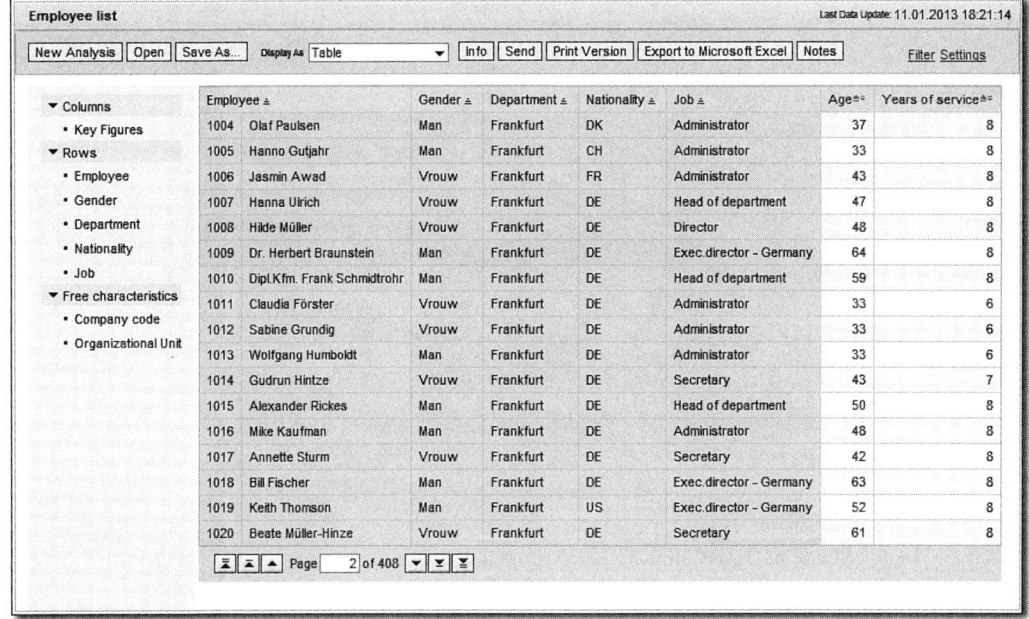

Figure 2.4 BEx Web Analyzer

In this section, we'll give you a brief overview of BEx Web Application Designer by walking you through some of the most important things you should know about the tool. As with SAP BusinessObjects Dashboards, if you're already familiar with BEx Web Application Designer, skip on ahead.

2.2.1 Setting Up a Web Application Template

Let's have a look at BEx Web Application Designer to get some basic knowledge of how this tool works. BEx Web Application Designer looks a bit like the development environment of SAP BusinessObjects Dashboards (see Figure 2.5). On the left there is a list of available web items.

These can be dragged into the web application layout. In contrast to adding components to the SAP BusinessObjects Dashboards canvas from the components list, here it is not possible to place a web item precisely where you want it. If you add a second web item, it will be positioned right next to the first component. To adjust the positioning of the web items, you can use special container web items. You can also add HTML tables in which to arrange web items. (It must be noted that is quite a challenge to create advanced application layouts.) A web application is saved as a web template, and the result of these actions is saved in a web template object.

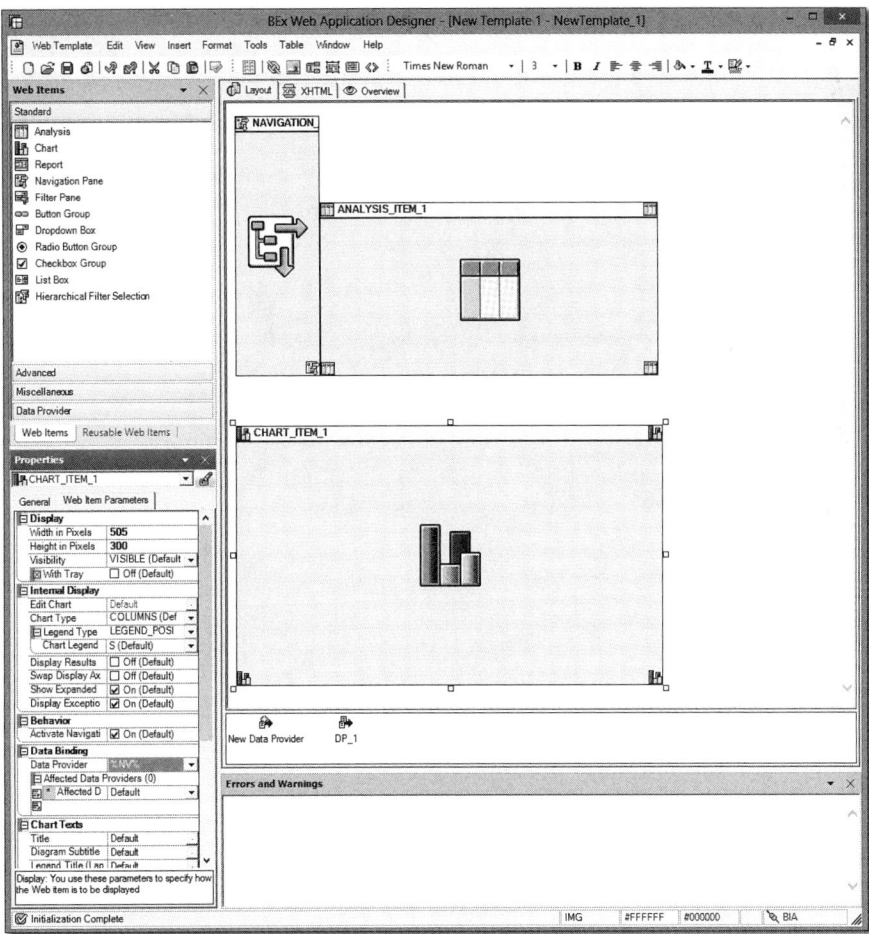

Figure 2.5 BEx Web Application Designer Design Environment

Data providers   The data provider plays a central role in the creation of web applications. After you drag one of the web items to the layout, the web application only contains a placeholder. No data will be shown, as no connection with a data source has been defined yet. A data provider will bring the web application to life and provide it with data from the SAP NetWeaver BW system. The source for such a data provider can be a BEx query, a BEx query view, or an SAP NetWeaver BW InfoProvider like an InfoCube or InfoSet. A web application can have multiple data providers, and a data provider can be connected to multiple web items in a web application (Figure 2.6). For example, a data provider connected to a BEx query on HR data can provide an analysis table with data and a filter pane with filter options. When the user of the web application sets a certain filter (e.g., his own organizational department) in the filter pane, the data provider updates the query result with this input. Accordingly, the analysis table will be updated and now show only data on the user's organizational department. So changing the input on a web item can affect all the web items connected to the same data provider.

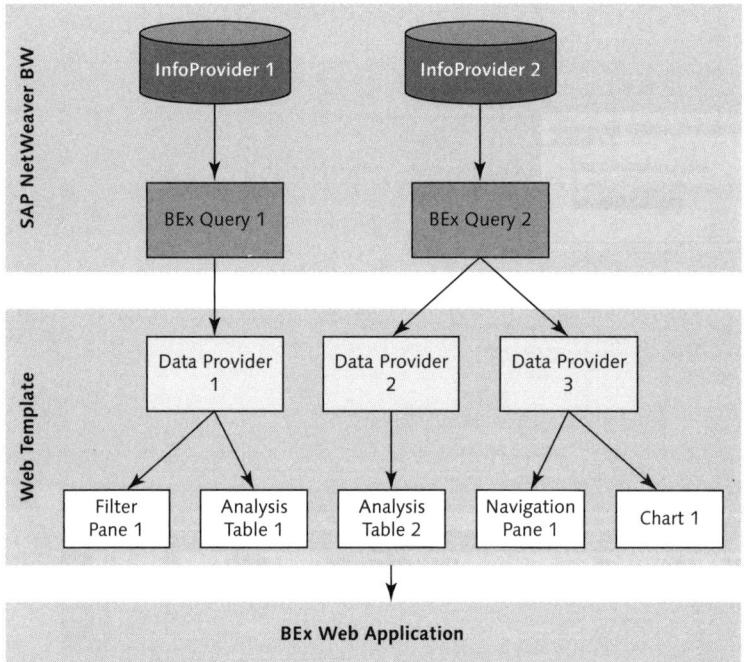

Figure 2.6 Application Layers in BEx Web Application Designer

The properties of the selected web item are shown under the list of web items in BEx Web Application Designer (refer back to Figure 2.5). A new data provider can be created here, and existing ones can be connected to the web item. In the web item parameters, some web-item-specific settings can be adjusted, such as the width and height of the web item and the maximum number of displayed values.

The XHTML tab shows the web items and some corresponding settings. This XHTML is fully editable, so this can be used to edit a web application. All used objects are listed in the OVERVIEW tab.

XHTML

2.2.2 Web Items

BEx Web Application Designer provides a number of web items, which are divided into three categories: standard, advanced, and miscellaneous web items. These web items can be compared to the components in SAP BusinessObjects Dashboards and are the building blocks of a web application. Below we briefly outline the three categories of web items.

Web items

Standard Web Items

The standard web items are as follows:

▶ **Analysis**
This is a table-like item that presents the data provider result in rows and columns.

▶ **Chart**
BEx Web Application Designer offers a wide range of chart types:

- ▶ Horizontal line chart
- ▶ Vertical line chart
- ▶ Bar chart
- ▶ Column chart
- ▶ Horizontal area chart
- ▶ Vertical area chart
- ▶ Pie chart

- ▶ Doughnut chart
- ▶ Split pie chart
- ▶ Polar chart
- ▶ Radar chart
- ▶ Scatter
- ▶ Time scatter
- ▶ Speedometer (gauge)
- ▶ Portfolio chart
- ▶ Histogram
- ▶ GANTT chart
- ▶ MTA chart
- ▶ Heat map
- ▶ Delta chart

▶ **Report**
Reports created with BEx Report Designer can be embedded into a web application using this web item.

▶ **Navigation pane**
This item shows the available characteristics and their positions (columns, rows, free). A characteristic can be dragged from this pane into the analysis table.

▶ **Filter pane**
This item allows the user to easily set up filters on one or more characteristics.

▶ **Button group**
Buttons can be programmed with standard commands or a custom script.

▶ **Dropdown box, radio button group, checkbox group, list box**
These web items function as custom filters.

▶ **Hierarchical filter**
This item lets a user navigate through a hierarchy for a specific characteristic and set up filters on hierarchical nodes.

Advanced Web Items

The advanced web items are, in contrast to the standard web items, more focused on grouping and placing web items than on displaying data. For this purpose, a container item, a container layout item, a tab pages item, and a group item are available. All these web items are able to arrange other web items in a certain layout.

With the map item, the BEx Map feature can display data in a map. There are also web items for displaying system messages and info fields to show all kinds of BEx query–related information (i.e., the most recent data update date of the InfoProvider).

The input field item is interesting because it can be used for SAP NetWeaver BW Integrated Planning (IP) web applications to enter values. It can also be used to enter a filter by typing the filter value in a field.

Integrated Planning

Miscellaneous Web Items

With the list of conditions and list of exceptions items, all available conditions and exceptions that are available in the connected BEx query can be displayed. The user of the web application can activate and deactivate the conditions and exceptions from this web item.

A ticker item can present data as a moving ticker, like the ones news channels use at the bottom of the screen. There is a text item to add text objects to the web application, and, with the menu bar item, a number of buttons with commands can be created. Furthermore, this category consists of web items that work on the background and can, for example, add custom scripts to the web application and select which options should be shown in the context menus (right click) of the other web items.

2.2.3 Publishing

A web template for a web application has to be published to the SAP NetWeaver BW environment. The web template then becomes an object that can be run from the SAP NetWeaver BW Java portal, the same way you can execute BEx queries as web queries or, as we have seen earlier, dashboards from SAP BusinessObjects Dashboards. The web application can be run from a web URL address.

2.3   Key Differences

Now that you have a basic understanding of the features of SAP BusinessObjects Dashboards and BEx Web Application Designer, we can compare them with Design Studio. Table 2.1 compares the three tools in a number of categories.

	SAP BusinessObjects Dashboards	BEx Web Application Designer	SAP BusinessObjects Design Studio
Platform	SAP NetWeaver BW Java Portal, SAP Business-Objects 4.0 BI Launch Pad, SWF file (standalone or embedded in PDF, HTML, Adobe Air, MS Word, MS Outlook, MS PowerPoint).	SAP NetWeaver BW Java Portal.	SAP NetWeaver BW Java Portal, SAP Business-Objects 4.0 BI Launch Pad.
Output Format	SWF file or HTML5 (mobile).	Java.	HTML5.
Components	Very wide range of charts, maps, containers, and selection and other graphical components.	Large set of charts, containers, and customizable buttons; limited graphical components.	Limited number of charts, selection, and graphical components.
Component Adjustment Options	Very high: All components have a lot of options to tweak their functionality, looks, and interactivity options. In the Excel spreadsheet, Excel formulas can be used for custom calculations.	High: Components can be adjusted with high detail.	Medium: Components have some adjustment options, but scripting and CSS are required for advanced adjustments.

Table 2.1 Key Differences

	SAP BusinessObjects Dashboards	BEx Web Application Designer	SAP BusinessObjects Design Studio
Layout Development Flexibility	High flexibility: Drag and drop components to the exact preferred position (WYSIWYG).	Low flexibility: Containers and HTML tables/code have to be used for positioning.	High flexibility: WYSIWYG, including relative positioning of components.
Data Connectivity	SAP BusinessObjects universe (UNX), SAP NetWeaver BW connection (BICS), web service query (Query as a Web Service), web service connection, XML data and Excel XML maps, Live Office connections.	BEx query, BEx query view, SAP NetWeaver BW InfoProvider.	BEx query, SAP NetWeaver BW InfoProvider, SAP HANA.
Data Input Options	Interactive scenarios can be developed using the Excel spreadsheet.	BI Integrated Planning options can be incorporated.	Not available yet.
Scripting Options	Excel spreadsheet.	XHTML, JavaScript, and ABAP coding.	JavaScript and CSS coding.
SDK	SDK available for development of custom components and connectivity options.	No SDK available.	SDK available in Design Studio version 1.2.
Mobile	HTML5 export for a limited number of components and connectivity options. These dashboards can be viewed via SAP BusinessObjects Mobile.	No options for mobile.	Applications are viewable on any device with an HMTL5 browser or via SAP BusinessObjects Mobile.
SAP HANA	No support for direct access to SAP HANA data sources.	No support for direct access to SAP HANA data sources.	Direct access to SAP HANA analytic views and calculation views.

Table 2.1 Key Differences (Cont.)

The remainder of this section describes three images of dashboards/applications created with the three tools we compared in this chapter. As demonstrated here, the three versions look a lot alike and have the same functionality. Each dashboard/application contains two charts, a number of filters, some tabs, and a text object that shows the latest refresh date of the data.

Comparing the tools

Figure 2.7 shows the SAP BusinessObjects Dashboards version, Figure 2.8 is the BEx Web Application Designer version, and Figure 2.9 displays the Design Studio application.

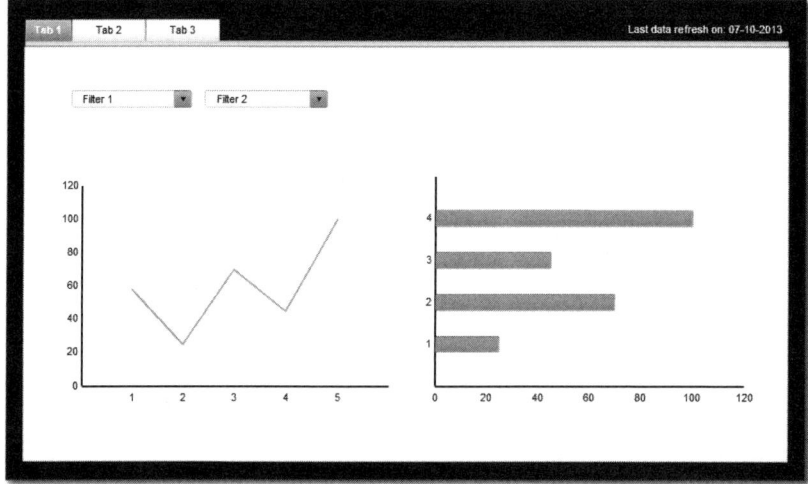

Figure 2.7 Simple Dashboard in SAP BusinessObjects Dashboards

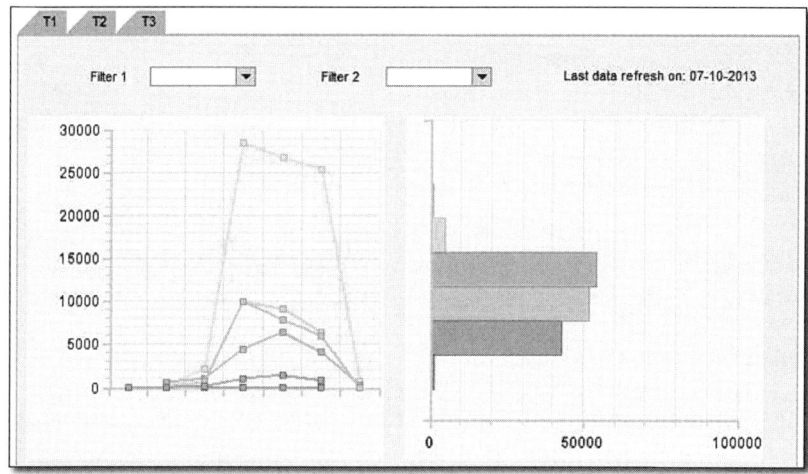

Figure 2.8 Simple Application in BEx Web Application Designer

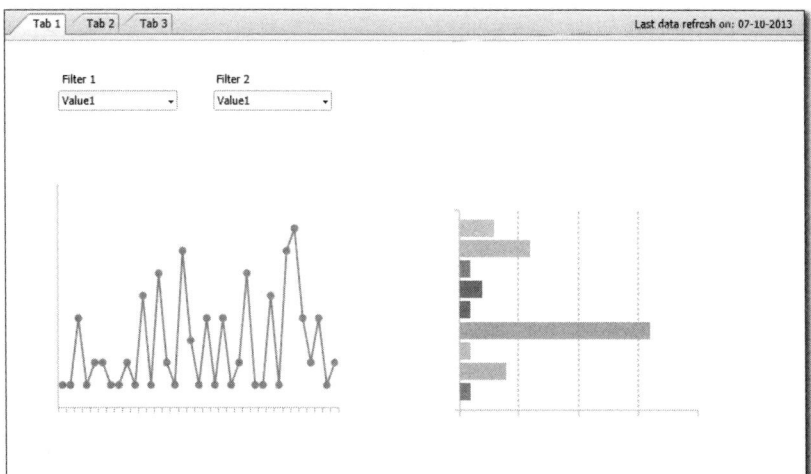

Figure 2.9 Simple Application in Design Studio

2.4 Summary

In this chapter, we introduced two tools from the SAP BI portfolio that overlap with the features and purpose of Design Studio: SAP Business-Objects Dashboards and BEx Web Application Designer. We took a quick dive into the steps and activities required to create a report, dashboard, or BI application. Next, we reviewed the different components of the tools that form the building blocks of the development process. Additionally, we examined the data connectivity options and the publishing possibilities for each tool. Finally, we discussed the key differences among the three tools.

This chapter shows use case scenarios where applications have been developed in Design Studio and are used by end users in diverse business scenarios.

3 Usage Scenarios

In this chapter, we will walk through a variety of examples that show you how applications developed in Design Studio can be used in different business scenarios. Each scenario will tell a story of an end user who is using an application designed for his particular role or task. The scenarios will show that Design Studio is able to deliver process support in very different situations, varying from real-time operational support to in-depth strategic analysis.

In Section 3.1, Section 3.2, and Section 3.3, we will show very practical hands-on applications that have been designed to support an operational workflow: information where you need it and when you need it. In Section 3.4, we will show an application of Design Studio as a reporting tool: an annual company report created for its stakeholders. Finally, Section 3.5 and Section 3.6 show applications that have been designed to enable managers to be in control of their business and support in-depth analysis. For all examples, we will walk you through the basic functionality of the most important screens in the application.

3.1 Customer Relationship Management

In this first scenario, we will assume the role of a gym trainer. The main responsibility of the gym trainer is to look after the clients and help them achieve the goals they have set for themselves. The role of the trainer is to assess clients' progress, help them with their training program, and try to motivate people to keep coming back to the gym. One

Gym application

of the main key performance indicators for a gym is the rate of subscription renewals.

In this section, we will we will walk you through a Design Studio application developed for an iPad that allows the trainer to walk around the gym and immediately access information about a particular customer.

3.1.1   Main Screen

At the start of the day, the trainer immediately wants to get going and help customers. On the application's main screen (Figure 3.1), he taps the CUSTOMERS button, and a screen opens with a list of the customers currently logged into the gym. When customers enter the gym, they have to access the gym with a subscription card. The application has access to the login data and can provide this list.

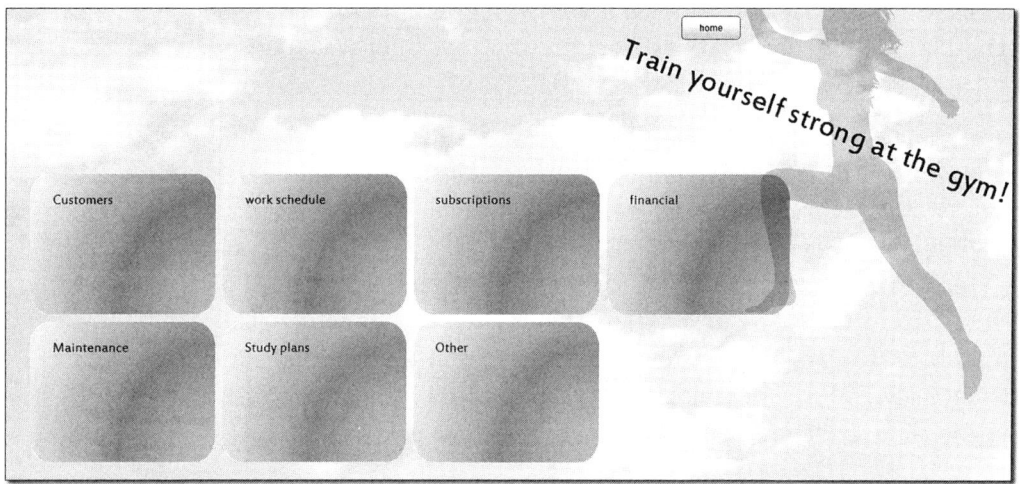

Figure 3.1 Main Screen

Customer list screen On the customer list screen, a long list of customers currently at the gym is available to view. As you can see in Figure 3.2, it is a busy day. A lot of regulars are in, but the trainer is mostly interested to know if there are people in that haven't been in the gym many times before. On the left side of the screen, there are a few predefined filter buttons for easy filtering of the customers. When you tap the NEW CUSTOMER button, a filter is placed on the customer list, and only currently present customers that have visited the gym fewer than 10 times will show up on the list.

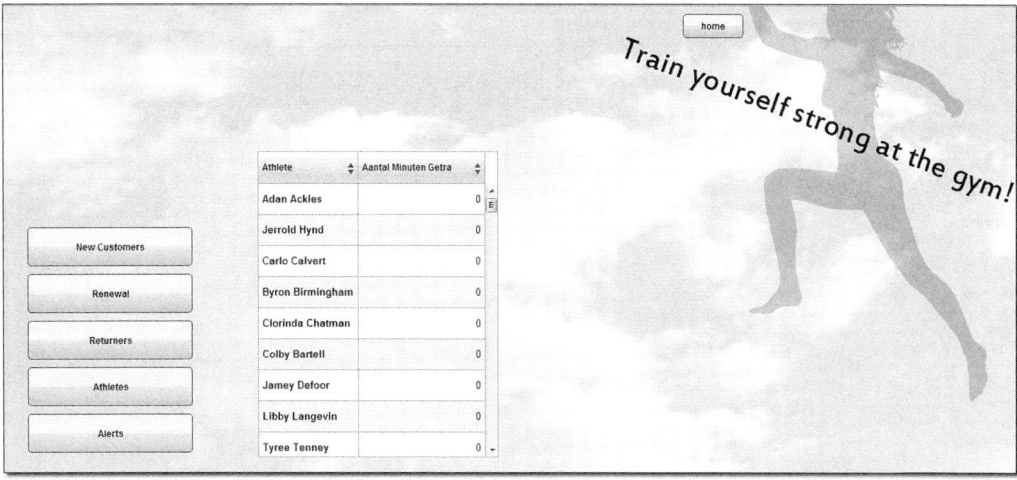

Figure 3.2 Customer List Screen

The other buttons are Renewal (for present customers whose subscriptions are running out), Returners (for those customers who are back after not visiting for quite some time), and Athletes (for those who have visited the gym frequently in the last few weeks). An Alerts button on the bottom of the button list is available to show only those customers for whom an alert is triggered. Such an alert can be triggered for a number of reasons, which we will discuss later on in this section.

3.1.2   Helping Out New Customers

The list now shows only those customers who have visited the gym 10 or fewer times. It is good practice to follow these customers closely, as beginners are prone to making mistakes, which could result in an injury or discouragement. With this list, the trainer on duty is able to watch this group of customers and help them out where needed (Figure 3.3).

When looking at the list, the trainer sees that there is an alert on a customer. To view more detailed information about this particular customer, he taps that record in the list. A new screen opens (Figure 3.4).

Customer alerts

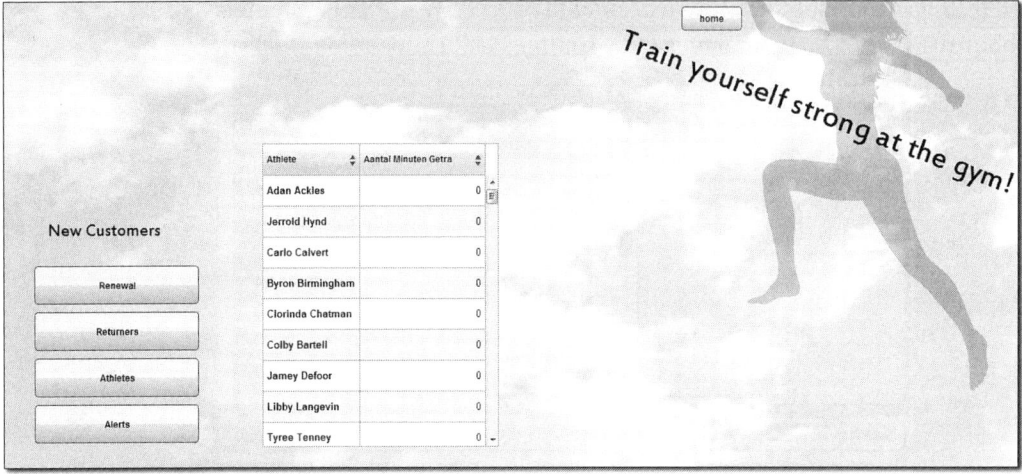

Figure 3.3 New Customers Screen with Alerts

Figure 3.4 Customer Information Screen

The customer information screen shows a lot of information about the customer: personal information, measurements, goals, and the workouts the customer has done in the past few weeks. If alerts are active, the reasons will be shown at the bottom of the screen.

In this case there are three reasons for an alert: The intake wasn't completed, the weight measurement hasn't been done yet, and the customer hasn't been assigned to a workout yet. Based on these alerts, the trainer will talk to the customer to see if he would like to make an appointment to finish the intake tasks. As the picture of the customer is also visible on the customer information screen, the trainer is able to recognize the customer in the gym.

3.1.3 Workout Evaluation

Going back to the main customer screen, the trainer can see that there is another alert. He navigates to the customer information screen, and sees that the alert is on the workout. Tapping the workout alert opens the workout screen (Figure 3.5). From here, he can see that the workout was scheduled for three times a week, but the customer has not managed to train on all scheduled days for the last few weeks.

Figure 3.5 Workout Evaluation

Talking to the customer, the trainer learns that he was on vacation and couldn't come to the gym. While they are talking, the customer mentions that he is planning to run more. A new three days per week workout is assigned to him, with more emphasis on exercises for running.

The trainer taps the EDIT WORKOUT routine button. Here he can select from a list with premade workout schedules. He selects the running workout, and the workout details are displayed. The trainer taps the ASSIGN button, and, from now on, the customer will be working with the running workout schedule (Figure 3.6).

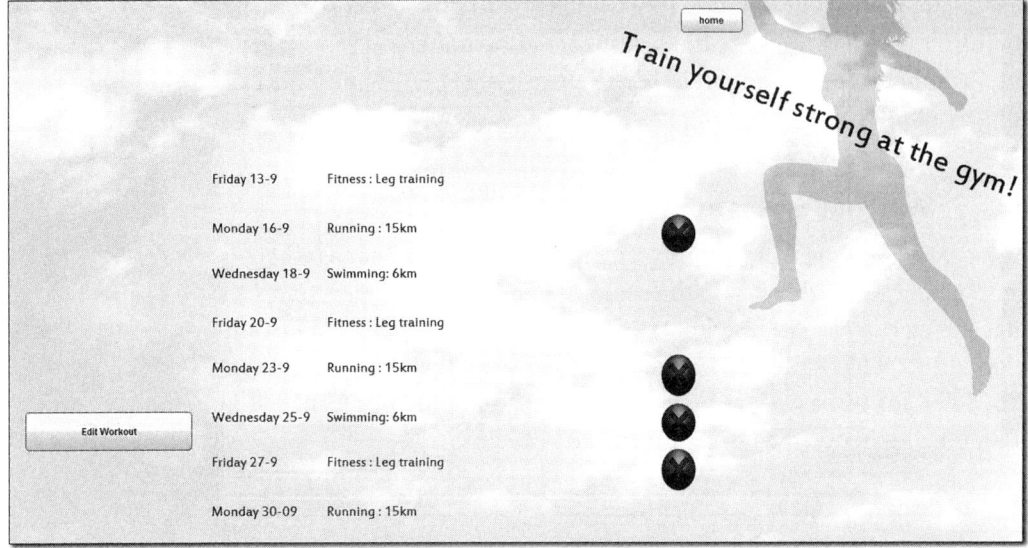

Figure 3.6 Assign Workout Screen

SAP NetWeaver BW Integrated Planning

As of the time of this writing, SAP NetWeaver BW Integrated Planning will be part of Design Studio in Q2 of 2014. In this scenario, integration with Integrated Planning could mean that the trainer would be able to alter the weights, the number of sets, and the number of repetitions before assigning the workout plan to the customer.

3.2 Employee Management

Call center application

In this section, we will assume the role of the team lead of a team of call center agents. The team lead will be constantly monitoring the progress of the call center. He needs to keep an eye on the number of customers that are on hold and see if there are agents struggling to make the number of calls necessary. Apart from the operational management, the team lead is also responsible for planning the shifts for the agents.

The most important aspect of the job of team lead is to act when customers have to wait too long before someone answers their call. To be able to constantly monitor how long customers are waiting, there is an operational view in the team lead's Design Studio application. Here, he can see the number of customers waiting and how long the top five waiters have been on hold.

3.2.1 Main Screen

As you can see in Figure 3.7, which shows the application's main screen, eight customers are waiting at the moment. That is a few more than there should be, but the top five customers haven't been waiting longer than three minutes — so the throughput of the calls at the moment is big enough to cope with the number of customers that are currently calling.

Monitoring wait times

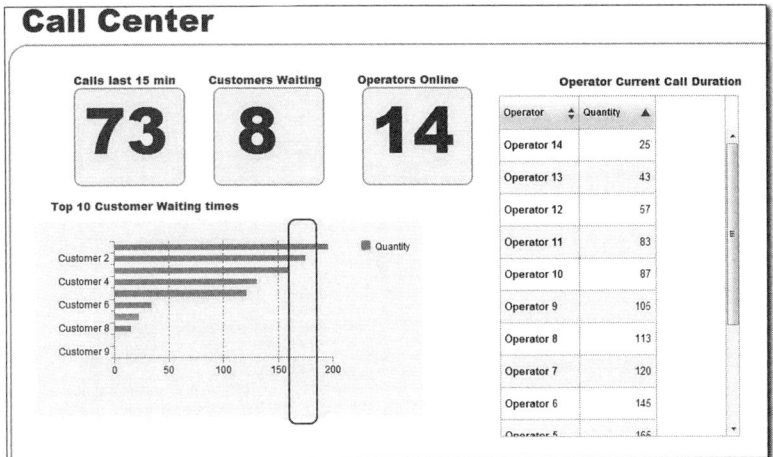

Figure 3.7 Call Center Application Main Screen

The team lead concludes that there are currently no issues he has to address immediately, so he goes on to review some other key figures.

3.2.2 Analyzing Calls by Volume

To review the number of customers that have been calling today, the team lead taps the customer part of the screen. A new screen opens that shows him how the number of waiting customers has been during the day. He can also see how many customers have been calling and see the maximum waiting times for the day.

This customer screen (Figure 3.8) is of particular value to recognize if there are any patterns in the incoming calls. If the team lead can identify any, he will be able to better schedule his agents to align them with that pattern. If he wants to compare this shift to similar shifts, he can turn the number of waiting charts and the number of customers calling charts into combined charts.

For example, if he is looking at a shift on a Wednesday, he can now look at how this shift compares to other Wednesdays. Or, in a more advanced example, he can compare it to Wednesdays in a week before a holiday or two weeks after a major release of a new software version of the product the call center is supporting. These kinds of effects can be analyzed and combined in the source data for this application. If these analysis data sets are available, the application can visualize them in the screen next to the actuals or predictions. This predicted pattern would help the team lead to better analyze the situation.

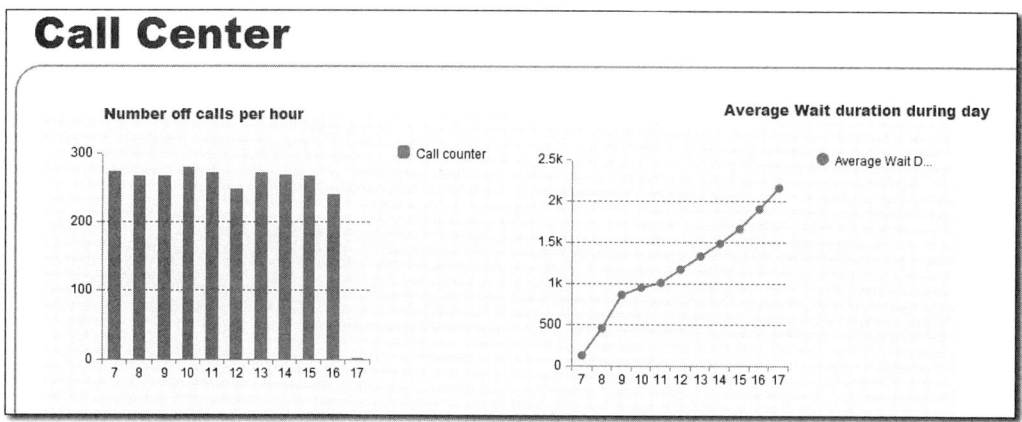

Figure 3.8 Customer Screen

In this example, there is a clear problem: The operators cannot cope with the number of calls, and the waiting time increases throughout the day to an unacceptable length.

Predictive Analytics

If you're interested in getting even further in this analysis, you could try to make predictions about the estimated number of customers who will be calling.

SAP offers a product that would enable this, which is SAP Predictive Analysis. Based on data from the past, this tool makes it possible to create a model and predict future outcomes. This prediction can then be shown as a comparison in a chart within the application.

For more information about SAP Predictive Analysis, see *Predictive Analysis with SAP* by John MacGregor (SAP PRESS, 2014).

3.2.3 Analyzing Calls by Subject

Now the team lead wants to know more about the telephone calls. He would like to know why customers are calling, and if there is a pattern in the subjects customers are calling about. He would also like to know how long it is taking the operators to handle calls about different subjects.

Grouping the calls by subject helps the team lead to identify issues he can address with the project teams. Then he can better focus his training budget with this knowledge. For example, the screen in Figure 3.9 clearly shows that subject 6 produces the most calls, and that taking those calls uses the longest amount of time. The team lead is then able to filter by month so he can compare the subjects with other months.

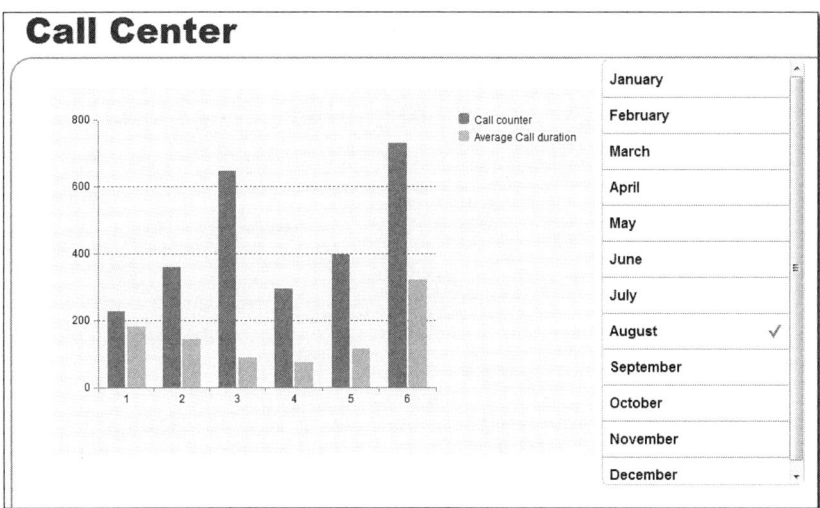

Figure 3.9 Call Analysis by Subject

3.2.4 Planning

Managing staff
capacity

For planning purposes, the team lead has a short-term and a long-term responsibility. For the short term, he needs to plan available staff so there is enough capacity to handle incoming calls. On the planning screen (Figure 3.10), he can see the planned staff capacity, the staff that isn't available, and the staff that is on leave. On the line chart, he can see the predicted amount of work (in full-time equivalents) for easy comparison to the available staff.

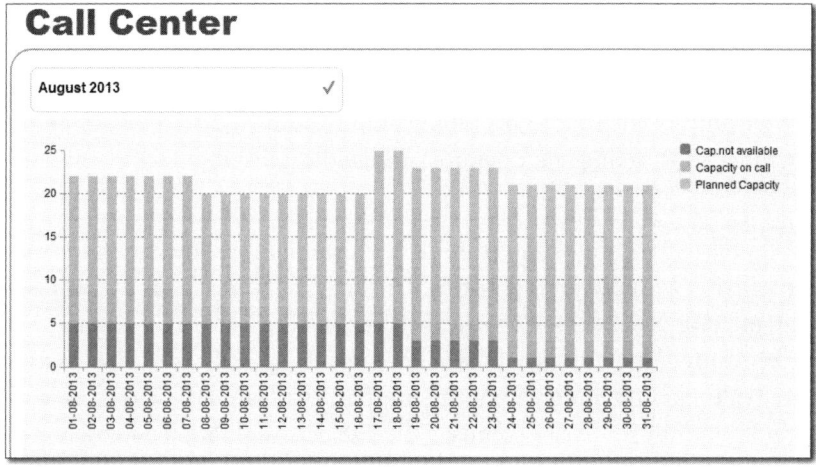

Figure 3.10 Short- and Long-Term Planning Screen

For the long-term, the team lead needs to see the total average staff capacity shown against the estimated workload for the coming months. Based on this, the team lead can decide if he needs to hire new agents or if he can't afford to renew contracts.

3.2.5 Employee Assessment

Now the team lead wants to look how his team is doing; specifically, he wants to look at the calls they handled today (Figure 3.11).

Evaluation

On the employee assessment screen, the team lead sees a list of his employees. Next to each employee's name is a graph showing the calls they've handled and how long the calls took. If the evaluation by the customer was unsatisfactory, the graph bar is a different color.

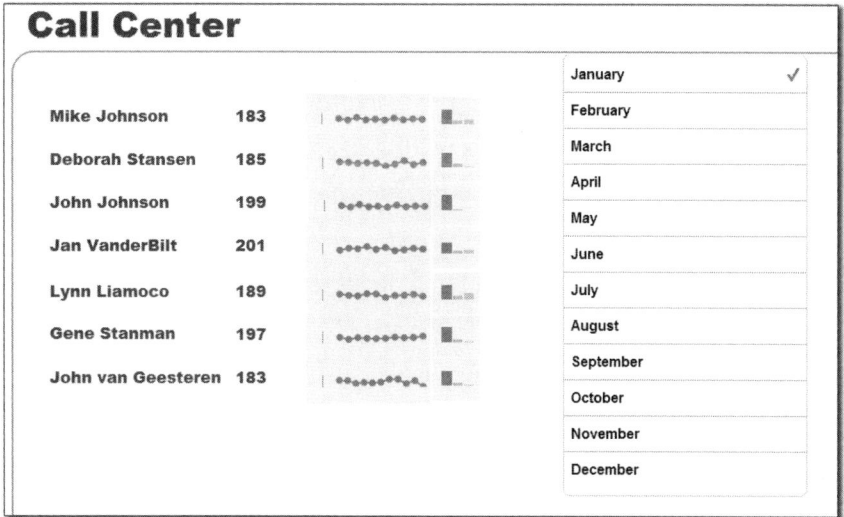

Call Center

			January ✓
Mike Johnson	183		February
			March
Deborah Stansen	185		April
John Johnson	199		May
Jan VanderBilt	201		June
Lynn Liamoco	189		July
Gene Stanman	197		August
			September
John van Geesteren	183		October
			November
			December

Figure 3.11 Employee Assessment

Color Images

Please note that, though the print book shows the application images in gray-scale, full color versions are viewable in the e-book.

3.3 Field Sales

A real estate agent spends his day talking to prospective buyers and sellers. To do so intelligently, he needs information about the buyer, the seller, and the property. In addition, because many of his meetings are out of the office, he needs a portable device from which he can get the necessary information to be able to better negotiate the terms of a possible deal. For example, if the real estate agent has an appointment with a prospective buyer, he wants to know the following pieces of information:

Real estate application

▶ How much interest the buyer has shown.

▶ Whether there are other prospective buyers.

▶ The build quality of the property.

- The maintenance quality of the property.
- The current asking price and the history of the asking price.
- When the property came on the market.
- The lowest price the seller is willing to accept.
- Whether there are similar properties on sale in the area, and what their history and quality is.

This is a lot of information, but it all helps the agent to be better able to discuss and negotiate a possible sale.

3.3.1 Main Screen

Agenda for the day First things first. The real estate agent has to know where and when the next appointment is. Therefore, the main screen of the application is the agenda for the day. He can tap the agenda for his next appointment (Figure 3.12).

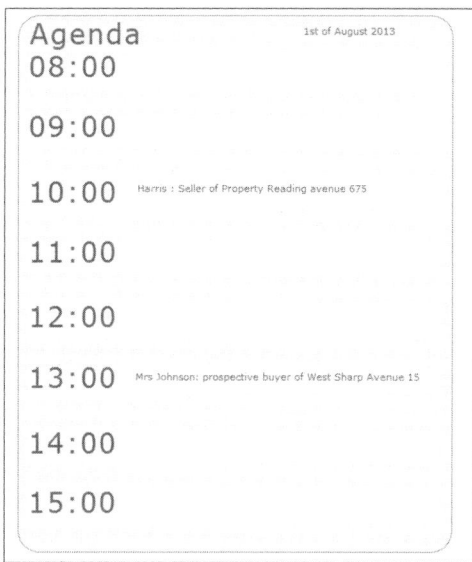

Figure 3.12 Real Estate Agenda

When he taps the agenda, he sees the selected appointment with the customer or seller he will be meeting and the property that will be discussed. Some general contact information about the customer or seller is visible in case the agent needs to contact them about the appointment (Figure 3.13).

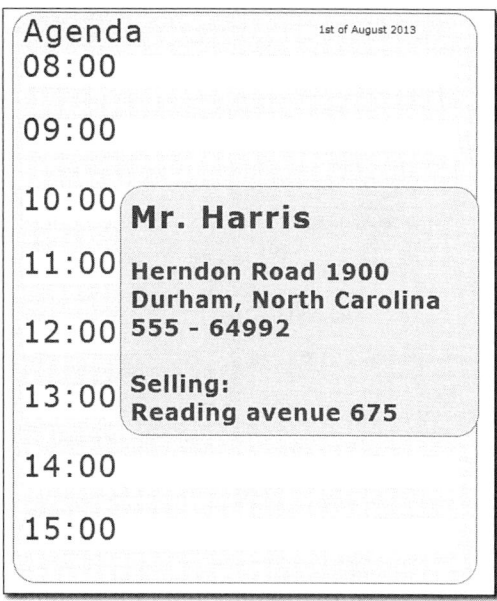

Figure 3.13 Detailed Appointment Information

3.3.2 Customer Information

If the agent taps the customer's name, he will see information about the customer's known history. Has the customer inquired about other properties? How many contacts already took place? What is the estimated value of a potential buyer in terms of annual income? How interested did the customer seem during previous appointments? In the case of Mr. Harris, as he is selling his house, it is interesting to know how many prospective buyers there are, how negotiations went in the past, and if there are circumstances that are important to know about.

In the customer information screen (Figure 3.14), the real estate agent can see that the current asking price for Mr. Harris's property is now $265,000. The property has been on the market for a long time; since January, the asking price was dropped several times. However, now there seems to be interest in the property: six customers have visited the property, and three of them made an offer. Rodrigo Delosantos made the highest offer of about \$250,000, but this is still somewhat lower than the asking price.

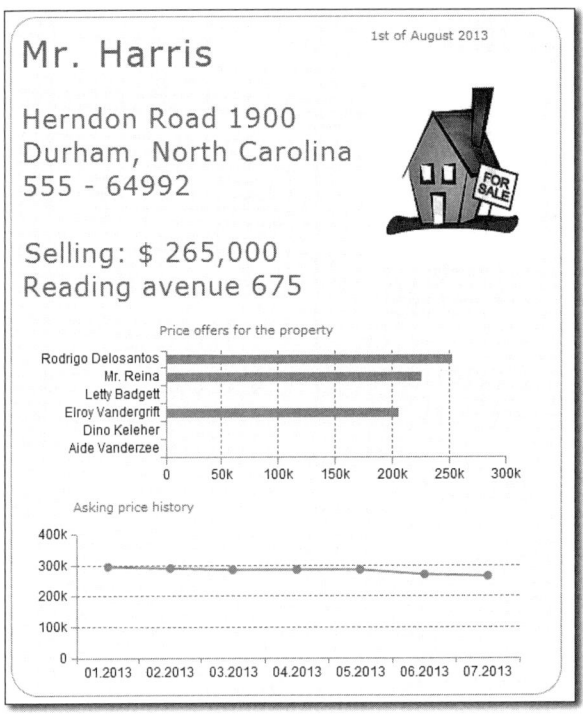

Figure 3.14 Customer Information Screen

3.3.3 Neighborhood Information

To be able to assess the market correctly, a real estate manager needs information about the neighborhood of the home. He can access this information by tapping the home address. When he does this, the neighborhood information screen (Figure 3.15) opens.

Neighborhood house prices

The first information presented to the real estate manager is the mean house prices per house type. This is the most important information, as this is the market price to which buyers will compare this house. Under the house type value numbers, he can see some more measures. There is some information about population, median income, and housing prices. These three measures give some information about how the area has been developing over the last few years.

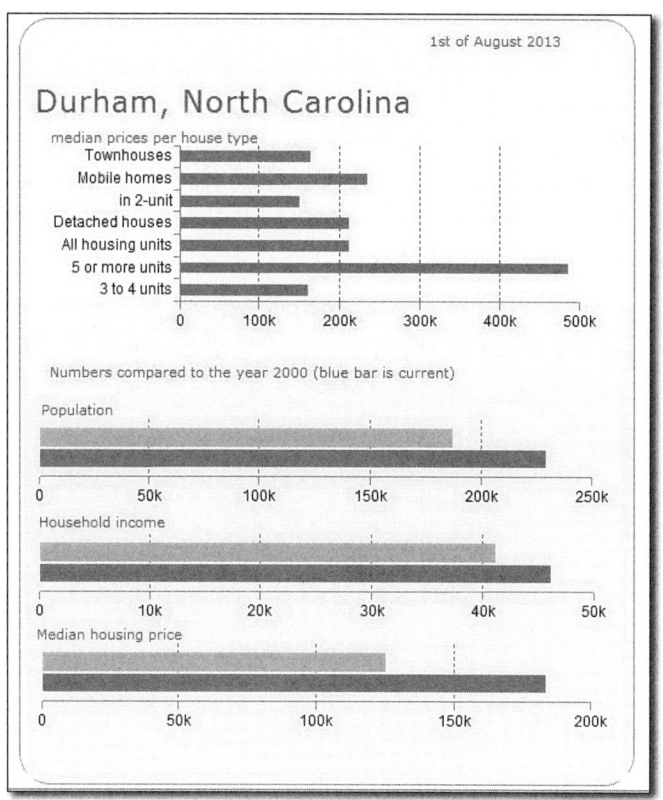

Figure 3.15 Neighborhood Information Screen

3.4 Financial Reporting

After looking at three operational scenarios, we will now focus on a reporting scenario: an annual company report. Typically, annual reports are highly formatted documents with a lot of key figures about the performance of the company. Additionally, the financial statements are presented.

Annual company report application

In this scenario, a company is publishing its annual report in a Design Studio application. As the annual report is arguably the most important communication from the company to the stakeholders, the application really has to shine in layout, navigation, and readability.

3.4.1 Main Screen

The main screen does not contain much information, but it is still important because it is the first thing the stakeholders see when they look at the annual report (Figure 3.16). On the left is a menu that helps to navigate to the part of the annual report that the reader is interested in. This navigation help is important, as annual reports can be more than 100 pages long.

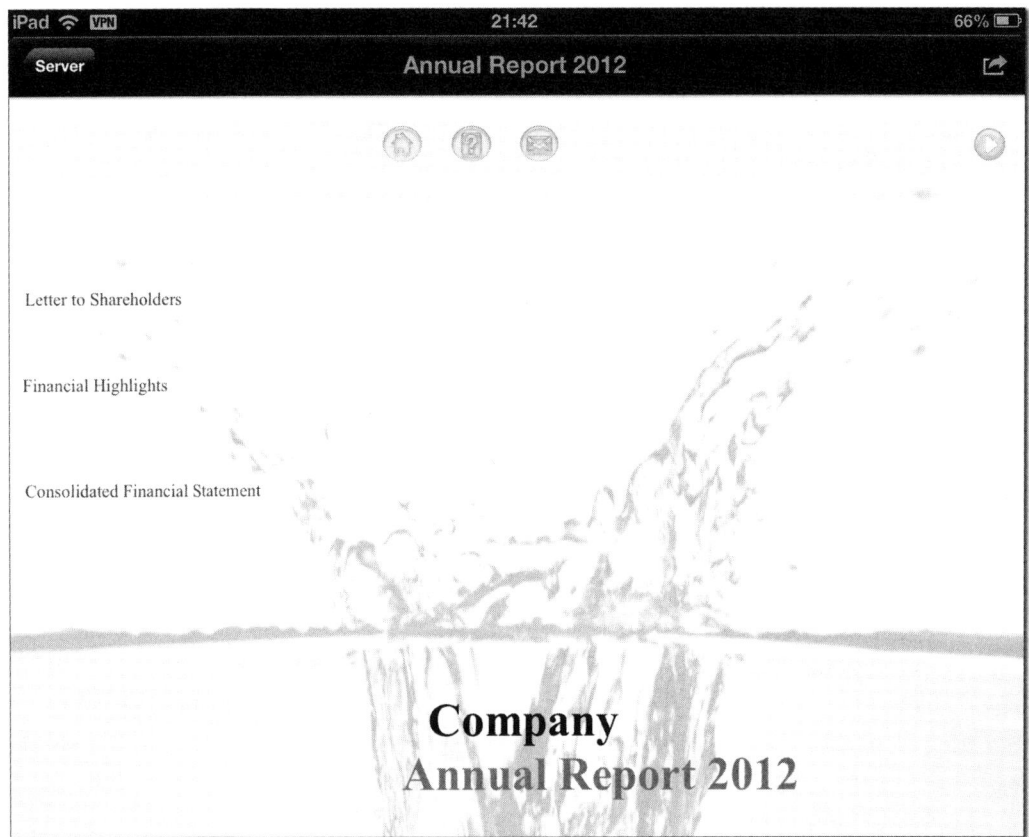

Figure 3.16 Annual Report Main Screen

3.4.2 Financial Highlights

The financial highlights are a short summary of the financial figures the company is presenting to the stakeholders (Figure 3.17). In this example,

the top of the screen shows three highlighted key figures about the performance of the company over the past five years. Below that, a number
of the most important financial key figures are displayed.

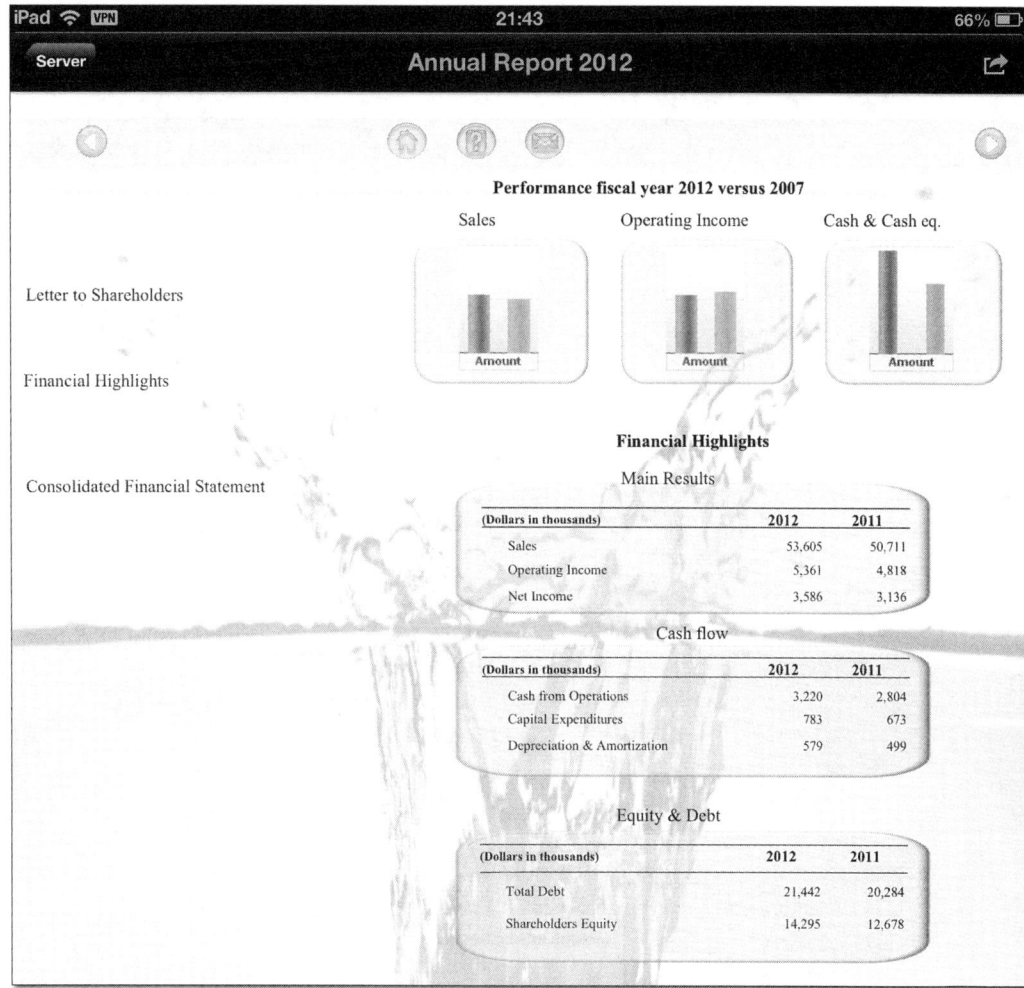

Figure 3.17 Financial Highlights

3.4.3 Letter to the Shareholders

The letter to the shareholders is very different in layout (Figure 3.18)
from the rest of the application; it is a representation of a letter from the

CEO of the company to the shareholders, and it provides a broad overview of the company. The letter covers the company's current financial state, its position in the market, and some future plans. The company uses this letter to show the company in the best possible light for the financial analysts who will advise investors about the stock value.

Figure 3.18 Letter to Shareholders

Income statement   An income statement is one of the company's financial statements and shows the company's revenues and expenses during a particular period. It shows the revenues from products and the costs and expenses charged against these revenues (Figure 3.19). There are official guidelines for these statements. In this example, you can see that the statement looks very different from the layout in the previous sections. It is very basic: just the numbers.

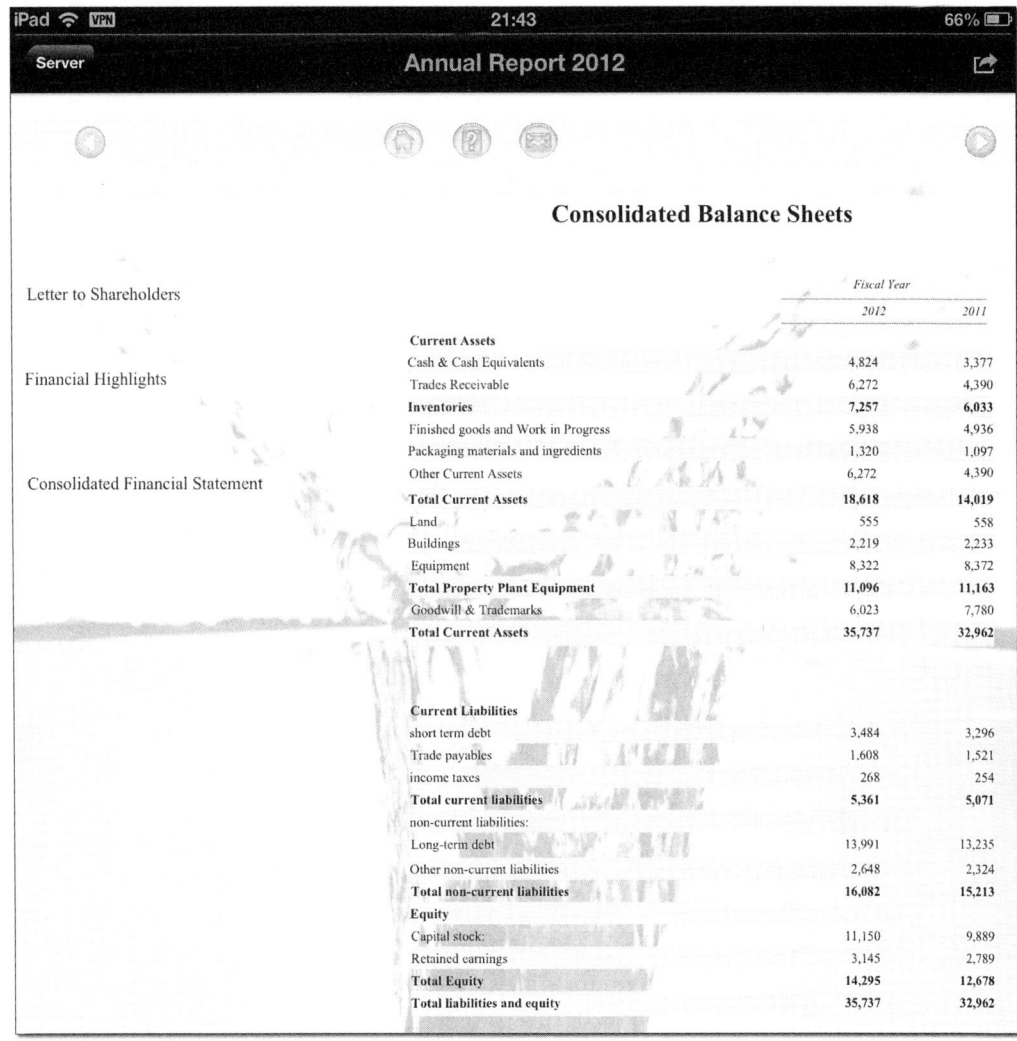

Figure 3.19 Financial Statement

3.5 Sales Analytics

In the first sections of this chapter, we looked at highly operational applications and a report for stakeholders. This section is more analytical, as in this example the branch manager of a supermarket uses an application (Figure 3.20) to analyze his business.

Supermarket application

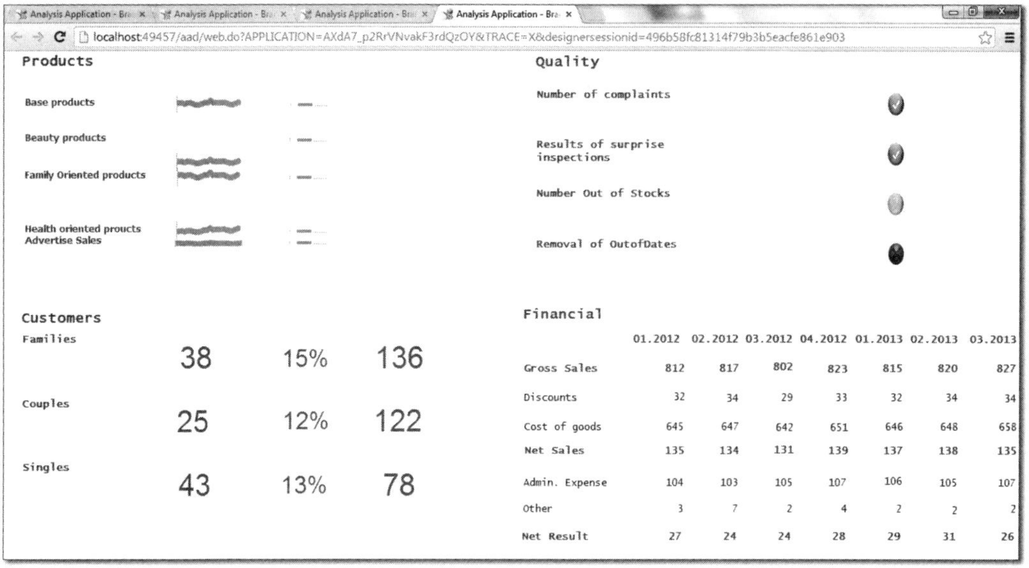

Figure 3.20 Supermarket Application Main Screen

3.5.1 Main Screen

The branch manager is responsible for the results of a single supermarket store within a chain of stores. He reports to the area manager, who is responsible for 50 stores within the area. To be able to run the store, the branch manager works with a dashboard that shows him how the shop is doing. The dashboard is divided into four segments: products, customers, financial, and quality. On the top left you see the numbers related to products. Below are numbers dividing customers into segments such as families, singles, and couples. On the top right we have the numbers related to quality. Finally, the financial numbers are on the bottom right.

Product

On the product part of the screen, the manager is able to see how sales are doing in relation to margin. Is a large enough part of his sales high margin? How are advertised sales going? How is each category doing over time? The store manager can see his sales divided by product category and divided by low-, medium-, and high-margin sales. Furthermore, he can see the *advertised* sales, which are sales of products that have been advertised in local or national media in the previous two weeks.

Customer

On the customer part of the screen, the manager is able to see how well he is doing in terms of acquisition, percentage of wallet, and retention of customers. He sees the customers grouped into segments: families, couples without children, and single-person households. The first number shows the number of new customers in the supermarket. The second number shows the percentage of customers that have not bought anything in the store for the last three months. The last number shows the average spending per week for the customers in that segment.

Financial

On the financial part of the screen, the manager can look at the results over the past seven quarters. He can look at a basic representation of the profit and loss statement for his store.

Quality

Quality is an important measure in a supermarket. To monitor this, the manager can look at key figures related to quality, such as number of complaints, results of surprise inspections, number of out-of-stocks, and number of removed out-of-date products. Finally, he can look at the perceived neatness and cleanliness of the supermarket.

For each of these four segments, a finger tap will open a new screen with further detail on that segment. Let's look a little closer at two of the most important segments: the product segment and the customer segment.

3.5.2 Product Segment

In the product segment screen (Figure 3.21), the manager is able to drill down to look at sales within the segment, as well as individual products.

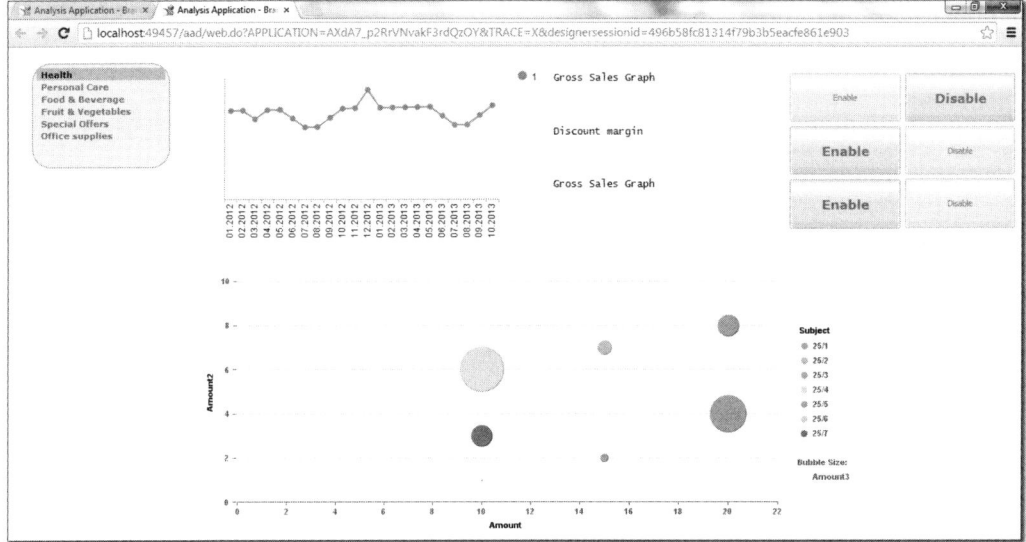

Figure 3.21 Product Segment Screen

In the list box, he can tap one of the product segments, which shows the corresponding detailed analysis. First, there is a line chart that shows the gross sales, discounts margin, and cost of goods sold over the past 24 months. On the right, the manager has the option to enable or disable each line for clarity. Below this graph is a bubble graph that shows each product based on margin, percentage of total sales in the segment, and growth. If the manager taps one of the dots, the screen automatically changes to a screen where a detailed product analysis is shown.

Detailed product analysis

In Figure 3.22, we see a list box on the left. If the manager taps one of the dots on the bubble chart in the product segment screen (refer back to Figure 3.21), that product is selected. He can also just swipe to this screen and manually select a product. Below the product selection list box is the PREFILTER button. This button places a filter on the items that are visible in the list box component. As the list box places the filter on the data source, we look at the button as a prefilter. When tapped, this button opens a popup screen with several options to prefilter the products.

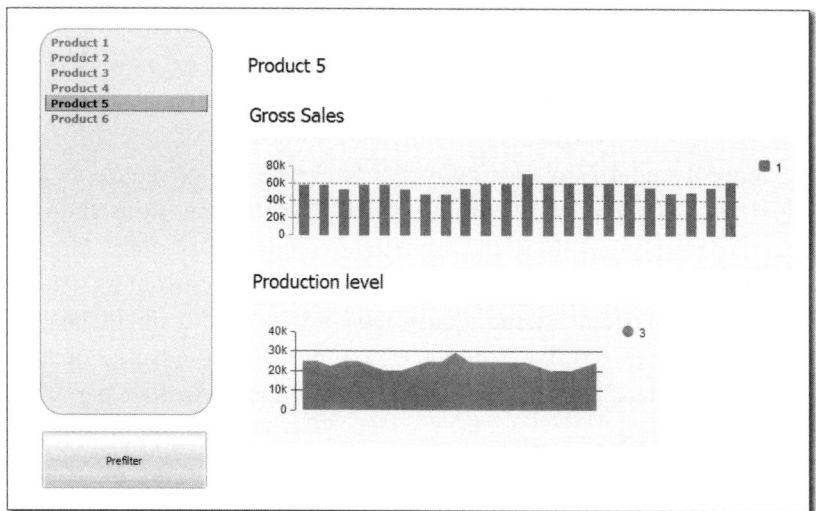

Figure 3.22 Product Analysis Screen

The options in the popup screen (Figure 3.23) are top sales, most discounts, margin, production quality, and shelf life. The list box on the left side of the product analysis shows only the products that fall within the filters made in the popup screen. Tapping one of those filters shows the analysis of that product.

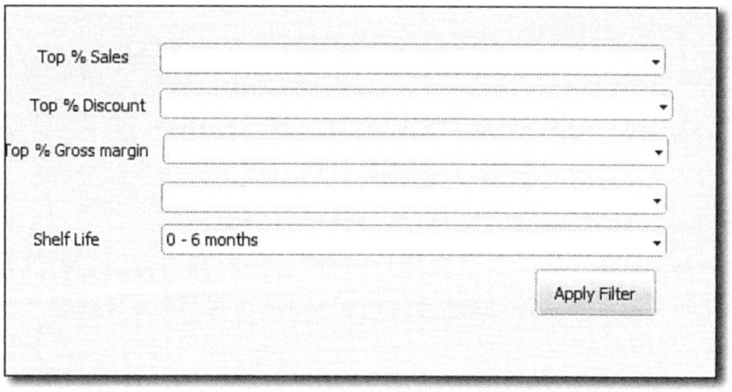

Figure 3.23 Popup Screen with Filter Options

Below the timeframe, there is a chart showing the discounts given and promotion actions made for that product. Clicking on one of the promotions or discounts resets the timeframe of the line chart; it shows from four weeks before to four weeks after the promotion or discount.

Discounts and promotions

85

3.5.3   Customer Segment

In the customer segment screen, the manager can have a more detailed look at the customer segments in his area. To help him analyze his customers, the screen (Figure 3.24) shows a recency-frequency matrix. This is a more detailed view of his customers. For customer retention, it is important to look at those customers that haven't been in his shop for some time, especially those that used to be frequent customers. Alternatively, it is interesting to see if there are a lot of recent customers that are not frequent customers; these customers are new and might be persuaded to become regular customers. Tapping one of the panels opens a detailed report of the customers that were assigned to that particular segment.

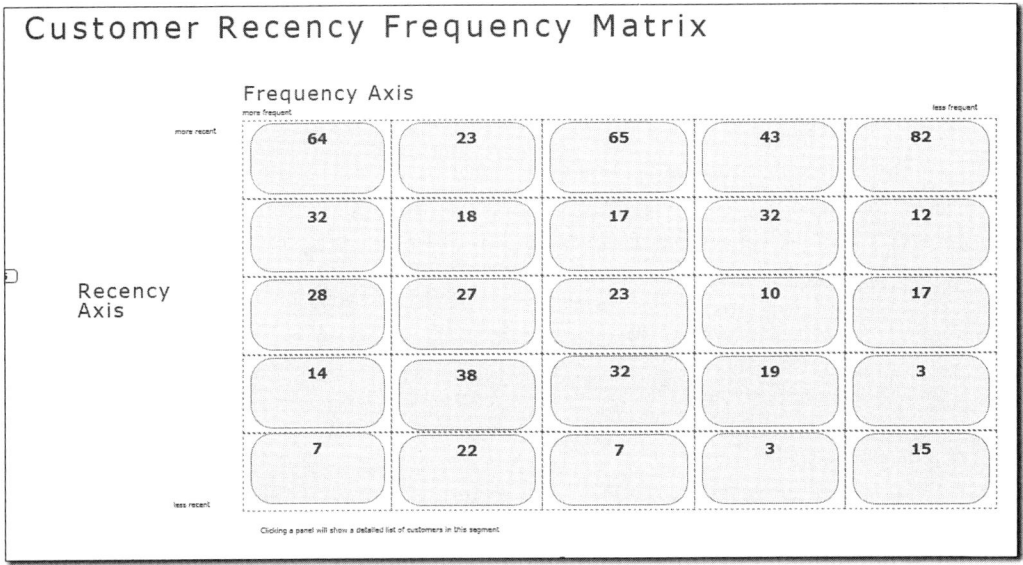

Figure 3.24 Customer Segment Screen

3.6   Business Balanced Scorecards

A business balanced scorecard is a framework of activities that managers can use to track their execution and results. The most visible part of the balanced scorecard is the visualization of both financial and nonfinancial key figures. The balanced scorecard is most effective in tracking the relationships between inputs and processes, and it helps to focus on managing these components to achieve the goals of the organization. In an implementation of a balanced scorecard framework, there are a lot of relationships among components that, in the end, should result in achieving the defined strategy. The goal of the balanced scorecard is usually to increase stockholder value. Stockholder value can be increased in several ways; for example, by improving cost structure, using your assets more effectively, developing more ways to produce income, or increasing your customer value.

For the example in this section, we are going to assume the role of the board of directors of a vegetable company. We will see a couple of strategic initiatives that can be checked, and then discuss how they interact in all the business balanced scorecard perspectives. The company in our example wants to keep growing, so they will look at initiatives to add value for their customers (i.e., supermarkets) and improve usage of assets to increase shareholder value. Specifically, their goal is twofold:

▸ To improve the turnaround time for processing stock. By reducing turnaround time in the factory, the number of harvests the company can process should increase. This means that they can process some products twice a year, instead of once a year, which dramatically cuts down the necessary stock for that finished product.

▸ To reduce instances of supermarkets both running out of stock, as well as having so much stock that it passes its expiration date. This added value for the customer will result in the vegetable company being able to ask for higher prices.

3.6.1 Main Screen

Figure 3.25 shows the main screen of the application. In the financial perspective, the board sees the gross margin percentage, the stock amount of finished goods, and the investment in machinery. It seems that the gross margin percentage and investments are doing okay, but the stock amount has a red signal. Naturally, they want to take a closer look to understand why this is.

Vegetable application

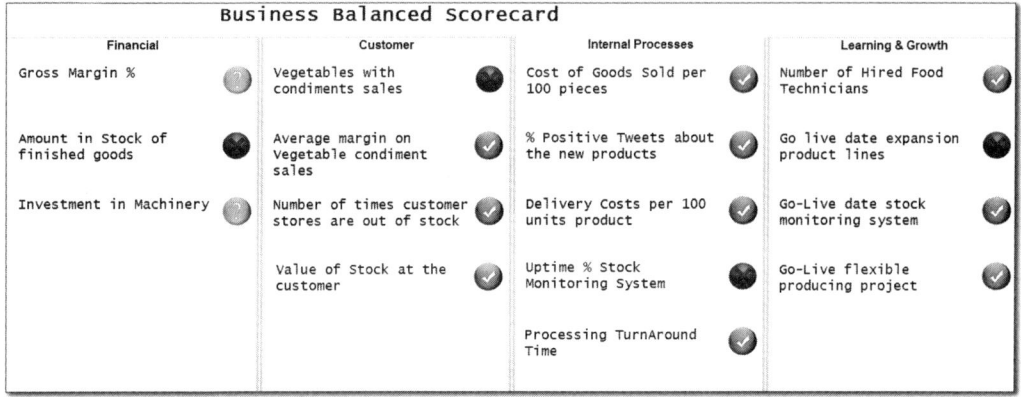

Figure 3.25 Business Balanced Scorecard Main Screen

Color Images

Please note that, though the print book shows the application images in gray-scale, full color versions are viewable in the e-book.

3.6.2 KPI: Amount in Stock of Finished Goods

Key performance indicators

Clicking the stock amount KPI shows a new screen where the board can look at a more detailed analysis of the stock amount KPI (Figure 3.26). Clicking the stock amount shows that the stock amount at the warehouse was decreasing steadily, but at some point during the year it stayed even. This is a problem, because the first goal of the company was to keep decreasing stock at the warehouse by improving processing turnaround time.

What's puzzling about the scenario is that the KPI for turnaround time is being achieved—as you can see from the green checkmark—but it is not having the desired result of reducing stock at the warehouse. Clicking the Project box should shed more light on why there is a red signal on the stock amount.

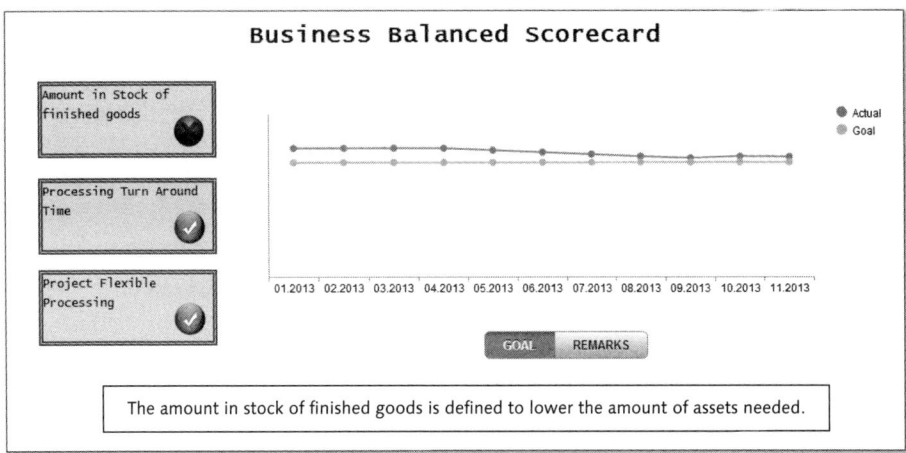

Figure 3.26 KPI Analysis Amount Stock Finished Product

The result of clicking the PROCESSING TURN AROUND TIME box is shown in Figure 3.27. As you can see, clicking the REMARKS tab on this screen gives some insight about why the faster turnaround time for deliveries wasn't resulting in lower stock numbers. It seems that the results of the turnaround time are fine—the problem is that the stock reduction is off-set by the company's other goal, which was to reduce stock at supermarkets. In other words, even though the company is succeeding at improving turnaround time, they are not reducing the necessary stock in their warehouse—because they are also sending less stock to supermarkets.

Project result

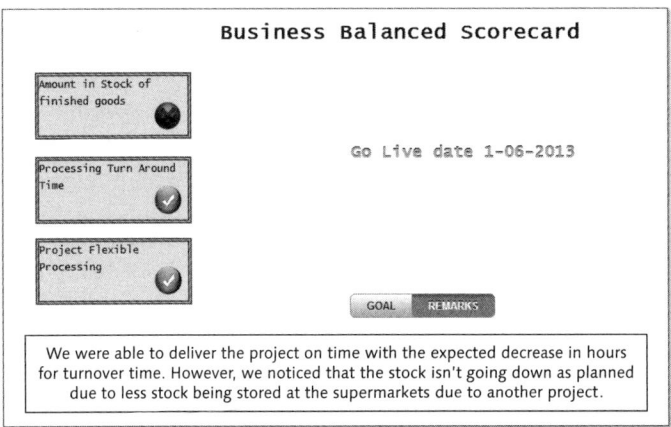

Figure 3.27 Project Turnover Time with Remarks

3.6.3   KPI: Value of Stock at the Customer

The board returns to the main screen to take a look at the KPI for VALUE OF STOCK AT THE CUSTOMER. This KPI is green. The company has succeeded in lowering the stock of its customers; i.e., the supermarkets. However, because this KPI has been achieved at the expense of a different KPI—to reduce stock in the warehouse—the board of directors wants to find out how much this has helped them. They click on the KPI to get more information; this screen is shown in Figure 3.28.

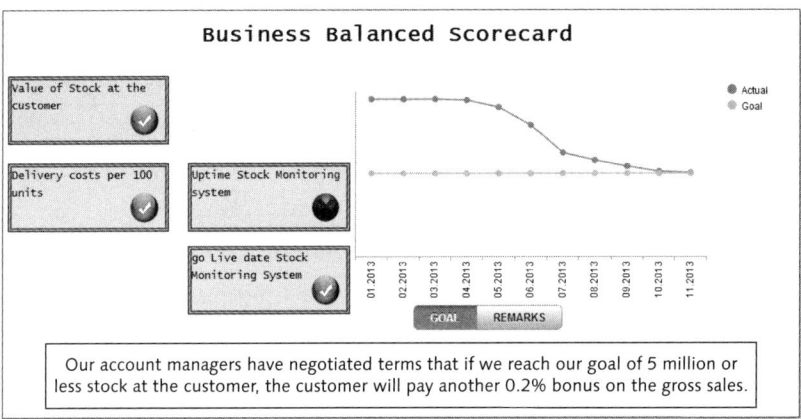

Figure 3.28 Less Stock in Supermarkets

In the graph, they see that the stock level declined from 10 million to 5 million in the last few months. In addition, by clicking the REMARKS button, they can read that their account managers were able to negotiate an extra 0.2% price increase because of the stock level decline. Knowing this, they now have enough information to determine whether the money gained with respect to this KPI balances out the money lost because the company wasn't able to lower stock in the warehouses.

In this example, a company was able to set up a business balanced scorecard with KPIs and define causes and effects. They were also able to analyze why an expected result failed to materialize, even though the KPI that was supposed to cause this result was achieved.

3.7 Summary

In this chapter, we looked at several use cases for Design Studio applications, and discovered that Design Studio can be used in many scenarios.

In the gym scenario, we saw a workflow that was supported by a real-time application. Further, because the application was viewable on an iPad, the employee could go anywhere on the premises and still have all the information he needed to help customers.

The call center scenario showed that an application can be a combination of operation information and tactical analysis. The team lead was able to use an application to see in real time if calls were being answered in an orderly fashion. At the same time, he could sit down and have a look at the planning for the next weeks, or even look months ahead for personnel management.

The real estate scenario showed the advantage of mobility. The agent could travel from place to place without having to go back to the office to collect the needed information. Because the information was so readily available, the agent could use the information more and could make better deals because of it.

The branch manager scenario showed how a Design Studio application can support managers. The manager had access to several different types of information, and could drill down to very detailed operational data.

Finally, the board of directors scenario showed that Design Studio can support a complicated balanced scorecard implementation. The application could provide insight about how one KPI influences another, and how sometimes the relationships between KPIs work out differently than was anticipated during the strategic design process.

This chapter will guide you through the steps to install the server-side add-on components for the SAP BusinessObjects BI platform and SAP NetWeaver BW system as well as the client tool for Design Studio.

4 Installation and Configuration

In this chapter we will take you through the steps to install and set up Design Studio within your SAP BI environment. We will start with an overview of the Design Studio architecture, including system requirements (Section 4.1). Then we will explain how to gather the material you need for the installation (Section 4.2).

In the most important sections in the chapter, we will use a step-by-step approach to show you how to install and configure the SAP BusinessObjects BI platform and SAP NetWeaver BW to run Design Studio (Section 4.3, Section 4.4, Section 4.5, and Section 4.6). After everything is installed and configured, you will perform your first login with the Design Studio client tool (Section 4.7).

> **Versioning**
>
> This chapter is based on SAP BusinessObjects Design Studio 1.1, service pack 02. The content of the following sections is aligned with this software version and might change in future editions of Design Studio.

4.1 Architecture, Components, and Prerequisites

Figure 4.1 shows a high-level overview of the Design Studio architecture. Three layers can be defined. Starting at the bottom of the figure is the first layer with the data sources that contain the data, i.e., an SAP NetWeaver BW or SAP HANA system. Architecture

Design Studio can be integrated in two platforms: the SAP Business-Objects BI platform and SAP NetWeaver BW. This is the second layer, where the connections to the data sources are set up, and the Design Studio applications can be stored here.

On the top layer the end users of the Design Studio applications can run the applications in a browser or on a mobile device. In addition, from this layer application developers can use the Design Studio client tool for development purposes.

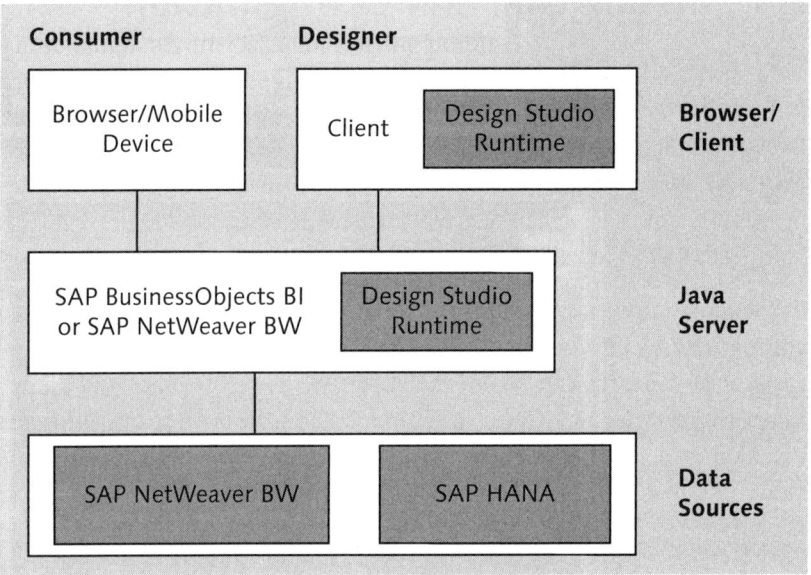

Figure 4.1 Design Studio High-Level Architecture Overview

Components — Design Studio consists of four components that can be installed and/or configured:

▶ **SAP BusinessObjects BI platform and add-on**
In addition to the platform itself, there is an add-on for Design Studio that must be installed.

▶ **SAP NetWeaver BW**
To integrate Design Studio in SAP NetWeaver BW, some configurations need to be made in the system.

▶ **SAP NetWeaver Portal**

To be able to deploy Design Studio applications to SAP NetWeaver Portal, you need to install a component and perform some additional configurations.

▶ **Design Studio client tool**

The Design Studio client tool is an application that has to be installed locally on a Microsoft Windows computer.

Note that when you choose to use the SAP BusinessObjects BI platform as the platform for Design Studio, you don't need to set up SAP NetWeaver BW and SAP NetWeaver Portal. Similarly, if you want to connect directly to the SAP NetWeaver BW system and host your Design Studio applications there, you don't need to set up the SAP BusinessObjects BI platform.

With the SAP BusinessObjects BI platform, you can use the data connections that are defined in the Central Management Console (CMC) as OLAP connections. (Later in this chapter, we will set up such OLAP connections to connect to an SAP NetWeaver BW system and an SAP HANA system; this is discussed in Section 4.4.5 and Section 4.4.6.) When you connect directly to an SAP NetWeaver BW system, the data connections are defined in your local SAP Logon. In this scenario it is only possible to connect to a single SAP NetWeaver BW system at a time.

To move Design Studio applications and files from the development environment to other environments (QA, production), the SAP BusinessObjects BI platform uses Promotion Management, also known as Lifecycle Management Console (LCM). In SAP NetWeaver BW scenarios the SAP Transport Management System (STMS) can be used.

Another important difference between the two scenarios is that running a Design Studio application on mobile devices is only supported by the SAP BusinessObjects BI platform.

Of course, these components all have some landscape prerequisites, and the actual execution of Design Studio applications has browser requirements. We'll look at all of these next.

> **Product Availability Matrix (PAM)**
>
> An updated list of all operation systems, browsers, and mobile devices that are supported for Design Studio is available in the Product Availability Matrix (PAM). The PAM can be found on the SAP Service Marketplace at *http://service.sap.com/pam*.

4.1.1 SAP BusinessObjects BI Platform

For the SAP BusinessObjects BI platform, the following versions are supported:

▶ SAP BusinessObjects BI platform 4.0 with at least service pack 05

▶ SAP BusinessObjects BI platform 4.1

The following conditions have to be met:

▶ Your account for the operating system has administrative rights.

▶ The machine has a 64-bit operating system.

▶ The Adaptive Processing Server is installed.

▶ The Multidimensional Analysis Service component is installed.

▶ The SAP BusinessObjects BI platform Web Applications component is installed.

▶ The Mobiles Services component is installed.

> **SAP BusinessObjects BI Platform Services**
>
> Section 4.4 will further discuss how to set up these necessary services in the Central Management Console.

4.1.2 SAP NetWeaver BW

The following versions of SAP NetWeaver BW are supported:

▶ SAP NetWeaver BW 7.30 with at least service pack 09

▶ SAP NetWeaver BW 7.31 with at least service pack 07

▶ SAP NetWeaver BW 7.40 with at least service pack 02

4.1.3   SAP NetWeaver Portal

To use SAP NetWeaver Portal with Design Studio, the following conditions must be met:

▶ SAP NetWeaver Portal is installed with the BI Java or Enterprise Portal Core usage type.

▶ BI Java is configured for use with SAP NetWeaver BW.

4.1.4   Design Studio Client Tool

To install the client tool for Design Studio on your local machine, you need the following components to be installed:

▶ MS Windows Vista SP2 or Windows 7 SP1, 32-bit or 64-bit

▶ Java Runtime Environment 1.6 or 1.7, 32-bit

▶ MS Internet Explorer 9.0

It is also recommended to have SAP GUI 7.30 installed on your local machine. This will prevent possible problems with connections to SAP NetWeaver BW systems that communicate through a message server.

4.1.5   Browsers

Finally, as we mentioned, there are browser requirements for running Design Studio applications. The following browsers are supported:

▶ MS Internet Explorer 8

▶ MS Internet Explorer 9

▶ MS Internet Explorer 10

▶ Google Chrome 21.0 and higher for Windows

▶ Firefox 17.0 and higher for Windows

▶ Apple Safari 5.1 and higher for Mac

Running a Design Studio application on a mobile device is at the moment reserved for the Apple iPad and iPhone only:

▶ Apple iPad with iOS 5.1.1 and higher

▶ Mobile Safari browser 5.1.1 and higher for iOS

Other mobile devices and platforms are not yet supported.

4.2 Preparing for Installation

In this section you will find all the material that you require to install Design Studio in your SAP BI environment.

4.2.1 Accessing Document Guides

SAP Service
Marketplace

Table 4.1 provides a list of the standard SAP product documentation guides for Design Studio. To access these documents, you require an SAP Service Marketplace account (*http://service.sap.com*).

Material	Location
Administrator Guide: Version for SAP BusinessObjects Business Intelligence (BI platform)	SAP Help Portal *http://help.sap.com/ boad* • INSTALLATION, CONFIGURATION, SECURITY AND ADMINISTRATION INFORMATION • ADMINISTRATOR GUIDE
Administrator Guide: Version for SAP NetWeaver	SAP Help Portal *http://help.sap.com/ boad* • INSTALLATION, CONFIGURATION, SECURITY AND ADMINISTRATION INFORMATION • ADMINISTRATOR GUIDE
Application Designer Guide	SAP Help Portal *http://help.sap.com/ boad* • APPLICATION HELP • ADMINISTRATOR GUIDE
What's New Guide	SAP Help Portal *http://help.sap.com/ boad* • APPLICATION HELP • WHAT'S NEW
Business Intelligence Platform Administrator Guide	SAP Help Portal *http://help.sap.com/ bobip40* • SYSTEM ADMINISTRATION AND MAINTENANCE INFORMATION • ADMINISTRATOR'S GUIDE
SAP BusinessObjects Mobile Administrator and Report Designer's Guide	SAP Help Portal *http://help.sap.com/ bomobileios* • INSTALLATION, ADMINISTRATION, CUSTOMIZATION AND REPORT DESIGNING INFORMATION • ADMINISTRATOR'S GUIDE

Table 4.1 Standard SAP Product Guides

4.2.2 Downloading Software Components

Table 4.2 shows the paths to the download locations for the Design Studio software components. To download these files, your SAP Service Marketplace account needs to be linked to an SAP customer number that owns a license for the Design Studio software.

To check which SAP software your company has access to, you can go to the SAP Software Download Center at the SAP Service Marketplace Support Portal. Go to *http://service.sap.com/swdc* • SAP SOFTWARE DOWNLOAD CENTER • INSTALLATIONS AND UPGRADES • MY COMPANY'S APPLICATION COMPONENTS • MY COMPANY'S SOFTWARE. Here a complete list of authorized software is given.

Checking your company's software

Software Component	Download Location
SAP GUI for Windows 7.30	SAP Software Download Center *http://service.sap.com/swdc* • SOFTWARE DOWNLOADS • SAP SOFTWARE DOWNLOAD CENTER • INSTALLATIONS AND UPGRADES • BROWSE OUR DOWNLOAD CATALOG • SAP FRONTEND COMPONENTS • SAP GUI FOR WINDOWS • SAP GUI FOR WINDOWS 7.30 CORE • INSTALLATION
SAP BusinessObjects Design Studio 1.1 Design tool and BI platform add-on	SAP Software Download Center *http://service.sap.com/swdc* • SOFTWARE DOWNLOADS • SAP SOFTWARE DOWNLOAD CENTER • INSTALLATIONS AND UPGRADES • BROWSE OUR DOWNLOAD CATALOG • ANALYTICS SOLUTIONS • SBOP DESIGN STUDIO SBOP DESIGN STUDIO 1.1 • INSTALLATION

Table 4.2 Software Components Locations

If you are updating from a previous version of Design Studio, you can download the service pack update from the download locations in Table 4.3. Here you will find the download locations for future releases of service packs and patches.

Updating from a previous version

Software Component	Download Location
SAP BusinessObjects Design Studio 1.1 BI platform add-on service pack	SAP Software Download Center *http://service.sap.com/patches* • SOFTWARE DOWNLOADS • SAP SOFTWARE DOWNLOAD CENTER • SUPPORT PACKAGES AND PATCHES • BROWSE OUR DOWNLOAD CATALOG • ANALYTICS SOLUTIONS • SBOP DESIGN STUDIO • SBOP DESIGN STUDIO 1.1 COMPRISED SOFTWARE COMPONENT VERSIONS • DESIGN STUDIO BIP ADD ON 1.1 • AIX 64BIT, LINUX ON X86_64 64BIT, SOLARIS ON SPARC 64BIT OR WINDOWS ON X64 64BIT
SAP BusinessObjects Design Studio 1.1 SAP NetWeaver BW add-on service pack	SAP Software Download Center *http://service.sap.com/patches* • SOFTWARE DOWNLOADS • SAP SOFTWARE DOWNLOAD CENTER • SUPPORT PACKAGES AND PATCHES • BROWSE OUR DOWNLOAD CATALOG • ANALYTICS SOLUTIONS • SBOP DESIGN STUDIO • SBOP DESIGN STUDIO 1.1 • COMPRISED SOFTWARE COMPONENT VERSIONS • DESIGN STUDIO NW 1.1 • # OS INDEPENDENT
SAP BusinessObjects Design Studio 1.1 BI platform add-on service pack	SAP Software Download Center *http://service.sap.com/patches* • SOFTWARE DOWNLOADS • SAP SOFTWARE DOWNLOAD CENTER • SUPPORT PACKAGES AND PATCHES • BROWSE OUR DOWNLOAD CATALOG • ANALYTICS SOLUTIONS • SBOP DESIGN STUDIO • SBOP DESIGN STUDIO 1.1 • COMPRISED SOFTWARE COMPONENT VERSIONS • DESIGN STUDIO BIP ADD ON 1.1 • AIX 64BIT, LINUX ON X86_64 64BIT, SOLARIS ON SPARC 64BIT OR WINDOWS ON X64 64BIT

Table 4.3 Service Pack and Patch Locations

4.2.3 Helpful SAP Notes

Table 4.4 shows a number of important SAP Notes that are related to Design Studio. To be able to access the SAP Notes, you need an SAP Service Marketplace account. You can find SAP Notes at *http://service.sap.com/notes*.

SAP Note Number	SAP Note Title
1177020	SAP BusinessObjects Design Studio: Sizing Information
1760372	SAP BusinessObjects Design Studio: Release Schedule
1768160	Reduced WAN Performance of Designer Client
1773751	SAP BusinessObjects Design Studio Support
1786081	Continuous Resizing on iPad
1807142	How to Enable HTTPS/SSL Designer against BIP
1811747	TLOGO Integration for Analysis Applications (Design Studio)
1814084	Additional Corrections: Analysis Applications/Design Studio
1816941	TLogo Integration for Analysis Applications #2
1822009	Support for Design Studio TLOGO Object Browsing in Roles
1843646	SBOP Design Studio 1.1: Release Note for First Delivery
1849128	Internet Explorer Version for Design Studio
1855350	Limitation: Restricted Internet Explorer in BI Platform
1866425	Analysis Applications on BIP Do Not Run on IE
1868232	SBOP Design Studio 1.1: Release Limitations Note
1869560	SAP BusinessObjects BI Support Matrix for SAP NetWeaver BW

Table 4.4 Important SAP Notes

4.2.4 Extracting Installation Files

Before we start with the actual installation of the various components, we have to download and extract the Design Studio software. Follow the steps below:

1. Make sure you have downloaded all the files from the SAP Software Download Center (see Table 4.2 for the exact download location). As you can see in Figure 4.2, there are three files:

   ▸ *51045997_part1.exe*

   ▸ *51045997_part2.rar*

   ▸ *51045997_part3.rar*

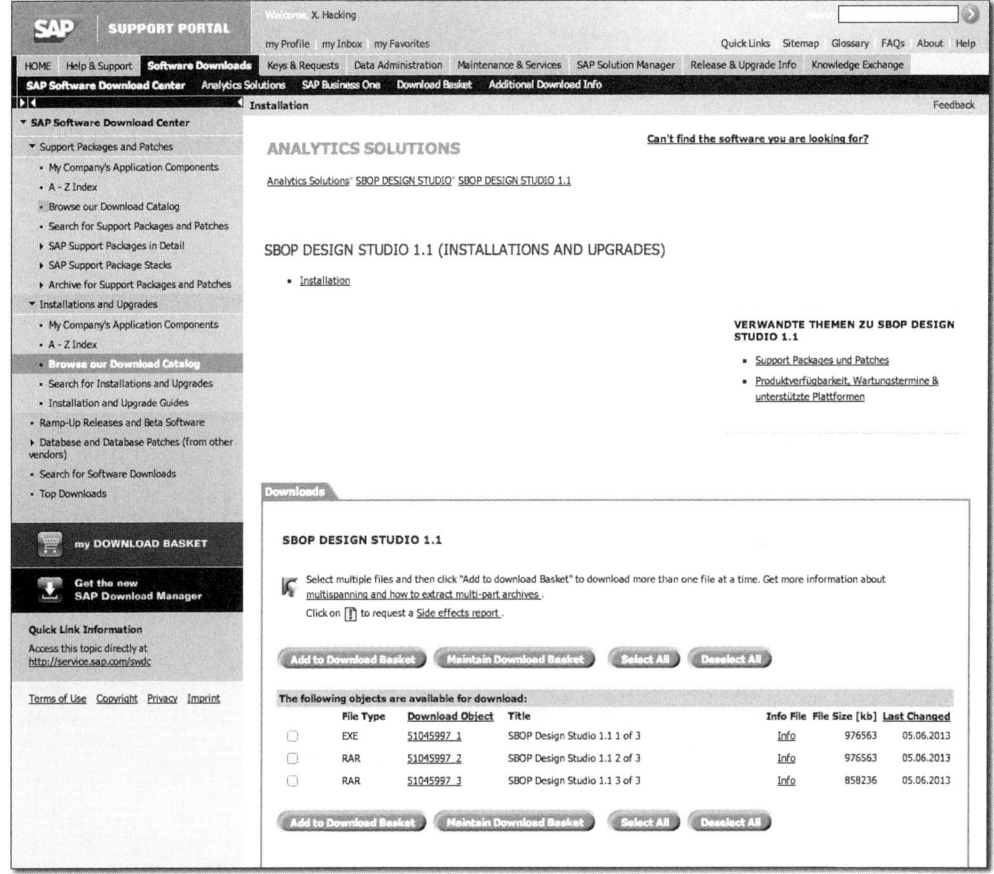

Figure 4.2 Design Studio Download Files on SAP Support Portal

2. Start 51045997_PART1.EXE to extract the files. Here you can choose a destination folder for the extracted files (see Figure 4.3).

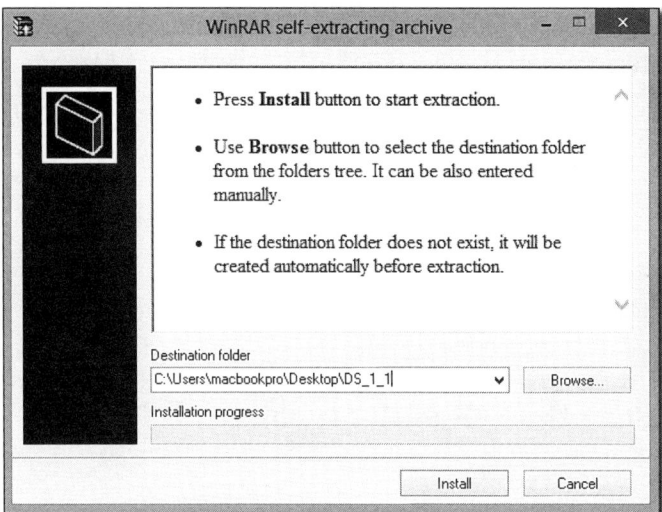

Figure 4.3 Extraction Destination Folder

3. Click INSTALL to start the extraction (see Figure 4.4).

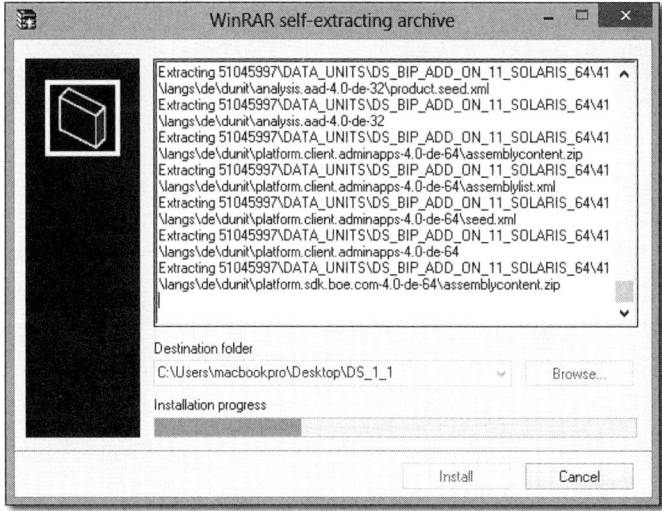

Figure 4.4 Extraction of Installation Files

4. Browse through the extracted files to the DATA_UNITS folder. Here you will see the server-side installation files for the four server environments that are supported for the SAP BusinessObjects BI platform, the server-side installation files for SAP NetWeaver BW, and the installation files for the Design Studio client tool (Figure 4.5).

DS_BIP_ADD_ON_11_AIX_PPC64	5-6-2013 10:46
DS_BIP_ADD_ON_11_LINUX_X64	5-6-2013 11:09
DS_BIP_ADD_ON_11_SOLARIS_64	5-6-2013 11:36
DS_BIP_ADD_ON_11_WINDOWS_X64	5-6-2013 11:47
DS_CLIENT_11	5-6-2013 10:24
DS_NW_APP_11	5-6-2013 10:24

Figure 4.5 Contents of DATA_UNITS Folder

4.3 Installing the SAP BusinessObjects BI Platform Add-On

In this section we will discuss the installation steps for the SAP BusinessObjects BI platform add-on for Design Studio. To complete this server-side installation, follow the steps below.

Operating Systems

In this book we will only follow the installation steps for installing Design Studio on a Microsoft Windows environment.

1. Open folder DS_BIP_ADD_ON_11_WINDOWS_X64. If you are running version 4.0 of the SAP BusinessObjects BI platform, open the 40 folder. If you are running version 4.1 open the 41 folder.

2. Double-click SETUP.EXE to start the installation.

3. Select a setup language and click OK (Figure 4.6). This is the language for the Installation Wizard only, not for the Design Studio installation itself. In this example, we selected ENGLISH as the setup language.

4. A prerequisite check is performed on the SAP BusinessObjects BI platform and server environment (Figure 4.7). The installation cannot start unless all of the critical prerequisites are met.

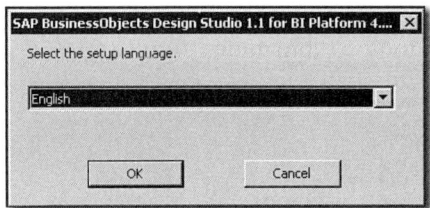

Figure 4.6 Setup Language Screen

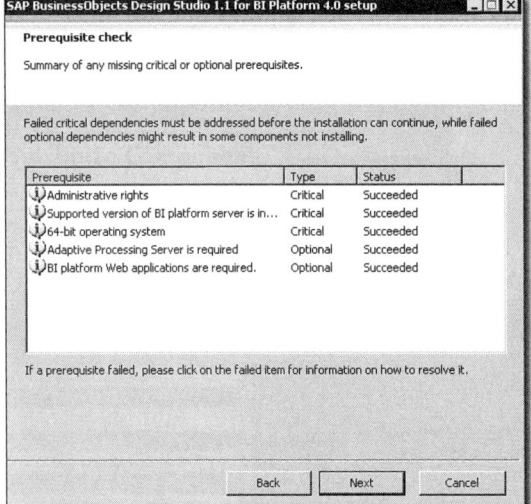

Figure 4.7 Prerequisite Check

Optional and Critical Prerequisites

Some of the optional prerequisites might become critical, depending on the specific SAP BusinessObjects BI platform installation and the installed components.

5. The next screen shows the Installation Wizard (Figure 4.8). Click NEXT to start the installation.

Installation Wizard

6. The Software License Agreement is displayed (Figure 4.9). If you accept the terms, click the I ACCEPT THE LICENSE AGREEMENT line and the NEXT button to continue.

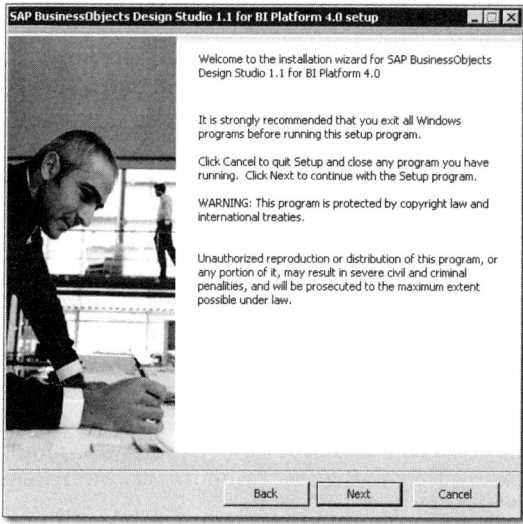

Figure 4.8 Installation Wizard

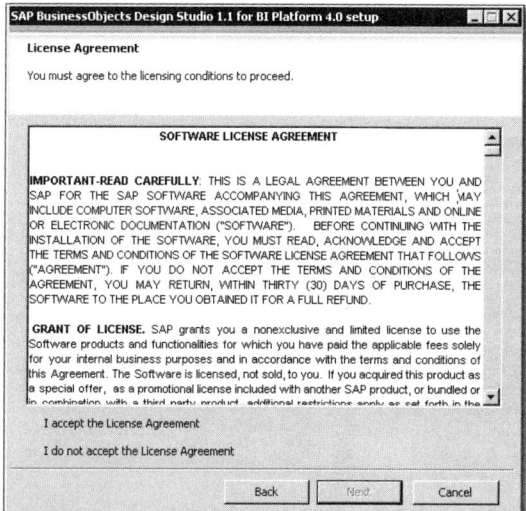

Figure 4.9 Software License Agreement

7. The destination folder location for the installation opens next (Figure 4.10). Since this directory is based on the SAP BusinessObjects BI platform installation directory and it cannot be changed, the only thing we can do here is click NEXT.

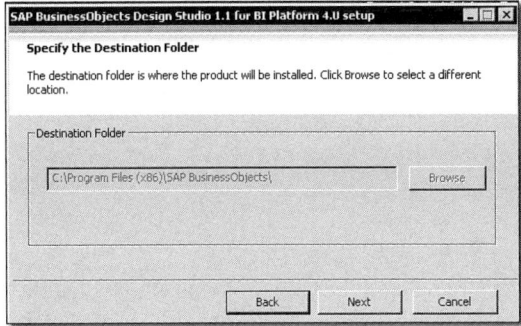

Figure 4.10 Destination Folder

8. In the following screen (Figure 4.11), you have the choice to perform either a full installation or an installation including only some specific features:

Full or partial installation

▶ Analysis Application Web Components

▶ Analysis Application Service

▶ Analysis Application support for Mobile Services

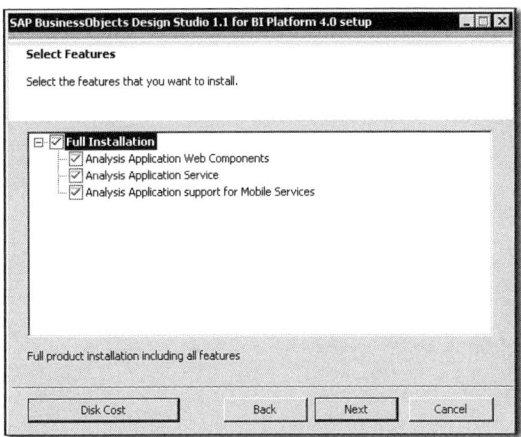

Figure 4.11 Installation Features Selection

Table 4.5 describes these features. With the DISK COST option, you can calculate the required amount of disk space (Figure 4.12). Select the features you want to install and click NEXT to continue.

Feature	Description
Analysis Application Web Component	This feature enables the integration of Design Studio applications in the BI Launch Pad environment, so they can be used like any other BI document. Open-Document links are supported. The feature also allows the Design Studio client tool to communicate with the SAP BusinessObjects BI platform to save and execute Design Studio applications.
Analysis Application Service	This feature enables the execution of Design Studio applications. It includes the Analysis Application Service in the Adaptive Processing Server.
Analysis Application support for Mobile Services	This feature includes mobile support for Design Studio applications. It enables users to access Design Studio applications through SAP BusinessObjects Mobile on mobile devices such as the iPad.

Table 4.5 Installation Features

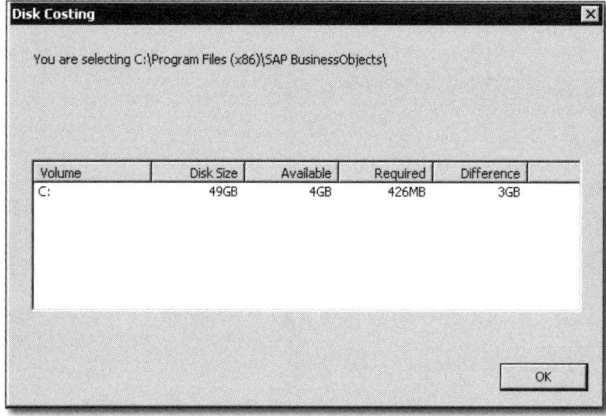

Figure 4.12 Installation Disk Costing

9. Now you are asked to enter some information on the SAP Business-Objects BI platform you are using for this installation (Figure 4.13):

▶ CMS name

▶ CMS port number

▶ CMS administrator user password

After entering the right credentials, click NEXT to continue.

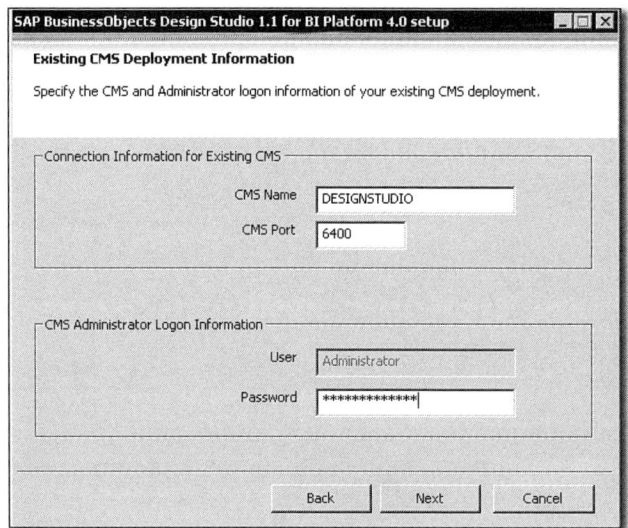

Figure 4.13 BI Platform Information

10. You are one NEXT click away from the installation finally starting (Figure 4.14)! Click NEXT.

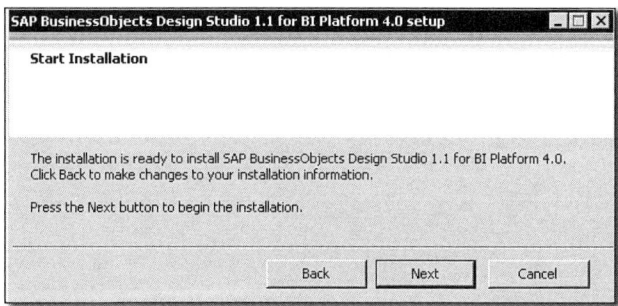

Figure 4.14 Start Installation Screen

11. Now you can sit back, enjoy something to drink, and let the machine do its work (Figure 4.15).

12. When the installation is finished, a post-installation instruction is displayed (Figure 4.16). If you use multiple Web Application Service nodes or you do not use the default Tomcat server or Web Application Container Services (WACS), you need to perform a post-installation step using the WDeploy tool.

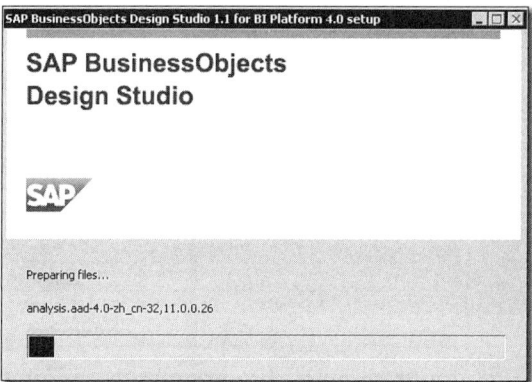

Figure 4.15 Running Installation

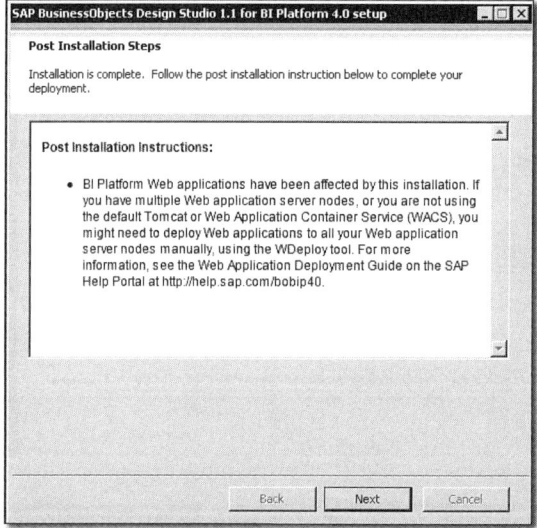

Figure 4.16 Post-Installation Instruction

> **WDeploy**
>
> For more information on the WDeploy tool, see *the Business Intelligence Platform Web Application Deployment Guide* on the SAP Help Portal at *http://help.sap.com/bobip40*.
>
> If you choose to run the WDeploy tool later, you can find it via Start • All Programs • SAP Business Intelligence • SAP BusinessObjects BI Platform 4 • WDeploy.

13. You have successfully installed the SAP BusinessObjects BI platform **WDeploy** add-on for Design Studio (Figure 4.17). If you wish to launch the WDeploy tool, just select the Automatically launch WDeploy tool after install checkbox.

Next we will continue the installation process with the configuration of the SAP BusinessObjects BI platform.

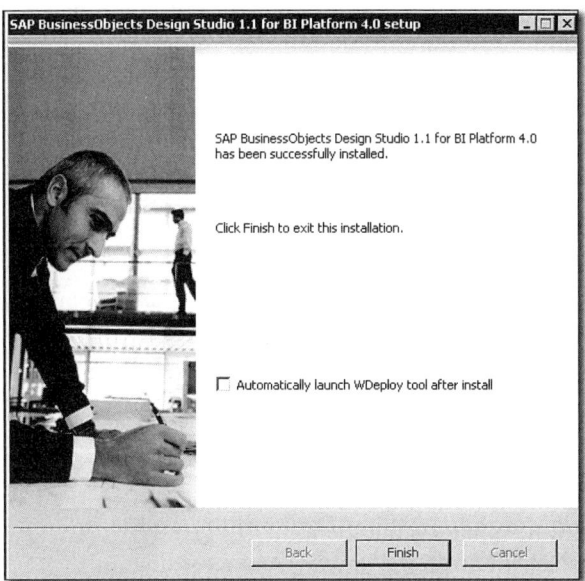

Figure 4.17 Installation Finished

4.4 Configuring the SAP BusinessObjects BI Platform

Now that the SAP BusinessObjects BI platform add-on for Design Studio has been installed, a number of configurations can be set on the platform itself. These configurations include the following:

▶ Initializing the Analysis Application Service
▶ Setting the number of client sessions
▶ Assigning user authorizations
▶ Establishing a Mobile category

111

After these steps are accomplished, we will show you how to set up OLAP connections to an SAP NetWeaver BW and SAP HANA environment.

4.4.1 Initializing the Analysis Application Service

CMC
To run Design Studio applications from the SAP BusinessObjects BI platform, the Analysis Application Service has to be successfully initialized. You can check this in the Central Management Console (CMC).

1. Log in to the CMC via START • ALL PROGRAMS • SAP BUSINESS INTELLIGENCE • SAP BUSINESSOBJECTS BI PLATFORM 4 • SAP BUSINESSOBJECTS BI PLATFORM CENTRAL MANAGEMENT CONSOLE. This is a shortcut to the URL of the CMC, which is *http://<host>:8080/BOE/CMC*.

2. Go to SERVERS.

3. Check if there is an Adaptive Processing Server available under SERVICE CATEGORIES • ANALYSIS SERVICES (Figure 4.18).

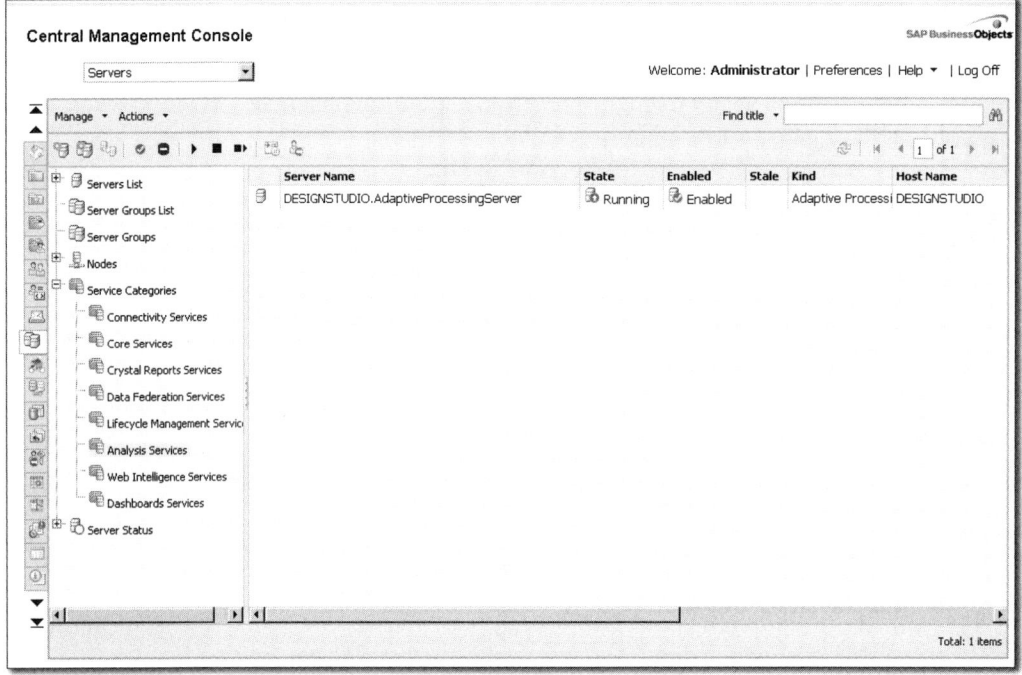

Figure 4.18 Adaptive Processing Server Is Running

4. If this Adaptive Processing Server is not available, you have to add one. To do this, go to MANAGE • NEW • NEW SERVER (Figure 4.19).

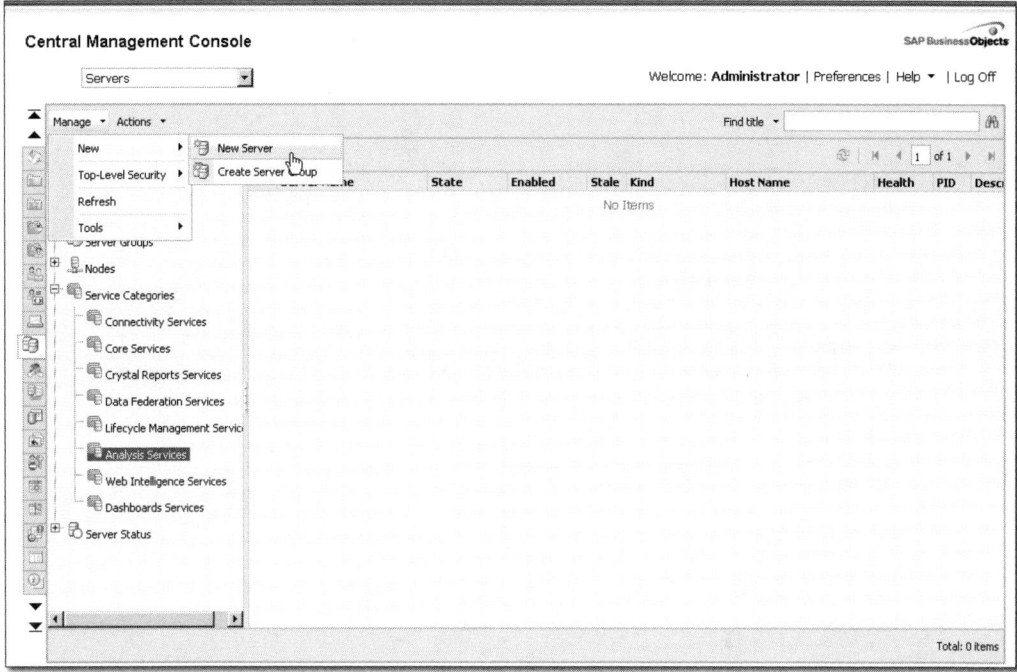

Figure 4.19 Add a New Server

5. Select ANALYSIS SERVICES as the service category (Figure 4.20).

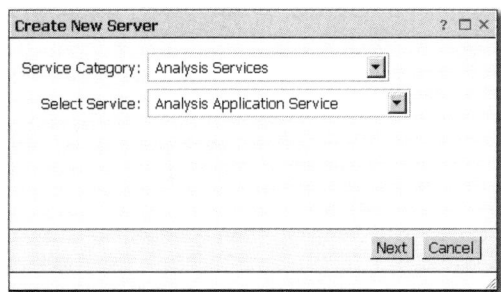

Figure 4.20 Select Service Category

6. Select the ANALYSIS APPLICATION SERVICE and click NEXT (Figure 4.21).

7. You can edit the server name if you like. Click CREATE to continue.

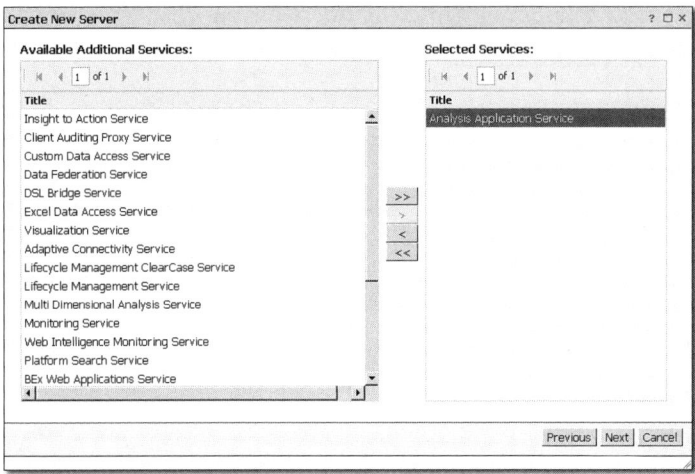

Figure 4.21 Select Service

8. As you can see in Figure 4.22, the Adaptive Processing Server is now available, but it is still inactive. Right-click the Adaptive Processing Server and select ENABLE SERVER (Figure 4.23).

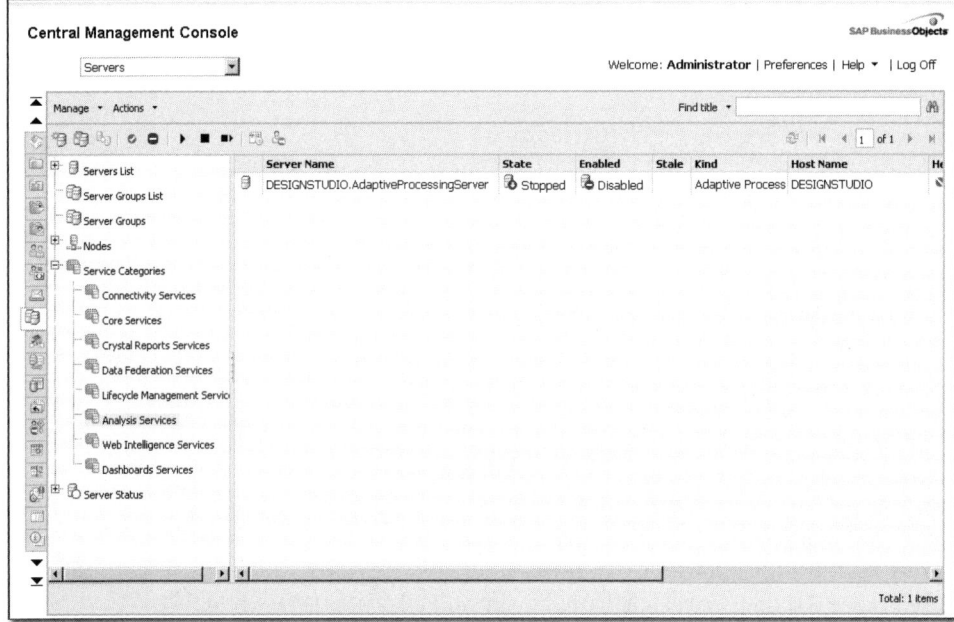

Figure 4.22 Adaptive Processing Server Created

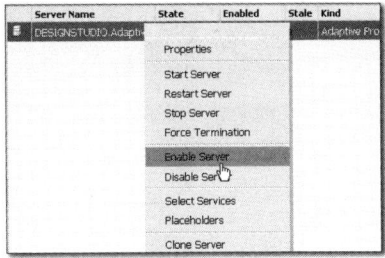

Figure 4.23 Enable Server

Enabling the
server

9. When the server is enabled, you can start it. Right-click the Adaptive Processing Server and choose START SERVER (Figure 4.24).

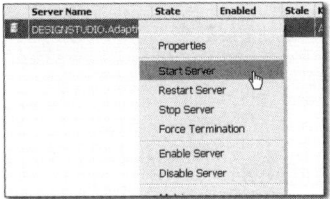

Figure 4.24 Start Server

10. Now right-click the Adaptive Processing Server and choose PROPERTIES to check the initialization status of the server. Scroll all the way down to the ANALYSIS APPLICATION SERVICE area (Figure 4.25).

11. The message that should appear here is SERVICE IS HEALTHY. If the service is not successfully initialized, it shows SERVICE INITIALIZATION FAILED. In this case, you should check the server log files to fix the issue.

Managing and Configuring Logs in the SAP BusinessObjects BI Platform

For more information about logging traces, you can check the Managing and Configuring Logs chapter in the *Business Intelligence Platform Administrator Guide*. This document can be downloaded from *http://help.sap.com/bobip40*.

For more information about SAP BusinessObjects BI administration in general, see *SAP BusinessObjects BI System Administration*, by Greg Myers and Eric Vallo (SAP PRESS, 2013).

---

12. Click SAVE & CLOSE to finish.

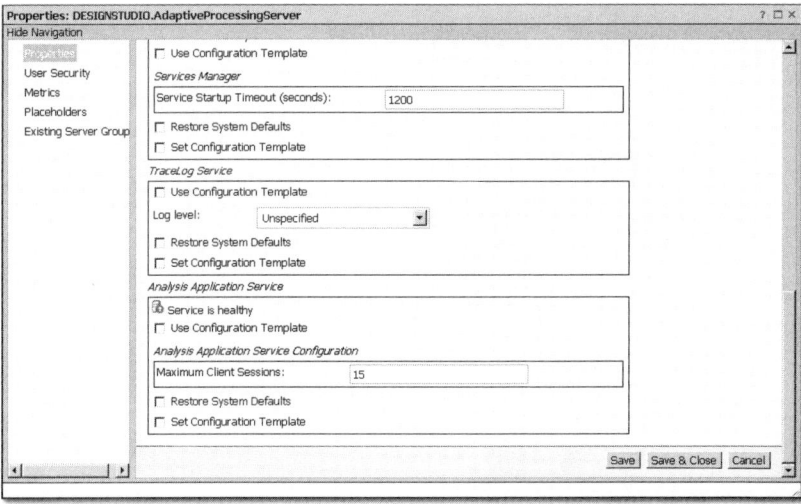

Figure 4.25 Check Server Status

4.4.2 Setting the Number of Client Sessions

The maximum number of client sessions that can be active simultaneously can be altered for the Analysis Application Service. When the number of active sessions reaches this number, any further attempts to use Design Studio applications will be cancelled. An error message like the one in Figure 4.26 will be shown.

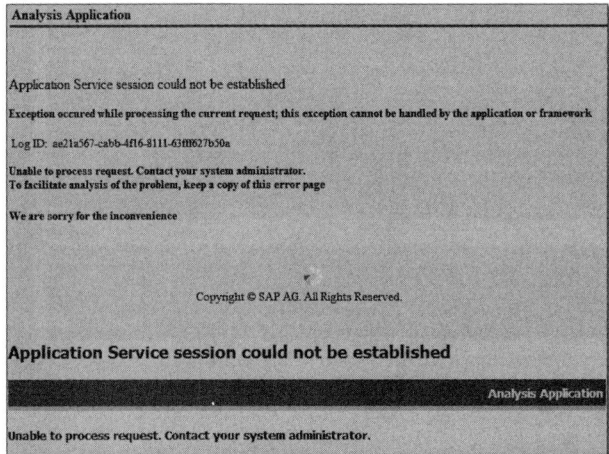

Figure 4.26 Error Due to Maximum Number of Client Sessions Reached

1. Log in to the CMC and go to SERVERS.

2. Go to SERVICE CATEGORIES • ANALYSIS SERVICES (Figure 4.18).

3. Right-click ADAPTIVE PROCESSING SERVER and choose PROPERTIES. Scroll all the way down to the Analysis Application Service area (Figure 4.25).

4. Check the MAXIMUM CLIENT SESSIONS and change the default value if required.

4.4.3 Assigning User Authorizations

Design Studio application designers and users need specific authorizations to be able to access and work with applications. We'll now explain how to create a new user group for these Design Studio users and assign the appropriate authorizations to it:

1. First you need to create a new user group. Log in to the CMC and go to USERS AND GROUPS.

2. Select MANAGE • NEW • NEW GROUP and enter a group name, for example, "Design Studio Users" (see Figure 4.27). Click OK to save the new user group.

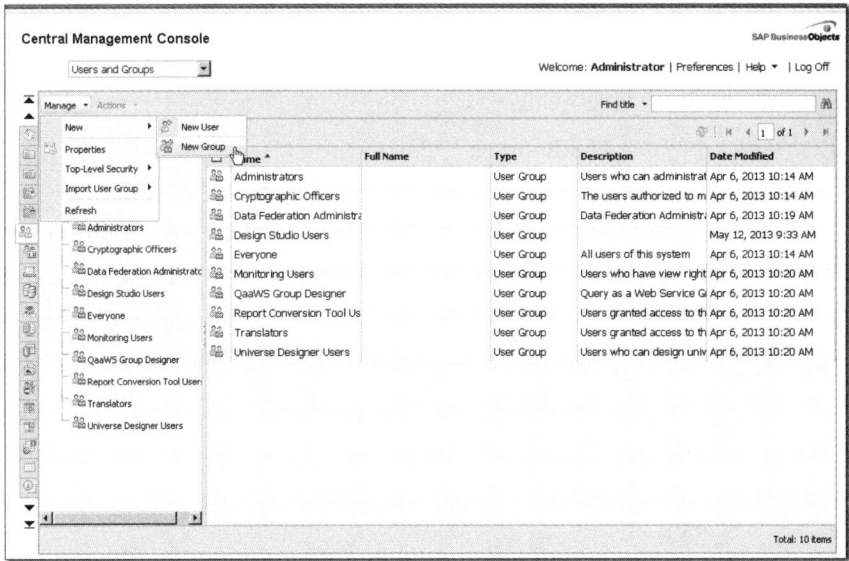

Figure 4.27 Adding a New User Group

Add members to group

3. You can add existing users to this group by right-clicking the group and selecting ADD MEMBERS TO GROUP (see Figure 4.28). Select the users you want to add and click OK to finish.

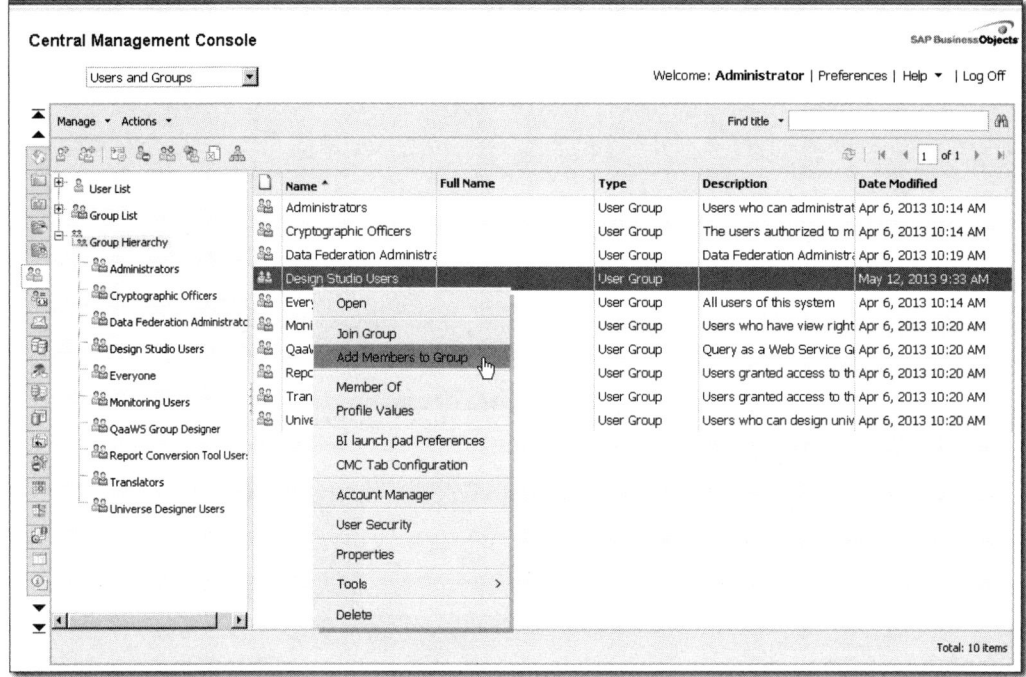

Figure 4.28 Adding Members to a User Group

4. Now go to the APPLICATIONS menu in the CMC.

5. Right-click DESIGN STUDIO RUNTIME and select USER SECURITY (see Figure 4.29). Now you will add the group you just created to this application's user security configuration.

Principals

6. Click ADD PRINCIPALS.

7. Select GROUP LIST and add DESIGN STUDIO USERS group to the SELECTED USERS/GROUPS (see Figure 4.30). Click ADD AND ASSIGN SECURITY.

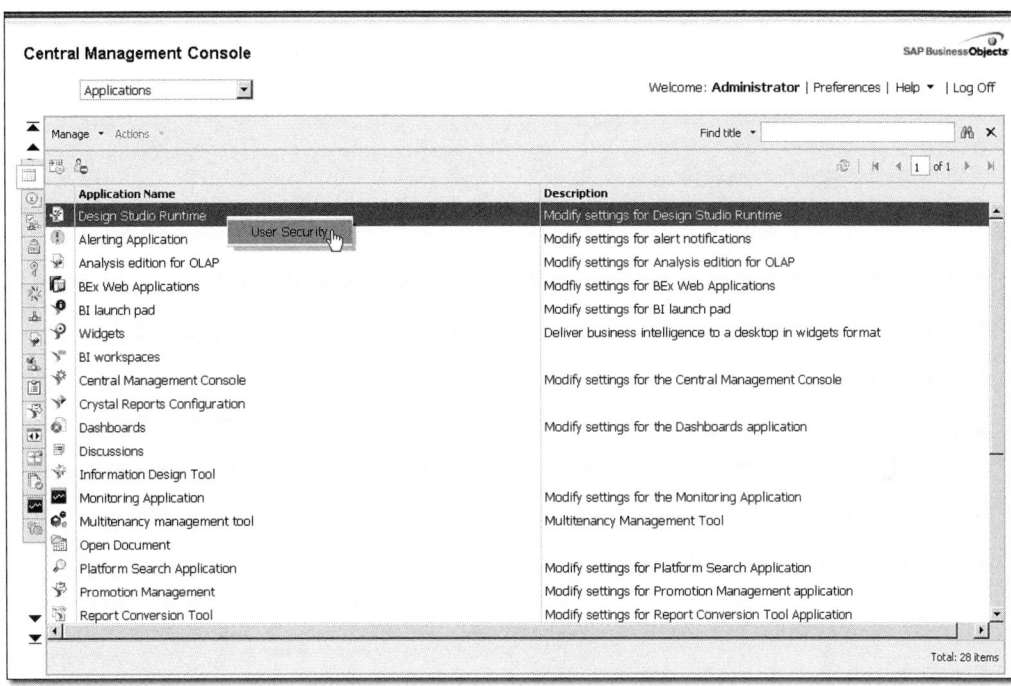

Figure 4.29 User Security for Design Studio Runtime Application

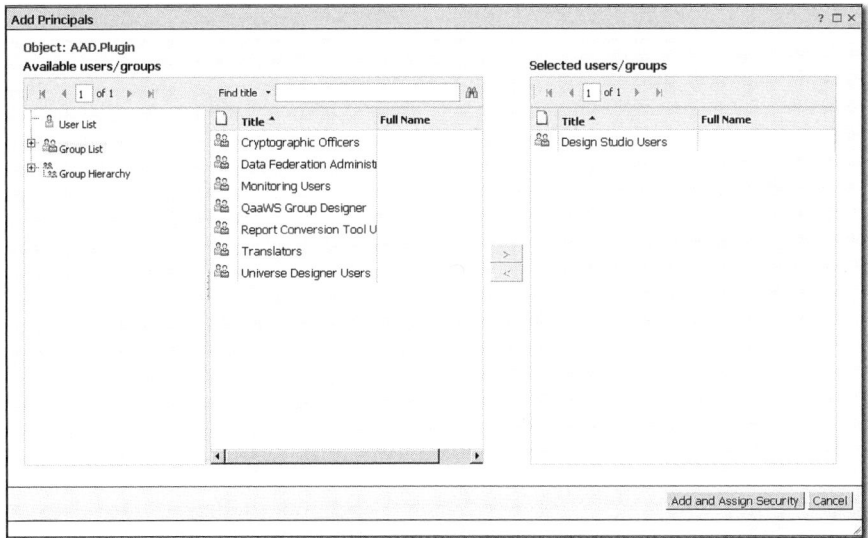

Figure 4.30 User Group Selection

8. Select the VIEW access level and add it to the ASSIGNED ACCESS LEVELS (see Figure 4.31). Click OK to finish.

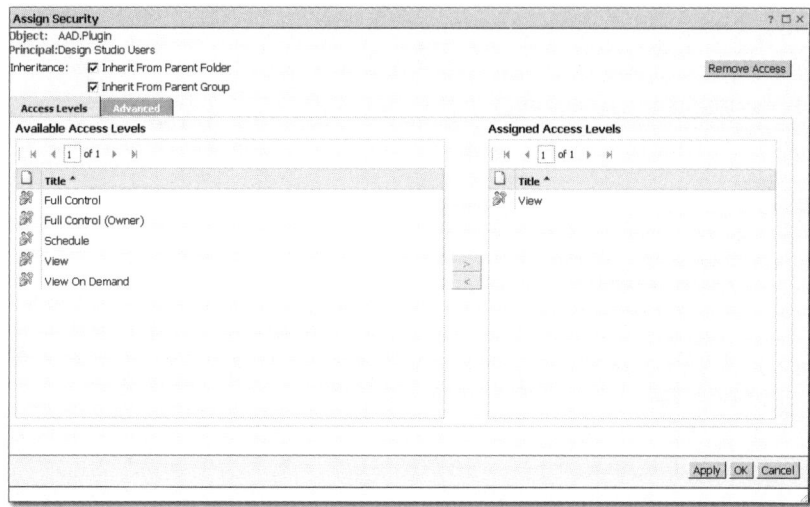

Figure 4.31 Access Level Selection

Your users have been granted the authorization rights for Design Studio. But remember, you will also have to configure the authorizations for other parts of the SAP BusinessObjects BI platform, like the OLAP connections and the document folders you want this user group to use.

4.4.4 Creating a Mobile Category

SAP BusinessObjects Mobile application

Design Studio applications can be accessed through the SAP BusinessObjects Mobile application on mobile devices (see Appendix C). To enable this feature, a Design Studio application should be filed to the MOBILE category on the SAP BusinessObjects BI platform. In this section we will check if this category exists, and, if not, we will create it.

1. Log in to the CMC and go to CATEGORIES.

2. Check if there is a MOBILE category.

3. If not, select MANAGE • NEW • CATEGORY (Figure 4.32).

4. Enter "Mobile" as the new category name and click OK (see Figure 4.33).

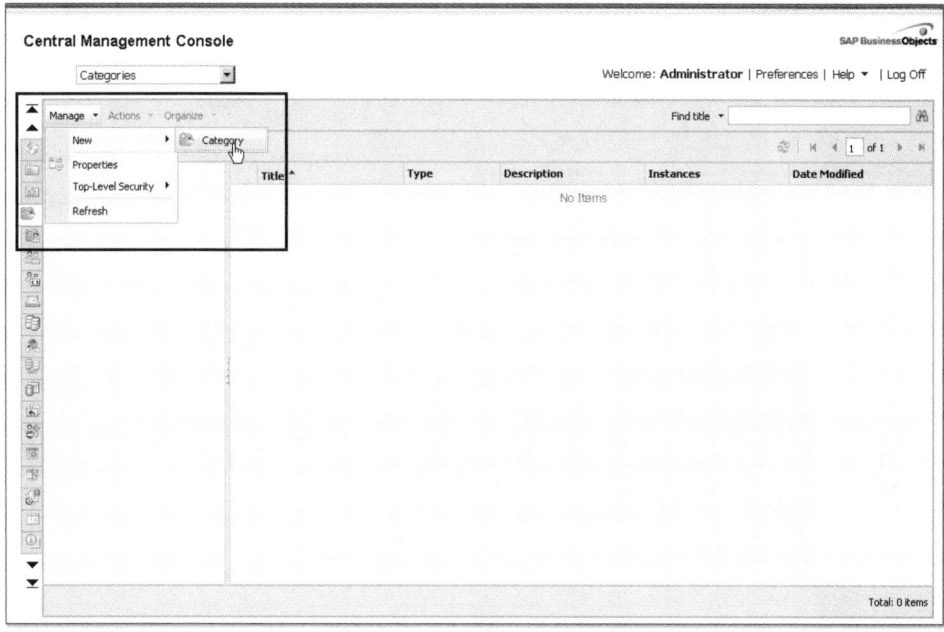

Figure 4.32 Add New Category

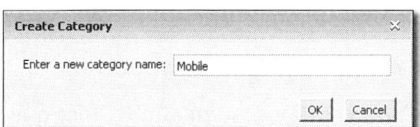

Figure 4.33 Mobile Category Name

5. The MOBILE category is now available (Figure 4.34).

6. You can add Design Studio applications to this category by right-click-   Add to category
ing the MOBILE category and choosing ADD TO CATEGORY. You can also
right-click the Design Studio application document itself and choose
CATEGORIES.

Configuring Categories on the Mobile Server

The default name for the mobile category is MOBILE. For more information on
how to change this category name and organize and display the mobile content, check the *Configuring Categories on the Mobile Server* section in the *SAP
BusinessObjects Mobile Administrator and Report Designer's Guide*. This document can be downloaded from *http://help.sap.com/bomobileios*.

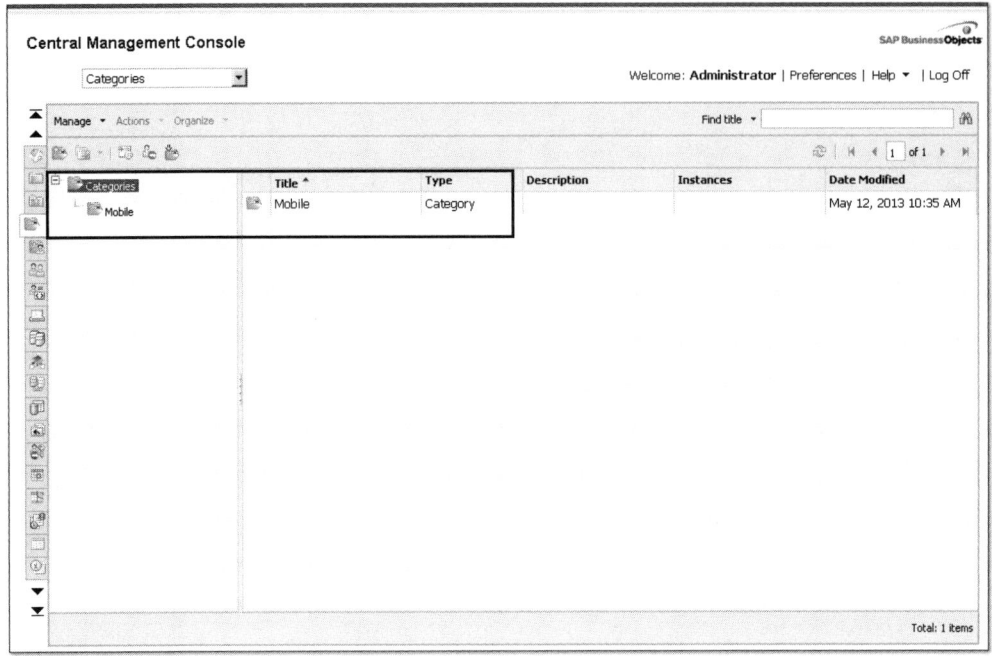

Figure 4.34 Mobile Category Added

4.4.5 Creating an SAP NetWeaver BW OLAP Connection

BEx queries and InfoProviders

To be able to connect to an SAP NetWeaver BW system and its BEx queries and InfoProviders, an OLAP connection has to be created on the SAP BusinessObjects BI platform. Such an OLAP connection can give access to the whole SAP NetWeaver BW system or to a specific BEx query, BEx query view, or SAP NetWeaver BW InfoProvider (like an InfoCube or DSO). To set up an OLAP connection, follow the steps below:

1. Log in to the CMC.

2. Go to OLAP CONNECTIONS and click NEW CONNECTION (Figure 4.35).

3. In the configuration screen that appears, enter the name and a description (optional) for the connection.

4. Choose SAP NETWEAVER BUSINESS WAREHOUSE as the provider for the OLAP connection.

5. Enter the SAP NetWeaver BW server information of the server to which you want to connect (Figure 4.36).

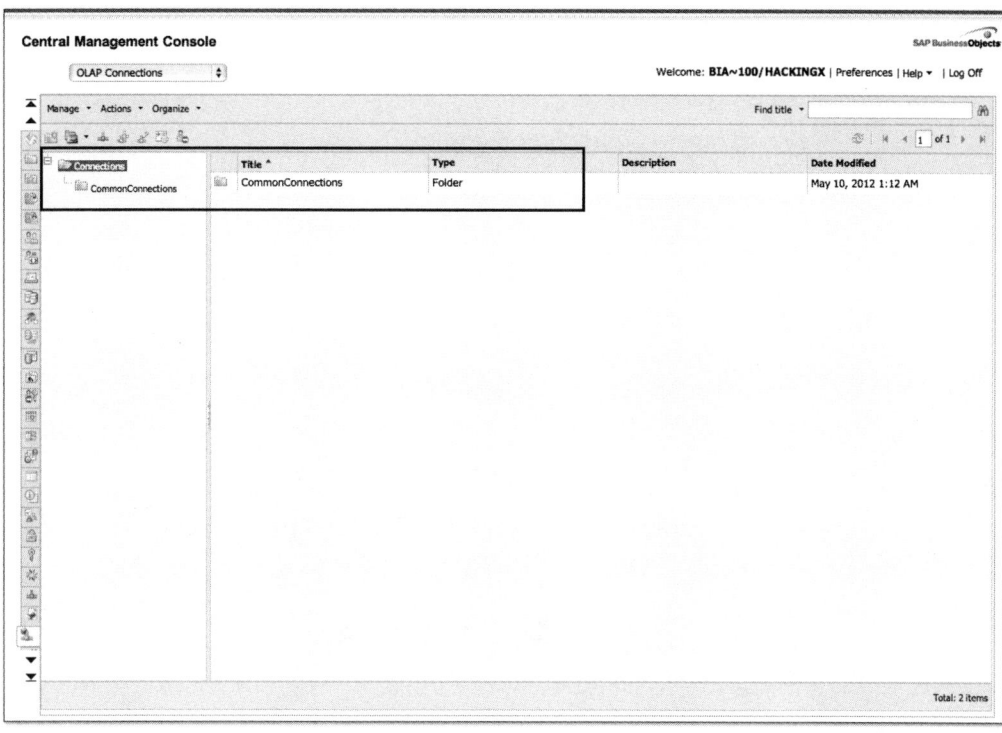

Figure 4.35 OLAP Connections in the CMC

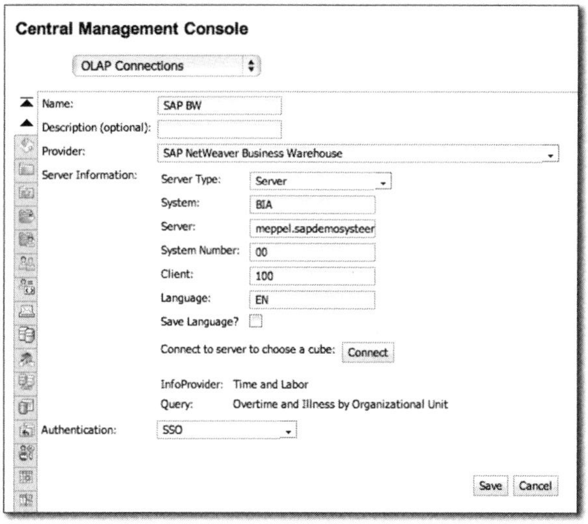

Figure 4.36 OLAP Connection Settings for SAP NetWeaver BW

6. To define an OLAP connection to a specific SAP NetWeaver BW object, click the CONNECT button. Enter your SAP NetWeaver BW credentials in the popup to log on here and click OK (Figure 4.37).

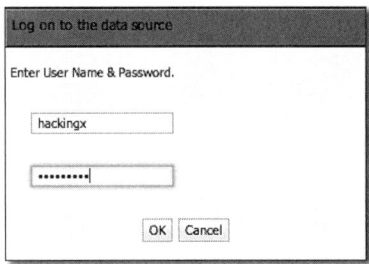

Figure 4.37 Log on to the Data Source Popup

7. With the CUBE BROWSER, you can now browse to a BEx query, BEx query view, or SAP NetWeaver BW InfoProvider. Click SELECT after you make your selection (Figure 4.38).

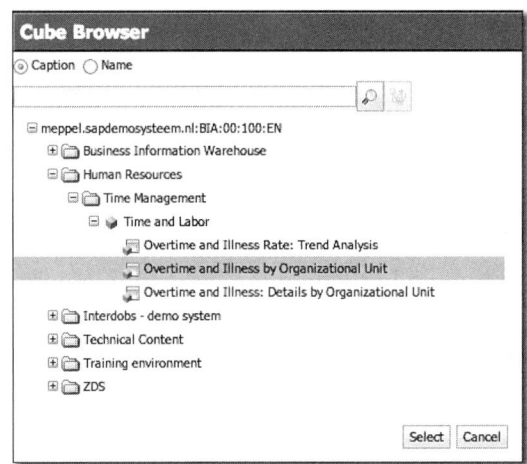

Figure 4.38 Cube Browser

Defining authentication method

8. Finally, the authentication method has to be defined. There are three possible options here:

  ▶ PROMPT

  ▶ SSO

  ▶ PRE-DEFINED

With PROMPT, the users have to log on with their own user credentials. They can change the client and the language in the logon screen. With single sign-on (SSO), the users don't have to enter their credentials, but they still can change the client and language in the logon screen. The users of an application can access the SAP NetWeaver BW objects and data that they are authorized for by the SAP NetWeaver BW authorization concept. With the PRE-DEFINED option, the credentials of a specific user account have to be entered. This means that the authorization profile of this user will be used whenever this connection is used.

9. Click SAVE to save the new OLAP connection. The OLAP connection is now added to the list of available connections (see Figure 4.39).

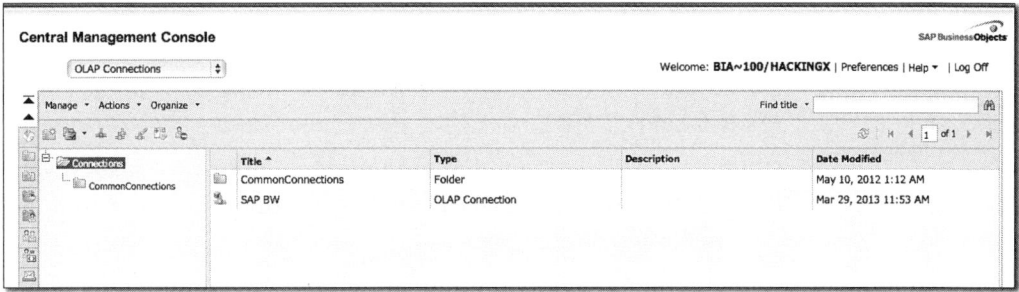

Figure 4.39 OLAP Connections

4.4.6 Creating an SAP HANA OLAP Connection

Setting up an OLAP connection from the SAP BusinessObjects BI platform to an SAP HANA system requires most of the same steps as in the previous section. You can connect to an SAP HANA system as a whole, an analytic view, or a calculation view.

Analytic and calculation views

1. Log in to the CMC, go to OLAP CONNECTIONS, and click NEW CONNECTION (Figure 4.35).

2. Enter a name and a description (optional) for the connection.

3. Choose SAP HANA as the PROVIDER for this OLAP connection (Figure 4.40).

4. Enter the server address and port.

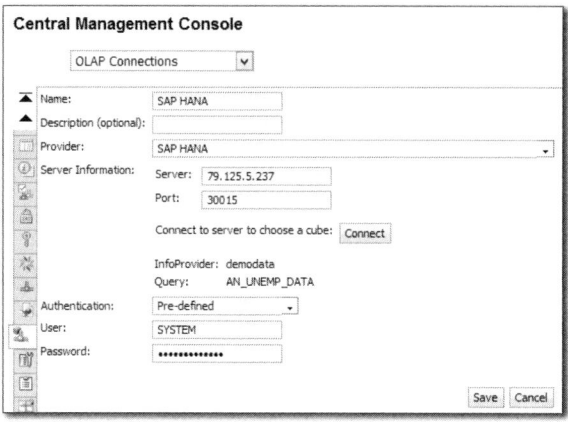

Figure 4.40 OLAP Connection Settings for SAP HANA

5. To define this OLAP connection for a specific SAP HANA object, click the CONNECT button. Enter your SAP HANA credentials in the popup to log in and click OK.

6. Use the CUBE BROWSER to browse to the analytic or calculation view you want to use in this OLAP connection. Click SELECT to continue (Figure 4.41).

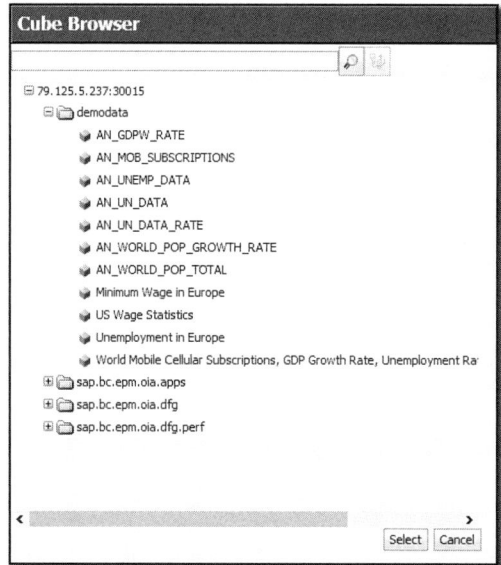

Figure 4.41 Cube Browser

7. Next you have to set the authentication method. Depending on the version of the SAP BusinessObjects BI platform you are running, you will see different options here:

  ▶ SAP BusinessObjects BI platform 4.0: PROMPT and PRE-DEFINED.

  ▶ SAP BusinessObjects BI platform 4.1: PROMPT, PRE-DEFINED, and SSO (single sign-on).

8. Click SAVE to store this OLAP connection.

4.5   Configuring SAP NetWeaver Portal and SAP NetWeaver BW

In this section, we will walk through the installation steps to enable the use of Design Studio within an SAP NetWeaver BW environment. To do this, you have to set some configurations and installations on SAP NetWeaver Portal and set up the authorization objects in SAP NetWeaver BW.

SAP NetWeaver BW 7.30 SP09 and 7.31 SP07

When running SAP NetWeaver BW version 7.30 with service pack 09 or version 7.31 with service pack 07, SAP Note 1811747 must be applied. This is necessary to save, delete, and load Design Studio applications from the SAP NetWeaver BW system. Later service packs already include these features.

If you try to log on to an SAP NetWeaver BW environment that does not have the correct service pack level, an error message like the one in Figure 4.42 will be shown, preventing you from continuing with the logon.

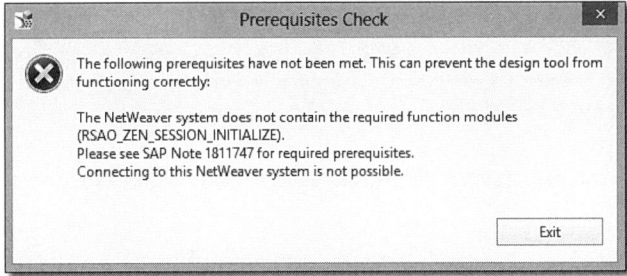

Figure 4.42 Prerequisites Check Error when Logging on to SAP NetWeaver BW 7.30

> **Connecting to Multiple SAP NetWeaver BW Systems**
>
> When using the SAP NetWeaver BW platform, it is only possible to use a single SAP NetWeaver BW system as a source for your Design Studio application's data sources. If you want to connect to multiple SAP NetWeaver BW systems, you should use the SAP BusinessObjects BI platform.

1. Go to the SAP NetWeaver Administrator (NWA) with the following URL: *http://<host>:<port>/nwa*.

2. Navigate to CONFIGURATION • INFRASTRUCTURE • JAVA SYSTEM PROPERTIES.

3. In the next screen click the SERVICES tab in the DETAILS section (see Figure 4.43).

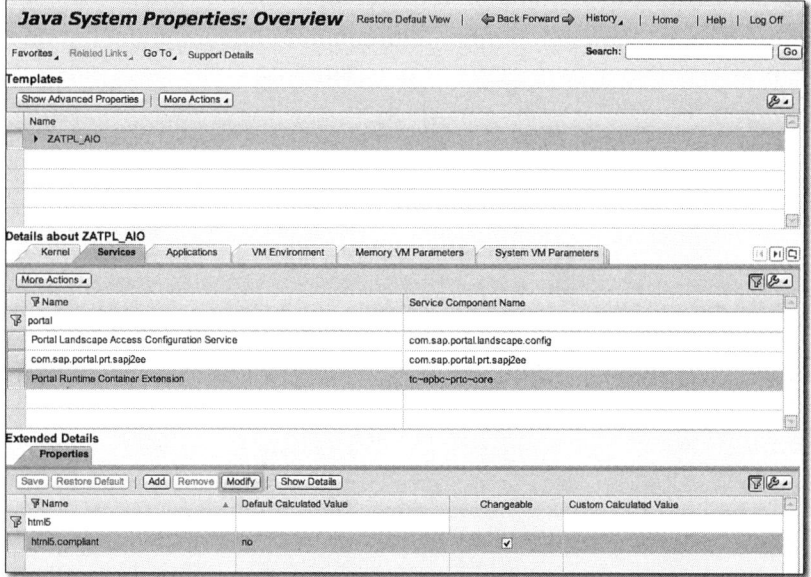

Figure 4.43 Selecting html5.compliant in Java System Properties

4. Search for PORTAL RUNTIME CONTAINER EXTENSION. Make sure it is selected.

5. In the EXTENDED DETAILS section search for HTML5.COMPLIANT and select it.

6. Click the MODIFY button.

7. A popup window appears (Figure 4.44). Here you have to enter "iViewDependent" and click the SET button.

Figure 4.44 Modify html5.compliant Custom Value

8. Click the SAVE button in the EXTENDED DETAILS section.

9. Next you have to grab the *DESIGNSTUDIONWAPP00_0.sca* file from the installation files you downloaded earlier in Section 4.2.2. This file is located in the DATA_UNITS • DS_NW_APP_11 folder. Transfer it to the JSPM inbox directory on the SAP NetWeaver Portal environment. By default this is *<DIR_EPS_ROOT>\in*.

10. Open the Java Support Package Manager (JSPM) on the SAP NetWeaver Portal environment.

11. Log in with an SAP NetWeaver Portal administrator account (Figure 4.45).

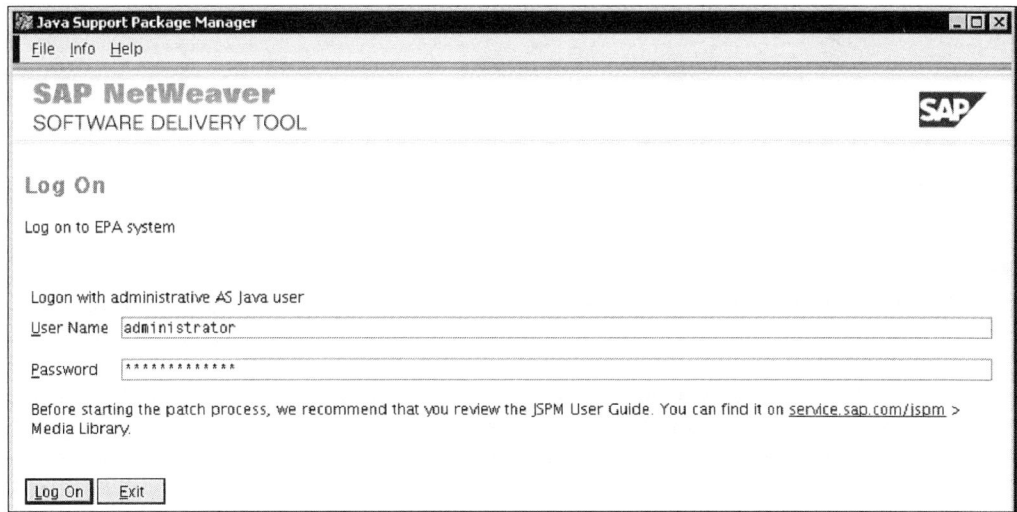

Figure 4.45 Logging in to JSPM

12. Select the package type NEW SOFTWARE COMPONENTS (Figure 4.46).

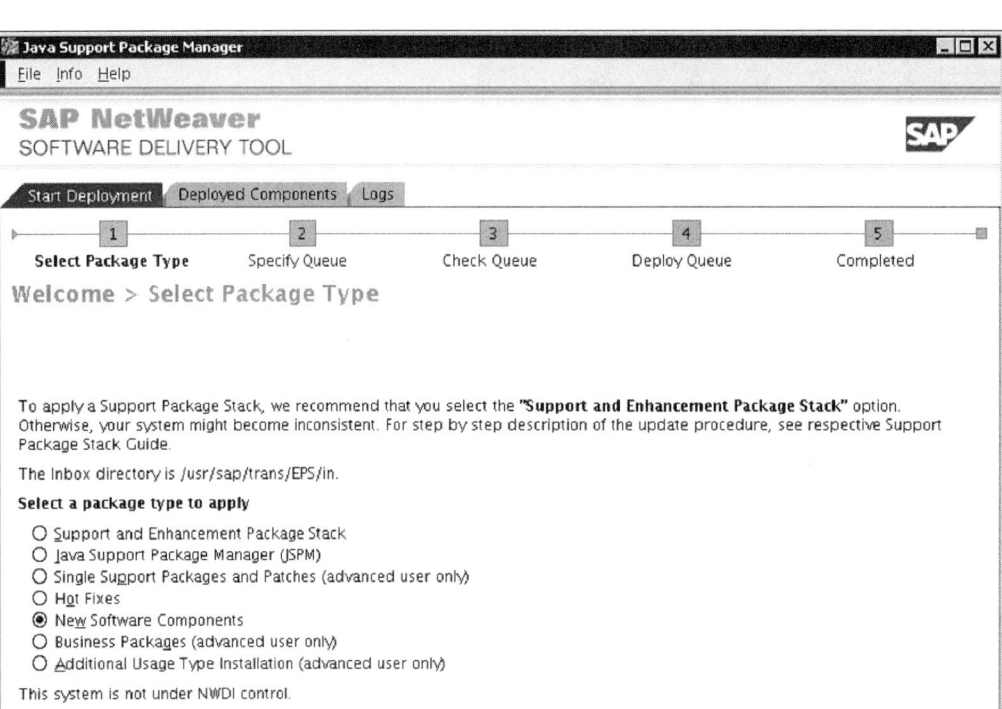

Figure 4.46 Package Type Selection in JSPM

13. The SPECIFY QUEUE screen appears. Since you only have a single software component archive to deploy, you can click NEXT to continue.

14. In the CHECK QUEUE screen, click START to begin the deployment.

15. The COMPLETED screen appears and shows the status DEPLOYED (Figure 4.47). The installation is now finished. Click EXIT to close the JPSM.

Now that you are finished with the installation and configuration of SAP NetWeaver Portal for Design Studio, a new iView template for Design Studio is available (Figure 4.48). This can be used to integrate Design Studio applications in SAP NetWeaver Portal.

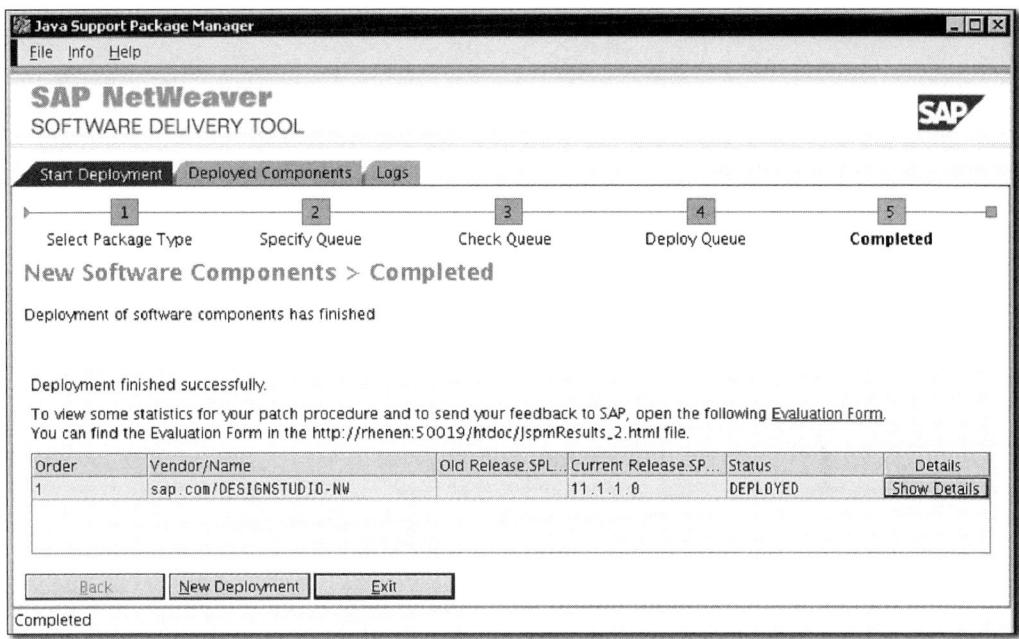

Figure 4.47 Deployment Finished Successfully

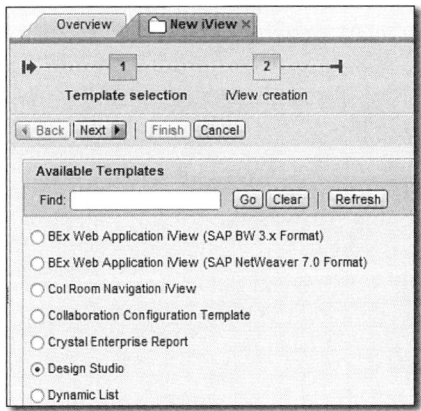

Figure 4.48 Design Studio iView

To provide Design Studio application users and developers with the correct authorizations, the authorization object S_RS_ZEN can be used. (Figure 4.49). Table 4.6 explains the authorization fields.

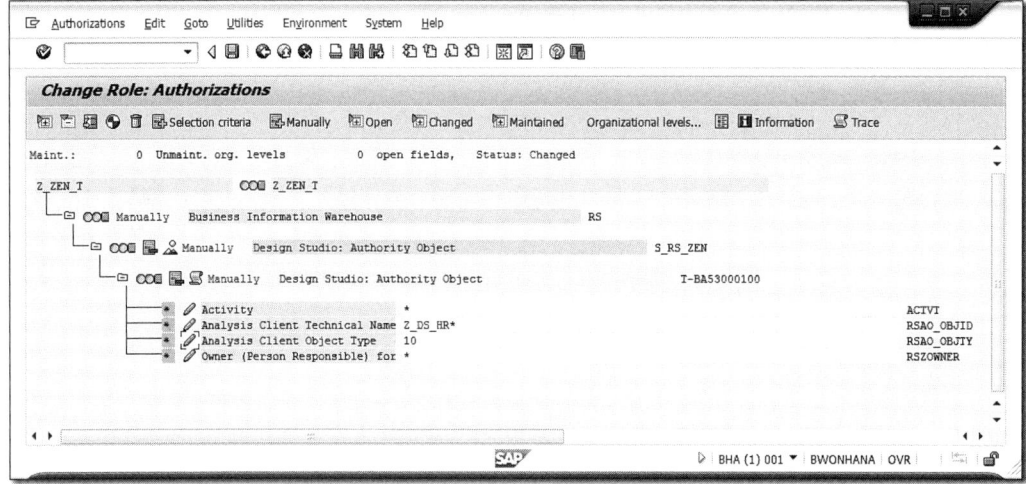

Figure 4.49 Authorization Object S_RS_ZEN Settings

Authorization Field	Description
ACTVT (Activity)	Design Studio application developers need all activity values. Application users only need DISPLAY (03) and EXECUTE (16).
RSAO_OBJID (Analysis Client Technical Name)	Technical name of the Design Studio application. You can use an asterisk (*) to limit the access to a specific range of applications (for example Z_DS_HR_*).
RSAO_OBJTY (Analysis Client Object Type)	The object type value should be 10 (ANALYSIS APPLICATION) for Design Studio applications.
RSZOWNER (Owner (Person Responsible) for a Reporting Component)	With this option you can limit access based on the owner of the Design Studio applications.

Table 4.6 Authorization Object S_RS_ZEN Settings

4.6   Installing the Design Studio Client Tool

In this section we will cover the installation of the Design Studio client tool.

To install the Design Studio client tool, follow the steps below.

Frontend installer

1. Browse to the DS_CLIENT_11 folder and execute the *SetupAll.exe* file. The SAP FRONT-END INSTALLER screen appears (Figure 4.50).

Figure 4.50 Installation Wizard

2. Click NEXT to continue to the following screen. Here you can select the Design Studio component (Figure 4.51). Select it and click NEXT to advance to the following screen.

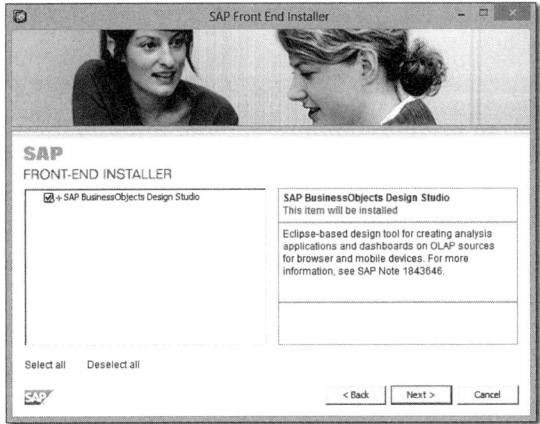

Figure 4.51 Component Selection

3. Click the Browse button to configure the target directory for the installation files (Figure 4.52).

Figure 4.52 Target Directory for Installation

4. After you click the Next button, the installation will start (Figure 4.53).

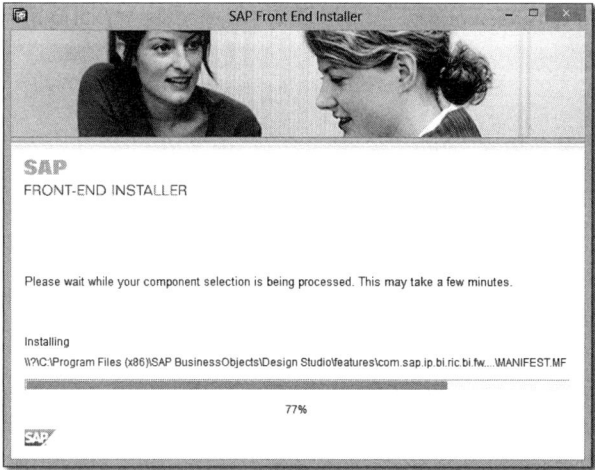

Figure 4.53 Running the Installation

5. If the installation has been executed successfully, the installer will show a screen like the one shown in Figure 4.54. Click the Close button to exit the wizard.

Figure 4.54 Installation Completed Successfully

4.7 Logging In

Congratulations! Design Studio is officially installed. The next step is to run the client tool and log in for the first time.

1. Open Design Studio via START • ALL PROGRAMS • SAP BUSINESS INTEL-
   LIGENCE • SAP BUSINESSOBJECTS DESIGN STUDIO • DESIGN STUDIO.
   Design Studio will start (Figure 4.55).

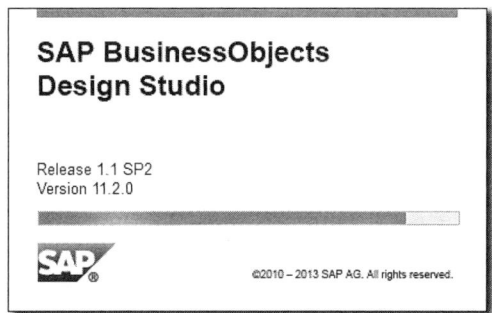

Figure 4.55 Design Studio Starting Up

2. The LOGON TO SAP BUSINESSOBJECTS BI PLATFORM screen appears (Figure 4.56). You can enter your user name and password here. Also enter the web service URL. This URL describes the connection to the SAP BusinessObjects BI platform and has the following format: *http://<host>:<port>/dswsbobje/services/Session*.

Figure 4.56 Logon to SAP BusinessObjects BI Platform

3. Select the AUTHENTICATION type you want to use for your connection. Remember that for access to SAP NetWeaver BW objects you'll need to use the SAP authentication method.

4. Click the OK button to log in. If you choose SKIP, the Design Studio client tool will start in local mode, with no active connectivity. You should now see the Design Studio welcome page, as shown in Figure 4.57.

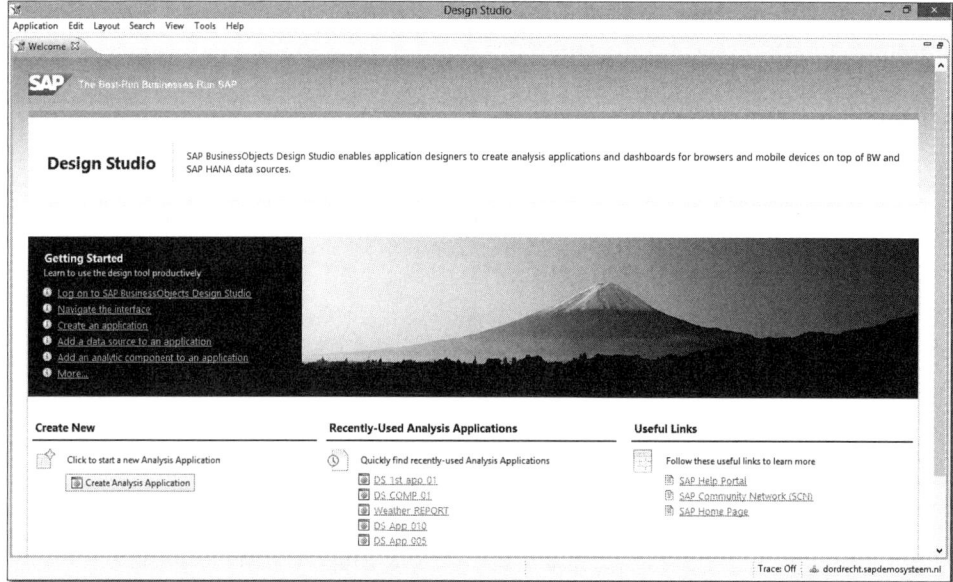

Figure 4.57 Design Studio Welcome Page

4.8   Summary

In this chapter we went through all the preparation steps required to start using Design Studio to build applications. We started with an architectural overview of Design Studio, including its components, environments, and prerequisites. Then we provided some information about what you need to do and have to prepare for installation. In the heart of the chapter we provided step-by-step instructions for installation, configuration, and your first logon.

Before you can start building dashboards and applications with Design Studio, you should know your way around the development environment. This chapter introduces the Design Studio workspace and its elements.

5   The Integrated Development Environment

Design Studio allows developers to create interactive applications and dashboards. With its integrated development environment (IDE) the developer can create a user interface using components from a predefined library, configure the properties of these components, and set up data connections with the source systems. Finally, the application can be published to SAP NetWeaver BW or the SAP BusinessObjects BI platform. Design Studio is fully WYSIWYG (*what you see is what you get*), which eases the development process.

What you see is what you get

Figure 5.1 shows the Design Studio development environment, including the menus, toolbar, and Layout Editor. The views for components, outline, properties, additional properties, error log, search results, and script problems are also visible. This chapter will introduce you to all these features of the Design Studio IDE and help you to get familiar with the menus, toolbars, and views available in this tool.

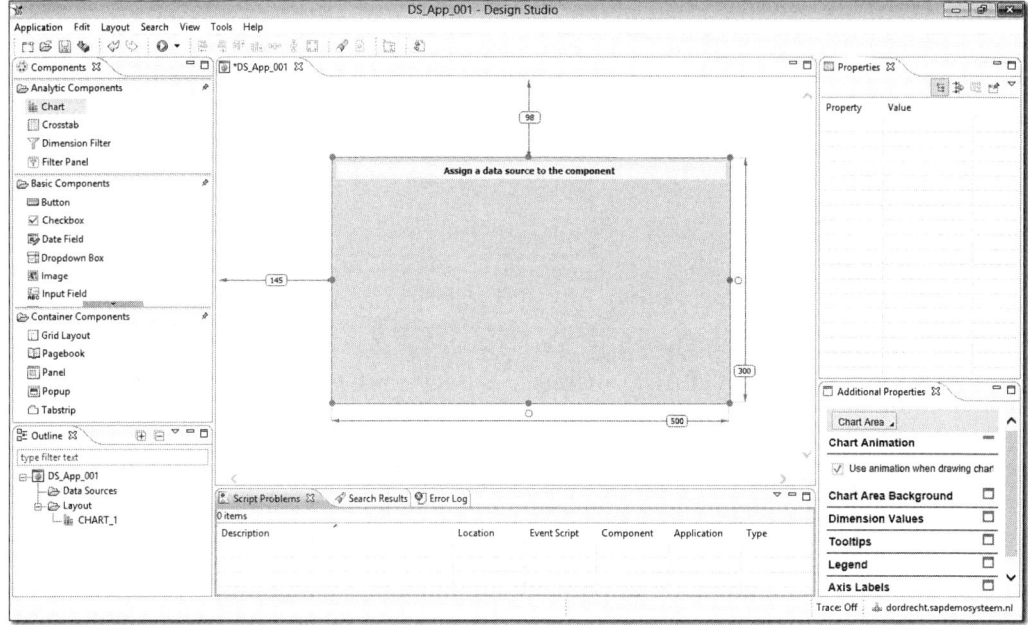

Figure 5.1 Design Studio Development Environment

5.1 Menu

The menu bar can be found at the top of the Design Studio window, and it has six dropdown menus. We will discuss each of these menus and their items next.

5.1.1 Application

Create, open, save, or execute

The application menu is the menu with the most options in Design Studio. Here you can create, open, save, or execute a Design Studio application, as you can see in Figure 5.2.

New...

Create a new application

With the NEW... command you can create a new Design Studio application from scratch or start with one of the device-specific templates. The hotkey combination for this option is $\boxed{\texttt{Ctrl}}$ + $\boxed{\texttt{N}}$.

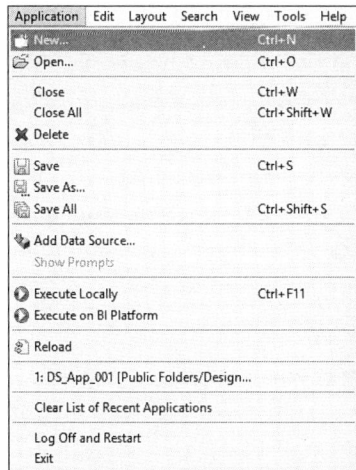

Figure 5.2 The Application Menu

If you are logged in to an SAP BI platform, the BROWSE button will be shown, which can be used to select the folder in which to store the application. (If you started in local mode, this option is not available.) Here you also can enter a unique technical name for the application and give a description (see Figure 5.3). With the TARGET DEVICE option you can choose for which user platform you want to create the application: desktop browser, iPad, or iPhone.

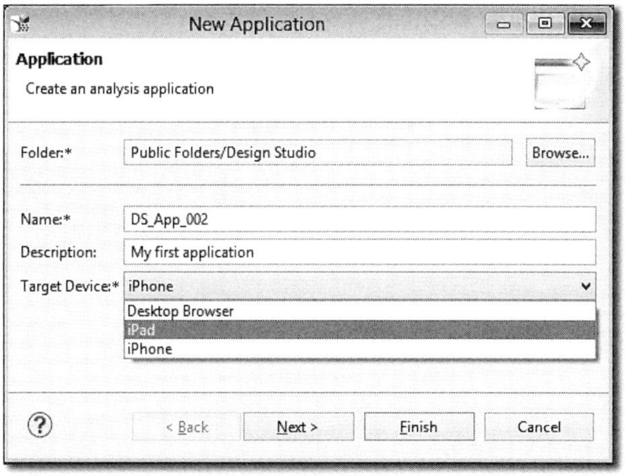

Figure 5.3 New Application Screen

You can click the FINISH button to create a blank application instantly.

If you select NEXT, you'll be given the option to choose from a set of predefined application templates (see Figure 5.4). These templates provide fully working interactive application layouts. If you create a new application based on a template and execute it without editing, you can directly check its interactive features like swiping through the pagebook pages or clicking/tapping a button that shows or hides a popup menu. Since there are no data sources defined and assigned to the application components, the application won't show any data yet.

These templates are excellent starting points when creating a new application. They can also be used as learning examples for new Design Studio developers.

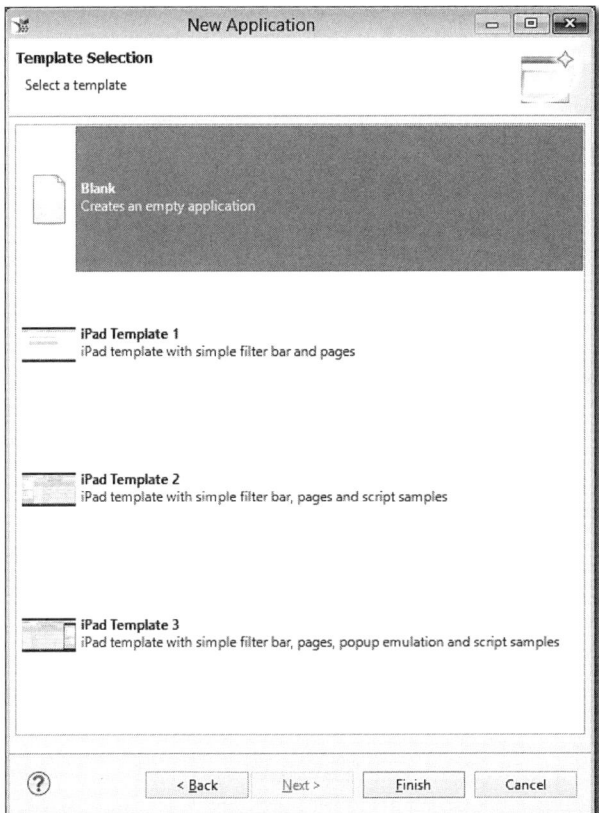

Figure 5.4 Template Selection Screen

Based on the target device you chose, a set of device-specific templates is shown. Figure 5.4 shows the template options for the iPad. The following templates are available:

Desktop, iPad, iPhone templates

▶ Desktop

   ▶ Desktop template 1: simple filter bar, side panel, and tabstrip

▶ iPad

   ▶ iPad template 1: simple filter bar and pages

   ▶ iPad template 2: simple filter bar, pages, and script samples

   ▶ iPad template 3: simple filter bar, pages, popup emulation, and script samples

▶ iPhone

   ▶ iPhone template 1: simple filter and charts using tabs

   ▶ iPhone template 2: simple filter using pagebook and panels

After you select a template and click the FINISH button, the application will be generated. Figure 5.5 shows the Layout Editor and the OUTLINE section for iPad template 3.

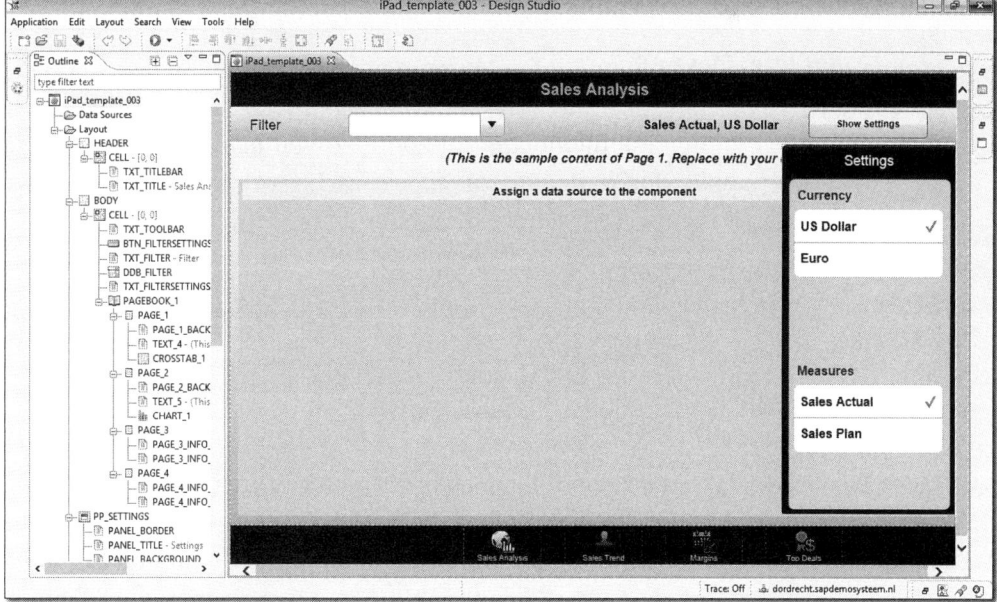

Figure 5.5 iPad Template 3

Open

You can use the OPEN command to open existing applications, which have been saved before. Depending on how you logged in, you can open these applications from either an SAP BI platform or your local system. Figure 5.6 shows this OPEN APPLICATION window for the SAP Business-Objects BI platform. The hotkey for this option is $\boxed{\texttt{Ctrl}}+\boxed{\texttt{O}}$.

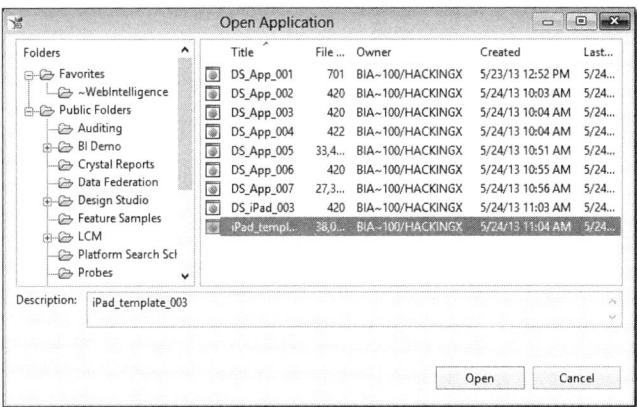

Figure 5.6 Open Application Window for SAP BusinessObjects BI Platform

Close, Close All

To close the application you are working in, you can select the CLOSE command or use the hotkey $\boxed{\texttt{Ctrl}}+\boxed{\texttt{W}}$. If you made some changes to your application, a popup will appear asking you if you want to save these changes before closing the application.

The CLOSE ALL option has the same purpose as the CLOSE command, but it will close all of your open applications. The hotkey for this option is $\boxed{\texttt{Ctrl}}+\boxed{\texttt{Shift}}+\boxed{\texttt{W}}$.

Delete

The DELETE command completely (!) removes your application, from either an SAP BI platform or your local system. So make sure you use this option with care because after you click the confirmation button there is no way back. Probably for this very reason there is no shortcut available for this command.

Save, Save As..., Save All

If you want to keep the changes you made to an application, you can use the SAVE command to overwrite the original saved file with the newer version. The hotkey for this command is Ctrl+S.

Save changes to an application

If you don't want to overwrite your original saved file, you should use the SAVE AS... option. You will be prompted for a new (unique) technical name and a description (optional), and you have to select the location on the BI platform where the application will be saved.

When you are working with multiple applications at the same time, the SAVE ALL command can save all changes for all these applications at once. The hotkey for this option is Ctrl+Shift+S.

Add Data Source

A *data source* is a gateway to get data from a certain part of your BI source system to the components in your Design Studio applications. Data sources are very important objects in Design Studio: Without at least one data source, there won't be any data to present in your application. Depending on the kind of platform you logged into when starting up Design Studio, you can use different objects as data sources. If you are logged in to an SAP NetWeaver BW system, you can use SAP NetWeaver BW BEx queries, query views, and InfoProviders. If you are connected to an SAP HANA platform, you can use analytic and calculation views.

Manage data sources

> **Other Data Source Types**
>
> When we compare the connectivity options of Design Studio to those of other tools in the SAP BusinessObjects BI portfolio, like SAP Crystal Reports and SAP BusinessObjects Dashboards, these are quite limited. Additional connectivity options are planned but won't be available before 2014.
>
> Universes will be the next connectivity option that will be supported by Design Studio. This will be a huge step forward, especially for SAP Business-Objects customers, because Design Studio can then also be used to access non-SAP databases.

If you click the ADD DATA SOURCE command, a popup window will appear giving you a few options (Figure 5.7). First you have to select a connection with the top-right BROWSE... button. The SELECT CONNECTION window (Figure 5.8) lists all connections that are defined on the SAP BI platform listed. Click the RELOAD button to refresh the list.

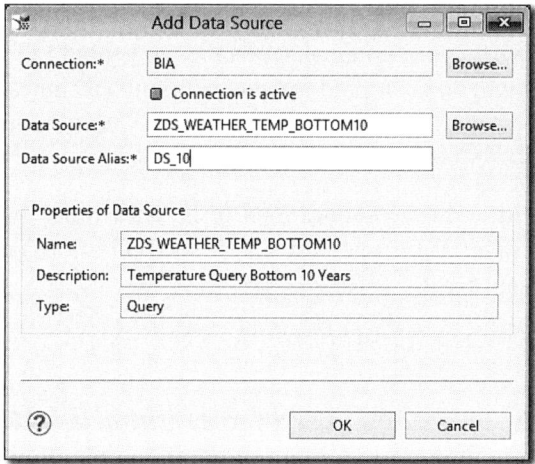

Figure 5.7 Add Data Source

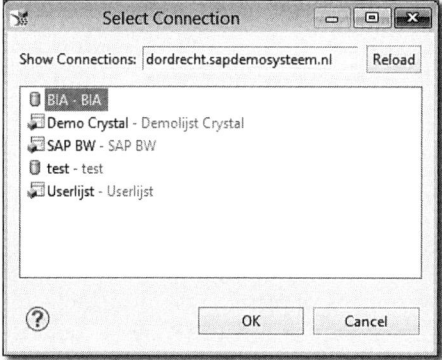

Figure 5.8 Select Connection

Next you can choose a data source. If you already know the exact name of the data source that you want to use, you can enter this in the DATA SOURCE field. Otherwise click the BROWSE... button to search and select it. For SAP NetWeaver BW systems, you can browse through ROLES or INFOAREAS, or use the SEARCH option. In the FOLDERS tab, you can select a data source from a hierarchical structure. This is grouped by either SAP

NetWeaver BW InfoAreas or roles (Figure 5.9). In the SEARCH tab you can search by the technical name and description of the available data sources.

To find a data source in SAP HANA, you can either look in the FOLDERS tab, where the data sources are displayed in a hierarchical structure, or search for the data source in the SEARCH tab.

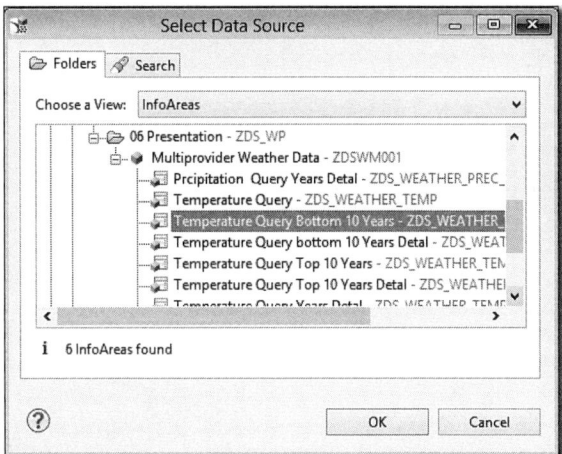

Figure 5.9 Select Data Source InfoAreas View

After you select a data source, the PROPERTIES OF DATA SOURCE area is filled in (see Figure 5.7). It shows the name and description of the selected data source and its object type. In the DATA SOURCE ALIAS field, a default name for the data source is entered, starting with DS_1 and counting up every time you add another data source. If you want to change this default name, make sure you use logical names for your data sources—you might later be using the data source name later in scripts.

After you click OK, the data source is defined and can be assigned to one or multiple components.

Tip

To quickly assign a data source to a component that is already added to the application, you can drag and drop the data source on top of that component. This can be done either in the item in the OUTLINE view, or on the component in the Layout Editor.

Show Prompts

Input variables

If you added a BEx query as a data source for the application and that BEx query contained one or more input variables, these prompts can be displayed by choosing the SHOW PROMPTS option. Figure 5.10 shows a BEx query with the input variable `Select month` on the characteristic CAL. YEAR / MONTH. This same variable is shown as a prompt in the Design Studio prompt window (Figure 5.11).

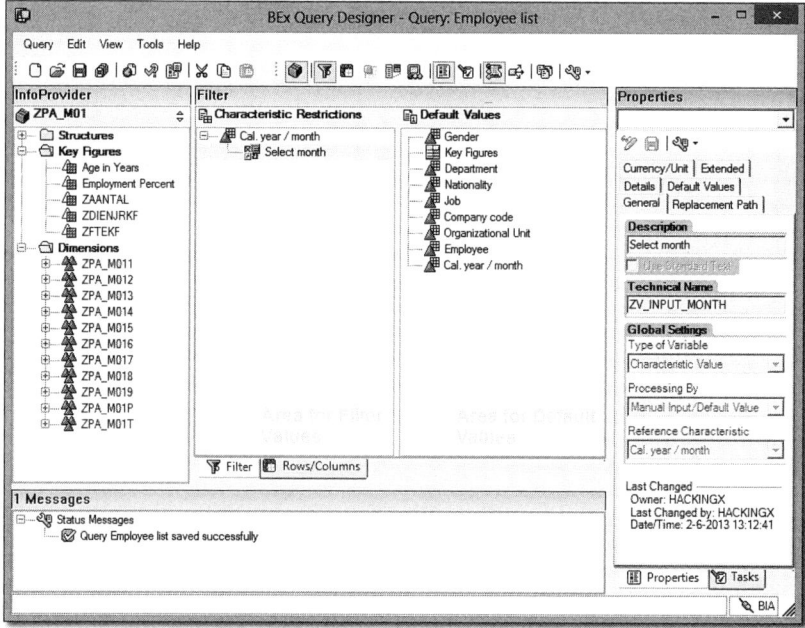

Figure 5.10 BEx Query with Input Variable

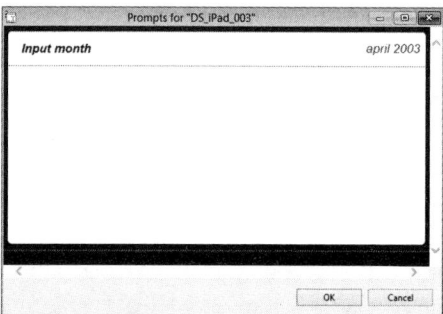

Figure 5.11 Prompt Window

In the prompt window, you can also edit the selected values for each prompt by double-clicking the selected values. The selection window shown in Figure 5.12 will appear.

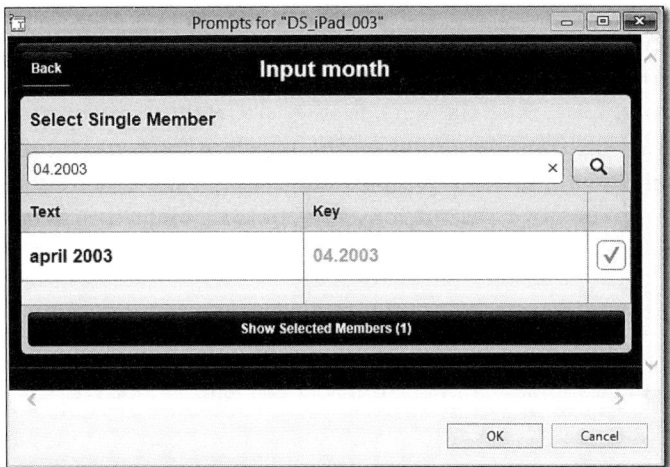

Figure 5.12 Select Prompt Value Window

Execute Locally

To check what your application looks like and how its interactive features work, you can execute it. If you choose the EXECUTE LOCALLY option, the application will be run using a local web server that is embedded in Design Studio. A new window of your default web browser will open and load the application. With this option, there is no need to save changes you made to the application before executing it. The shortcut for this command is Ctrl+F11.

Execute applications

Execute on SAP BI Platform

If you want to execute the application on the SAP BI platform you are connected to, you can use the EXECUTE ON BI PLATFORM option. The application will be run in a new browser window and is executed with the login credentials you used when logging into Design Studio. If you haven't saved your application before using this command, Design Studio will ask you to save. If you decline, the last saved version of the application will be executed.

Reload

Refresh components

The RELOAD command refreshes all components you are using in your current Design Studio application, which can be useful. For example, let's say you use an SAP NetWeaver BW BEx query as a data source in your application. Then, while you are working on your Design Studio application, you decide to make some changes to this BEx query. After you save the BEx query, the components that are assigned to this data source still show the initial data output. If you select the RELOAD command, the components will be refreshed and the adjusted data output (as a result of the changes in the BEx query) will be shown.

Open Repository Folder

Open Repository Folder for local mode

The OPEN REPOSITORY FOLDER option is only available when starting up Design Studio in local mode. It opens Windows Explorer and goes to the following directory:

C:\<users>\Analysis-workspace\com.sap.ip.bi.zen\repository

Here you can find the files of your locally stored applications.

Recent Applications, Clear List of Recent Applications

Five most recent applications

In the RECENT APPLICATIONS section of the APPLICATION menu, a list of the five most recently used applications is shown. From here you can quickly open these applications.

The CLEAR LIST OF RECENT APPLICATIONS option erases this list.

Log Off and Restart, Exit

Change SAP BusinessObjects BI platform, work locally

You can use the LOG OFF AND RESTART command if you want to log in to another SAP BI platform or want to work locally without a connection to an SAP BI platform. If you want to switch between a platform type—let's say you are working with an SAP BusinessObjects BI platform but want to log in to an SAP NetWeaver BW system—you first have to change the preferred startup mode in the application design preferences (see Section 5.1.6).

When you select the Log Off and Restart command, Design Studio will quit and start up again, and a logon window will appear. Now you can log in to the platform you chose or click the Skip button to start up in local mode.

5.1.2 Edit

The Edit menu (Figure 5.13) provides the basic productivity features that are common in desktop applications. You can quickly undo or redo a certain operation, or copy and paste an object.

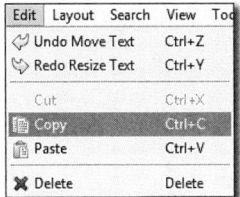

Figure 5.13 Edit Menu

Undo, Redo

You can use the Undo option to reverse an action you performed. For example, if you deleted a Button component from your application by accident, you can easily go back to the state of your application before you hit the Delete command. The hotkey for undo is `Ctrl`+`Z`.

Undo or redo edits

If you used the Undo feature but still want to use the change, you can use Redo. The hotkey for redo is `Ctrl`+`Y`.

In Design Studio you can go back and forth across multiple steps with these options.

Cut, Copy, Paste

Some other well-known features are Cut, Copy, and Paste. When you use the Cut option on a selected component, the component will be cut from the application and stored in your system's clipboard. You can use the Paste option to paste it again in a desired location. The Copy option does the same thing, except the original object isn't cut.

You can use these commands on multiple selected components at the same time. The hotkeys are $\boxed{\text{Ctrl}}$+$\boxed{\text{X}}$ for cut, $\boxed{\text{Ctrl}}$+$\boxed{\text{C}}$ for copy, and $\boxed{\text{Ctrl}}$+$\boxed{\text{V}}$ for paste.

Delete

The DELETE command erases the selected component or components from the application. The hotkey for this action is $\boxed{\text{Del}}$.

5.1.3　Layout

The LAYOUT menu (Figure 5.14) is all about positioning components within a Design Studio application.

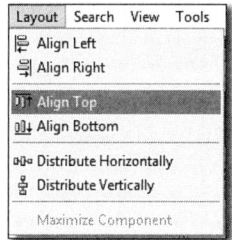

Figure 5.14 Layout Menu

Align

Position components

With the four ALIGN commands, you can position two or more components on the same left, right, top, or bottom edge. To do this, you have to select two or more components in the OUTLINE view (see Section 5.3.2) by using $\boxed{\text{Ctrl}}$-click or $\boxed{\text{Shift}}$-click. Next, select the ALIGN command for the alignment that you want to execute.

Design Studio uses the outermost component as the leading place-holder. Let's say you have three components in your application: component A positioned on the left of the application, component B in the middle, and component C on the right. If you select these three components and choose the ALIGN LEFT command, components B and C will be aligned with the left side of component A, since that component provides the outermost position for the ALIGN LEFT command. If you choose the ALIGN RIGHT command, components A and B will be aligned with the right side of component C.

Distribute

With the DISTRIBUTE HORIZONTALLY and DISTRIBUTE VERTICALLY options, a set of three or more selected components can be spaced evenly. The two outer components remain in position, but the components lying in between are arranged such that the distance between the center point of each component is the same.

Evenly space components

Maximize Component

The MAXIMIZE COMPONENT command enlarges a component to its maximum size. When you use this option, the layout properties of the component will be set as shown in Figure 5.15, with zero margin and auto width and height.

Increase the size of components

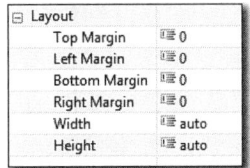

Figure 5.15 Layout Properties after Maximize Component Command

5.1.4   Search

The SEARCH menu (Figure 5.16) brings some very powerful developer features to Design Studio, which will come in handy when working with more complex applications: SEARCH APPLICATION... and FIND REFERENCES.

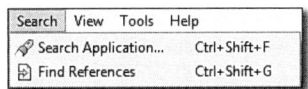

Figure 5.16 Search Menu

Search Application...

Search every text string

With the SEARCH APPLICATION... option, you can search every text string that is used throughout the complete application—whether it is a part of code, a component name, or a property value. The result box displays the search results while you are typing. If you want the search to be case-sensitive, you can select this option after clicking the OPTIONS << button. You can also select if you want to search through the components that are hidden.

As you can see in Figure 5.17, 11 matches are available when searching for the string "false". The results are grouped by component, showing the corresponding component icon and its name. The items underneath the component show the properties, scripts, or CSS styles in which a match has been found.

You can double-click a component or property to select it. If you double-click a script or a CSS style, its editor will open instantly.

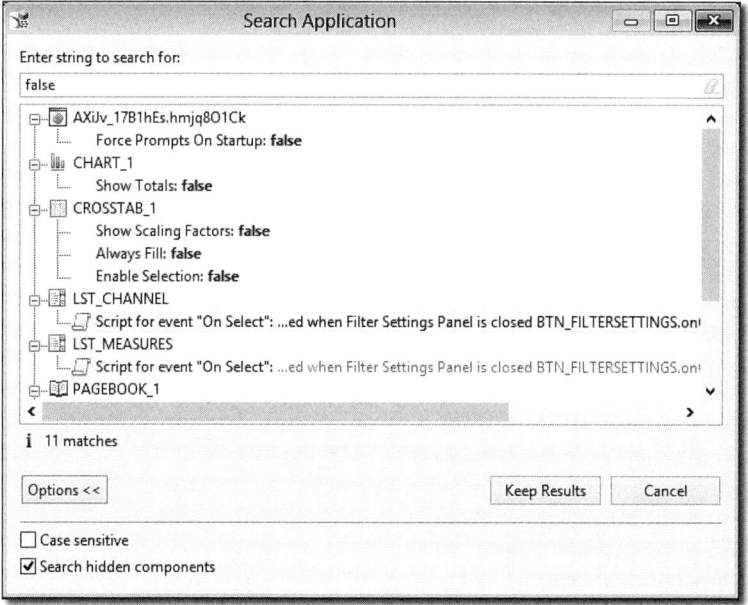

Figure 5.17 Search Application

If you click the KEEP RESULTS button, the SEARCH APPLICATION window will close and the search results will appear in the SEARCH RESULTS view (see Figure 5.18). You can also press ⌈Enter⌋ to do this.

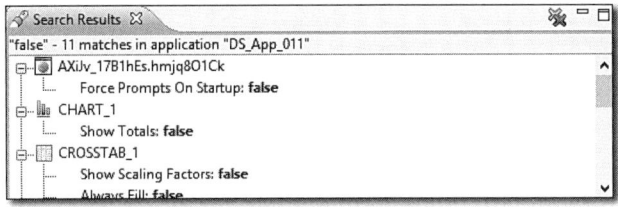

Figure 5.18 Search Results View

The hotkey for SEARCH APPLICATION... is ⌈Ctrl⌋+⌈Shift⌋+⌈F⌋.

Find References

The FIND REFERENCES option lets you easily find the components and their scripts that have a linkage to the currently selected component. The results are displayed in the SEARCH RESULTS view (Figure 5.19). The hotkey for this command is ⌈Ctrl⌋+⌈Shift⌋+⌈F⌋.

Find components and linked scripts

Just as with the SEARCH APPLICATION... results, you can double-click a component to select it, and double-clicking a script or a CSS style will open its editor.

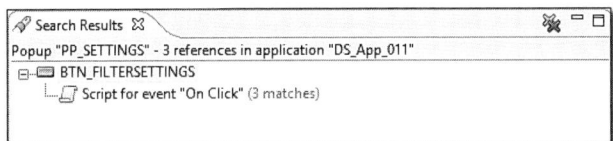

Figure 5.19 Search Results View with References

5.1.5   View

The VIEW menu enables you to show or hide the views that are present in Design Studio (Figure 5.20). We will discuss these views in depth later on in this chapter, so here we will only briefly mention the key purpose of each view.

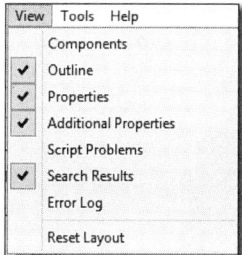

Figure 5.20 View Menu

Components

The COMPONENTS view lists all the components you can use to create a user interface in the Layout Editor for your Design Studio application.

Outline

The OUTLINE view lists all the data sources and components that are currently used in the Layout Editor of the Design Studio application.

Properties

The PROPERTIES view shows the properties of the Design Studio application or one or more selected components.

Additional Properties

Unlike other components, the chart components have additional properties to further configure the looks and features of the chart. The ADDITIONAL PROPERTIES view displays these settings.

Script Problems

The SCRIPT PROBLEMS view shows script errors if there are any available in the application.

Search Results

The SEARCH RESULTS view lists the search results from the SEARCH APPLICATION... command in the SEARCH menu.

Error Log

The ERROR LOG view lists general errors in the Design Studio application itself.

Reset Layout

The RESET LAYOUT command rearranges the views around the Layout Editor. All views are shown except the SEARCH RESULTS view and the ERROR LOG.

5.1.6 Tools

The TOOLS menu has two options: UPLOAD LOCAL APPLICATION and PREFERENCES (Figure 5.21).

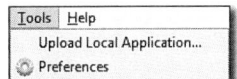

Figure 5.21 Tools Menu

If you created an application in the local mode and you want to use this application on an SAP BI platform, you can use the UPLOAD LOCAL APPLICATION command to upload the application's .biapp file.

Upload local application

To get the application working you also have to change the data source connections from the local mode into data source connections on the SAP BI platform. If you use any images, you must also upload them to the SAP BI platform and change the paths to the images.

In the PREFERENCES menu (Figure 5.22) you can review and change the settings for Design Studio. On the left side of the window, you can choose between the following menus:

Review and change settings

▶ APPLICATION DESIGN

    ▶ BACKEND CONNECTIONS

    ▶ SUPPORT SETTINGS

▶ SCRIPTING

    ▶ SYNTAX COLORING

    ▶ TEMPLATES

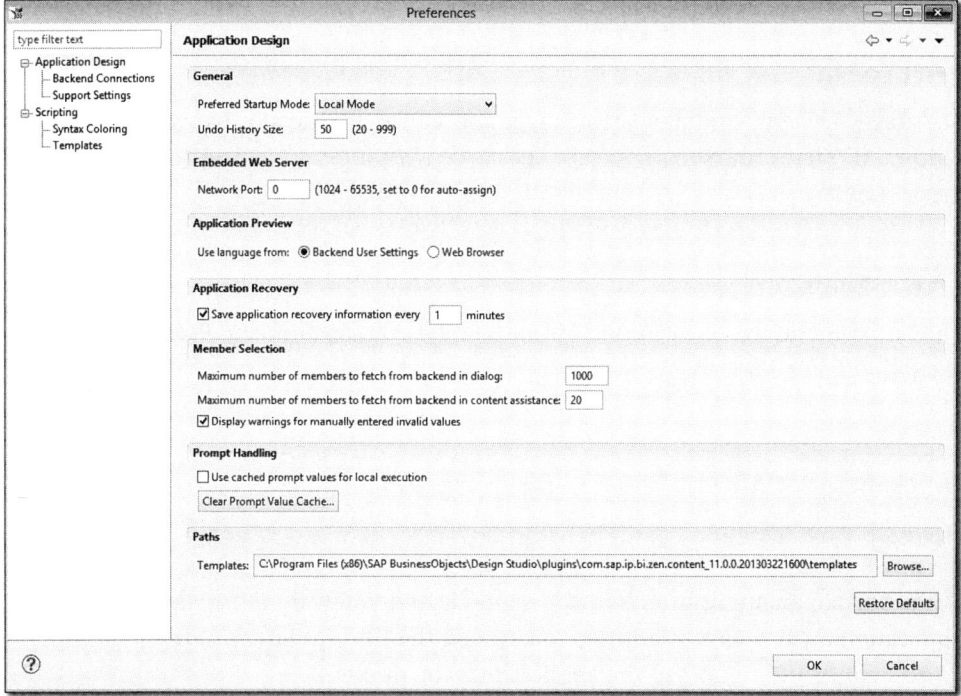

Figure 5.22 Design Studio Preferences

Since the bulk of the functionality in the TOOLS menu is within this PREFERENCES option, we will devote some time to it here.

Application Design

First let's have a look at the APPLICATION DESIGN settings.

Choose startup mode

In the GENERAL section you can change the preferred startup mode for Design Studio. You can choose between the following options:

- Local mode
- SAP BusinessObjects BI Platform
- SAP NetWeaver (SAP NetWeaver BW)

The Undo History Size setting determines how many changes can be undone by using the Undo command from the Edit menu.

In the Embedded Web Server section, you can see that the network port for the web server that is embedded in Design Studio to execute applications locally can be defined here. If you use the default value of 0, Design Studio assigns a network port.

Define network port

In the Application Preview section, you define which language settings should be used when executing an application: Backend User Settings, which are the language settings in the BI Launch Pad, or Web Browser, which are the language settings that are defined in the web browser. The selected language is used for message texts, tooltips, and determining the correct formatting of numbers, dates, and times.

Language settings

The Application Recovery section gives you the option to have Design Studio create a recovery copy of your application. To enable this, check this option and define the time interval between each copy.

Application recovery

The Member Selection section allows you to define how many members of a dimension are shown when using the Script Editor. Figure 5.23 shows the Script Editor creating a script on a button component.

Define dimension members

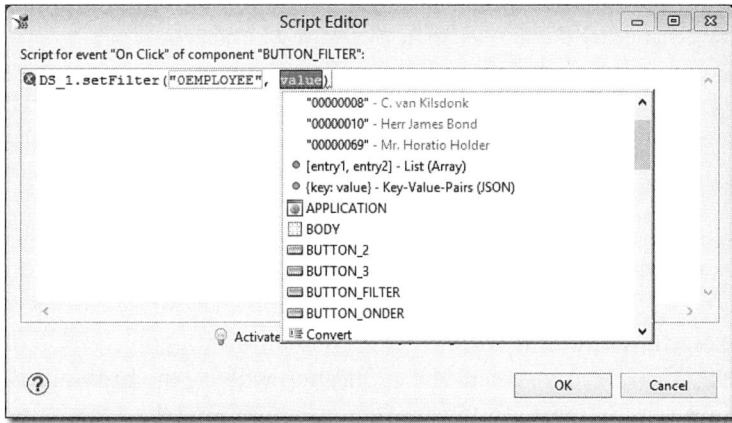

Figure 5.23 Script Editor Member Selection: Fewer than 20 Members

As you can see, the CONTENT ASSISTANCE feature (hotkey Ctrl+Space) has been used to show a list of members for the 0EMPLOYEE dimension. Since this list consists of fewer than 20 members, it is shown here. You can change this value by editing the MAXIMUM NUMBER OF MEMBERS TO FETCH FROM BACKEND IN CONTENT ASSISTANCE number setting.

In the example in Figure 5.24, more than 20 members for the 0CALMONTH dimension are available. In this case the SELECT MEMBER... option is shown instead of a list of members. When you select this option, the SELECT MEMBER window appears, giving a list of a maximum of 1,000 members, as shown in Figure 5.25. You can adjust this value by editing the MAXIMUM NUMBER OF MEMBERS TO FETCH FROM BACKEND IN DIALOG setting.

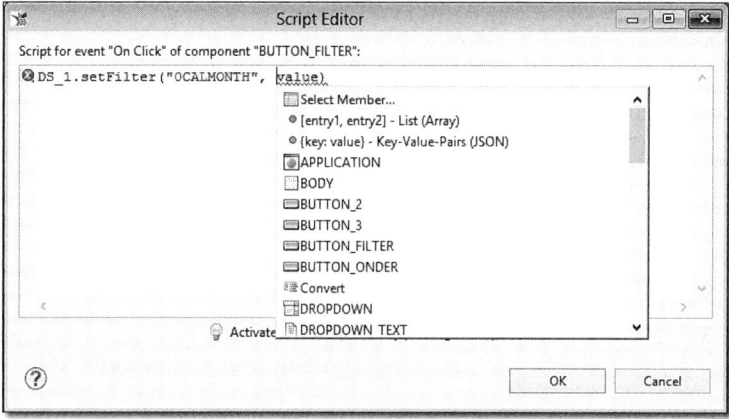

Figure 5.24 Script Editor Member Selection: More than 20 Members

Display warnings Finally, you can select the DISPLAY WARNINGS FOR MANUALLY ENTERED INVALID VALUES setting to let Design Studio display warnings in the Script Editor when nonexistent values are entered.

Prompt values If your application uses a BEx query with input variables as a data source, you can use the SHOW PROMPTS command from the APPLICATION menu to select the prompt values. If the USE CACHED PROMPT VALUES FOR LOCAL EXECUTION option is selected in the PROMPT HANDLING section of the APPLICATION DESIGN screen, the application will use the prompt values that are already set in Design Studio when executing the application locally.

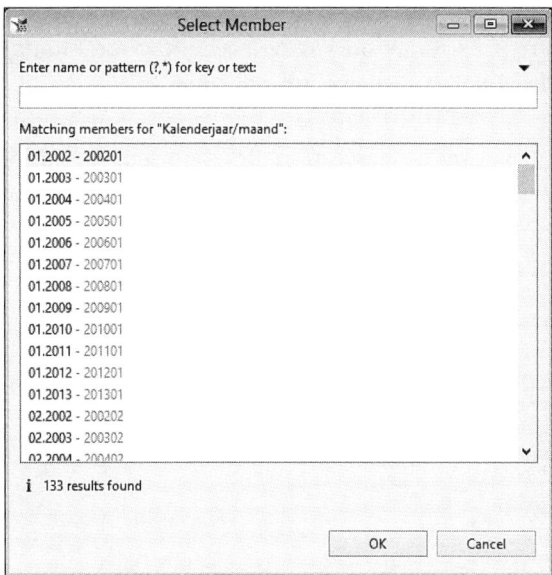

Figure 5.25 Select Member Window

You can clear these prompt values with the CLEAR PROMPT VALUE CACHE... button. The dialog screen gives you the option to choose the applications for which the cache should be emptied (Figure 5.26).

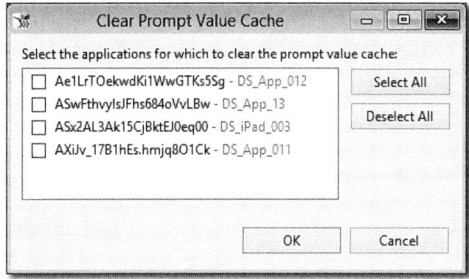

Figure 5.26 Clear Prompt Value Cache

The PATHS section is where you set the path to the application templates folder. These are templates you can choose from when creating a new application.

This brings us to the end of the options on the APPLICATION DESIGN screen.

Backend Connections

Now refer back to Figure 5.22. Click on BACKEND CONNECTIONS under APPLICATION DESIGN. This section displays the available BACKEND CONNECTIONS, which you can use to create data sources. The contents of this section can differ depending on the startup mode you used. In Figure 5.27 the backend connections are shown when connecting to an SAP BusinessObjects BI platform. The connections can be edited in the SAP BusinessObjects BI platform Central Management Console (CMC).

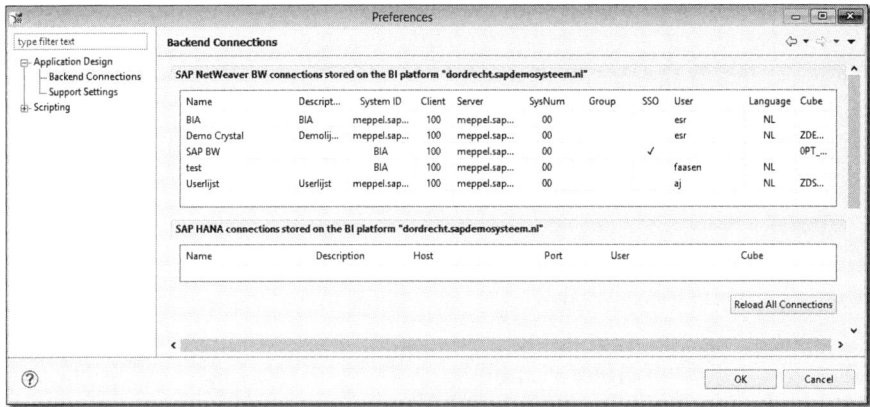

Figure 5.27 Backend Connections on BI Platform

Figure 5.28 shows the connections that are defined in SAP Logon (SAP NetWeaver BW) and the ODBC Data Source Administrator (SAP HANA). You can go to these tools by clicking the icon with the gear wheels in the upper right.

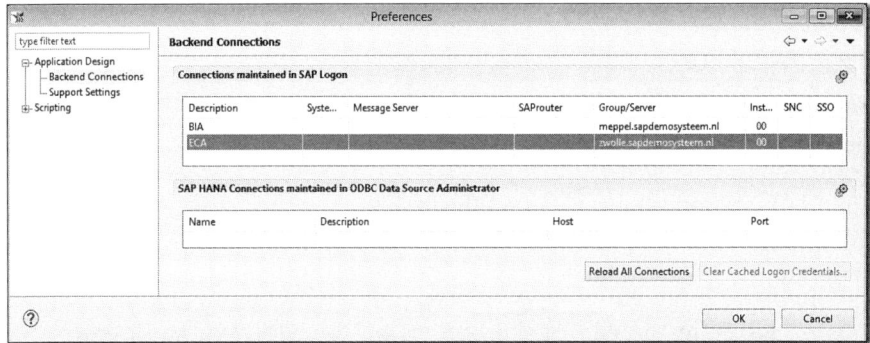

Figure 5.28 Backend Connections in SAP Logon and ODBC Data Source Administrator

Support Settings

Now click the SUPPORT SETTINGS option. The options in SUPPORT SET-
TINGS can provide help in case of problems or errors (Figure 5.29).

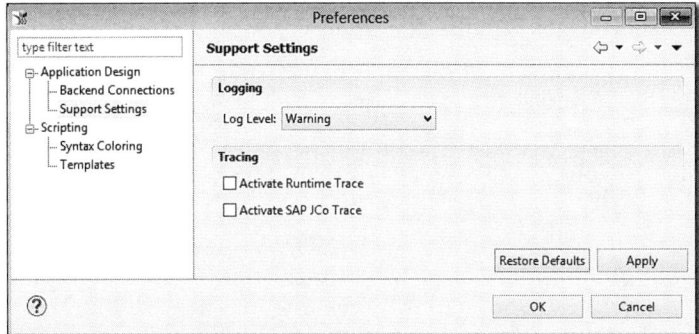

Figure 5.29 Support Settings

With the LOG LEVEL setting, you can define the level of detail of logs that are shown in the ERROR LOG view.

Define log levels

To generate a trace file that can be used for an in-depth analysis of the activities that are performed in Design Studio and in the executed application, you can select the ACTIVATE RUNTIME TRACE checkbox. The trace file is stored on the following location: *C:\<user>\Analysis-work-space\.metadata\.plugins\com.sap.ip.bi.zen\logs\RSTT*

You can also record SAP JCo traces by checking the ACTIVATE SAP JCO TRACE setting. The trace level is set to 8, and the trace files can be collected with the COLLECT SUPPORT INFORMATION option (see Section 5.1.7).

SAP Java Connector (SAP JCo)

More information on SAP JCo and SAP JCo traces can be found here: *http://wiki.sdn.sap.com/wiki/display/SI/Java+Connectivity*.

Scripting

In the SCRIPTING section, some settings that support the coding activities can be adjusted.

Syntax Coloring

With SYNTAX COLORING (Figure 5.30), you can adjust the styling of scripts to make the code easier to read.

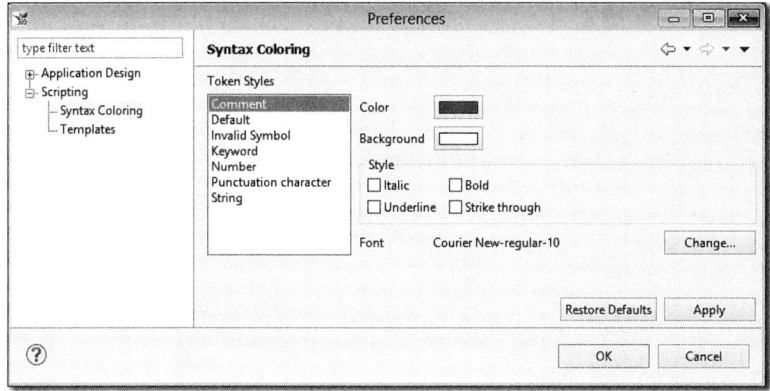

Figure 5.30 Syntax Coloring

Templates

Templates for scripts (Figure 5.31) can be used in the Script Editor to generate a predefined code template, as shown in Figure 5.32.

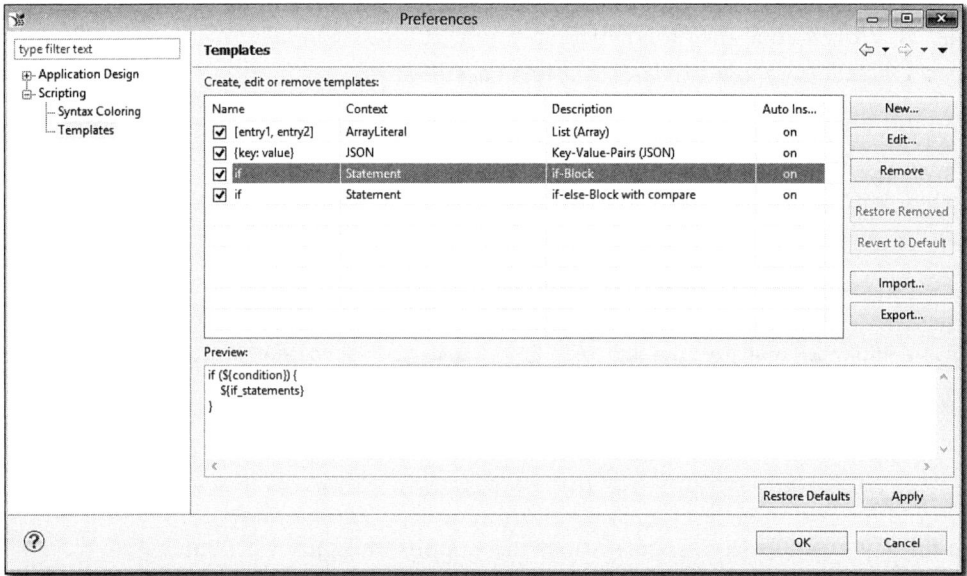

Figure 5.31 Scripting Templates

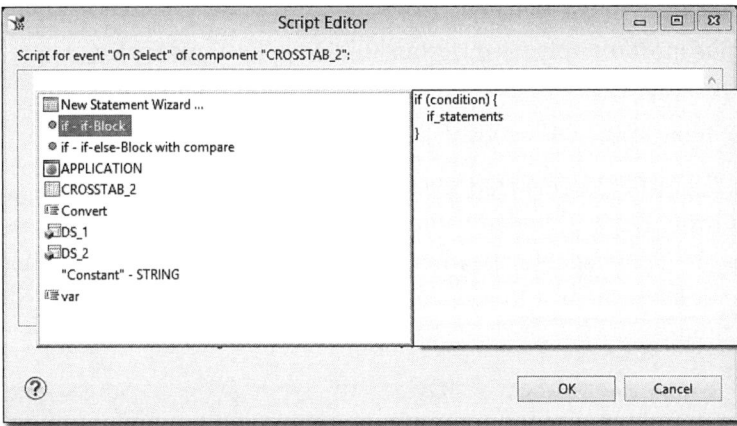

Figure 5.32 Template in Script Editor

5.1.7 Help

The HELP menu (Figure 5.33) is the final item in the menu bar. Here several support options for Design Studio are provided, as well as some more detailed information about your current Design Studio installation.

Figure 5.33 Help Menu

Welcome

The WELCOME option shows the welcome page that you also see when you start Design Studio (Figure 5.34). It consists of four sections:

▶ GETTING STARTED
This section provides a number of links to introductory video tutorials. The MORE... link redirects to SAP's official product tutorial website for Design Studio.

▶ CREATE NEW
The button in this section closes the welcome page and creates a new Design Studio application.

▶ RECENTLY-USED ANALYSIS APPLICATIONS
The five most recently used Design Studio applications are listed here.

▶ USEFUL LINKS
Some links to the SAP website are listed here.

Disable welcome page As you might have concluded for yourself already, this welcome page doesn't bring any real added value to Design Studio, since most of its features are also available elsewhere. Luckily, in the bottom left corner you can deselect the box to disable showing this page at each startup of Design Studio.

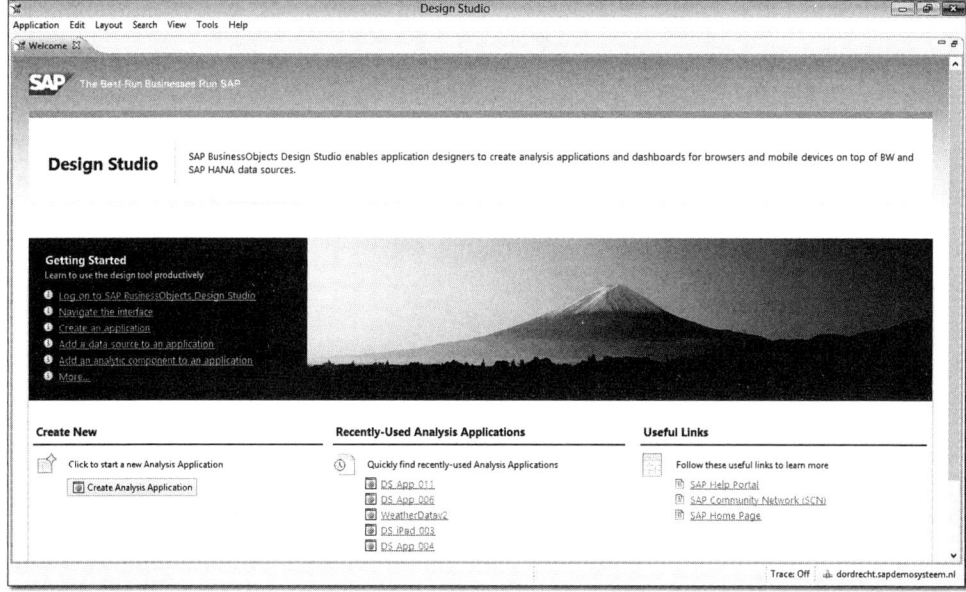

Figure 5.34 Welcome Page

Help Contents

The HELP CONTENTS option provides the default guide for Design Studio created by SAP.

Support

If you run into problems with Design Studio, the SUPPORT menu offers ways to collect information that can be shared with the SAP support department. When you select the COLLECT SUPPORT INFORMATION... option, a ZIP file will be created, which includes several configuration settings and logs.

With DOWNLOAD APPLICATION... you can download the complete Design Studio application from the BI server to your local environment.

About...

You can use the ABOUT... option to check the installation and versioning details of your Design Studio setup (Figure 5.35).

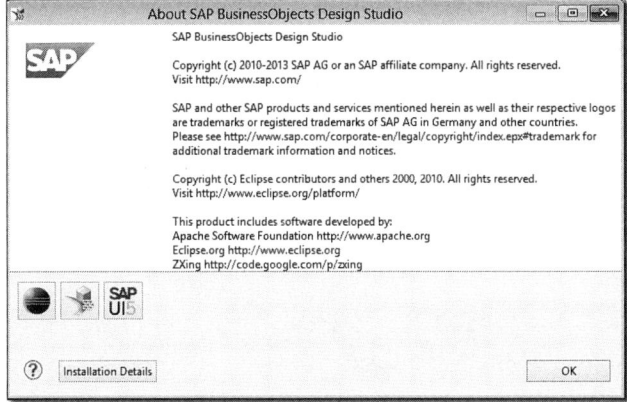

Figure 5.35 About Design Studio Window

5.2 Toolbar

The toolbar is positioned just below the menu bar. It includes a lot of the commands that are also available in the menus, but from the toolbar they are just a bit easier and faster to access (Figure 5.36).

Figure 5.36 Design Studio Toolbar

You can use a toolbar button by simply clicking it. Just as with the commands from the menus, depending on the component or components you have currently selected, some of the buttons are enabled and some are disabled. For example, the alignment buttons are only active when two or more components are selected.

Seven command
groups

The toolbar is divided into seven command groups. Each new group starts with a vertical line of dots. You can rearrange these command groups by selecting the vertical line of dots and dragging it to the desired position on the toolbar.

Send to Mobile
Device

The only command that is listed in the toolbar but is not available in one of the menus is the SEND TO MOBILE DEVICE (USING QR CODE®) command (see Figure 5.37). This function generates a QR code (quick response code) of the URL of the Design Studio application (Figure 5.38). This QR code can be read by a QR code scanner application on a mobile device. Free applications with this functionality are widely available in app stores. After scanning the QR code, you can run the application URL in a browser on the mobile device to execute the Design Studio application.

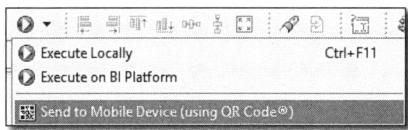

Figure 5.37 Send to Mobile Device Toolbar Command

Figure 5.38 Generated QR Code

Table 5.1 lists all of the toolbar buttons with a short description of their commands.

Toolbar button	Command description
	Create a new Design Studio application
	Open an existing application
	Save the current application
	Add a new data source to this application
	Undo an operation
	Redo an operation
	Execute the application locally
	Execute the application on the BI platform
	Generate a QR code to send the application's URL to a mobile device
	Left-align two or more selected components
	Right-align two or more selected components
	Top-align two or more selected components
	Bottom-align two or more selected components
	Distribute three or more selected components horizontally
	Distribute three or more selected components vertically
	Maximize the size of a selected component
	Search the application
	Find references to a selected component
	Show prompts
	Reload the application

Table 5.1 Toolbar Buttons and Their Commands

5.3 Layout Editor

The Layout Editor is the central area of Design Studio (refer back to Figure 5.1). Because it functions as the visual representation of an application, this is the place to design your applications in a WYSIWYG format.

When you make changes to your application, an asterisk (*) is placed in front of the technical name that is shown on top of the Layout Editor. This indicates that the current version of the application hasn't been saved yet.

The Layout Editor is affected by what views you select in the VIEW menu, which we briefly introduced earlier (Section 5.1.5). Now, we'll go into a lot more detail about what each of these views means for you.

5.3.1   Components View

The COMPONENTS view (Figure 5.39) houses all the visual building blocks to create an application, including an interactive user interface. To add a component to an application, just drag and drop the component from the COMPONENTS view into the Layout Editor.

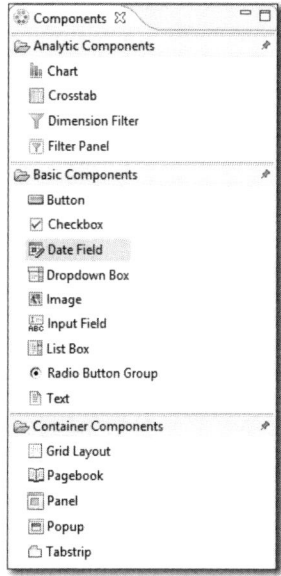

Figure 5.39 Components View

Analytic, basic, and container components

The components are grouped in three categories:

▶ **Analytic components**
These components present data through charts and tables and deliver standard filtering options.

▶ **Basic components**

This category consists of components to create more advanced filters and interactivity, as well as components to display images and texts.

▶ **Container components**

These components are used to define the framework of an application by grouping and structuring the other components.

5.3.2 Outline View

The OUTLINE view provides a structured overview of all the components and data sources that are used in the application. As shown in Figure 5.40, there are two folders under the top application level: DATA SOURCES and LAYOUT. As the name indicates, all data sources are displayed in the DATA SOURCES folder. Components are shown in the LAYOUT folder. As you can see, this happens in a structured way. In the example of Figure 5.40, we are using a TABSTRIP component with two tabs. Since this is a container component, other components can be placed within it. Tab 1 contains a CROSSTAB, BUTTON, and FILTER PANEL component. Tab 2 contains a CHART and FILTER PANEL component.

Structured overview of components and data sources

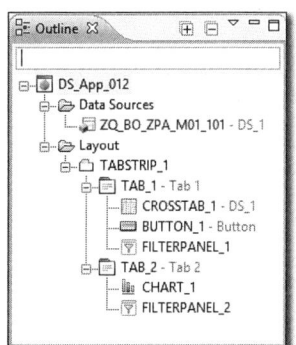

Figure 5.40 Outline View

Not only does the OUTLINE view give you a very clear overview of the application and its components and data sources, but it can also be used to select and rearrange these items. With ⌈Ctrl⌉-click you can select multiple items, and with ⌈Shift⌉-click you can select a range of items. With the search box on top of the OUTLINE view, you can quickly look for an item. The search results will appear as soon as you start typing.

Select and rearrange items

When you right-click an item, its context menu is shown, which provides a number of quick commands. These commands differ according to the type of item that is selected and the number of items that are selected. The options for COPY, PASTE, RENAME, DELETE, and FIND REFERENCES are available for all items.

For the data source items here, the options EDIT INITIAL VIEW and RESET INITIAL VIEW are also available (Figure 5.41). The INITIAL view of a data source represents the formatting of the data source. The RESET INITIAL VIEW command sets the output of a data source back to its original state by eliminating all the changes you made using the EDIT INITIAL VIEW option.

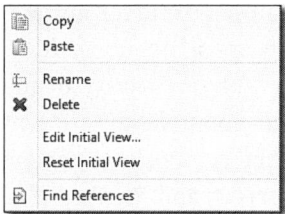

Figure 5.41 Context Menu for Data Sources

Initial view You can change the INITIAL view of a data source with the EDIT INITIAL VIEW option, which brings you to the screen shown in Figure 5.42. This screen can be divided into the following three areas:

- The available dimensions and measures are placed on the left, including their attributes and hierarchies (when available). To add an attribute, right-click the attribute and select ADD from the context menu. An attribute is only visible in the result set when its dimension is also added to the columns or rows. If a dimension has a hierarchy, you can go to the context menu of this hierarchy to activate and deactivate it, and you can set its expansion level.

- The middle column is the area to place and arrange the dimensions and measures that should be shown in the columns and rows of the result set. In the BACKGROUND FILTER section, measures can be added that are being filtered but do not appear in the result set.

- On the right side of the window a LIVE PREVIEW of the result set is given with the number of data cells. In the upper-right corner a PAUSE

REFRESH checkbox is available. Selecting this option suspends the automatic refreshing of the result set. This comes in handy when you need to make a lot of alterations to the INITIAL view and there is no need for an updated preview of the result set after each change. When all changes are done, deselect the checkbox again to refresh the preview of the result set.

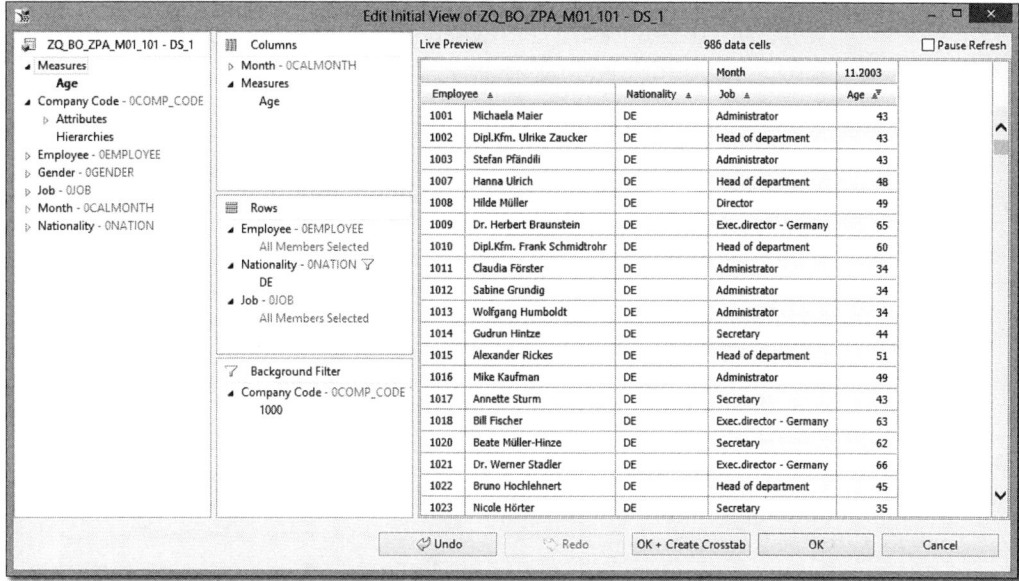

Figure 5.42 Edit Initial View of Data Source

For each measure, you can change the following by right-clicking the measure:

▸ Number of decimal places

▸ The scaling factor

▸ How the totals are calculated

▸ The sorting order

For each dimension, you can change the following by right-clicking the dimension:

▸ Additional attributes to be displayed

▸ The active hierarchy and its initial expansion level

- A member to be filtered
- The filter by input string
- Member presentation (key, text, key + text, etc.)
- The totals display mode

In the context menu of a measure, you can change the number of decimal places, the scaling factor, how totals should be calculated (sum, average, median, etc.), and whether the measure should be sorted in ascending or descending order.

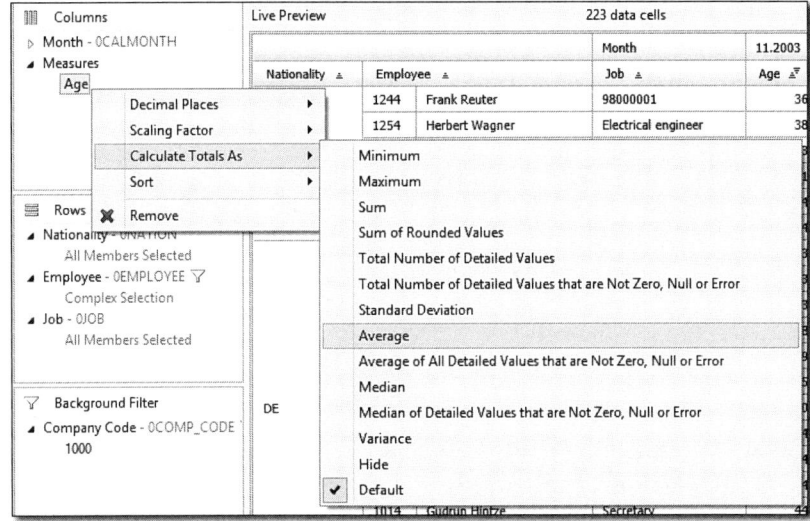

Figure 5.43 Context Menu of a Measure

In the context menu of a dimension (Figure 5.44), you can change the display settings. Use the MEMBER DISPLAY option to define whether the text and/or key value of a dimension should be shown, its order, and which text type should be used. You can also choose FILTER MEMBERS, which allows you to add filters from a list of values. If you want to make a complex filter, you can choose the option FILTER BY INPUTSTRING. An editor will open, and you will be able to type a filter expression yourself. For example, if you want the product numbers 0001 through 0005, product number 0008, and all above 0010 in your selection, you can type this filter into the editor: "[0001;0005],0008,[>0010]". To remove all filters, use SELECT ALL MEMBERS.

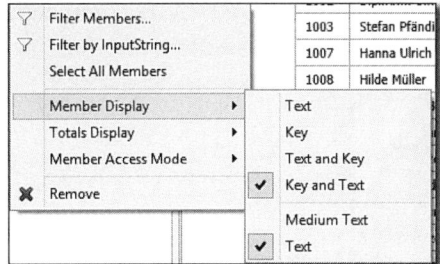

Figure 5.44 Context Menu of a Dimension

The TOTALS DISPLAY option determines if a totals column or row should be shown for the dimension. Here you can choose among SHOW TOTALS, HIDE TOTALS, and HIDE TOTALS IF ONLY ONE MEMBER.

Finally, the MEMBER ACCESS MODE defines whether all available members in the master data should be shown or only those members for which values can be posted.

The context menu of a component has the option to hide a component (Figure 5.45). This is a very important feature for developers. Applications that consist of a large number of components, which are also nested within each other and form multiple interface layers, quickly lead to an overcrowded Layout Editor. This might make it hard for a developer to oversee the application. With the HIDE feature, the selected component or components can be hidden from the Layout Editor. When a component is hidden, the HIDE option is replaced with the SHOW option, which can be used to reveal the component again. The HIDE option has no effect on the application when executing it.

Hide a component

Figure 5.45 Context Menu for Components

When you select two or more components, the ARRANGE command is added to the context menu, providing the commands for alignment.

Align and distribute

175

When you select three or more components, the DISTRIBUTE commands are available (see Figure 5.46).

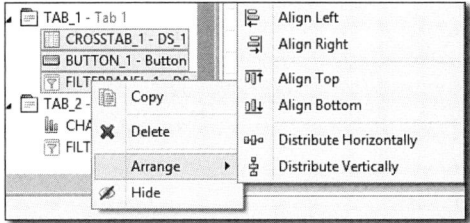

Figure 5.46 Arrange Commands in the Context Menu for Components

From the context menus of the DATA SOURCES folder and LAYOUT folder, new items can be added to the application and copied items can be pasted. In addition, the context menu for the LAYOUT folder has the option SHOW ALL HIDDEN COMPONENTS, to undo all the HIDE settings on the hidden components in one click.

5.3.3   Properties View

The PROPERTIES view contains all the settings that can be edited for a selected item. This can be a data source, a component, or the application itself. When multiple items are selected, only those properties that are common to all selected items are shown.

In the remainder of this section, we will give a short overview of the properties that are available in the various PROPERTIES views in Design Studio. In Chapter 7 we will discuss in detail the item-specific properties for all available components.

The PROPERTIES view of a data source consists of two sections (Figure 5.47):

▶ GENERAL
The data source name.

▶ DATA BINDING
Loading settings and source information about the data source.

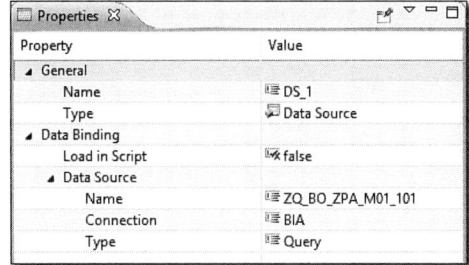

Figure 5.47 Properties View of the Data Source

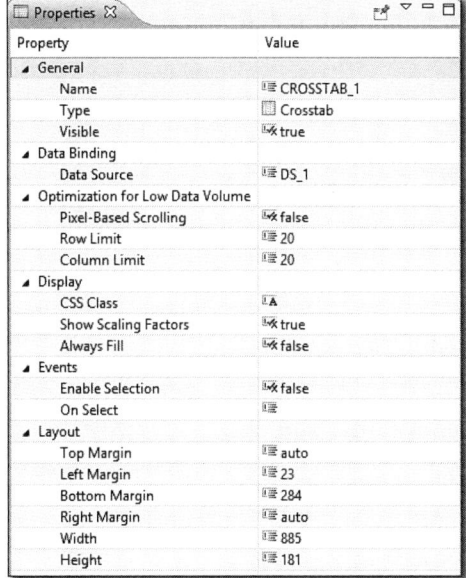

Figure 5.48 Properties View of the Crosstab Component

The PROPERTIES view of a component can consist—depending on the type of selected component—of the following sections (Figure 5.48):

▶ GENERAL
Name and type of component, plus a visibility setting.

▶ DATA BINDING
The data source assigned for this component.

▶ OPTIMIZATION FOR LOW DATA VOLUME
Settings to improve usability.

▶ DISPLAY

Formatting and display features.

▶ EVENTS

Options to create interactivity on this component.

▶ LAYOUT

Size and positioning options.

Finally, the PROPERTIES view for the application consists of the following sections (Figure 5.49):

▶ GENERAL

Name, location, and application file information.

▶ DISPLAY

Formatting and display options.

▶ PROMPTS

Setting to display prompts when starting the application.

▶ SCRIPTING

Definition of global variables.

▶ EVENTS

Scripts that have to run when the application starts.

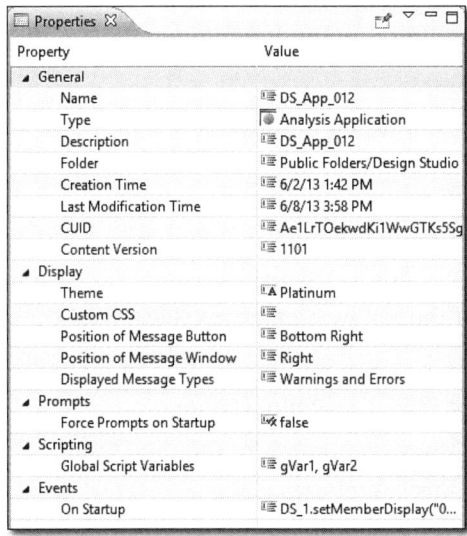

Figure 5.49 Properties View of the Application

5.3.4   Additional Properties View

The ADDITIONAL PROPERTIES view is an extension of the PROPERTIES view for charts. This is the only type of component for which the ADDITIONAL PROPERTIES view has a function.

In the CHART AREA pane (Figure 5.50), you can define the appearance of the chart framework. With the use of several checkboxes you can determine whether a chart should be displayed with an animation, if tooltips should be active, if a legend has to be shown, and whether the axis labels and values have to be visible. This is also where you can set the background color of the chart area. If you select SOLID FILL, the color that is defined in the application theme will be used. Finally, there is an option to either use or override the display options for dimensions as defined in the INITIAL view of the data source that is assigned to this chart.

Customizing the chart framework

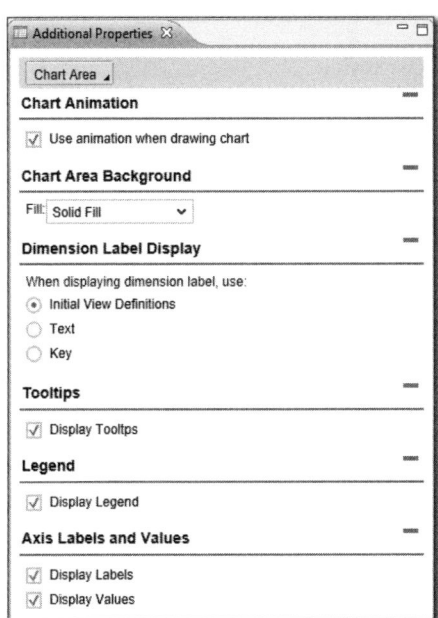

Figure 5.50 Additional Properties Chart Area

The DATA SERIES panel (Figure 5.51) provides some settings to adjust the presentation of the data. In the DISPLAYED SERIES FORMAT section, you can edit the color of each series by clicking the colored squares.

The combination charts have an additional DISPLAYED MEASURES section. Here you can set a series to be displayed as a line or a bar/column.

Waterfall charts — Waterfall charts have an additional DATA SERIES SEQUENCE section. With this feature, you can switch between the options to display a dimension's value as a cumulative value (floating in the waterfall) or as a total value (starting at the x-axis).

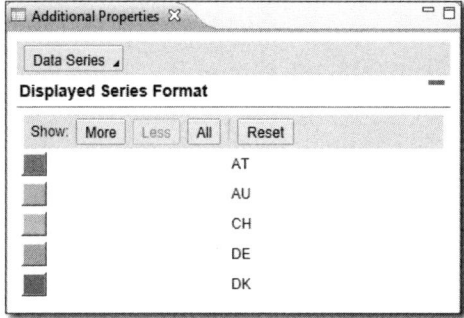

Figure 5.51 Additional Properties Data Series

5.3.5 Error Log View

In the ERROR LOG view, all Design Studio system and application errors are displayed (Figure 5.52). In addition, messages are displayed when script validation methods are used in scripts. If you double-click an error, more details about the event are given in a popup window.

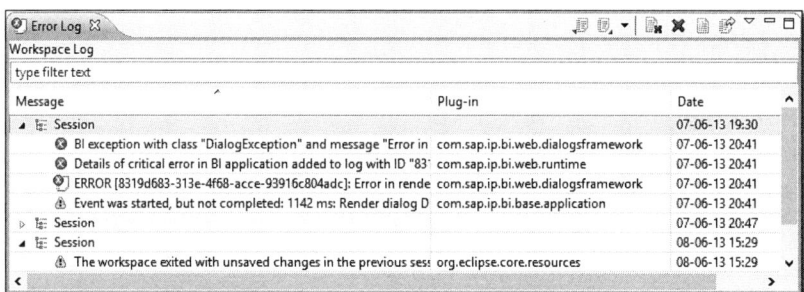

Figure 5.52 Error Log View

5.3.6   Script Problems View

The SCRIPT PROBLEMS view displays script errors encountered during script validation (Figure 5.53). This view is only updated when you open and save an application, so a problem can remain in the SCRIPT PROBLEMS view after it has been fixed. Double-clicking a problem opens the script editor of the component concerned.

Description	Location	Event Script	Component	Application	Type
Script Problems					▽ ▭ ◻
4 errors, 0 warnings, 0 others					
Couldn't resolve reference to Member "setText"	Line 14	On Select	LST_CHANNEL	ZHR_DS_001	Design Studio Script Problem
Couldn't resolve reference to Member "setText"	Line 14	On Select	LST_MEASURES	ZHR_DS_001	Design Studio Script Problem
Couldn't resolve reference to Variable "TXT_FILTERSETTI	Line 14	On Select	LST_CHANNEL	ZHR_DS_001	Design Studio Script Problem
Couldn't resolve reference to Variable "TXT_FILTERSETTI	Line 14	On Select	LST_MEASURES	ZHR_DS_001	Design Studio Script Problem

Figure 5.53 Script Problems View

5.4   Summary

In this chapter we took a detailed look at the Design Studio application, with the goal of getting more familiar with its integrated development environment. We discussed all the available menu options in detail, from creating a new Design Studio application to checking the Design Studio software version in the ABOUT... menu. We also learned that some of the most important commands are incorporated in the toolbar.

In the remainder of the chapter we went through the Layout Editor and all the views in Design Studio: COMPONENTS, OUTLINE, PROPERTIES, ADDITIONAL PROPERTIES, ERROR LOG, SEARCH RESULTS, and SCRIPT PROBLEMS.

In the next chapter we will put this knowledge to use by creating our first simple Design Studio application.

Now that you've been introduced to the Design Studio development environment, it is time to get your hands dirty. In this chapter we will walk you through the basic steps in building a Design Studio application.

6 The Application Design Process

At this point you know what Design Studio is, what its abilities are, and how it compares to similar tools in the SAP business intelligence portfolio. You have also been introduced to the Design Studio development environment. The next step is to learn about the general process of building a Design Studio application. This chapter serves as a tutorial to guide you through this process. Keep in mind that this is just a high-level overview to help you understand the process of building an application—all the specific details about the relevant components, properties, and methods will come in the next chapters.

Before we can build anything, we have to know what information the application should show and in what way it will be used. In this example scenario, we will build an application for a human resources manager. The manager wants to see the monthly trends for the headcount and the full-time equivalent (FTE) amount for each department. He also wants to see a list of employees for each department. This list should show the employee number, name, department, gender, nationality, and age for each employee. Finally, the application has to be accessible and usable on a mobile device.

Human resources application

The application in our scenario consists of three main sections:

- Monthly trend visualization for the two measures
- Employee list
- Filter for department selection

In this scenario we will use a TABSTRIP component to format the two visualizations. The first tab will contain the monthly trend visualization, and the second tab will show the employee list.

Application components

To visualize the monthly trend for the two measures—headcount and FTE amount—we are going to use a CHART component of the LINE type. To make this example a bit more interesting, we will add an option to switch between these two measures, so the CHART will show the trend of only one measure at a time. We can use a RADIO BUTTON GROUP component to achieve this. The list of employees, including all of the employee dimensions and measures, can be displayed with a CROSSTAB component. Finally, we need a filter to select the department for which the data should be shown. We will use a DROPDOWN BOX component to achieve this. The filter should set the selection for both the CHART and the CROSSTAB. The DROPDOWN BOX component has to be visible all the time, so we won't add this component to the TABSTRIP component.

Now that you know the requirements, we'll use the rest of the chapter to walk you through the major development steps:

▸ Setting up the user interface and visualizations
▸ Adding the data
▸ Making it interactive
▸ Formatting and fine-tuning it
▸ Executing the application

Now let's build an application!

6.1   Setting Up the User Interface and Visualizations

In this first step of building an application, we'll start by setting up the components. You can do this by following the steps below:

1. Open Design Studio and log in to your SAP BI platform.

Create a new application

2. Select APPLICATION • NEW... to create a new application.

3. Enter a name and description for your application (Figure 6.1). Then select iPAD as a TARGET DEVICE, since you want to use this application on a mobile device. Click NEXT to continue.

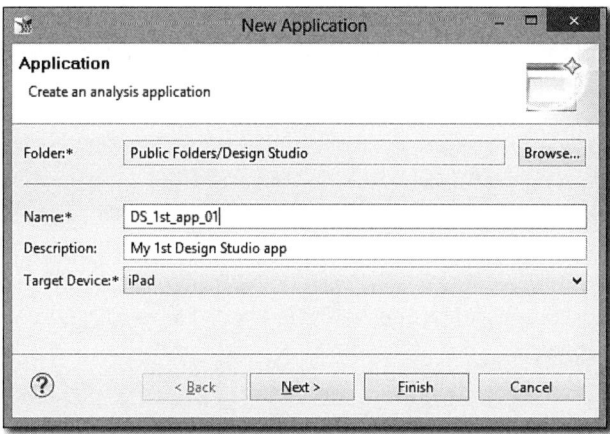

Figure 6.1 Create a New Application

4. You are going to create an application from scratch, so don't use a template. Choose the BLANK option and click the FINISH button (Figure 6.2).

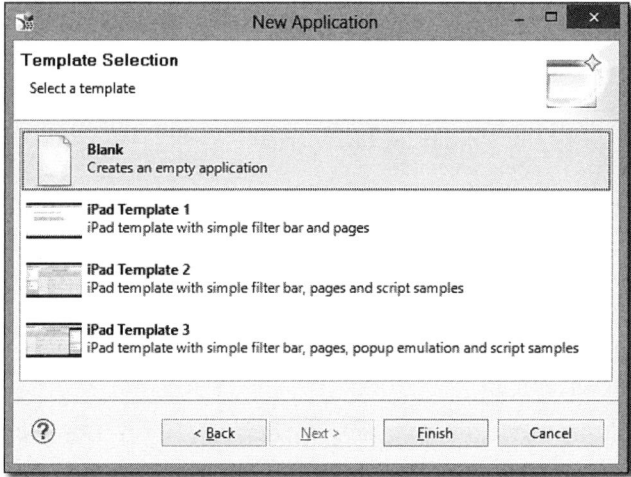

Figure 6.2 Template Selection

5. A clean Design Studio Layout Editor appears. Now it is time to add some components to create the user interface. First you want to add the TABSTRIP component. Select the TABSTRIP component from the CONTAINER COMPONENTS section in the COMPONENTS view. Drag it to

the Layout Editor and release the mouse button to drop this component. The component will appear in the Layout Editor but also in the OUTLINE view in the bottom-left corner of the screen (Figure 6.3).

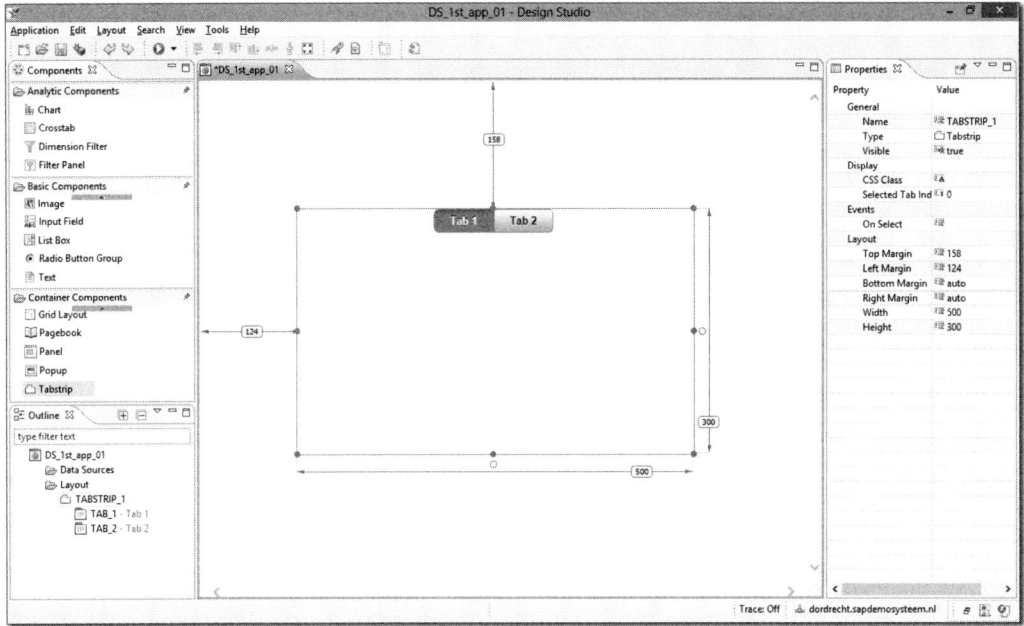

Figure 6.3 Tabstrip Component Added to the Layout Editor

6. This component should be as large as the whole application. To do this you can use the MAXIMIZE COMPONENT feature. Select the TABSTRIP component in the Layout Editor or in the OUTLINE view and select LAYOUT • MAXIMIZE COMPONENT from the menu bar. If you are familiar with the icons in the toolbar, you can use the MAXIMIZE SELECTED COMPONENT icon.

7. The TABSTRIP component has two tabs by default. Select TAB 1 by clicking it in the Layout Editor or select it from the OUTLINE view.

8. Rename the tab label by entering "KPI trends" in the DISPLAY • TEXT field in the PROPERTIES view. You can also do this from the OUTLINE view by right-clicking the tab and choosing the RENAME option.

9. Rename the other tab label "employee list".

10. Select a CHART component from the ANALYTIC COMPONENTS section **Select components** in the COMPONENTS view and drag it into the first tab of the TABSTRIP component.

11. In the PREFERENCES view of this CHART component, select DISPLAY • CHART TYPE to LINE. You will notice that nothing happens. This is because you didn't assign a data source to this component yet. We will further format the CHART component later on in this chapter.

12. To the first tab, add a RADIO BUTTON GROUP component from the BASIC COMPONENTS section in the COMPONENTS view. Your screen should now look like Figure 6.4.

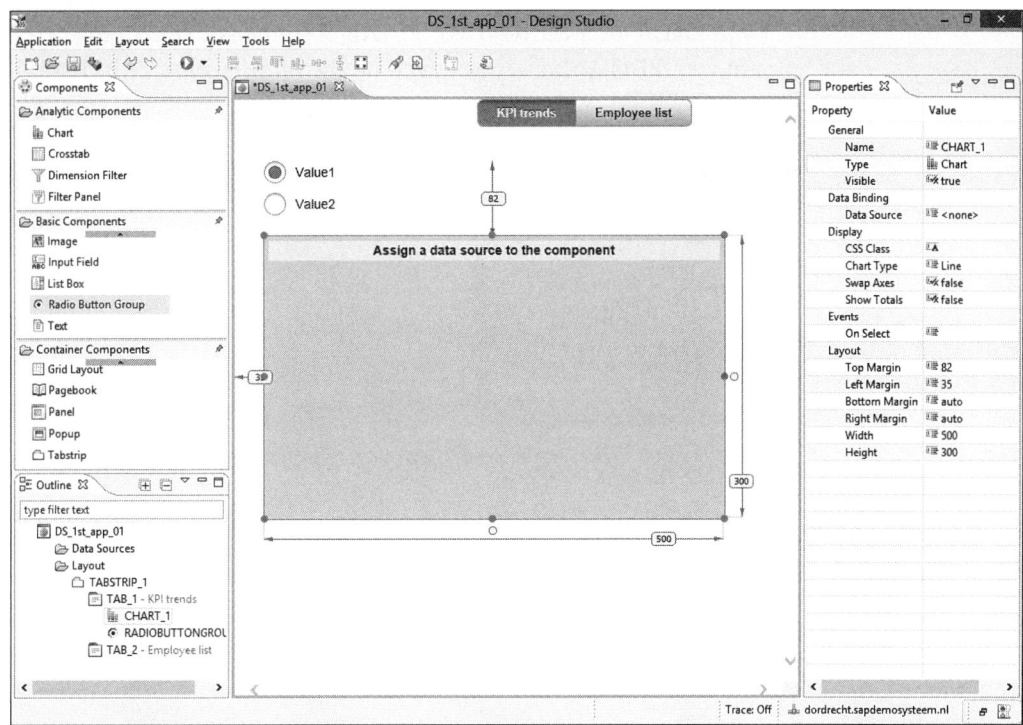

Figure 6.4 Tabstrip Component with Two Child Components

13. Select the second tab and add a CROSSTAB component to it. You can find this component in the ANALYTIC COMPONENTS section of the COMPONENTS view. Make the CROSSTAB component as big as the tab by using the MAXIMIZE COMPONENT option.

14. Next you need to drag a DROPDOWN BOX component into the layout editor. You will use this component to select the department for which the data has to be shown. The DROPDOWN BOX component is located in the BASIC COMPONENTS section of the COMPONENTS view. Make sure that the DROPDOWN BOX component is not placed within one of the two tabs. Remember, you want this dropdown box to be visible all the time, independent of which tab is selected. It should therefore be positioned on the same level as the TABSTRIP component. If you are not sure about this, check the OUTLINE view.

In Figure 6.5 you can clearly see that the TABSTRIP_1 component contains two tabs (TAB_1 and TAB_2). TAB_1 contains the items CHART_1 and RADIOBUTTONGROUP_1. TAB_2 contains CROSSTAB_1. The item DROPDOWN_1 is positioned on the same level as TABSTRIP_1.

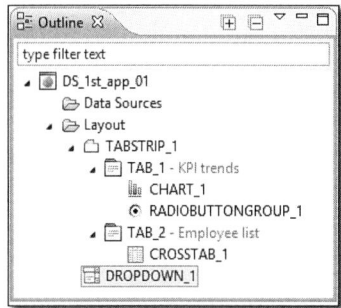

Figure 6.5 Outline View with Multiple Component Levels

If your OUTLINE view looks like the one in Figure 6.5, you are ready to add some data to the application!

6.2 Adding the Data

Bring in data sources

To bring data into the application, you need to add some data sources. In this example, we'll use a BEx query as the data source. This BEx query contains six dimensions and three measures (Figure 6.6). The measures are located in the COLUMNS, and the CAL. YEAR / MONTH dimension is placed in the Rows. The other dimensions are in the FREE CHARACTERISTICS section. The BEx query provides data for a 12-month period.

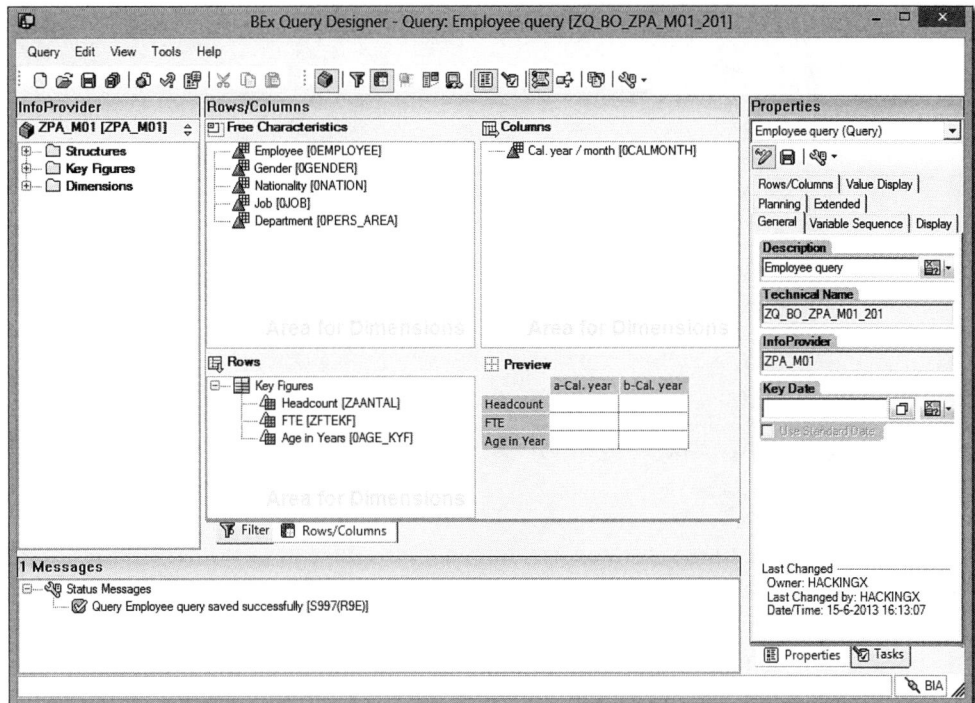

Figure 6.6 BEx Query Setup

Follow the steps below:

1. In Design Studio, select APPLICATION • ADD DATA SOURCE... or right-click the DATA SOURCES folder in the OUTLINE view to add a new data source. Connect to the SAP BI platform by clicking the first BROWSE... button.

2. Enter the technical name of the BEx query in the DATA SOURCE field. You can also use the second BROWSE... button to search for the query (Figure 6.7). The data source gets the alias name DS_1 by default, and you can leave it that way.

Connect to a BEx query

3. Now drag and drop this data source from the DATA SOURCES folder in the OUTLINE view onto the CHART component in the KPI TRENDS tab. As soon as you release the mouse, the CHART component will be assigned to the data source. You can also achieve this result from the DATA BINDING option in the PROPERTIES view of the CHART component.

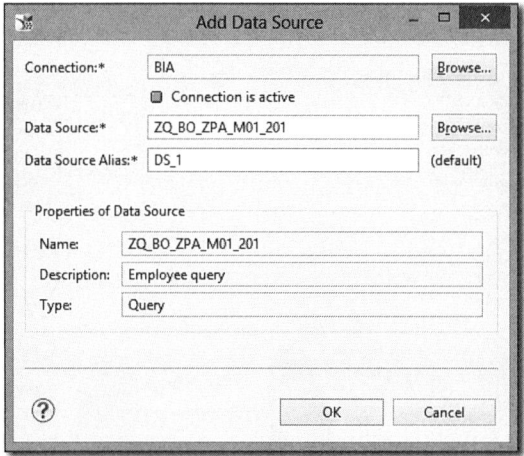

Figure 6.7 Add Data Source

4. The CROSSTAB component contains a different set of dimensions and measures than the CHART component, so you need to add another data source, specifically set up for the CROSSTAB. Since the BEx query contains all the dimensions and measures you need, you can reuse it. Copy and paste the data source (right-click the data source or use the EDIT menu). A new data source with the alias name DS_2 will appear.

5. Right-click data source DS_2 and select EDIT INITIAL VIEW (Figure 6.8).

Initial view

6. Now you have to rearrange this initial view. First drag dimension CAL. YEAR / MONTH from the COLUMNS area to the BACKGROUND FILTER. You want the CROSSTAB to show data for only one month. Right-click it and set a filter on a single month. For this example we created a filter on 01.2003.

> **Note**
>
> To keep this example scenario simple we use a fixed filter here. In real-life you would add an additional selection option or a generated selection value instead.

7. Move the measures from the ROWS to the COLUMNS area. Since you need only the AGE IN YEARS measure, expand MEASURES by clicking the little arrow on the left and drag the other two measures out of the COLUMNS area into the panel on the left.

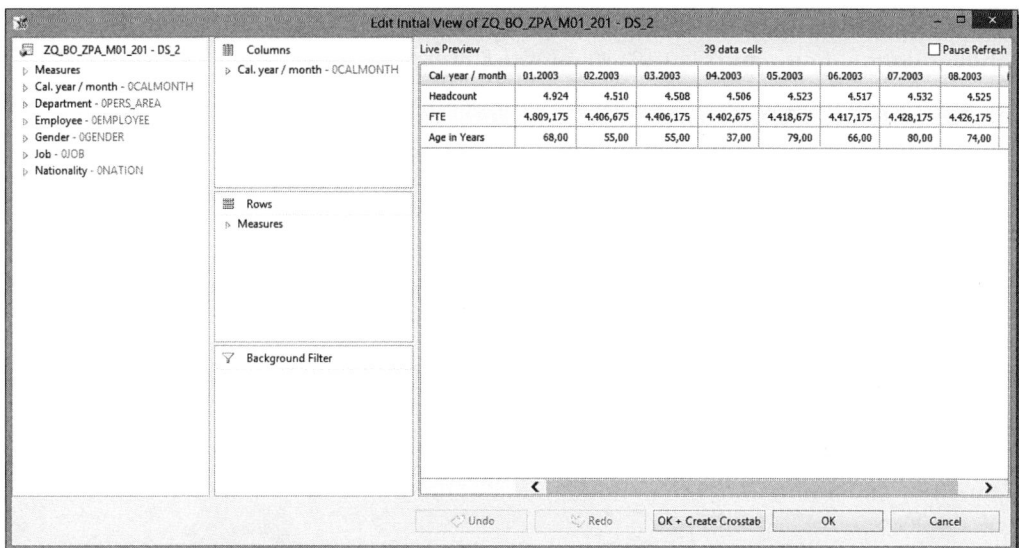

Figure 6.8 Initial View of Data Source DS_2

8. Add the dimensions EMPLOYEE, DEPARTMENT, JOB, NATIONALITY, and GENDER to the ROWS area.

9. The INITIAL VIEW should now look like Figure 6.9. Click the OK button to save these changes.

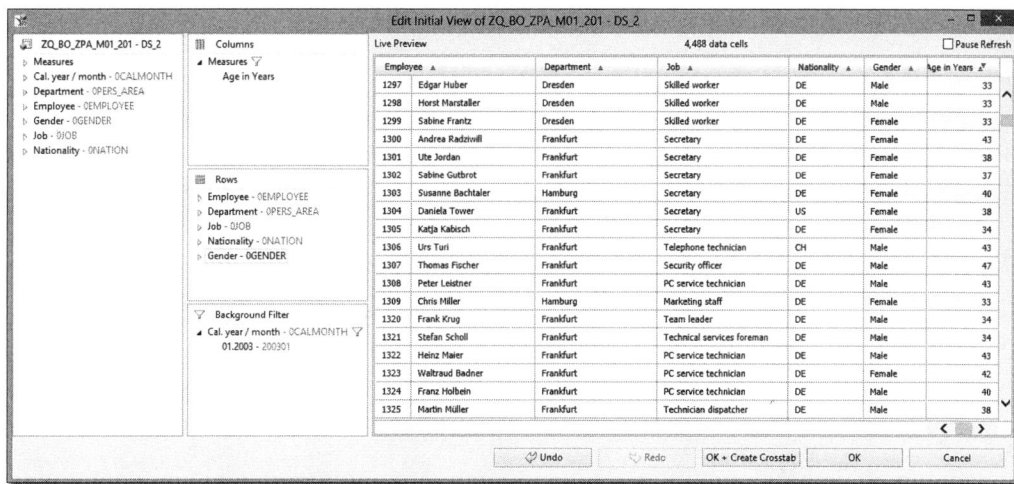

Figure 6.9 Rearranged Initial View of Data Source DS_2

10. Assign data source DS_2 to the CROSSTAB in the EMPLOYEE LIST tab. As you can see, the CROSSTAB is now populated with a list of employee attributes (Figure 6.10).

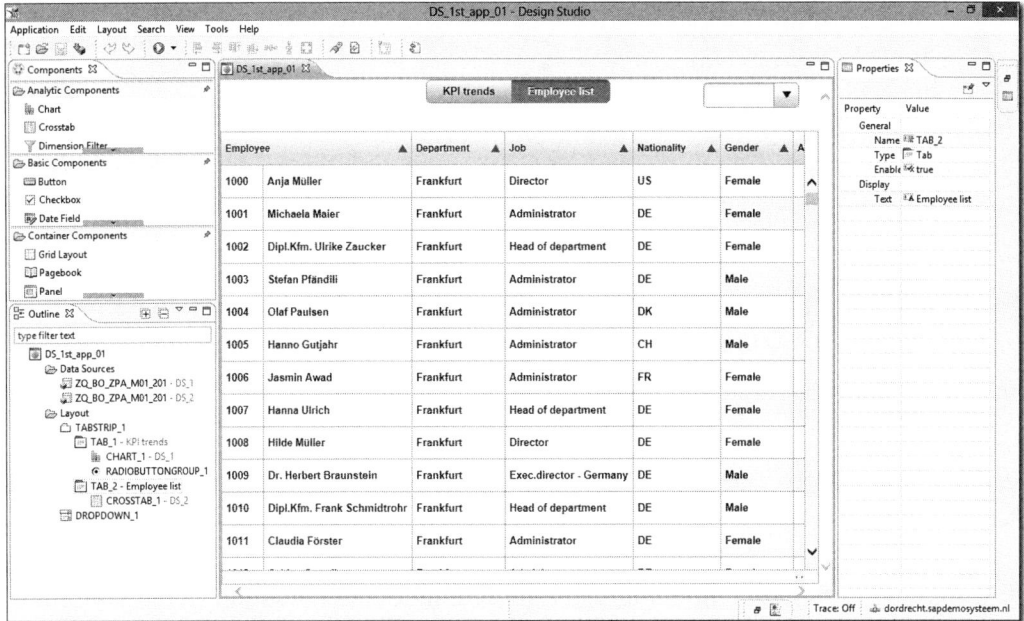

Figure 6.10 Crosstab Populated with Data

6.3 Making It Interactive

You now have the components all set up in the Layout Editor, and the application is already connected with a BEx query, delivering the data you want to show. In this section, we will use some scripts to add interactivity to the application and to set up the filters.

Scripting Don't worry if you are a bit overwhelmed by the coding we're going to discuss here. Later in the book, we will explore scripting in a far more detailed way and will actually explain what is happening. For now, we're just giving you the big picture. The following things need to happen:

▶ When the application first starts up, the labels of the DROPDOWN BOX component have to be populated with the values for the departments.

▶ You have to set the initially selected label of the DROPDOWN BOX component, since you want to see the data for only one department at a time.

▶ Not only do you need to show the initially selected label, but you also have to make sure both data sources are actually filtered for this initial value on the department dimension.

▶ When a department is selected from the DROPDOWN BOX component, the CHART and CROSSTAB components should show the values for that department.

▶ The RADIO BUTTON GROUP component must determine which measure should be presented in the CHART component. Only one of the two measures should be shown when the application starts.

Now let's code!

1. Select your application from the OUTLINE view. This is the top level.

2. In the PROPERTIES view, all the way down, click the EVENTS • ON STARTUP button to edit the script. This script will be executed when the application first starts up.

3. To populate the DROPDOWN BOX component with labels from the DEPARTMENT dimension, use the following script:

```
DROPDOWN_1.setItems(DS_1.getMemberList("0PERS_
AREA", MemberPresentation.EXTERNAL_KEY, MemberDisplay.KEY_
TEXT, 50));
```

4. In this example, use department 1300 (Frankfurt) as the initially shown department. First make sure the DROPDOWN BOX component shows this value initially. Add the following script on a line beneath the script from the previous step:

```
DROPDOWN_1.setSelectedValue("1300");
```

5. The next step is to filter both data sources so they will give only the data for department 1300 (Frankfurt) when the application starts up. On a new line write this script:

```
DS_1.setFilterExt("0PERS_AREA", "1300");
DS_2.setFilterExt("0PERS_AREA", "1300");
```

6. The code for the On Startup event is now finished (Figure 6.11). Click the OK button.

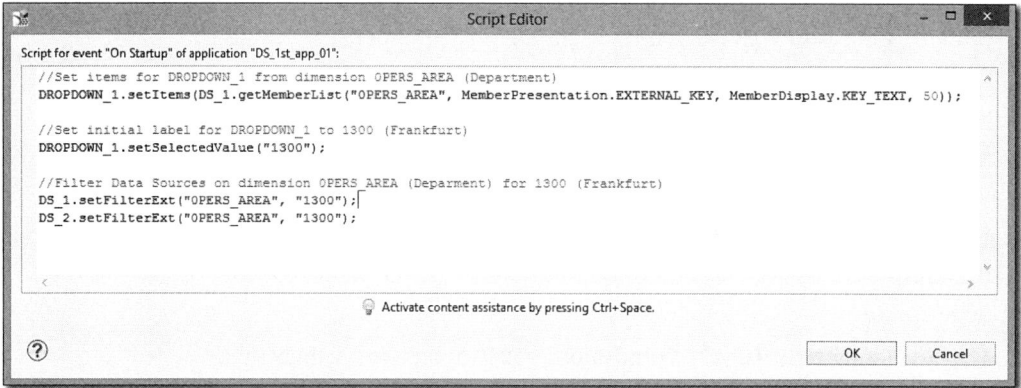

Figure 6.11 On Startup Event Script

7. Now head over to the DROPDOWN BOX component. Select it and in its PREFERENCES view choose EVENTS • ON SELECT.

8. Add the following code to execute a filter on both data sources, with a value that is selected from the DROPDOWN BOX labels.

```
DS_1.setFilterExt("OPERS_AREA", DROPDOWN_1.getSelected-
Value());
DS_2.setFilterExt("OPERS_AREA", DROPDOWN_1.getSelected-
Value());
```

9. Click OK to close the Script Editor (Figure 6.12).

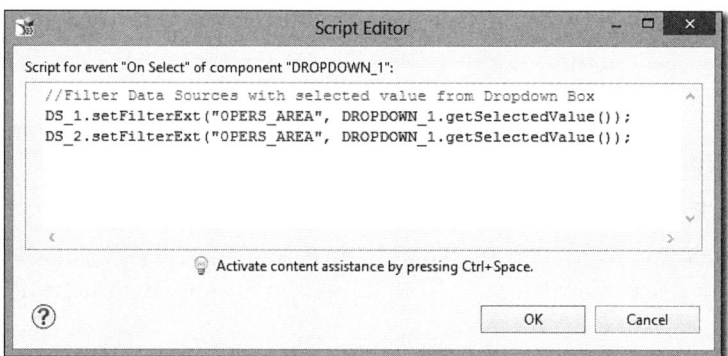

Figure 6.12 Dropdown Box On Select Event Script

10. Finally, you have to set up the Radio Button Group component. Select the component and navigate in its Properties view to Display • Items.

11. Here you will add the two selection values for the measures FTE and headcount. In the Text (optional) fields enter "FTE" and "Headcount" (Figure 6.13).

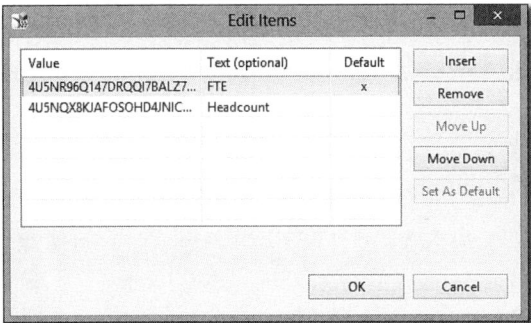

Figure 6.13 Edit Display Items for the Radio Button Group Component

12. You need to get the values for the Value fields from the BEx query you used earlier as a data source for the application. Open BEx Query Designer and open the BEx query.

13. Select the key figure for FTE from the Rows section and go to the Extended Tab in the Properties view. Here you can find the enterprise ID of this key figure (Figure 6.14). You need this to create the filter in the Radio Button Group component. Copy the enterprise ID and paste it in the Value field for FTE in the Edit Items window in Design Studio.

Figure 6.14 BEx Query Designer Properties for Key Figure FTE

14. Repeat these steps for the HEADCOUNT key figure and click OK to close the EDIT ITEMS window.

15. Now go to EVENTS • ON SELECT to open the Script Editor.

16. Enter the following code, where <Enterprise ID KF> should be changed with the enterprise ID of the key figures structure in your BEx query (Figure 6.15). You can find this the same way you got the enterprise IDs for the two key figures, only now you have to select the KEY FIGURES structure instead. You can also press Ctrl + Space while typing the code to select the dimension from the context menu.

```
DS_1.setFilterExt("<Enterprise
ID KF>", RADIOBUTTONGROUP_1.getSelectedValue());
```

Figure 6.15 Radio Button Group on the Select Event Script

17. Close the Script Editor by clicking OK.

18. If you were to execute the application at this point, three lines would still be shown in the CHART. This is because the event script you just created for the RADIO BUTTON GROUP is only executed when a selection is made. Therefore, you need to add another line of code to the On Startup event of the Design Studio application to set an initial filter on the measures. Select the application from the OUTLINE view.

19. In the PROPERTIES view go to EVENTS • ON STARTUP.

20. Add the next piece of code. Again, you have to change <Enterprise ID KF> to the enterprise ID of the KEY FIGURE structure and <Enterprise ID FTE> in the enterprise ID for the FTE key figure.

```
DS_1.setFilterExt("<Enterprise ID KF>", "<Enterprise ID FTE>");
```

21. The complete Script Editor for the On Startup event should now look like Figure 6.16. Click OK.

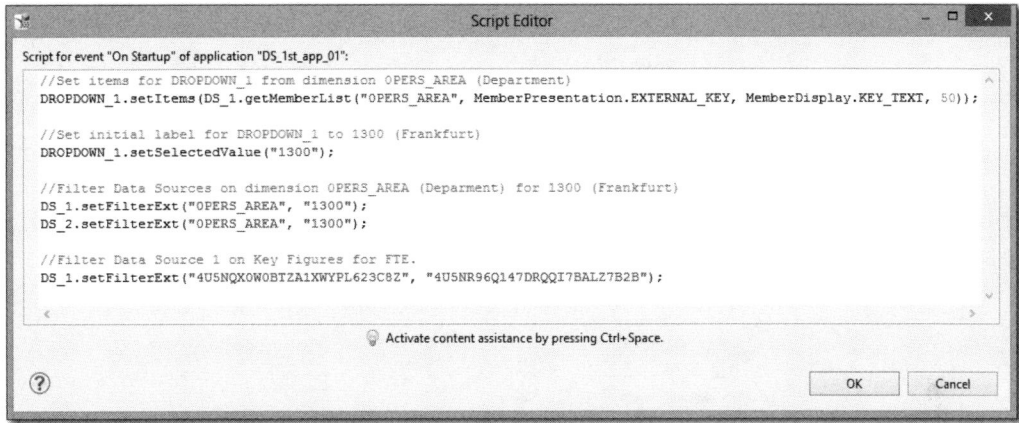

Figure 6.16 On Startup Event Script

Congratulations: Your Design Studio application is now fully operational! But before you can start using it, you should take some time to focus on the application's appearance to create a superb user experience.

6.4 Formatting and Fine-Tuning

Until this point of the example scenario, we didn't take a lot of time to have you format the application in the right way. You just added the building blocks you needed and made sure the application worked and the components did what they had to do.

If an application meets all its functional requirements but is designed such that the user doesn't understand what he sees or how things work, or it just doesn't look nice, the application quickly loses its value. It may frustrate the user and eventually lead to a situation in which the application won't be used at all.

User experience

Luckily, Design Studio provides a lot of options to customize and format the looks of an application. In this section we will go through a few of the features that would apply to our example application. Follow the steps below:

Customize an application

1. Place the DROPDOWN BOX component on the same height position as the TABSTRIP component. Select both components from the OUTLINE view by Ctrl-clicking them.

2. From the LAYOUT menu select the ALIGN TOP option. The DROPDOWN BOX is now moved to the top of the application.

3. Now you want this DROPDOWN BOX component to always keep the same margin from the right side of the application. Select the DROPDOWN BOX component.

4. In the PROPERTIES view set LAYOUT • RIGHT MARGIN to "20" (Figure 6.17).

Figure 6.17 Dropdown Box Component Properties View Layout Section

5. Select the CHART component. In the PROPERTIES view set LAYOUT • HEIGHT to "450".

6. Set LAYOUT • LEFT MARGIN to "30" and set the same value for BOTTOM MARGIN and RIGHT MARGIN. You'll see that the WIDTH is set to AUTO (Figure 6.18). The CHART component's width will now automatically resize when the user increases or decreases the application size.

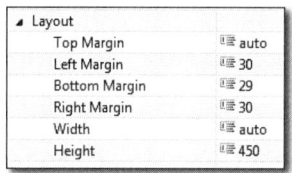

Figure 6.18 Chart Component Properties View Layout Section

7. Select the RADIO BUTTON GROUP component. In the PROPERTIES view set LAYOUT • WIDTH to "200".

8. Set DISPLAY • COLUMNS to "2" (Figure 6.19).

9. Now drag the RADIO BUTTON GROUP component to a position just above the CHART component.

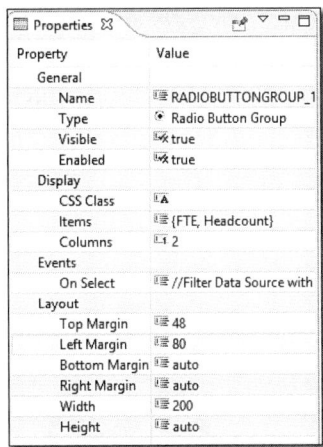

Figure 6.19 Properties View of the Radio Button Group Component

10. Once again, go to the PROPERTIES view and set LAYOUT • LEFT MARGIN to "80" (Figure 6.19).

11. Since you already maximized the size of the CROSSTAB component in the EMPLOYEE LIST tab of the application, you don't have to edit the LAYOUT settings for that component. Now that all the components are in place, you can edit the appearance of the CHART. Select the CHART component.

12. Open the ADDITIONAL PROPERTIES view from the VIEW menu.

13. In the ADDITIONAL PROPERTIES view, go to the LEGEND section and deselect the DISPLAY LEGEND checkbox (Figure 6.20). Since you already have a RADIO BUTTON GROUP component that indicates which measure the CHART is displaying, you don't need an additional legend.

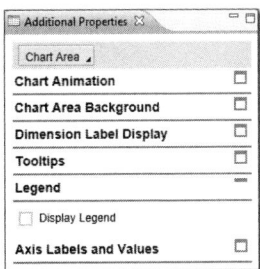

Figure 6.20 Legend Section in the Additional Properties View

14. Click the CHART AREA button, which is located above the ADDITIONAL PROPERTIES view, and select DATA SERIES.

15. Click the colored square and pick a color you like from the palette (Figure 6.21).

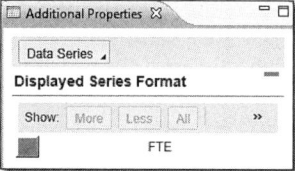

Figure 6.21 Data Series Pane in the Additional Properties View

The application you created is now nicely formatted and looks like Figure 6.22.

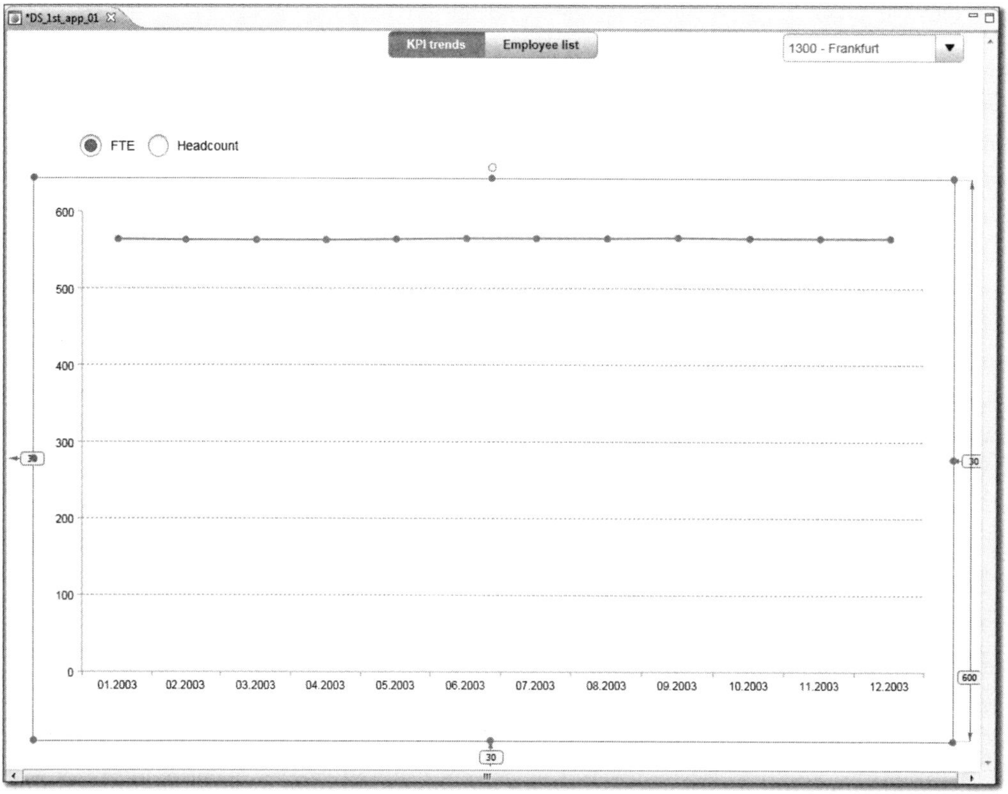

Figure 6.22 Layout Editor after Formatting

6.5 Executing the Application

It is time to check out your first application in Design Studio! Although we waited until the end to walk you through this process, keep in mind that you don't have to wait until the application is completely finished to do some test runs. During the development process you constantly want to see how the application behaves and how the changes you make affect the application.

Test run

To execute the application, follow the steps below:

1. Select the EXECUTE LOCALLY option from the APPLICATION menu to check the application in a browser window. The result is shown in Figure 6.23 and Figure 6.24.

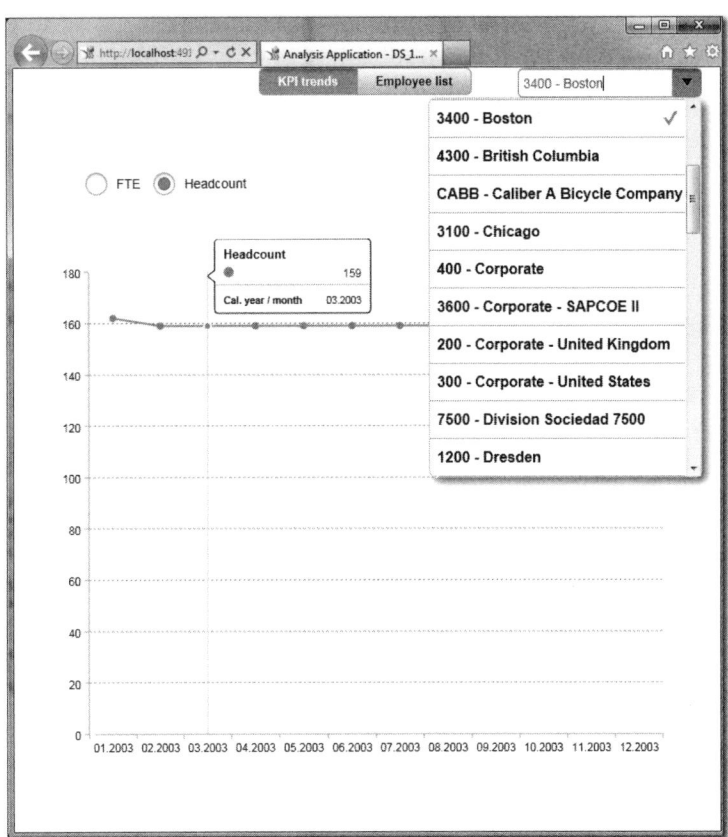

Figure 6.23 Application Running in a Browser (KPI Trends Tab)

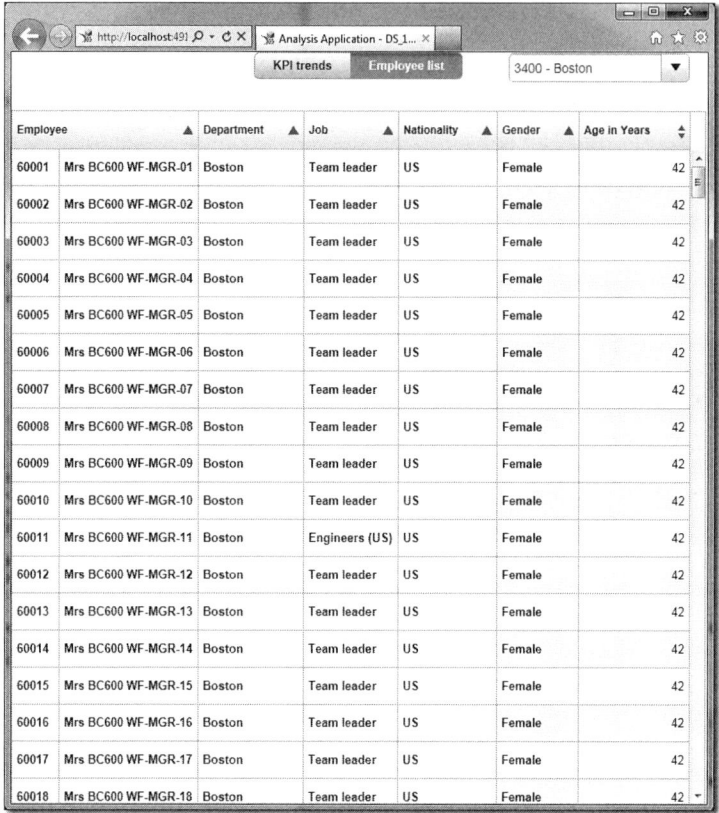

Figure 6.24 Application Running in a Browser (Employee List Tab)

2. Switch tabs, set a filter on another division, and switch between the two chart measures.

3. Check the application on your mobile device by selecting the SEND TO MOBILE DEVICE (USING QR CODE®) command in the toolbar.

6.6 Summary

In this chapter we went through a step-by-step tutorial to build a simple application with Design Studio. We used a CHART component and a CROSSTAB component to visualize and display data from a BEx query data source. To set up the overall layout of the application, we used a

TABSTRIP component, which allows the user to switch between the CHART and the CROSSTAB. With a DROPDOWN BOX component, a RADIO BUTTON GROUP, and some associated event scripts, we created the interactive elements in this application to filter the data and select the measures to be presented in the chart. Finally, we executed the application and checked its functionality.

The components and properties in Design Studio are your basic tools for enhancing your applications. In this chapter, we'll introduce you to them.

7 Components and Properties

In this chapter, we will look at all the building blocks—in other words, the components and their properties—of Design Studio. We start by talking about the properties of the APPLICATION component, then move on to the properties of the DATA SOURCE ALIAS component. In the heart of the chapter, we discuss the properties of all the visual components of Design Studio. Finally, we end the chapter with some tips and tricks about working with all these pieces and parts.

7.1 Application Component Properties

The APPLICATION component (Figure 7.1) is the main component in Design Studio, as it is the application itself. It is the top-level node in the OUTLINE view, and its PROPERTIES view contains settings that cover the whole application. Variables are maintained in this component, and a script can be added that will start up at the start of the application. Furthermore, you can insert a central CSS file that will allow you to have a single source of layout classes that you can use for every component within the application.

Common properties
Main component

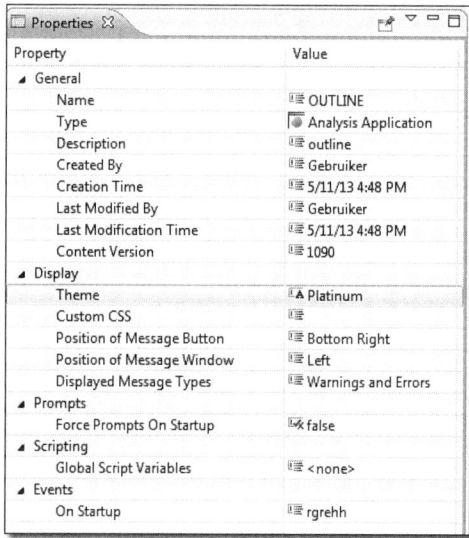

Figure 7.1 Application Component Properties

Table 7.1 shows the changeable properties of the APPLICATION component.

Properties	Usage
DESCRIPTION	The description of the application. You set this when you create a new application, but it can be changed at design time.
THEME	Specifies the theme of the application. The theme is a set of layout choices that apply to all the components used in the application. SAP recommends using the SAP Platinum theme for desktop applications and the SAP Mobile theme for iPad and iPhone applications.
CUSTOM CSS	You can upload a CSS file to the root folder of the application (local) or the SAP BI platform. In the CUSTOM CSS property, you can point to this CSS file. In this CSS file, CSS classes are defined that can be used by other components that have a CSS class property.

Table 7.1 Changeable Properties of the Application Component

Properties	Usage
POSITION OF MESSAGE BUTTON	Location of the button in a message. The button can be located on the top left, top right, bottom left, or bottom right of the application screen. The message button informs the user about information, warnings, and errors at runtime of the application.
POSITION OF MESSAGE WINDOW	Location of a message on the application during runtime. This message can be positioned on the top left, top right, bottom left, or bottom right of the application.
DISPLAYED MESSAGE TYPES	With this setting you can set the kind of messages that will show up at runtime of the application. The available message types are: ► NONE: No messages will be shown. ► ERRORS: Only errors will be shown. ► WARNINGS: Warnings and errors will be shown. ► ALL: All information messages will be shown.
FORCE PROMPTS ON STARTUP	When set to TRUE, this setting forces the application to prompt for new variable values at the start of the application when SAP NetWeaver BW or SAP HANA variables are used in the application.
GLOBAL SCRIPT VARIABLES	Here you can define global variables that are available in all the scripts in each component. You can also define the variable as a URL parameter so parameter values can be read from other applications.
ON STARTUP	Script code that will be run when the application starts. Editing this property will start the Script Editor. In the startup phase of the application, you typically insert code to work with external parameters or use data sources to populate the items of basic components.

Table 7.1 Changeable Properties of the Application Component (Cont.)

There are a number of cases when you might work with the properties of the APPLICATION component. These properties have a bigger impact than the properties of other components, because application components influence the behavior of scripting and layout of other components. Let's look at some examples.

7.1.1 Custom CSS

CSS text file The CUSTOM CSS property allows you to use the CSS classes defined in a CSS text file. You can either use a CSS file that is already uploaded to an SAP BI platform, or you can upload a CSS file to an SAP BI platform.

For example, you can create your own CSS file on your local computer with the code below. Next, you upload the CSS file to an SAP BI platform. The CUSTOM CSS property of the application should then point to this file, so the defined classes can be used by other components.

The CSS file consists of the following code:

```
.TextPanelOrange
{
background-color:#d0e4fe;
color:orange;
    text-align:center;
}
```

In each component, you can now assign the `TextpanelOrange` CSS class. Assigning this class to a component will result in the layout of the component changing to an orange text with a blue background.

There are specific applications available for editing CSS, for example, Notepad. Insert the code as shown in Figure 7.2.

Save the file as a .css file. In SAVE AS, select all files and name the file *mycssfile.css*.

Now go to the application in the Design Studio tool and go the properties of the APPLICATION component. Press the ... button on the right side of the CUSTOM CSS input box (Figure 7.3).

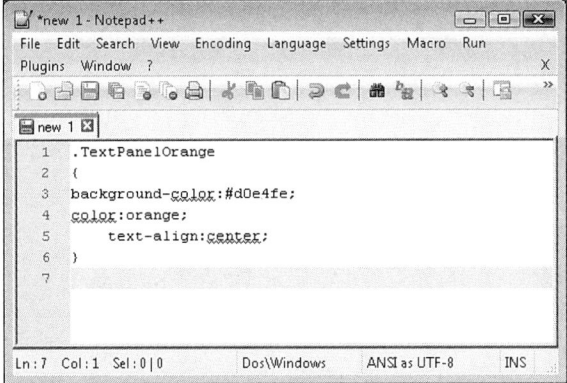

Figure 7.2 Create a CSS File

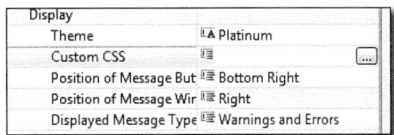

Figure 7.3 Custom CSS

You are now looking at the SAP BusinessObjects BI platform folders. We have selected a folder in the PUBLIC FOLDERS section, which means that other applications can access the CSS file we upload. To upload, click the button with the upward arrow on the top left of the window (Figure 7.4).

Public folder

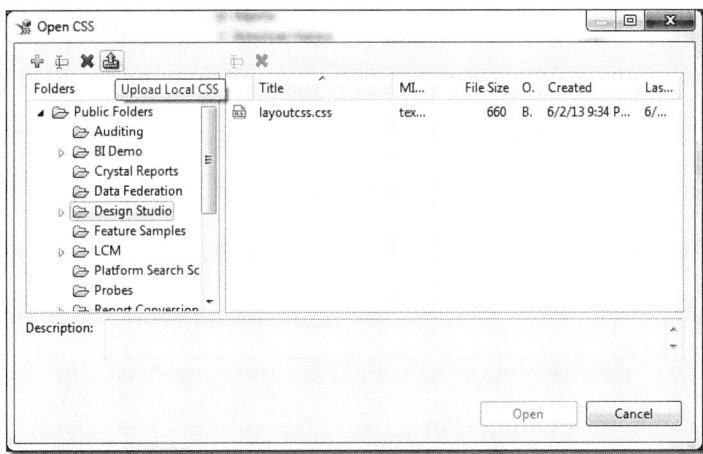

Figure 7.4 Public Folder on the SAP BusinessObjects BI Platform

You now see a window where you can select your CSS file. Navigate to the location where you saved your file and select the file by either double-clicking it or selecting it and clicking OPEN. In the SAP Business-Objects BI platform, you can now see your CSS file next to the already present CSS file. Select MYCSSFILE.CSS and click OPEN (Figure 7.5).

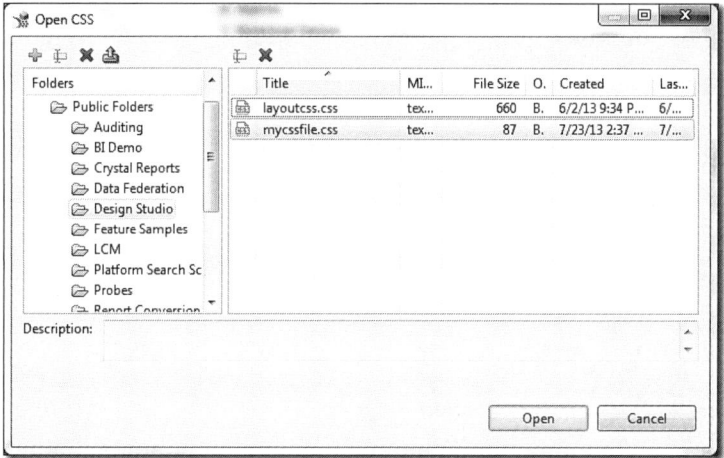

Figure 7.5 CSS File on SAP BusinessObjects BI Platform

After you've selected the CSS file, return to the application. You now see in the APPLICATION properties that the CUSTOM CSS property points to the file on the SAP BusinessObjects BI platform (Figure 7.6).

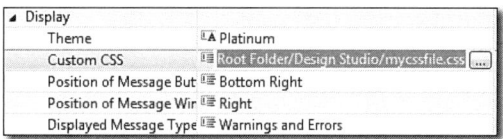

Figure 7.6 Custom CSS Property after Selection

As the final step, add a TEXT component to the application and set the CSS CLASS property to `TextPanelOrange` (Figure 7.7). You now can see how the TEXT component changes the background color and the font color.

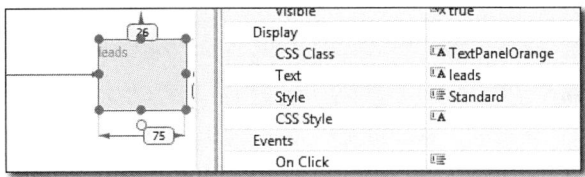

Figure 7.7 Applying the CSS Class

7.1.2 Global Script Variables and On Startup

As the number of applications in an organization grows larger, you will eventually need a way for the applications to communicate with each other. The best way to do this is via a few connected lightweight applications—this is easier to maintain then one very big application.

Communication between applications

Design Studio is able to open another website or another Design Studio application by using the APPLICATION.openNewWindow method. The URL of the new application can include parameters for the other application. With a global script variable, the other application will receive those parameters and can thus allow outside applications to influence that application.

We will set up an external parameter by adding it as a variable to the VARIABLES property of the APPLICATION component (Figure 7.8). This is done by adding the parameter in the URL, as we will show shortly. Once the application starts, it will automatically run the application's On Startup script. In this handler, we will insert script code. When the external parameter value is Green, the CSS class Green is set for the components in the application; otherwise, the CSS class TextPanelOrange is used. In the example we show only one code example, but in an application, you would put all the components in the On Startup handler.

External parameter

The On Startup script looks like this:

```
if (XvarTheme == "Green") {
    TEXT_1.setCSSClass("GreenText");
} else {
    TEXT_1.setCSSClass("TextPanelOrange");
}
```

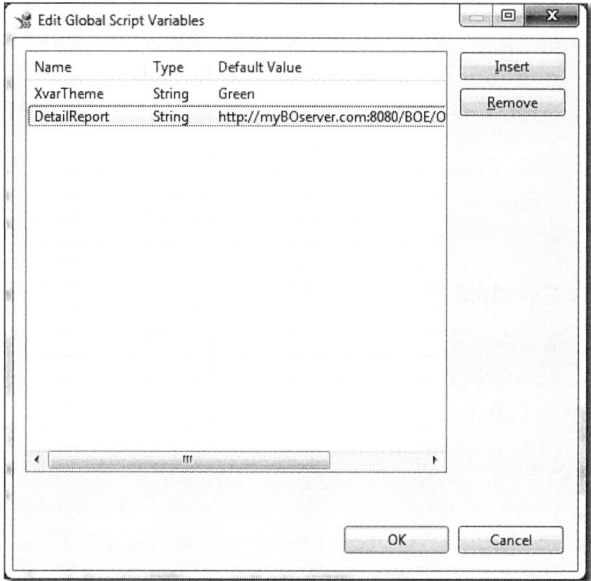

Figure 7.8 Edit Global Script Variable

Note

In Chapter 8, we will give you more specific instructions about scripting. For now, we're just using this as an example to show you how the VARIABLES property of the APPLICATION component can be used.

The application is now set up to check whether parameter values are passed. If they are, it will set the CSS classes based on the color passed in the parameter.

If an application wants to use the ability to pass the parameter, it can do this by using the `application.openNewWindow` method:

```
APPLICATION.openNewWindow("http://myBOserver.com:8080/BOE/Open-
Document/1302122240/OpenDocument/opendoc/
openDocument.jsp?sIDType=CUID&icdocID=ARlLC4JJgDxDujA4IODZobk"
+ "&XvarTheme=" + RADIOBUTTONGROUP_COLOR.getSelectedValue());
```

Radio Button Group component

In this method we use a RADIO BUTTON GROUP component that holds the possible values for the colors. When the `openNewWindow` method is used, the method will look at the component and use the value to pass it as a parameter to the first application.

As the URL with the CUID is quite complicated, the code above looks a bit messy. We want to make the script code more readable. To do this we add the variable `DetailReport` to the application. This variable holds the value of the URL of the application. This will be easier to read and maintain, especially when you want to link from several components.

The code now looks like this:

```
APPLICATION.openNewWindow(DetailReport +
        "&XvarTheme="+ RADIOBUTTONGROUP_COLOR.getSelected-
Value());
```

7.2 Data Source Alias Component Properties

The DATA SOURCE ALIAS component also has properties, which are shown in Table 7.2.

Property	Description
NAME	Name of the data source alias.
VISIBLE	Toggles the visibility of the component.
LOAD IN SCRIPT	Specifies if the data source is loaded immediately when initializing the application or is loaded in the script later. The standard setting is FALSE, meaning the data source will load immediately.
DATA SOURCE NAME, CONNECTION, AND TYPE	Click these fields if you want to change the data source underneath the data source alias. The ADD DATA SOURCE screen will open with the current settings.

Table 7.2 Data Source Properties

The LOAD IN SCRIPT property is worth a special mention as a property that allows you to delay the moment when the data is loaded. This property tells the application if the data will be immediately loaded at startup or will be triggered from a script at a later time. Reasons for delaying

Data source Load in Script

213

include wanting to reduce the start time of the application or wanting to apply filters before you load the data for performance reasons. When you want to load the data, add this script line:

```
DS_MYDATA SOURCE.loadData source();
```

7.3 Visual Component Properties

In this section, we'll discuss the properties of all the visual components of Design Studio. Visual components can be divided into three categories: analytic, basic, and container. We'll discuss the properties for each, but we'll begin with the common properties that all visual components share.

7.3.1 Common Properties

Some properties are shared among all the visual components. These involve the layout of the components—specifically, their sizes and margins. You can alter the layout and the relative positioning of a component by editing the numbers in the LAYOUT section of the properties. You can also use the mouse to drag the component or its borders to the desired size or position.

Property	Description
TOP MARGIN	The distance between the top of the component and the top of the parent component. Either a number in pixels or AUTO.
LEFT MARGIN	The distance between the left side of the component and the left side of the parent component. Either a number in pixels or AUTO.
RIGHT MARGIN	The distance between the right side of the component and the right side of the parent component. Either a number in pixels or AUTO.
BOTTOM MARGIN	The distance between the bottom of the component and the bottom of the parent component. Either a number in pixels or AUTO.

Table 7.3 Common Properties

Property	Description
HEIGHT	The height of the component. Either a number in pixels or AUTO.
WIDTH	The width of the component. Either a number in pixels or AUTO.

Table 7.3 Common Properties (Cont.)

By setting the layout properties to AUTO, you are telling the application which settings are allowed to shrink and grow along with the screen size. When a fixed number is entered for a property, then the value for that property remains constant.

Auto layout properties

For example, consider a component with the following layout parameters:

▶ TOP MARGIN: 10

▶ LEFT MARGIN: 10

▶ BOTTOM MARGIN: 10

▶ RIGHT MARGIN: 10

▶ WIDTH: AUTO

▶ HEIGHT: AUTO

The result of these settings is that the margins will remain equal in relation to the parent component, but the component itself will resize according to the screen size.

As another example, consider these parameters:

▶ TOP MARGIN: 10

▶ LEFT MARGIN: 10

▶ BOTTOM MARGIN: AUTO

▶ RIGHT MARGIN: AUTO

▶ WIDTH: 100

▶ HEIGHT: 100

The result of these settings is that the component size is fixed to 100x100 pixels with a margin of 10 pixels to the left and top. A bigger screen size will mean larger right and bottom margins.

7.3.2 Analytic Component Properties

Analytic components are components that use data to show numbers in either table or graphical form. These components are tied to data by assigning a data source to a component, and then using the component to visualize the data output that is defined in the INITIAL view of the data source.

We will describe the different types of analytic components next.

Chart Component

Graphically visualize data

CHART components (Figure 7.9) can be added to application to visualize data graphically. They can identify trends or outliers in data, and also help users to focus on those data points. The CHART component shows as soon you assign a data source to it, and the default CHART type is a column chart.

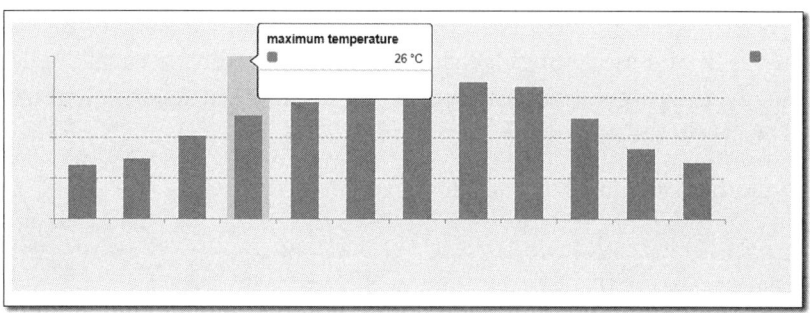

Figure 7.9 Chart Component Example

A CHART is meant to communicate data in a clear, concise way. The example in Figure 7.10 shows the maximum temperatures per month for a certain location. When you hover over a month, you see a tool tip with the exact data value.

Table 7.4 lists the properties of the CHART component.

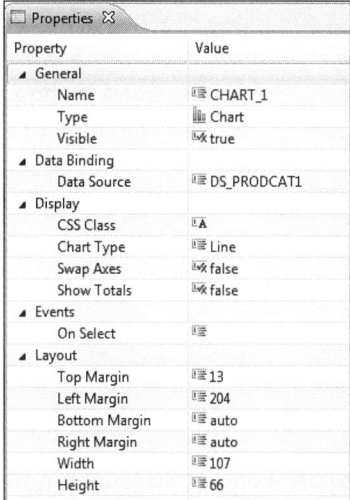

Figure 7.10 Chart Component Properties

Property	Description
NAME	The name of the component. This must be a unique name within the application.
VISIBLE	Toggles the visibility of the CHART component at runtime.
DATA SOURCE	Assigns data to the component to visualize. You can choose from the defined data source aliases that are added to the application.
CSS CLASS	When a custom CSS file is assigned to the APPLICATION component, you can assign a class here.
CHART TYPE	A number of chart types are available, as outlined in more detail below. In Figure 7.11, all the chart types are listed with a screenshot for reference.
SWAP AXES	Specifies whether the horizontal and vertical axes of the data source should be swapped before visualization.
SHOW TOTALS	When TRUE, the totals of the data source output will also be visualized.
ON SELECT	This will open the Script Editor. The On Select handler is triggered when a value is selected or deselected.

Table 7.4 Chart Component Properties

Types of charts
The types of charts are as follows:

▶ **Line**
A line graph shows a trend by showing a line with the labels in the x-axis and the values in the y-axis. In addition, there is a variation of a line chart:

  ▶ **Horizontal line**
  A horizontal line chart shows the line going in a vertical direction with the labels horizontal.

▶ **Bar**
A bar chart shows a bar for each value in the data source. There are several variations of bar charts:

  ▶ **Stacked bar**
  A stacked bar chart is a bar chart where you can also show how different values add up to the total of the bar. The length of the stacked bar depends on the sum of the values.

  ▶ **100% stacked bar**
  This shows bars, where each value is a part of the bar. This type of chart will always show the total bar length at 100%.

  ▶ **Bar combination**
  A combination of a bar chart and a line chart.

▶ **Column**
A column chart shows each value in a column. There are several variations of column charts:

  ▶ **Stacked column**
  A stacked column is a column chart where you can also show how different values add up to the total of the column. The total length depends on the sum of the values.

  ▶ **100% stacked column**
  This shows columns, where each value is part of the column.

  ▶ **Column combination**
  A column combination chart is a combination of a column chart and a line chart.

▶ **Area**
An area chart is like a line chart with the area under the line colored in. In addition, there is a variation of an area chart:

▸ **Horizontal area**
A horizontal area chart is an area chart where the line is vertical and the labels are horizontal.

▸ **Crosstab**
A crosstab is a table in which numbers are presented along rows and columns.

▸ **Bubble**
A bubble chart is a chart where you can map three key figures: one on the x-axis, one on the y-axis, and one that affects the size of the bubble.

▸ **Waterfall**
A waterfall chart is a bar chart where bars are shown in a cumulative way. The total value of bar 1 is the starting point of bar 2. There are two variations of a waterfall chart:

  ▸ **Stacked waterfall**
  A stacked waterfall chart is a waterfall chart with the added ability to add up several values in each bar.

  ▸ **Horizontal waterfall**
  A horizontal waterfall chart shows the bars going from left to right and the labels horizontal.

▸ **Pie**
A pie chart shows the relative size of entities compared to the whole. In addition, there is a variation of a pie chart:

  ▸ **Multiple pie**
  A multiple pie chart shows a different pie graph for each key figure and shows the relative sizes for each value on the graphs.

▸ **Radar**
A radar chart shows the relative size for each value. It is like a line graph with a round axis. In addition, there is a variation of a radar chart:

  ▸ **Multiple radar**
  A multiple radar chart shows a radar graph for each key figure.

▸ **Scatter**
A scatter chart shows combinations of key figures, where one key figure is plotted along the x-axis and the other along the y-axis.

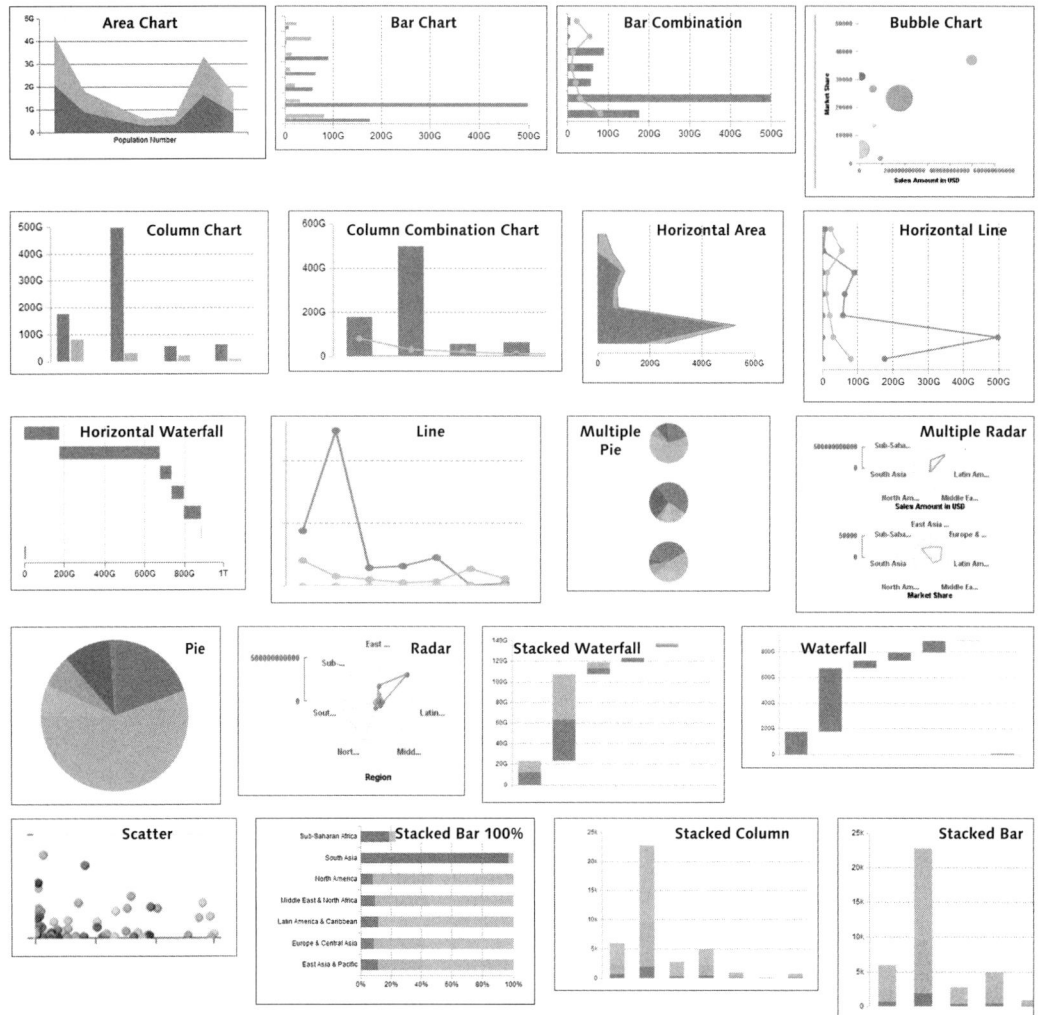

Figure 7.11 Chart Types

In the ADDITIONAL PROPERTIES section (Figure 7.12) of a chart, you can alter the look of the CHART component. In the CHART AREA, you can choose which labels you want to be visible, whether you want a tool tip, and whether a chart animation should be shown at application startup. You can also choose the fill of your background and how the dimension values are displayed in the chart.

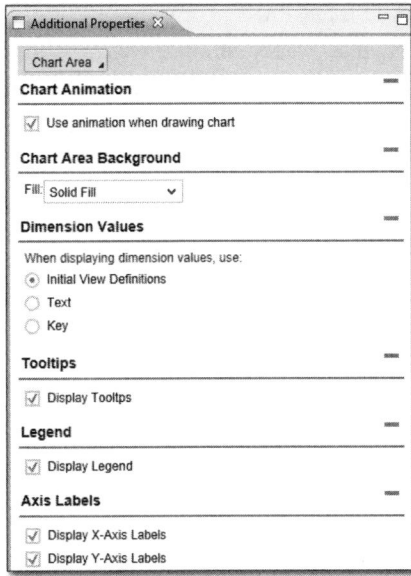

Figure 7.12 Additional Properties of a Chart Component

With the DATA SERIES properties of a chart (Figure 7.13), you can choose how many data series will be displayed. There is only a choice when more than five data series are available.

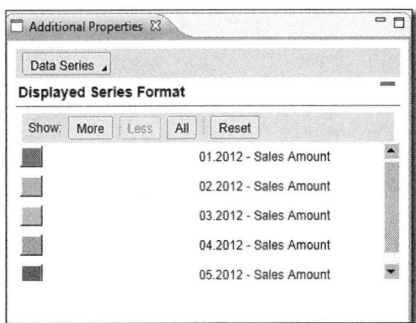

Figure 7.13 Data Series Properties

Crosstab Component

The CROSSTAB component (Figure 7.14) is useful for displaying detailed multidimensional data with analytic purposes. Used together with the

Multidimensional data

221

DIMENSION FILTER component and the FILTER PANEL component, which will be described later in this chapter, it is a very flexible way to show and work with data. You can use the CROSSTAB component to sort data, filter data, move or swap dimensions, and select cells that in turn can be scripted to add filters to data sources.

Region	Sales Amount in USD East Asia & Pacific	Europe & Central Asia	Latin America & Caribbean	Middle East & North Africa	North America	South Asia	Sub-Saharan Africa	Totaalresultaat
Calendar year/month	$	$	$	$	$	$	$	$
01.2011	500.817.375,53	1.923.048.432,13	240.262.114,95	418.617.309,53	83.203.021,83	5.563.385,10	67.850.969,12	3.239.362.608,19
02.2011	500.797.339,14	1.923.083.706,95	240.182.997,66	418.566.748,27	83.179.799,52	5.563.385,10	67.854.188,54	3.239.228.165,18
03.2011	550.741.217,96	2.115.462.573,92	264.249.713,53	460.559.324,84	91.538.669,91	6.119.723,61	74.637.020,72	3.563.308.244,49
04.2011	550.833.006,55	2.114.915.166,94	264.282.100,17	460.351.344,11	91.468.334,39	6.119.723,61	74.636.066,01	3.562.605.741,78
05.2011	500.704.546,46	1.922.673.653,07	240.279.587,97	418.506.787,05	83.174.067,45	5.563.385,10	67.852.994,92	3.238.755.022,02
06.2011	500.881.384,43	1.922.928.494,63	240.256.454,65	418.588.467,62	83.215.721,61	5.563.385,10	67.852.994,91	3.239.286.902,95
07.2011	400.602.115,93	1.538.115.720,80	192.205.163,75	334.817.858,91	66.552.768,89	4.450.708,06	54.279.848,94	2.591.024.185,28
08.2011	500.751.867,87	1.922.949.942,12	240.288.402,81	418.680.976,07	83.164.026,04	5.563.385,10	67.851.403,06	3.239.250.003,07
09.2011	500.746.032,86	1.922.754.258,90	240.282.742,52	418.540.271,89	83.161.841,92	5.563.385,10	67.849.811,23	3.238.898.344,42
10.2011	550.841.094,42	2.114.787.775,49	264.253.183,54	460.467.375,15	91.470.624,27	6.119.723,61	74.633.479,35	3.562.573.255,83
11.2011	550.926.572,51	2.114.971.694,84	264.233.684,12	460.640.291,15	91.528.177,14	6.119.723,61	74.633.479,33	3.563.053.622,70
12.2011	350.559.504,97	1.345.681.753,10	168.181.726,51	293.015.959,63	58.210.200,98	3.894.369,56	47.495.982,13	2.267.239.496,88
Total Result	5.959.202.058,63	22.881.573.172,89	2.858.957.872,18	4.981.352.714,22	989.867.253,95	66.204.282,66	807.428.238,26	38.544.585.592,79

Figure 7.14 Crosstab Component

Table 7.5 shows the properties of the CROSSTAB component.

Property	Description
NAME	The name of the component. This must be a unique name within the application.
VISIBLE	Toggles the visibility of the CROSSTAB component at runtime.
DATA SOURCE	Assigns data to the component to visualize it. You can choose from the defined data source aliases you added to the application.
PIXEL-BASED SCROLLING	Enables a smooth scrolling experience. This property is recommended when building an application for mobile devices or applications with a low data volume.
ROW LIMIT	Maximum number of rows for pixel-based scrolling.
COLUMN LIMIT	Maximum number of columns for pixel-based scrolling.

Table 7.5 Crosstab Component Properties

Property	Description
CSS CLASS	When a custom CSS file is assigned to the APPLICATION component's properties, you can assign a class here.
SHOW SCALING FACTOR	When this property is set to TRUE, the scaling factor will be shown in the column header.
ALWAYS FILL	If set to TRUE, the CROSSTAB component will be sized as defined in the LAYOUT properties. This means that if the number of cells is not sufficient to fill the space that was set for the CROSSTAB component, the cells will increase in size until the entire frame (the width and height of the component) is filled.
ENABLE SELECTION	When set to TRUE, users will be able to select cells in the CROSSTAB component by hovering over or clicking the inner members of the required dimension. This does not apply for result cells. Selecting a cell will result in an On Select handler where you can insert script to perform several actions based on the user's selection.
ON SELECT	This will open the Script Editor. The On Select handler is triggered when a value is selected or deselected.

Table 7.5 Crosstab Component Properties (Cont.)

As an example of when this component can come in handy, you can use the CROSSTAB component in combination with a GRAPH component. Users can click a value on the GRAPH component. The CROSSTAB component will then show detailed information about the selected value. The selected value then can be used as a filter that will be used for a second component for a more detailed view.

Clickthrough from Chart component to Crosstab component

For this example, let's assume that a second data source is being filtered based on the selection that is made in the CROSSTAB component. This results in an interactive screen that will pop up with additional information when a cell is being selected. Figure 7.15 shows an application where the user selected the decade 1950-1959 from below the graph and a CROSSTAB component appeared to show each year in that decade.

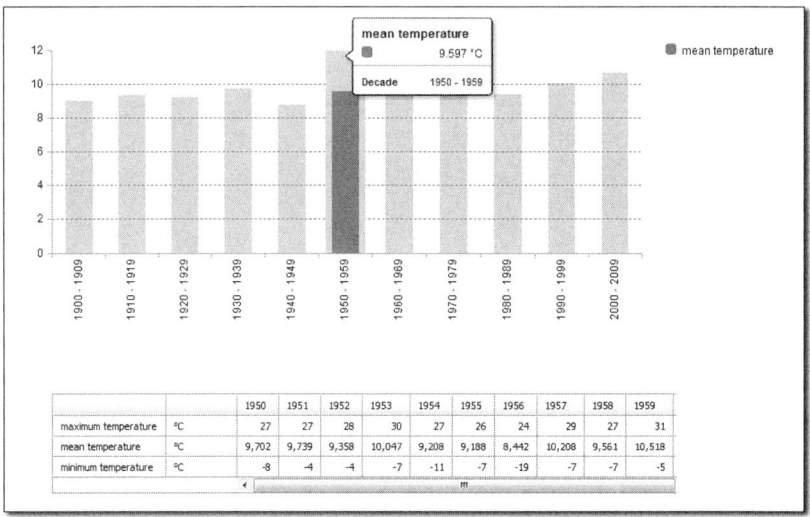

Figure 7.15 Clickthrough from Graph to Crosstab

The CROSSTAB component is placed inside a PANEL component that is not visible at the start of the application. When the user clicks on a bar in the chart, a filter is applied to the second data source and the PANEL component is set to visible.

The code for this is shown below:

```
DS_SECOND.setFilter("ZDECADE",
  CHRT_SELECTVALUE.getSelectedMember("ZDECADE"));
PNL_YEARS.setVisible(true);
```

Dimension Filter Component

Add a filter for one dimension

The DIMENSION FILTER component (Figure 7.16) is useful for adding a filter for one dimension. This filter can be applied to multiple data sources. When clicked at runtime, the component opens a popup in which the user is able to select a value or a range of values. In the SELECTION tab, you can choose filter values by selecting the members in the table, and you can limit the number of possible choices by entering a search string in the textbox. For example, if you want to be able to choose from all the products starting with N, enter "N*" in the text box.

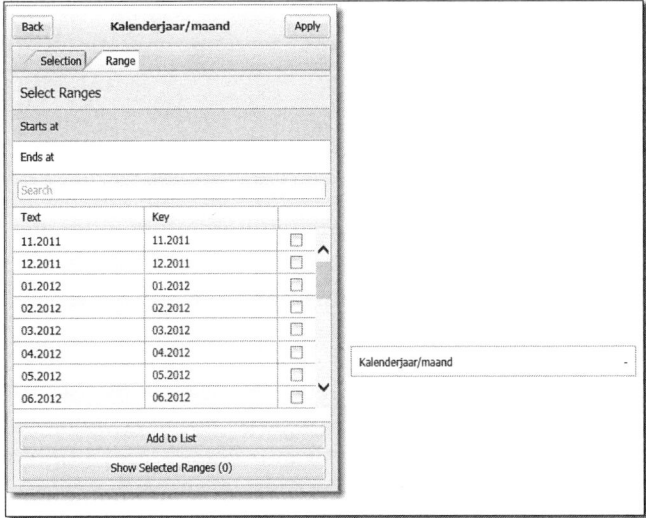

Figure 7.16 Dimension Filter Component

In the RANGE tab, you can build a range filter with a lowest and a highest value. First select the STARTS AT row and select the value. Then select the ENDS AT row and select the highest value. Click the ADD TO LIST button on the bottom of the popup screen. Now you can make a new range filter and add it to the list. When you're finished, click the APPLY button on the top right. When you click BACK, the last filter you entered will be ignored.

When you want the user to be able to filter on more dimensions, you have to add a DIMENSION FILTER component for each dimension to which you want to allow the user to apply filters. (Alternatively, you could use the FILTER PANEL component, which is discussed next.)

Table 7.6 shows the properties of the DIMENSION FILTER component.

Property	Description
NAME	The name of the component. This must be a unique name within the application.
VISIBLE	Toggles the visibility of the DIMENSION FILTER at runtime.

Table 7.6 Dimension Filter Properties

Property	Description
DATA SOURCE	Assigns data to the DIMENSION FILTER component. This data source delivers the items for which you can set a DIMENSION FILTER on the target data sources defined in the next property.
TARGET DATA SOURCES	With this property, the DIMENSION FILTER component can be applied to other data sources. Data sources must have the same dimension and must be defined in the application. If you have an application that shows sales, purchases, general ledger, and transport for regional offices, you have several data sources for each dataset. One DIMENSION FILTER component on a regional office dimension would set the correct filter on all these data sources.
DIMENSION	The dimension to be filtered.
CSS CLASS	When a custom CSS file is assigned to the APPLICATION component, you can assign a class here.
DIMENSION NAME	Shows the dimension name.
DISPLAY MODE	This property sets the way the filters are displayed: ▶ FILTER LIST: Filter values are displayed as comma-separated values. ▶ FILTER COUNT: The number of applied items is displayed.
POPUP WIDTH/HEIGHT/POSITION	The layout of the popup screen component that is used to define the DIMENSION FILTER component.
ON APPLY	The script that is executed when a filter is applied. A Script Editor opens for this property.

Table 7.6 Dimension Filter Properties (Cont.)

When you use multiple DIMENSION FILTER components, you can limit the usage by hiding the components that cannot be used. For example, if the user already filtered on products, you could stop him from also filtering on customers by hiding the DIMENSION FILTER component that handles the customer filter. This can be done using the following code:

```
DIMENSIONFILTER_CUSTOMER.setVisible(false);
```

Filter Panel Component

The FILTER PANEL component (Figure 7.17) is a component that allows you to apply filters on several dimensions to target data sources. The DIMENSION FILTER component, discussed previously, can also be used to apply filters to target data sources; the FILTER PANEL component, however, is able to put filters on more than one dimension.

Apply filters on multiple dimensions

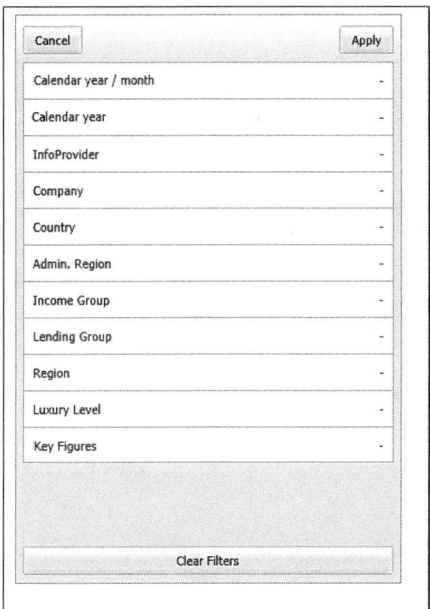

Figure 7.17 Filter Panel Component

The FILTER PANEL component shows all the dimensions of the data source to which it is assigned. The user can open an input box by clicking

227

the name of the dimension. By clicking the "-" sign on the right, the user can open a selection screen to pick values.

Table 7.7 shows the properties of the FILTER PANEL component.

Property	Description
NAME	The name of the component. This must be a unique name within the application.
VISIBLE	Toggles the visibility of the FILTER PANEL component at runtime.
DATA SOURCE	Assigns data to the component for filtering. You can choose from the defined data source aliases added to the application.
TARGET DATA SOURCES	With this property, the FILTER PANEL component can be applied to other data sources. Data sources must have the same dimension and must be defined in the application.
DIMENSIONS	Select and order the dimensions that will be available for the user.
CSS CLASS	When a custom CSS file is assigned to the APPLICATION component, you can assign a class here.
DIMENSION NAME	Shows the dimension name.
DISPLAY MODE	Shows the filters or the number of filters applied.
MEMBER DISPLAY	Sets member display mode, for example, *key + text*.
TITLE	Sets a title for the FILTER PANEL component.
ON APPLY	The script that is executed when a FILTER PANEL component is applied. A Script Editor opens for this property.
ON CANCEL	The script that is executed when the CANCEL button is clicked. A Script Editor opens for this property.

Table 7.7 Filter Panel Component Properties

Display dimensions

One of the things you can do using the FILTER PANEL component is control which dimensions you display. Although you could put all the dimensions in one filter panel, it is easier for the user of the application when you put dimensions that belong together in one filter panel. For example, in an application that shows sales data, you can put all the customer dimensions in one filter panel, the product dimensions in the second, and time dimensions in the third panel. You could also put a couple of FILTER PANEL components in one PANEL container component and, for example, allow the user to toggle the visibility of these PANEL components. That way you can create a dimension-like menu structure in which the user can navigate.

The FILTER PANEL component already has interactivity built into it, as it interacts with the data source. We can, however, add something to the layout to highlight that this component has been used to add a filter. In the On Apply handler, set the following code. This will assign a CSS class with, for example, a different font color to signal that this filter has been used.

```
FILTERPANEL_1.setCSSClass("Active");
```

7.3.3   Basic Component Properties

In this section we are going to look at the basic components. Basic components are buttons, text components, and image components. They do not have a direct link to a data source or allow child components.

No direct link to data source, no child components

Button Component

Buttons (Figure 7.18) allow the user to interact with the application. To build this interactivity, you add a script to the BUTTON component's ON CLICK property.

Figure 7.18 Button Component

Table 7.8 shows the properties of the BUTTON component.

Property	Description
NAME	The name of the component. This must be a unique name within the application.
VISIBLE	Specifies whether the BUTTON component is visible.
ENABLED	Specifies whether the BUTTON component is enabled. Disabled BUTTON components are not available for interaction.
TEXT	Specifies the text displayed on the BUTTON component. It is possible to display text, an icon, or a combination of both.
ICON	Specifies the icon to be displayed on the BUTTON component. If the icon image is in the application directory, providing the file name is sufficient. When the file is located somewhere else, click the ... button to the right of the textbox of the property to navigate to the image. If the image is located on the Internet or intranet, you can use a URL. For example: *http://www.image-server.com/myimage.jpg*.
CSS CLASS	When a custom CSS file is assigned to the APPLICATION component, you can assign a class here.
ON CLICK	Opens the Script Editor to add user interaction.

Table 7.8 Button Component Properties

Use the Enabled and/or Text properties for easier navigation

Having the appearance of the BUTTON component itself change when the user clicks the button can help the user to understand what is happening in the application. For example, if the user switches to another screen and comes back five minutes later, it is immediately apparent where he is in the application.

For a simple example, if you have a BUTTON component that, when clicked, excludes internal sales, it would be helpful if the BUTTON component showed that state. When you look at the examples in Figure 7.19, it is clear that internal sales and pipeline sales are included, but OEM sales and sold-but-not-delivered sales are not.

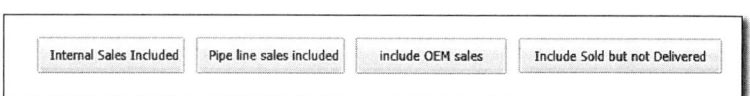

Figure 7.19 Button States

To make the switch between states possible, the script checks the BUT-TON component's current state and switches to the other state. The script for our internal sales example is as follows:

```
if (BUTTON_INTERNAL.getText() =="Include Internal Sales" ) {
    BUTTON_INTERNAL.setText("Internal Sales included");
    BUTTON_INTERNAL.setCSSClass("Included");
}
else
{
    BUTTON_INTERNAL.setText("Include Internal Sales");
    BUTTON_INTERNAL.setCSSClass("Included");
}
```

To further emphasize the state, we have added a script line to set the CSS class of the text object depending on its current state, so the user can see the state based on the appearance of the button.

Checkbox Component

CHECKBOX components (Figure 7.20) help the user to interact with the application. CHECKBOX components can be used as on/off buttons to support other components.

On/off buttons

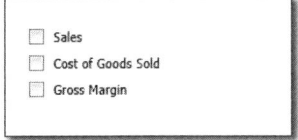

Figure 7.20 Checkbox Component

Table 7.9 shows the properties for the CHECKBOX component.

Property	Description
NAME	The name of the component. This must be a unique name within the application.
VISIBLE	Specifies whether the CHECKBOX component is visible.

Table 7.9 Checkbox Component Properties

Property	Description
ENABLED	Specifies if the checkbox is enabled. Disabled buttons are not available for interaction.
TEXT	Specifies the text displayed on the CHECKBOX component.
SELECTED	Specifies whether the CHECKBOX component is initially selected.
ON CLICK	Opens the Script Editor to add user interaction.

Table 7.9 Checkbox Component Properties (Cont.)

Showing key figures

To understand how the CHECKBOX component can improve an application, look at Figure 7.21. In this example, you can use the CHECKBOX component to manipulate the graph so that it only shows one of the three key figures based on the choice of CHECKBOX components. By using an On Click event for each CHECKBOX component, you can select and deselect key figures and see the graph change accordingly.

One could also imagine more complicated scenarios where some choices make other options unfeasible. An example is when a user has multiple CHECKBOX components to filter the data source. If you want to avoid a situation where the user applies a filter that results in 0 records, you can disable all the components that would lead to this result. Using the enabled and selected property in the script, you can manage the CHECKBOX components to reflect those scenarios.

In the ON CLICK property of Checkbox_1 the script would look like this:

```
CHECKBOX_1.setChecked(true);
CHECKBOX_2.setChecked(false);
CHECKBOX_3.setChecked(false);
```

Date Field Component

The DATE FIELD component (Figure 7.22) enables the user to select a date. The entered date can be used in other parts of the application. To enable this interactivity, a script has to be added to the On Select handler.

Table 7.10 shows the properties of the DATE FIELD component.

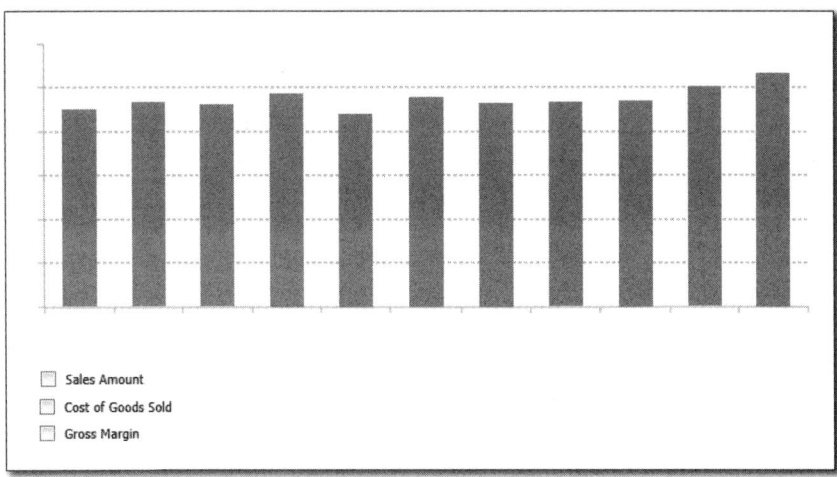

Figure 7.21 Example Checkbox for Key Figure Selection

Figure 7.22 Date Field Component

Property	Description
Name	The name of the component. This must be a unique name within the application.
Visible	Specifies whether the Date Field component is visible.
Enabled	Specifies whether the component is enabled. Disabled Date Field components are not available for interaction.
CSS Class	When a custom CSS file is assigned to the Application component, you can assign a class here.

Table 7.10 Date Field Component Properties

Property	Description
DATE	Sets the initial date.
ON SELECT	Opens the Script Editor to add user interaction.

Table 7.10 Date Field Component Properties (Cont.)

Set a date as a filter

The main use for the DATE FIELD component is to enable the user to set a date, which is then used to filter a data source dimension that holds calendar day values. The statement to do this is as follows:

```
DS_2.setFilter("0CALDAY", DATEFIELD_1.getDate());
```

Dropdown Box Component

DROPDOWN BOX components (Figure 7.23) enable the user to select items from a list. A common use for this component is setting a filter.

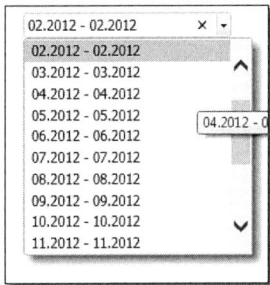

Figure 7.23 Dropdown Box Component

Table 7.11 shows the properties of the DROPDOWN BOX component.

Property	Description
NAME	The name of the component. This must be a unique name within the application.
VISIBLE	Specifies whether the component is visible.
ENABLED	Specifies whether the component is enabled. Disabled DROP-DOWN BOX components are not available for interaction.

Table 7.11 Dropdown Box Component Properties

Property	Description
CSS CLASS	When a custom CSS file is assigned to the application component, you can assign a class here.
ITEMS	With this property, the items available in the DROPDOWN BOX component can be edited. A key has to be entered for each value. Providing a text label and setting a default item is optional.
ON SELECT	Opens the Script Editor to add user interaction.

Table 7.11 Dropdown Box Component Properties (Cont.)

A common way to set the items you can select in a DROPDOWN BOX component is to populate the items of the component at runtime. To do this, we will add a script to the APPLICATION component at the On Startup handler:

Populate the Dropdown Box component with metadata

```
DROPDOWN_1.setItems(DS_1.getMemberList("0CALMONTH",
  MemberPresentation.EXTERNAL_KEY, MemberDisplay.KEY_TEXT, 20));
```

This script instructs the application to fill the items of dropdown_1 with the 0CALMONTH dimension of the data source DS_1.

Using the actual values in the data source will ensure that the DROPDOWN BOX component will only hold the values that are actually available in the data source. This will avoid situations where a user applies a filter and the result is an empty dataset. In this example, it could very well be that the current year hasn't ended yet and not all months are available. In this situation, there will be fewer than 12 months to choose from.

Avoid empty datasets

Image Component

With the IMAGE component (Figure 7.24), you can enhance the layout of the application. The IMAGE component also has a number of properties that make it very useful for interactivity purposes. One of the most useful properties is the ability to change the IMAGE component at runtime. This means you can change the look of the application based on the data values or as the result of specific user interactivity actions. IMAGE components can also respond to hovering and clicking.

Change image at runtime

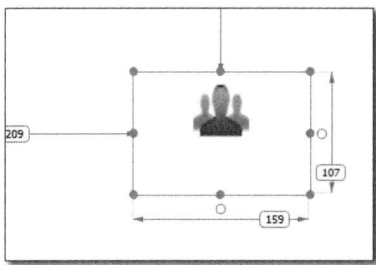

Figure 7.24 Image Component

Table 7.12 shows the properties of the IMAGE component.

Property	Description
NAME	The name of the component. This must be a unique name within the application.
VISIBLE	Specifies whether the IMAGE component is visible.
CSS CLASS	When a custom CSS file is assigned to the APPLICATION component, you can assign a class here.
IMAGE	The location of the main image file.
HOVER IMAGE	The location of the image file that shows when the user hovers over the image.
CLICK IMAGE	The location of the image file that is shown when the user clicks the image.
OPACITY %	By controlling this property, you can establish how transparent the IMAGE component is. 0% opacity means that the IMAGE component is not visible, and it becomes more opaque the closer to 100% you go. This property can be used for layout reasons; by setting the opacity of some IMAGE components a bit higher than others, you can send a subtle but clear message to the user. For example, if you have ON and OFF buttons, you can make the buttons that are in the ON position more opaque than those in the OFF position. This gives you the ability to convey a lot of information about the state of the buttons without using much room or color, thus keeping your design easy to grasp for the user.
ON CLICK	Opens the Script Editor to add user interaction.

Table 7.12 Image Component Properties

The IMAGE component can often come in handy, for example, when creating scorecards. For a scorecard, green, yellow, and red symbols are typically used. In the example below, the script evaluates the value of a key figure in the data source. If the value of the key figure is 1, then a green light image is used; if the value of the key figure is 2, then a yellow light will show; and for the value 3, a red light will show.

Using images for a scorecard

Instead of writing the location of the image in these statements, we have introduced three global variables holding the location of the images. The three variables are Greenlight, Yellowlight, and Redlight.

```
if (DS_1.getDataAsString("ZBB_NMBR","ZBB_KPIID=00001") == "1")
{IMG_FIN1_EVAL.setImage(Greenlight);}
else {
if (DS_1.getDataAsString("ZBB_NMBR","ZBB_KPIID=00001") == "2")
{IMG_FIN1_EVAL.setImage(Yellowlight);}
else {
if (DS_1.getDataAsString("ZBB_NMBR","ZBB_KPIID=00001") == "3")
{IMG_FIN1_EVAL.setImage(Redlight);}
}}
```

Input Field Component

The INPUT FIELD component (Figure 7.25) enables the user to type specific content into the application at runtime. For example, an INPUT FIELD component can be useful for filtering with wildcards (*). This kind of filtering is possible because the user is free to type anything he wants into the component's text box.

Input content at runtime

Figure 7.25 Input Field Component

Table 7.13 shows the properties for the INPUT FIELD component.

Property	Description
NAME	The name of the component. This must be a unique name within the application.

Table 7.13 Input Field Component Properties

Property	Description
Visible	Specifies whether the component is visible.
Enabled	Specifies whether the component is enabled. Disabled Input Field components are not available for interaction.
CSS Class	When a custom CSS file is assigned to the Application component, you can assign a class here.
Value	The initial value of the Input Field component.
On Change	Opens the Script Editor to add user interaction.

Table 7.13 Input Field Component Properties (Cont.)

Wildcard use

The Input Field component can come in quite handy, for example, if you do not want to restrict a user in setting a filter value. For example, if a user wants to select all the years in the range 2001–2009, he can input "20*", and with that value a filter can be set on the data source with this script:

```
1.setFilterExt("0CALYEAR",INPUTFIELD_1.getValue());
```

As another example, if you want to filter on products and you have a lot of different kinds of product types in your product line (red sauce, green sauce, sweet sauce, etc.), a user can input "*sauce" and apply the filter and see which products come up.

This also could set up a cascading filter where a List Box or Dropdown Box component is filtered based on the input in the Input Field component.

List Box Component

List Box components (Figure 7.26) enable users to select items. A selected item can be used to filter for or choose a particular functionality in the application. As the List Box component shows all the values in a list, it is advisable to limit the number of items.

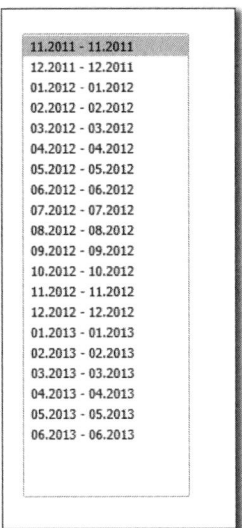

Figure 7.26 List Box Component

Table 7.14 shows the properties of the LIST BOX component.

Property	Description
NAME	The name of the component. This must be a unique name within the application.
VISIBLE	Specifies whether the LIST BOX component is visible.
ENABLED	Specifies whether the LIST BOX component is enabled. Disabled LIST BOX components are not available for interaction.
CSS CLASS	When a custom CSS file is assigned to the APPLICATION component, you can assign a class here.

Table 7.14 Properties of the List Box Component

Property	Description
ITEMS	With this property, the items available in the LIST BOX component can be edited. A key has to be entered for each value. Having a text and a default item is optional. Click the ... button on the right side of the property to open an EDIT SCREEN dialog box where you can add, edit, or remove items.
ON SELECT	Opens the Script Editor to add user interaction.

Table 7.14 Properties of the List Box Component (Cont.)

Build a cascading filter

Consider a case where a user has to navigate through a lot of data. In this situation, you probably want a way to drill down instead of finding your way through a lot of choices. With the help of LIST BOX components, you can achieve this. For example, you could first build a LIST BOX component that contains all the product categories. Then, a second LIST BOX component would contain all the products. When you select a product category from the first LIST BOX component, the second LIST BOX component will be populated with the products within that category. Using this technique, you can lead the user step by step through the possible choices.

Let's look at an example where we apply a category filter to the data source. Then the data source repopulates the items of the second LIST BOX component with the accompanying products and makes this second component visible, while the first LIST BOX component is set to invisible. Finally, when the user selects a product on the second LIST BOX component, the script in this component will filter the data source on that product. Other components that use that same data source will then only show the data for that one product.

The code is as follows:

```
DS_1.setFilterExt("0PRODUCTGROUP", LISTBOX_CATEGORY.getSelect-
edValue());
LISTBOX_PRODUCT.setItems(DS_
1.getMemberList("0PRODUCT", MemberPresentation.EXTERNAL_
KEY, MemberDisplay.TEXT, 20));
LISTBOX_CATEGORY.setVisible(false);
LISTBOX_PRODUCT.setVisible(true);
```

Radio Button Group Component

The RADIO BUTTON GROUP component (Figure 7.27) enables users to select items. A selected item can be used to filter or to make a choice for a particular functionality in the application. As the RADIO BUTTON GROUP component shows all the values in a list, it is advisable to limit the number of items.

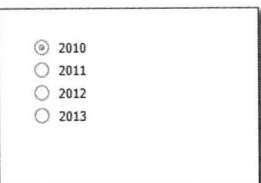

Figure 7.27 Radio Button Group Component

Table 7.15 shows the properties of the RADIO BUTTON GROUP component.

Property	Description
NAME	The name of the component. This must be a unique name within the application.
VISIBLE	Specifies whether the RADIO BUTTON GROUP is visible.
ENABLED	Specifies whether the RADIO BUTTON GROUP is enabled. Disabled RADIO BUTTON GROUP components are not available for interaction.
CSS CLASS	When a custom CSS file is assigned to the APPLICATION component, you can assign a class here.
COLUMNS	Number of columns used to display the RADIO BUTTON GROUP components.
ITEMS	With this property, the available items can be edited. A key has to be entered for each value. Having a text and a default item is optional.
ON SELECT	Opens the Script Editor to add user interaction.

Table 7.15 Radio Button Group Component Properties

The RADIO BUTTON GROUP component should be used when you need to give users a lot of different choices for navigation. For example, if you allow your sales team to navigate through the customer base, there are a lot of ways they might segment their customer base. Maybe they would like to look at married customers in their 50s who bought something in the last four weeks and show a pattern of purchases that puts them in the luxury buyers segment.

Two RADIO BUTTON GROUP components together with five options allows the user a lot of choices. Now imagine four RADIO BUTTON GROUP components, with each holding five options. This creates 625 different combinations for the user to choose from. In other words, this component offers a lot flexibility.

Text Component

The TEXT component (Figure 7.28) is used to add text, such as labels or values, to an application. TEXT components can be formatted at runtime by reassigning the CSS class. With all the possibilities of CSS, the TEXT component is a very flexible tool to use in an application.

this is component Text_1

Figure 7.28 Text Component Using CSS for Layout

> **Note**
>
> You are even able to set the width of the TEXT component using CSS, although this is also possible via the common properties of components.

Table 7.16 shows the properties of the TEXT component.

Property	Description
NAME	The name of the component. This must be a unique name within the application.

Table 7.16 Text Component Properties

Property	Description
VISIBLE	Specifies whether the TEXT component is visible.
ENABLED	Specifies whether the TEXT component is enabled. Disabled TEXT components are not available for interaction.
CSS CLASS	When a custom CSS file is assigned to the APPLICATION component, you can assign a class here.
STYLE	The style applied to the TEXT component.
CSS STYLE	You can insert CSS code to further enhance the layout of the component. The starting point for the CSS code inserted here will be based on the theme of the application and the assigned CSS class—so keep this in mind when setting this property. If the theme sets the font size a little higher, the class sets the font size a little higher, and you set the font size in this property a little higher, your font size might turn out to be enormous.
ON CLICK	Opens the Script Editor to add user interaction.

Table 7.16 Text Component Properties (Cont.)

CSS Tip

When applying formatting using CSS, try to use the CSS CLASS property as much as possible. When a class is altered in the central CSS file, all dependent components will automatically be updated. When using the CSS STYLE, however, you only influence the components where you have put the CSS code. This means that, when the same code is used in more than one component, any changes to the layout require that you manually change each component.

7.3.4 Container Component Properties

Container components are used to group components into meaningful groups. These grouped components can be managed together by manipulating the container component (also known as the parent component) and therefore making maintenance easier. Components inside a container component are dependent on that container component; for example, if the container component's visibility is set to false, then this setting will also apply to all the components inside the container component.

243

When the margin properties of components are set, they are set in relation to the borders of their container component. For example, when the left margin of a container component is set to 100 and the left margin of a TEXT component within that container component is set to 10, this will set the text box at 110 pixels from the left side of the screen.

Place components outside of a container and still be dependent

That being said, it is possible to place components outside their container component but still maintain dependency. For example, you can set the top, bottom, left, or right margin to a negative value. If you move the container component, the component outside will move along with the container, but remain outside. In this case, if the left margin is set to –50, the object will be placed to the left of the container component, but there will still be a dependency between them.

In the example in Figure 7.29, you see a main component with a left margin of 25, a container component with a left margin of 50, and another container component with a left margin of 100. The total left margin for the main component will then be 175.

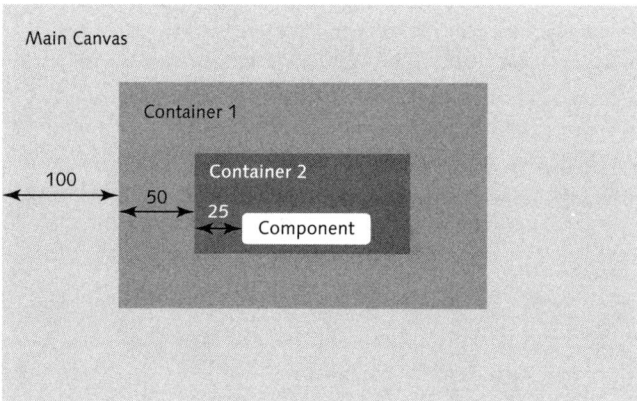

Figure 7.29 Layered Container Components with Their Respective Left Margins

There are five types of container components, all of which we discuss next.

Grid Layout Component

Divide screen into rows and columns

The GRID LAYOUT component (Figure 7.30) is used to group and order the components in a grid. (The grid itself is not shown at runtime.) The

Grid Layout component is very useful for dividing the screen into rows and columns. The sizes of the rows and columns can be adjusted by setting the relative size of each column and row.

Figure 7.30 Grid Layout Component

Table 7.17 shows the properties of the Grid Layout component.

Property	Description
Name	The name of the component. This must be a unique name within the application.
Number of Rows	The number of rows in the grid.
Row Height	The relative height of the row in comparison to the other rows. Each row starts with the value 1. Setting the rows' heights then divides the height of the grid according to the Row Height settings for each row.
Number of Columns	The number of columns in the grid.
Column Width	The relative width of the column in comparison to the other columns. Each column starts with the value 1. Setting the columns' widths divides the width of the grid according to the Column Width setting for each column.

Table 7.17 Properties of the Grid Layout Component

You can create advanced layouts using several Grid Layout components. For example, if you have a main Grid Layout component with three rows, of which the middle row is the largest, you can divide the top and bottom row by adding a new Grid Layout component in the top row and bottom row.

Create advanced layouts

Let's consider a case where you choose to divide the top row into three columns and the bottom row into five. In Figure 7.31, you can see how this layout would look to the user. In Figure 7.32, you can see the outline as it would look in Design Studio at design time.

Figure 7.31 Grid Layout View with Three Rows and Several Columns

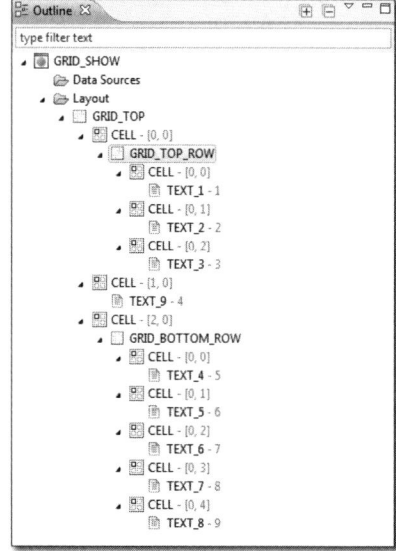

Figure 7.32 Outline View with Nested Grid Layout Components

Pagebook Component

The PAGEBOOK component (Figure 7.33) shows one page at a time and enables the user to switch to other pages by either swiping (iPad or iPhone) or dragging (computer mouse). It is also possible to switch pages by using the script language.

Swipe or drag to other pages

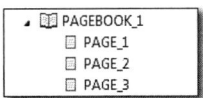

Figure 7.33 Pagebook Component in the Outline View

In Figure 7.33 you can see several pages connected to the PAGEBOOK component. In design mode, it is possible to add or remove pages from the component. Each page is an empty canvas. Only the canvas of the selected page is visible to the user.

Table 7.18 shows the properties of the PAGEBOOK component.

Property	Description
NAME	The name of the component. This must be a unique name within the application.
VISIBLE	Specifies whether the PAGEBOOK component is visible.
CSS CLASS	When a custom CSS file is assigned to the APPLICATION component, you can assign a class here.
SELECTED PAGE INDEX	Sets the initial visible page of the PAGEBOOK component. Note: 0 represents the first page of the PAGEBOOK component. 1 represents the second page, and so on.
TRANSITION EFFECT	Specifies the transition effect when a user swipes between pages. The options are: ▶ SLIDE IN ▶ FADE ▶ FLIP ▶ CUBE

Table 7.18 Pagebook Component Properties

Property	Description
TRANSITION DIRECTION	Specifies the transition direction when a user switches between pages. Options are HORIZONTAL or VERTICAL.
PAGE CACHING	Specifies the caching behavior of the PAGEBOOK component. If set to ALL, every page of the component will be cached. If set to ADJACENT, the page before and after the current page will be cached. Caching leads to a smoother swipe, but as more components are loaded it can lead to performance issues. Do test the different options before going to production, because this will always be a compromise between startup time and navigation speed.
ON SELECT	Opens the Script Editor.

Table 7.18 Pagebook Component Properties (Cont.)

Design menu items

The PAGEBOOK component often comes in handy when you're designing menus. In Figure 7.34, you can see three menu items on the left and the data that corresponds to the second menu item on the right. The application is made in such a way that when you tap one of the menu items, the content on the right side will fade away and new content relating to the menu choice will fade in. The fading effect is achieved by using the TRANSITION EFFECT property, which you can set to fade. The script in the text box contains the following line for the second menu:

```
PAGEBOOK_1.setSelectedPageIndex(1);
```

This will result in the current screen fading away and being replaced with another screen.

Numbering for Pagebook Pages

Although we mentioned it in Table 7.18, we want to emphasize this important fact: Because the numbering of PAGEBOOK pages starts at 0, the second page is actually listed as page 1.

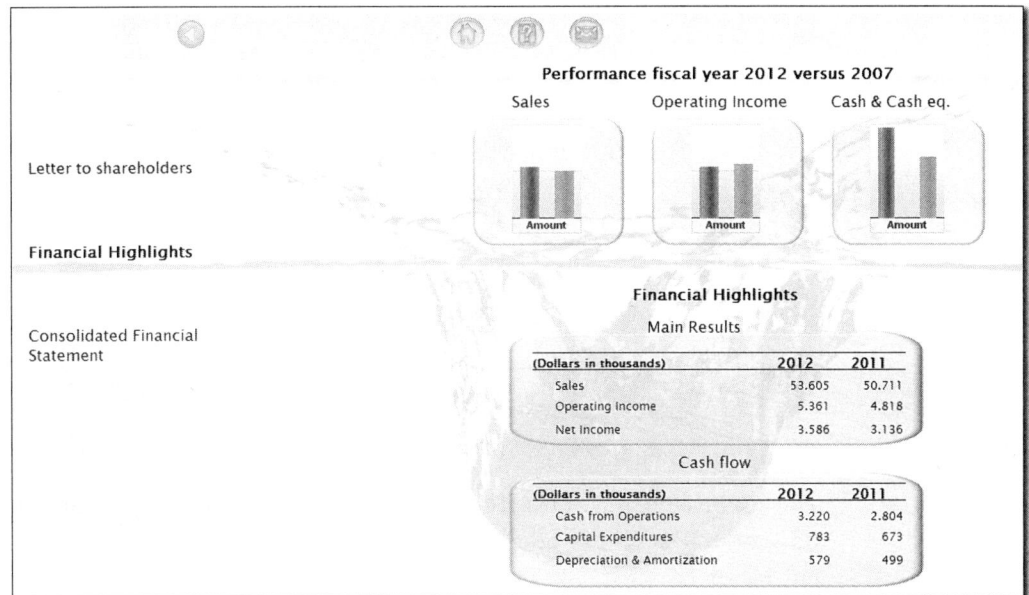

Figure 7.34 Example Using a Pagebook Component

Panel Component

A PANEL component is used to group components together. By using the methods of the PANEL component, including .setCssClass, it is possible to build interactivity into the application. As the number of components tends to grow quickly in an application, it is advisable to use these PANEL components often to group components that belong together, even if no interactivity is planned. Grouping allows you, for example, to hide a group of components at design time so your screen isn't cluttered when you are working on another part of the application.

Group components together

Table 7.19 shows the properties of the PANEL component.

Property	Description
NAME	The name of the component. This must be a unique name within the application.
VISIBLE	Specifies whether the PANEL component is visible.

Table 7.19 Panel Component Properties

Property	Description
ENABLED	Specifies whether the PANEL component is enabled. Disabled PANEL components are not available for interaction.
CSS CLASS	When a custom CSS file is assigned to the APPLICATION component, you can assign a class here.
CSS STYLE	Here it is possible to enter CSS code to change the layout of the PANEL component.
ON CLICK	Opens the Script Editor.

Table 7.19 Panel Component Properties (Cont.)

Popup Component

The POPUP component can be used to let a screen appear in the application, on top of all the other components, where users can make quick entries or configurations or create selections. POPUP components can also be quite helpful for help messages and for providing further information about elements. The main reason to use a POPUP component is to allow the user to perform a particular task and freeze the rest of the application until that task is done. You can ensure this by using the MODAL property of the component.

Popup component restrictions

There are two restrictions on the use of the POPUP component:

▶ The POPUP component can only be located in the root layout and not within another container element.

▶ The POPUP component can only be positioned in relation to the root layout.

Table 7.20 shows the properties of the POPUP component.

Property	Description
NAME	The name of the component. This must be a unique name within the application.

Table 7.20 Popup Component Properties

Property	Description
MODAL	If the POPUP component is set to MODAL, the user can only navigate within the POPUP screen. If the MODAL property is set to FALSE, the user can also interact with other elements of the application.
AUTOCLOSE	Specifies whether the popup screen automatically closes when the user interacts outside of the POPUP in the application.
ANIMATION	Specifies the animation effect when the POPUP is opened or closed: ▸ NO ANIMATION ▸ FLIP ANIMATION ▸ POP ANIMATION ▸ HORIZONTAL SLIDE ANIMATION ▸ VERTICAL SLIDE ANIMATION

Table 7.20 Popup Component Properties (Cont.)

A useful way to work with a POPUP component is to set up a BUTTON component in the application and have the POPUP component appear near the button. For example, if you want to show a POPUP component with some application settings, a BUTTON component to the top right of the screen can be combined with a POPUP component. The setting for animation can be set to VERTICAL SLIDE ANIMATION. When you use the POPUP component this way, it will look like the popup comes directly out of the button and immediately grabs the user's attention, as the user was already clicking that button.

Useful Popup component design

To show the POPUP component, add this code in the first BUTTON component:

```
POPUP_1.show();
```

You add a second BUTTON component in the POPUP component itself and set the following code in the second button component to hide the component again:

```
POPUP_1.hide();
```

Tabstrip Component

A TABSTRIP component (Figure 7.35) allows you to group your application into tabs. You can also use this component to create possibilities for user interaction. The TABSTRIP component works much the same way as the PAGEBOOK component, creating several tabs, only one of which is visible at a time. The difference with a PAGEBOOK component is the way it allows you to navigate. With the TABSTRIP component, you automatically have a direct way to go from one tab to any of the other tabs. With a PAGEBOOK component, you can only go to the previous or next page, or you have to write scripts and add BUTTON components to create this same functionality.

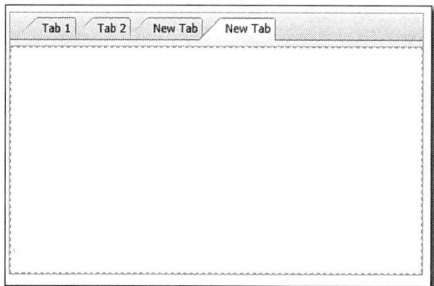

Figure 7.35 Tabstrip Component

Table 7.21 shows the properties of the TABSTRIP component.

Property	Description
NAME	The name of the component. This must be a unique name within the application.
VISIBLE	Toggles the visibility of the component.
CSS CLASS	When a custom CSS file is assigned to the APPLICATION component, you can assign a class here.
SELECTED TAB INDEX	Specifies the tab that will initially be shown at the start. Index 0 opens the first tab of the component, index 1 the second, etc.
ON SELECT	Opens the Script Editor. ON SELECT triggers each time a user selects a tab.

Table 7.21 Properties of the Tabstrip Component

If you want to go through the tabs step by step, you can add a BUTTON component outside the TABSTRIP. Each time the BUTTON component is clicked, the user goes to the next page until reaching the last (page 4, in our example). Then the TABSTRIP component jumps back to the starting tab.

```
var tabnumber = TABSTRIP_1.getSelectedTabIndex();

if (tabnumber == 4)
{
    TABSTRIP_1.setSelectedTabIndex(0);
} else {
    TABSTRIP_1.setSelectedTabIndex(tabnumber + 1);
}
```

You could use this for a wizard-like navigation through several steps, and if the final step is done, return to the starting page. A wizard-like solution is handy for when you want to enable users to do complicated tasks and guide them through the process.

7.4   Working with Components and Properties

As you work more and more with Design Studio, you'll want to adopt some best practices for working with all the components and properties available. In this section, we'll walk you through three important parts of this process: creating application templates, using container components, and adopting naming conventions for your components.

7.4.1   Create Application Templates

The longer you use Design Studio, the more applications you develop. Therefore, it's helpful to have a template in place with a basic component structure and all the right colors and settings. This can be helpful for developers, as they immediately have a base to work from, and a lot of repetitive work is removed from their workload.

Figure 7.36 shows an application structure. As you can see, this application already contains a lot of structure with panels. We want to save this as a template so that when we want to use this setup again we do not have to add all the container PANEL components again.

> **Themes in Future Releases**
>
> We expect that, in the future, you will be able to set up your own themes, so you don't have to rely on a template like we show here.

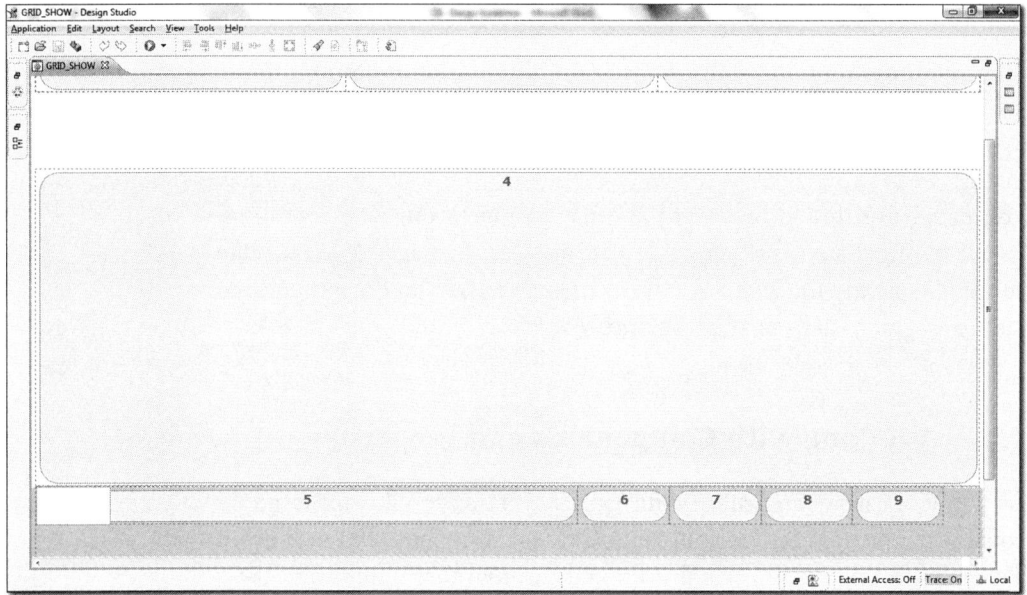

Figure 7.36 Application with Many Structure Elements

When you save an application locally, it is saved to a directory in the local repository. The location can be found from the APPLICATION • OPEN REPOSITORY FOLDER option, as you can see in Figure 7.37.

Copy an application to a template folder The name of the application is GRID_SHOW. There is a folder with that name in the repository folder. Copy this folder to the template folder, which you can find by going to PREFERENCES under the TOOLS menu (Figure 7.38).

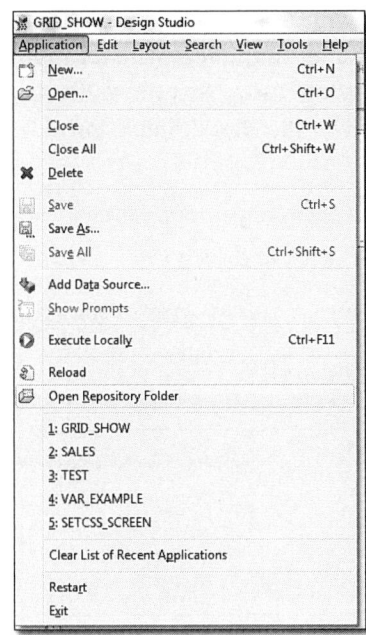

Figure 7.37 Application Menu with Open Repository Folder Option

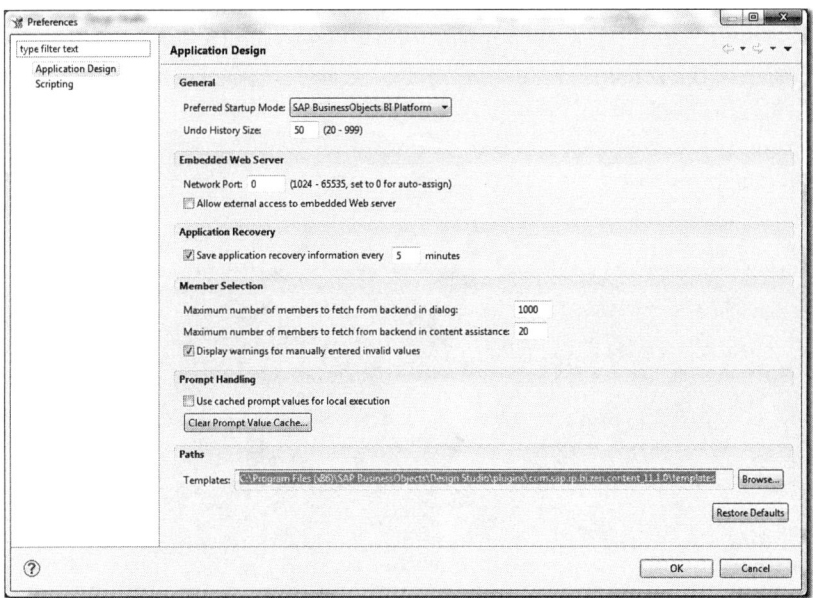

Figure 7.38 Preferences Menu with the Location of the Template Folder

In the TEMPLATE folder, there is a folder with the name DESKTOP. Copy the GRID_SHOW folder to the DESKTOP folder in the template location. Now the files are in place. The next step is to create a text file and a picture so the template will show up properly in the New Application Wizard.

1. Create a text file in Notepad, set a text as shown in Figure 7.39, and save the file as *GRID_SHOW.info* in the desktop directory.

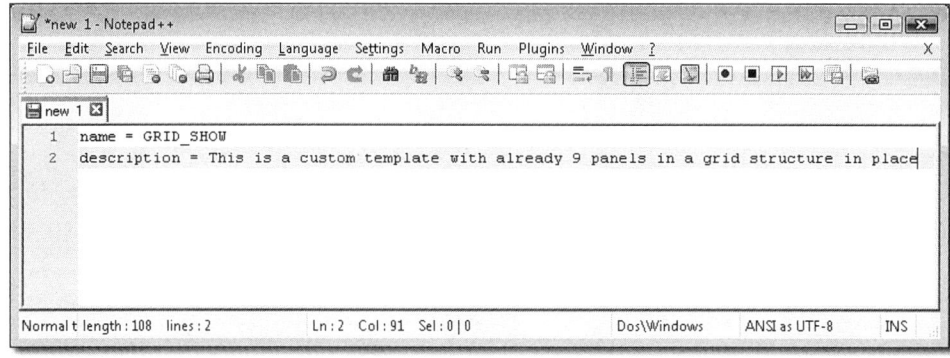

Figure 7.39 Text File

2. Next, create a screenshot image with an image editor and decrease the size of the screenshot to 42 pixels wide and 63 pixels tall, as shown in Figure 7.40.

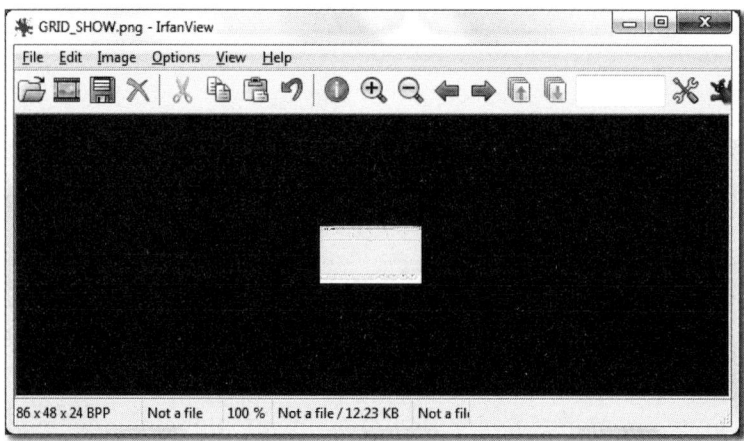

Figure 7.40 Screenshot File in the Image Editor

3. Put the text file and the image file in the TEMPLATE folder.

4. With these two files and the folder in the DESKTOP folder within the template location, you should be able to use the new template. In Design Studio select NEW in the APPLICATION menu.

5. Enter a name and description and click NEXT. In the TEMPLATE SELECTION window you now also see the template, as shown in Figure 7.41.

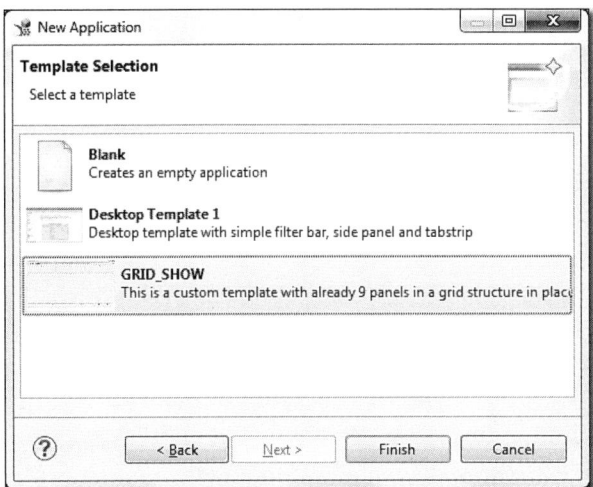

Figure 7.41 Template Selection Screen with Custom Template

7.4.2 Using Container Components

Whenever you have a small group of components that belong together, put them in a separate container component. If you have several components in one PANEL component, you can work with the PANEL component, and the components inside the PANEL component will keep their places relative to the container component. Furthermore, if you hide the container component during design time, you will immediately hide all the components within the container component. To set up this structure, follow the steps below:

Container and Panel components

1. Drag a PANEL component onto the canvas (Figure 7.42).

2. Next drag a BUTTON component and a TEXT component into the PANEL component. Drag another BUTTON component onto the canvas, outside of the PANEL component (Figure 7.43).

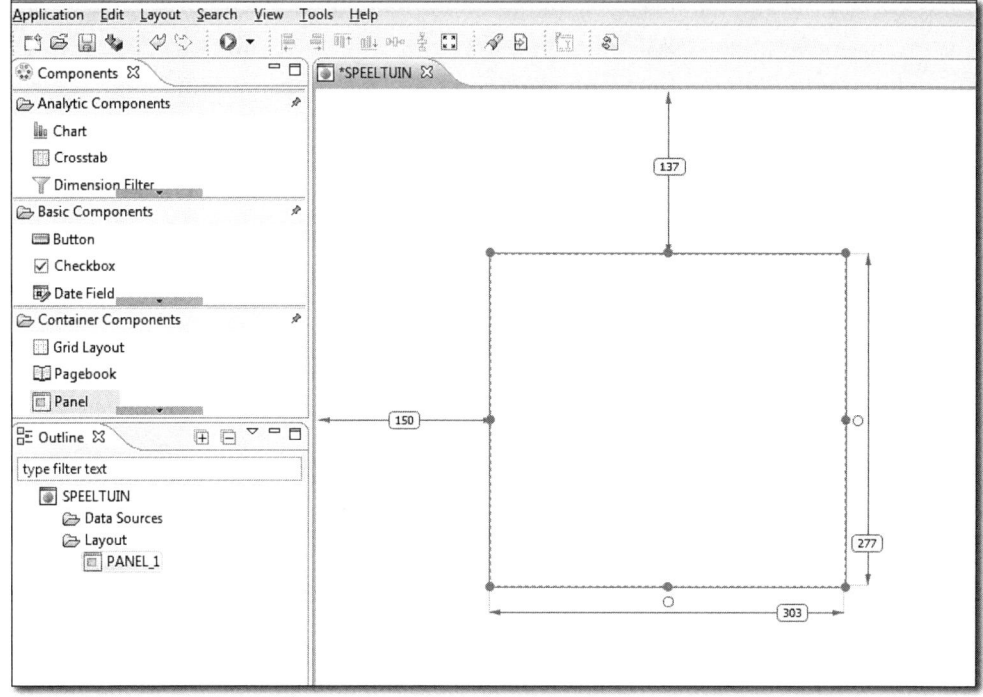

Figure 7.42 Panel Component Added

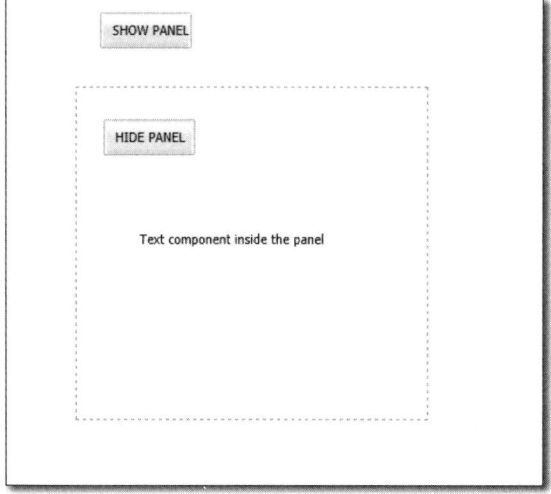

Figure 7.43 Add Components to the Panel

3. Name the button outside the PANEL component BUTTON_SHOW.

4. Set the text of this button to "SHOW PANEL".

5. Name the button inside the PANEL component `BUTTON_HIDE`.

6. Set the text of this button to "HIDE PANEL".

7. In `BUTTON_SHOW`, add the following script to the `On Click` handler:

   ```
   PANEL_1.setVisible(true);
   ```

8. In BUTTON_HIDE, add the following script to the `On Click` handler:

   ```
   PANEL_1.setVisible(false);
   ```

9. Run the application.

Now, when you click the SHOW PANEL button, the other components will become visible. Click the HIDE PANEL button, and the components will disappear again. By using a container component, you control multiple components with one script line.

At design time, you can also control the visibility of the container component from the OUTLINE view by right-clicking the component (Figure 7.44). With the HIDE option you can hide the PANEL component with all the components inside it.

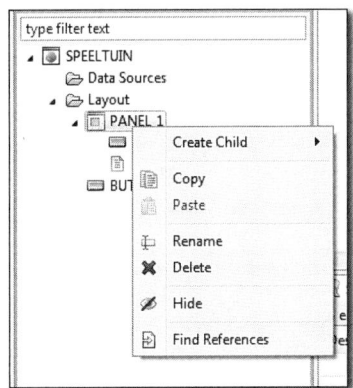

Figure 7.44 Possibilities in the Outline View

7.4.3   Using a Naming Convention for Your Components

Using a naming convention will help you to more easily find your way through all the components inside an application. Especially if someone else built the application, it will shorten the time you need to get acquainted with the application.

Figure 7.45 shows an example where all the components were dragged onto the canvas and the original names were kept.

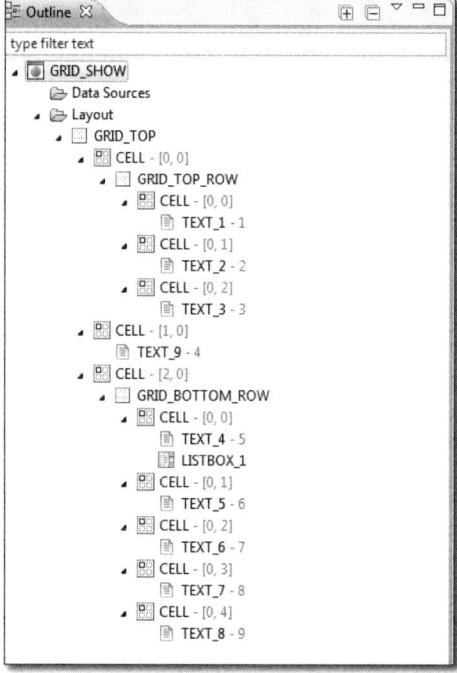

Figure 7.45 Bad Naming of Components

Bad naming   As you can see in this example, you would have a hard time finding out what each component is supposed to do, since the names give no clues. In Figure 7.46, the components were named based on the functions they perform. This helps you navigate through the list and know what each component does.

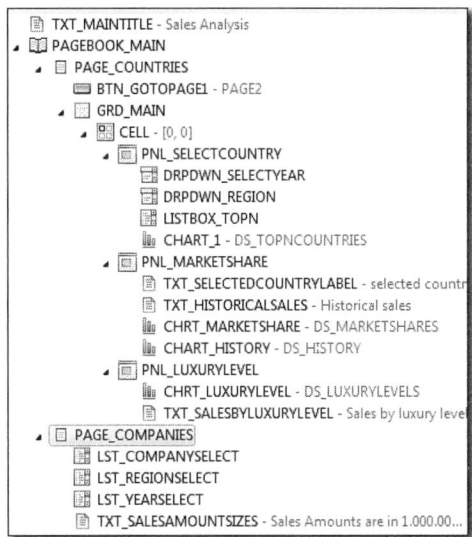

Figure 7.46 Better Naming

The bottom line is to agree on a naming convention within your application development team.

Renaming Components

You don't have to name the components immediately when you insert them. They can be renamed later. Script code referring to the component will automatically be altered, as the code points not to the name of the component but to a unique ID that is hidden from view.

When choosing a naming convention, we advise that you include the function of the component in the name. For example, you could name a PANEL component that holds the top 10 customers for sales:

```
SALES_TOP10CUSTOMERS
```

If you have a TEXT component that functions as a main header inside the PANEL component, you can name this:

```
SALES_TOP10CUSTOMERS_MAINHEADER
```

Note that we do not refer to the type of component but refer only to the function.

Good naming

Include function in name

Component Filter

At the top of the OUTLINE view is an input box that you can use to filter relevant components. If you use the naming method we described above, you can limit the structure to only the top 10 customers by typing "TOP10CUSTOMER".

7.5 Summary

In this chapter, we looked at all the components of Design Studio, from the APPLICATION component down to each individual visual component. In the last section, we gave you some tips and tricks for managing all these components and properties.

Interactivity is the key to Design Studio applications. In this chapter, we'll show you how it's done.

8   Scripting for Interactivity

Design Studio is a tool that is designed to create interactive applications. To support this interactivity, the tool uses a script language that is executed when the user performs an action in the application. In this chapter, we will have a closer look at the script language and will show examples of how to use the script in your application.

In Section 8.1, we will introduce you to the script language, including its elements and what you need to know to build your first script. In Section 8.2, we will explain the basics of script writing, including some Design Studio tools that will come in handy for this purpose. In Section 8.3, we will provide a comprehensive description of all the script methods and properties of the components in Design Studio. Finally, we will devote the entire second half of the chapter (Section 8.4, Section 8.5, Section 8.6, and Section 8.7) to showing you examples of how to build interactivity in applications.

> **Tips for CSS**
>
> This chapter uses CSS. For some additional tips about CSS, see Appendix A.

8.1   BI Action Language

The script language in Design studio is called *BI Action Language (BIAL)*. BIAL is a true subset of JavaScript, and is executed on the Analysis Application Design Service, which is a service that is installed on the SAP BusinessObjects BI platform server or SAP NetWeaver BW server. It is also present on the client computer to run the Design Studio tool

BIAL

locally. (This is unlike JavaScript, as the JavaScript is executed in the web browser.)

The BIAL script consists of individual statements in lines and is written inside event handlers. (As you'll recall from Chapter 7, all components have event handlers.) These event handlers are triggered by user interaction with Design Studio, such as clicking a button, navigating to another part of the application, or starting the application.

In this section, we will dive into the script language itself. We will look at the syntax and the general way the script language is built up, including expressions, script variables, and event handlers.

8.1.1   Syntax

To begin, we'll describe the official syntax of the script language, which is based on three types of statements: call statements, conditional statements, and assignment statements.

> **Note**
>
> Although this section is a bit theoretical, it provides very useful information, as this background knowledge will help you to more easily understand what is happening in the script.

Call Statements

Call statements call component methods by stating the name of the component followed by a method that the component has. Component methods are predefined reactions of the component, and control one of two things: Either the component method performs an action, or the component method returns a property value of the component. In the first case, call statements play a central role in writing scripts because the call statement is what makes the components behave as you want them to. In the second case, the call statements are essential because they return information about the state of the component. An example of this second type of method is `.getselectedvalue`. This method returns the currently selected value of the component, which you can then use in your further script. You can, for example, use the value you got back from the `.getselected` method to present it to the user or use it to add a filter to a data source.

The call statement has the following format:

```
<Component>.<Method><Arguments>;
```

Each element of this format is described in Table 8.1.

Format	Description
`<Component>`	This is the name of the component in the application with which you want to do something. This component can be the application itself, a data source, or a component that you have added to the application. When you add components, you want to name them properly—later on, when scripting, it makes a lot more sense if the name of the component suggests what functionality it delivers.

For example, `LISTBOX_1` does not provide the same information as `LISTBOX_PRODUCTFILTER`, although you can work with both names. You can always change these names later; references in scripts will change accordingly. |
`<Method>`	This is the operation that you want the component to do. Each component type has its own set of operations. Some operations, like `setVisible`, are quite common. Others, such as `setFilter`, are limited to a specific type of component.
`<Arguments>`	This is a comma-listed set of *expressions*. These expressions must match the requirement of the method. You can use functions or other call statements as an argument for another component.
`;`	Each statement has to end with a semicolon.

Table 8.1 Format of a Call Statement

Conditional Statements

Conditional statements can have two formats. The first is as follows:

Two formats for conditional statements

```
If (<condition>)
{
<Statements when the condition is met>
}
```

The second is:

```
If (<condition>)
{
<Statements when the condition is met>
}
else
{
<Statements when the condition is not met>
}
```

Boolean expressions In both of these formats, <condition> is a Boolean expression, meaning it must have a value of either `true` or `false`. The Boolean expression can be a constant, but it also can be a combination of expressions that together result in a `true` or `false` value.

There are a lot of possible constructions to build a Boolean expression resulting in a `true` or `false` value, as shown in Table 8.2. You are not limited to these constructions. You can combine them with other constructions as long the end result is `true` or `false`.

Construction Type	Construction Example
Constant	TRUE
Call statement	Button_1.isEnabled;
Comparison	Button_1.isEnabled == Button_2.isEnabled
Multiple comparisons where all the values must be TRUE (AND logic)	Button_1.isEnabled == Button_2.isEnabled && Button_3.isEnabled
Multiple comparisons where any of the values must be TRUE (OR logic)	Button_1.isEnabled == Button_2.isEnabled || Button_3.isEnabled

Table 8.2 Constructions that Result in a Boolean Value

Assignment Statements

Assignment statements assign values to variables. There are two formats to assign a value variable, as described in Table 8.3: a format for a global variable and another format for a local variable. For local variables you need to define the variable first with the VAR statement. For the global variable this isn't necessary, as you already defined the global variable in the application component.

Context	Format
Variable is not yet defined.	VAR <variable_name> = <Expression>;
Variable is defined.	<variable_name> = <Expression>;

Table 8.3 Assigning a Value to a Variable

Assigning values to variables in the application is very useful for storing values that you can reuse later. Variables can also be used extensively when calculations have to take place in the application. For example, you can pull the numbers from the components and store them in variables. Then perform the calculation and, finally, store the result in another variable and assign the value back to another component.

Doing it like this, step by step, helps you keep an overview of the code, making it very easy to read by reducing the complexity of each line.

8.1.2 Expressions

An *expression* is a combination of variables, component values, and subexpressions that together result in a value. Value results of an expression have a type, which indicates the format of the result (for example, string or integer). If an expression is used to produce a result that is used in another statement, that result type must match the requirement of that statement.

With operators you can combine several arguments into one result value. Table 8.4 describes all the operators that are supported in BIAL.

Operators

Operator	Description	Result type	Example
+	Concatenates	String	`"foo" + "bar"`
+	Adds two values	Integer, float	45 + 12
-	Subtracts two values	Integer, float	45 – 12
*	Multiplies two values	Integer, float	5*7
/	Divides one value by another	Integer, float	8 / 2
==	Checks if both values are equal	Any	`"A" == "A"`
!=	Checks if both values are not equal; this gives the opposite result of ==	Any	`"A" != "A"`
&&	Results in `True` when the expression to the left and right both result in `True`	Boolean	`"A" == "A"` `&&` `"B" == "B"`
||	Results in `True` when either the expression to the left *or* to the right results in `True`	Boolean	`"A" == "B"` `||` `"B" == "B"`
!	Turns the Boolean result around; if the result is `True`, it will be set to `False`; if the result is `False`, it will be set to `True`	Boolean	`! "A" == "B"`

Table 8.4 Supported Operators in BIAL

If an expression is to be used as an argument for a component method, the type of the expression must match the required expression for the component method.

Types of expressions

Table 8.5 describes the expression types.

Expression type	Description
Primitive types	These types are the basic types such as: ▶ Boolean: `True`, `False` ▶ String: `"foobar"` ▶ Float: `123.45` ▶ Integer: `123` ▶ Primitive types are also arrays. The following values are stored in a variable: ▶ String array: `["foo","bar"]` ▶ Integer array: `[14,15]` ▶ JSON: `{"key": "value"}`
BI types	These are special types such as data source alias, dimension, and measure, which are often combinations of primitive types to help you to enter the appropriate input in the component methods.
Component types	These are components. For example, BUTTON, PAGEBOOK, LIST BOX, and IMAGE.

Enum	An Enum is basically a set of values. Enums are BI types. A value is written as:
	`<EnumType>.<EnumValue>`
	Examples are the components themselves, which in a sense are expression types. For example, the APPLICATION component has methods, and if you want to address them, you write:
	`Application.getinfo`

Table 8.5 Expression Types

8.1.3 Script Variables

Script variables are used to store values for later use. Variables can be used in a number of ways, for example, storing results for calculation, keeping a tab on the current state of the application, and holding values that are used at several points in the application.

Like expressions, script variables are of a certain type depending on the assigned value. These types are the same as the types for expressions, which were described in Table 8.5. If you want to use a variable as a parameter for a method, the variable type must match the parameter type.

There are two kinds of script variables:

▶ **Local variables**

These are variables that are defined in a local script and cannot be used in other places. These kinds of variables are useful if you want to compute a result and need a place to store a temporary value. A local variable is defined by adding the following line:

```
var <variable> = <expression>;
```

The variable type is determined by the result of the expression. Local variables can be preferred over global variables if you want to perform only a local action. Using a local variable ensures that you do not alter something that will hurt another part of the application, as the local variable value disappears when the script in that component has ended. Using the same local variable name in another component does not result in an overlap.

▶ **Global script variables**

Global variables can be used in every script in your application. Global variables are used for storing values that will be used in multiple parts of your application. Constant values can be held in global variables; the maintenance of these values is less time-consuming. Additionally, a global variable can be defined as a URL parameter. If you set a global variable as a URL parameter, it is possible to add this variable as a parameter in the URL when someone calls the application. The value in the parameter will be stored in the variable.

8.1.4 Calling the Event Handler

Event handlers are placeholders for scripting and are defined for each component; for example, for a BUTTON component, the handler event is On Click, and for the APPLICATION component, it is On Startup. When the handler is triggered, the application will run the script that has been entered.

Event handlers are triggered by user interaction. For example, when a user changes a selected value in a component, the On Change handler will be triggered. Note, though, that when a script line performs the same action, the On Change handler will *not* be triggered.

If you do need to trigger an event handler using code, you can use the handler method for that component. For example, the PAGEBOOK component has an On Select handler. With the code Pagebook_1.onSelect(); you can trigger the handler and run the code that is in the On Select handler of the PAGEBOOK component.

Handler methods

> **Tip: Using Event Handlers**
>
> If you notice that you are using the same code in several components, event handlers can save you some time. Instead of writing the same code over and over again, try using a separate component with the sole purpose of holding that repeated code. For example, if you want to hide 20 components based on actions in various parts of your application, you write those 20 lines of script in one place (the extra component). Then, using an event handler, you can call the component from all the appropriate places.

8.2   Creating a Script

Now that you understand the basics of the scripting language, it's possible to build your first script. To dive right into writing statements, let's start by going to the properties of a component (Figure 8.1). Navigate to the ON CLICK, ON SELECT, or—for the APPLICATION component—the ON STARTUP section in the PROPERTIES view. Click the EDIT THE SCRIPT button next to the property.

Figure 8.1 Edit the Script Button

The Script Editor opens. On the top you can see the component and method handler you are editing (Figure 8.2).

Script Editor

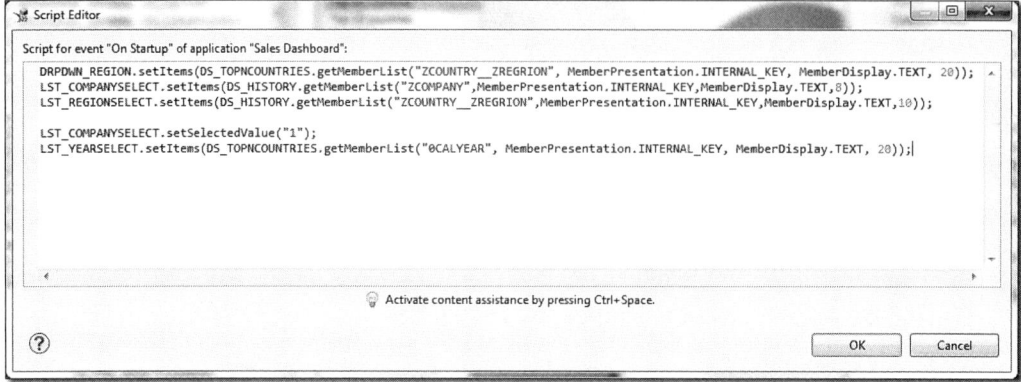

Figure 8.2 Script Editor Screen

In this screen, you can type statements as described in Section 8.1.1. When you are done typing, click OK. If you do not wish to save the script, click CANCEL.

In this section, we'll describe some essential functionalities of the Script Editor. Understanding these functionalities will be instrumental when you write your own script.

8.2.1 Using the Content Assistance Screen

Content Assistance When you are entering script lines, you can use the ⎡Ctrl⎤+⎡Space⎤ shortcut at any time. The CONTENT ASSISTANCE screen that appears will give you suggestions on how to continue writing code—it knows which continuations make sense, and will offer suggestions that are possible based on the script you already entered. For example, if you have already entered a data source alias name, the context-sensitive help will know this and propose specific data source methods (Figure 8.3).

If, in this case, you select the .getData method, you can press ⎡Ctrl⎤+⎡Space⎤ again, and you will see that the CONTENT ASSISTANCE screen gives you new options (Figure 8.4). Because the value in our example can be derived in multiple ways now, all the components show up in the CONTENT ASSISTANCE screen.

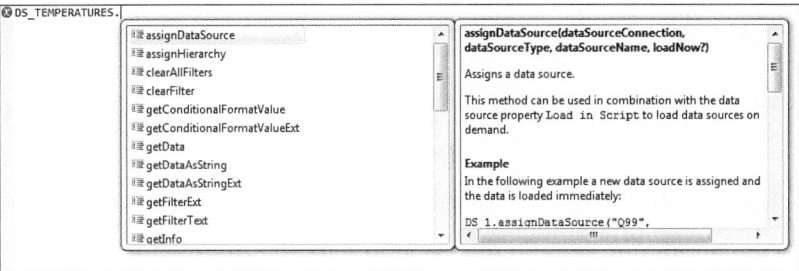

Figure 8.3 Content Assistance Offers Available Methods for the Data Source

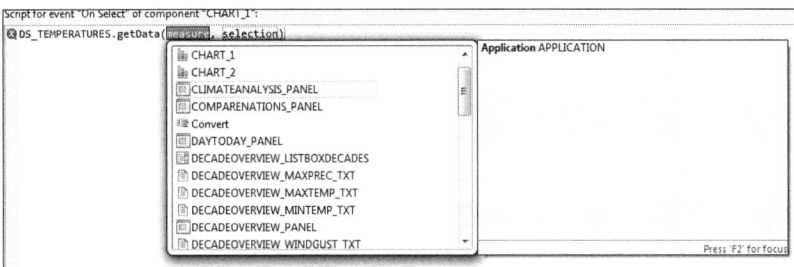

Figure 8.4 Content Assistance on Selecting the Measure

Within the CONTENT ASSISTANCE screen, there are a number of helpful options that you should know about. Let's discuss these next.

New Statement Wizard

When writing scripts, you'll find that the New Statement Wizard is an important tool. If you haven't yet entered any script code in the Script Editor, the CONTENT ASSISTANCE screen will show you the option to start the New Statement Wizard. Press Ctrl + Space to start up the New Statement Wizard, as shown in Figure 8.5. The New Statement Wizard will offer you a number of statements to choose from, and, when the desired statement is selected, the syntax will automatically be written in the Script Editor.

> **Note**
>
> If you already entered a part of a script line, then the option to start the New Statement Wizard will not be shown in the CONTENT ASSISTANCE screen, and you will only see context-relevant components and variables.

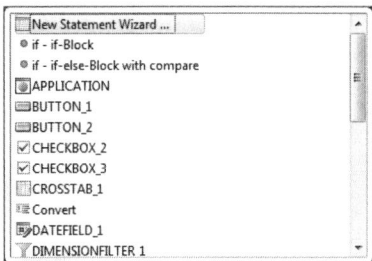

Figure 8.5 New Statement Wizard in the Content Assistance

The predefined statements in the New Statement Wizard are helpful for building more complex statements in a wizard-like way. To see an example of how to use the New Statement Wizard, follow the steps below.

1. Click NEW STATEMENT WIZARD. A screen opens where you can select a predefined statement.

2. You can choose from the statements in Figure 8.6. Choose CLEAR FILTER.

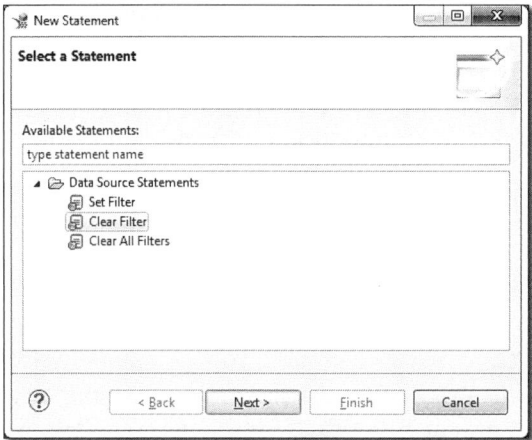

Figure 8.6 Select a Predefined Statement

Select parameters   3. You are now a step further in the New Statement Wizard and can select parameters as shown in Figure 8.7.

4. For the CLEAR FILTER statement, select a data source for the DATA SOURCE ALIAS component, as well as a dimension.

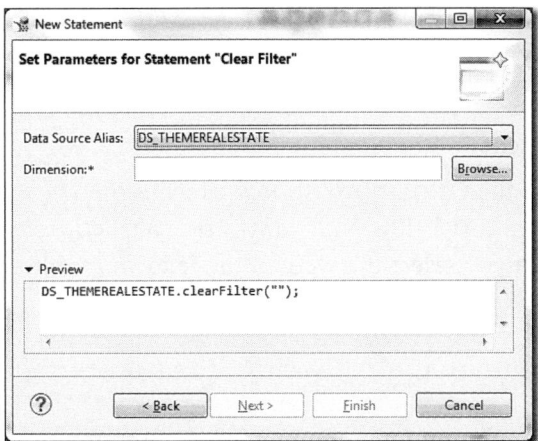

Figure 8.7 Select Parameters

5. Pressing [Ctrl]+[Space] or clicking the BROWSE button automatically shows the available dimensions in the method for the DATA SOURCE ALIAS component.

6. Select DS_THEMEREALESTATE as the data source alias and 0CALYEAR as the dimension. On the bottom of the screen, you can see the script code taking shape (Figure 8.8).

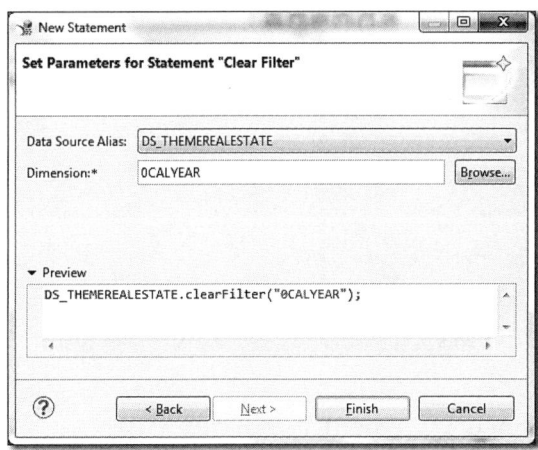

Figure 8.8 Parameters Filled

7. Click FINISH to close the wizard.

You can now see that the script line DS_THEMEREALESTATE.clearFilter("0CALYEAR"); has been added to the Script Editor.

IF – IF Predefined Statement

IF – IF block   Another helpful option in the CONTENT ASSISTANCE screen is the if – if block, which you can find just below NEW STATEMENT WIZARD (refer back to Figure 8.5). When you select this option, the following code is automatically inserted in the editor:

```
if (condition) {
    if_statements
}
```

Using this predefined statement puts the structure of the IF – IF statement in place. By double-clicking either condition or if_statements, you select that variable, and you can fill it with script code by using the ⎡Ctrl⎤ + ⎡Space⎤ shortcut (Figure 8.9).

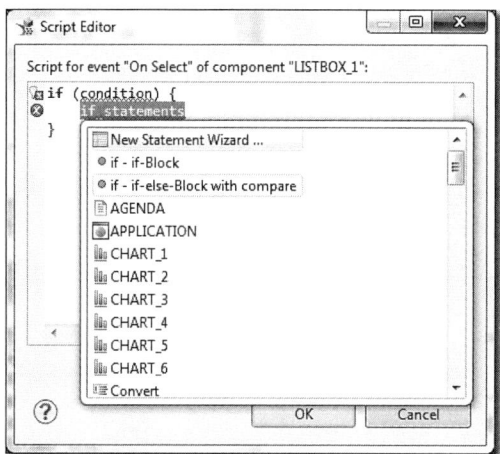

Figure 8.9 Using Predefined Statements

8.2.2   Creating Predefined Statement Templates

Add your own predefined statement templates   Design Studio's Script Editor has only two predefined statement templates. Fortunately, you can add your own predefined statements in the SCRIPTING TEMPLATES menu. Adding new predefined statements can increase your scripting speed, especially for those statements you use often. Follow these steps:

1. Go to PREFERENCES in TOOLS.

2. Open the SCRIPTING segment and click TEMPLATES.

3. In the screen (Figure 8.10), you see the currently predefined statements.

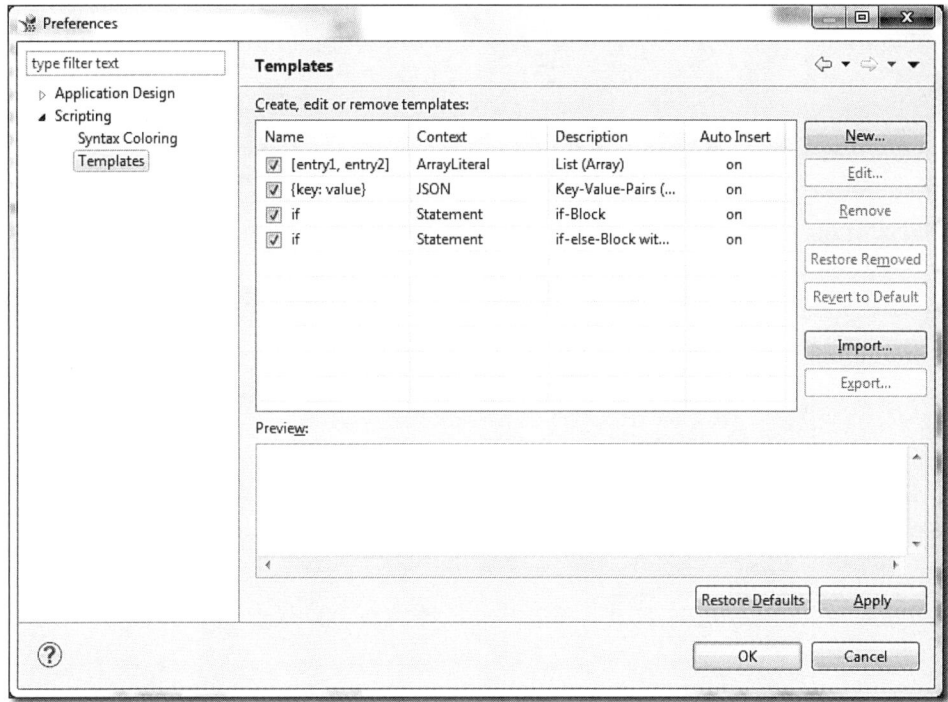

Figure 8.10 Predefined Statements Screen

4. In the CONTEXT column, you see two statement templates, which you saw when you used the New Statement Wizard earlier.

5. The JSON template is only visible when you use the ⌈Ctrl⌉+⌈Space⌉ shortcut on a place in the code where a json argument is needed (Figure 8.11).

6. For this example, you want to create a predefined JSON list of American states so you don't have to type them all. Click NEW.   **JSON**

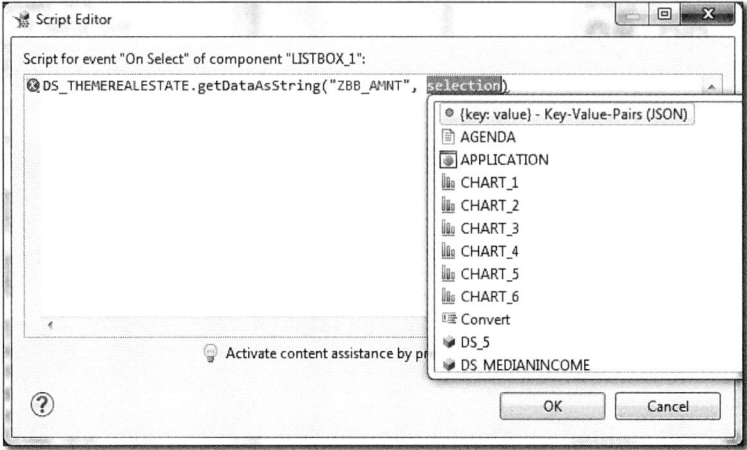

Figure 8.11 Using a JSON Predefined Statement Template

7. Fill in the fields as shown in Figure 8.12.

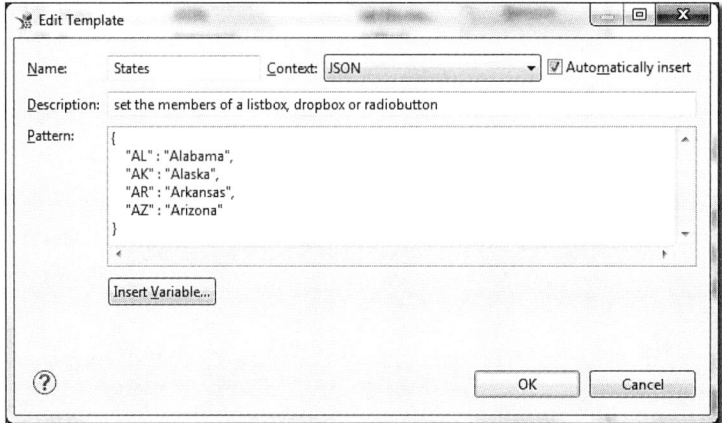

Figure 8.12 Template Code

8. Use the context JSON so you can insert these as a list.

9. Click OK.

10. You now see the states in the predefined statement templates (Figure 8.13).

11. Now when you go to the Script Editor, you can type in sample code to get data from a data source (Figure 8.14).

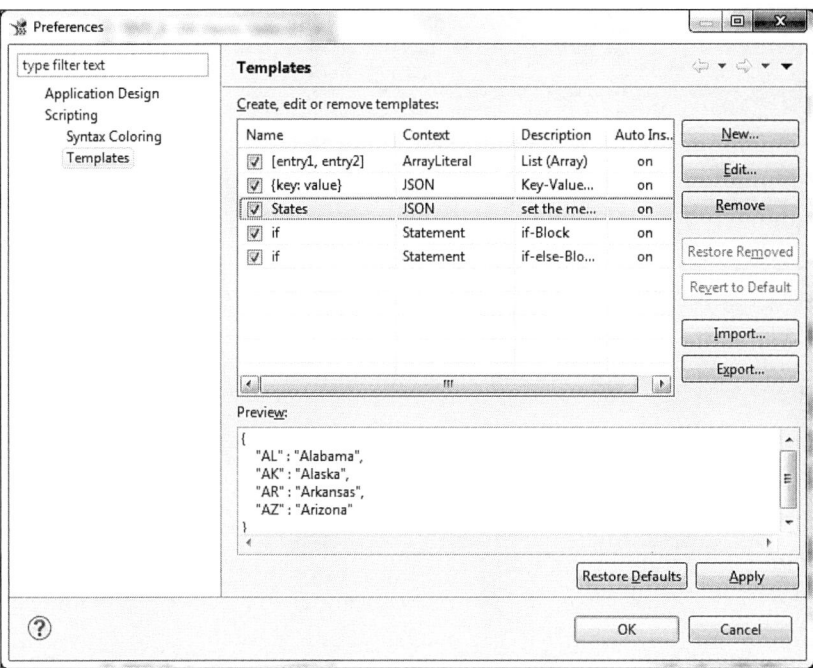

Figure 8.13 New Predefined Statement Ready

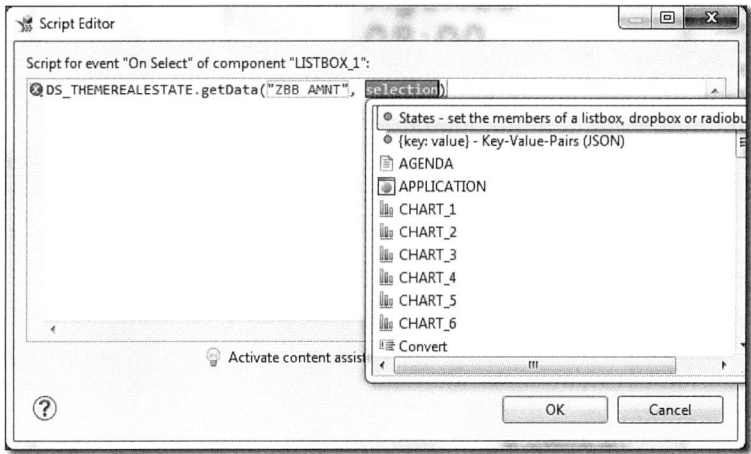

Figure 8.14 Using the New Predefined Statement

12. The end result is that the code from the predefined statement template is inserted into the script and looks like Figure 8.15.

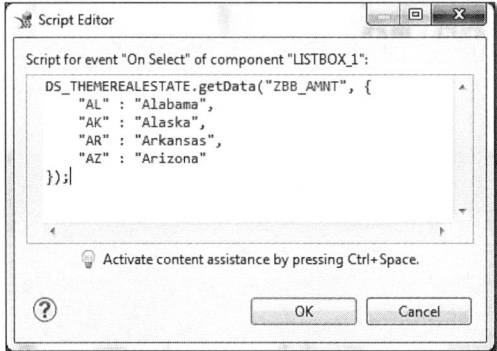

Figure 8.15 Script Editor after Inserting Predefined Code from the Template

8.2.3 Finding Script Errors

Script errors

Even after you've built your script, the Script Editor can still help—it identifies errors in your script by putting a marker at the beginning of the line (Figure 8.16). It also underlines the error with a red squiggle line.

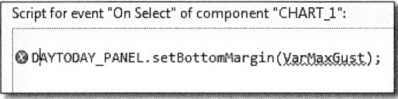

Figure 8.16 Syntax Error

When you hover your mouse pointer over the marker, the editor gives more information about the error. In Figure 8.17, you can see how the application delivers more information about the error. Even when there are multiple errors in the line, the Script Editor gives details about all the errors.

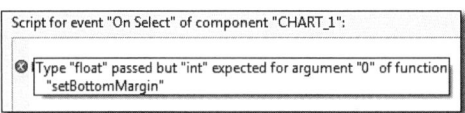

Figure 8.17 Syntax Error Explained

In this example, you can see that the variable `VarMaxGust` is of type `float`, but the API for the method `.setBottomMargin` requires a value of type `int`. You could repair this issue by either altering the variable or replacing the parameter in the line with an `integer` value.

8.3   Methods

Now that you understand the basics of BIAL and using the Script Editor to write script, let's take a close look at the scripting options in Design Studio. These are controlled using *methods*. In Section 8.3.1, we will look at the methods for the CONVERT component, which is a specific kind of component that is used to convert the value of an expression into another type. In Section 8.3.2, we'll discuss the methods of the DATA SOURCE ALIAS component. In Section 8.3.3, we'll look at the methods of the APPLICATION component. Finally, in Section 8.3.4, we will describe the methods and associated functions of all the visual components, starting with the common methods.

8.3.1   Convert Component

The CONVERT (Table 8.6) component is not a visual component, but is a global object that is designed to provide functions for data conversion. This is useful, for example, when you want to show a number in a text box and want to apply formatting.

Functions for data conversion

> **Note**
>
> As you may have noticed, the CONVERT component was not mentioned in Chapter 7. This is because you cannot see it or set any properties at design time. You can only use this component in script by referring to it using call statements.

You can use the CONVERT component to format a number so the number becomes more readable for users. If you have a number value `1234567`, you can use the convert method `floatToString`, which will result in a string value of `123,456.78 EUR`. When you set the text of a TEXT component using this resulting value, you present the user with an easy to comprehend value.

Convert a number to prepare it for viewing

The script line would look like this:

```
Convert.floatToString(123456.78, "###,###,##0.00 EUR");
```

In addition, if you have variables or parameters of different types and you need to change them so they will align, you use the CONVERT component to achieve this. You can view this object as a toolkit to handle all kinds of values. Table 8.6 lists all the CONVERT methods.

Method	Description
floatToString	Converts a float number type value to a string and applies a formatting pattern. English local is standard, but you can apply your own formatting in a parameter.
floatToStringUsingLocale	Converts a float number type to a string and applies the local formatting pattern. You can set the number of decimals.
stringLength	Returns the length of the string type value given in the parameter.
stringToFloat	Converts a string type to a float number.
stringToFloatUsingLocale	Converts a string type to a float number using the local formatting pattern.
stringToInt	Converts a string type to an integer.
Substring	Returns a substring of the original string based on the start and end positions set in the parameters.

Table 8.6 Convert Methods

8.3.2 Data Source Alias Component

Navigate and filter data

The DATA SOURCE ALIAS component has a lot of methods to navigate and filter the data (Table 8.7). In addition, you can assign a data source to the alias at runtime, meaning you can switch between the queries or views the data source is referring to, based on the interaction with the user.

Method	Description
assignDataSource	Assigns a new data source to the alias. You can select a system, a query, and whether it has to load immediately.
assignHierarchy	Assigns a hierarchy to a dimension.
clearAllFilters	Removes all filters on all dimensions.
clearFilter	Removes filter for dimension.
getConditionalFormatValue	Gives the conditional format applied. 0 is no format. 1-9 is the priority.
getConditionalFormat-ValueExt	Gives the conditional format with the use of external format keys.
getData	This results in the value of a single data cell from the dataset. A data cell holds information about the value, formatted value, scaling factor, and unit of measure.
getDataAsString	This results in the return of a single data cell from the dataset with external member keys.
getFilterText	This method results in the filter value of the filter in the dimension passed in the parameter.
getFilterText	Returns the filter value of a dimension. As this method returns the text of the value, you use this for displaying the filter.
getInfo	Returns data source information, for example, the key date or the technical name.
getMemberList	Returns a list of dimension members.
getStaticFilterExt	Returns the static filter value of a dimension.
getStaticFilterText	Returns the static filter value of a dimension. As this method returns the text of the value, you use it for displaying the filter.
getVariableValueExt	Returns the value of the variable in the external key format.

Table 8.7 Data Source Alias Methods

Method	Description
getVariableValueText	Returns the value of the variable. Use this method to display the value of the variable.
loadDataSource	Loads the assigned data source.
moveDimensionAfter	Adds the dimension after another dimension in the data source.
moveDimensionBefore	Adds the dimension before another dimension in the data source.
moveDimensionToColumns	Moves the dimension to a selected column in the data source.
moveDimensionToRows	Moves the dimension to a selected row in the data source.
reloadData	Reloads the data from the source. When the source data changes, this is a useful method.
removeDimension	Removes the dimension from the row or column.
setFilter	Sets a filter for a dimension in the internal key format. If there is already a filter on the dimension, that filter is removed.
setFilterExt	Sets a filter for a dimension in the external key format. If there is already a filter on the dimension, that filter is removed.
setMemberDisplay	Changes the member display for a data source dimension. Options are KEY, TEXT, KEY + TEXT, or TEXT + KEY.
swapDimensions	Two dimensions change place. This only works when at least one of the dimensions is placed in the row or column.
unassignHierarchy	Unassigns a hierarchy from the dimension.

Table 8.7 Data Source Alias Methods (Cont.)

8.3.3 Application Component

As you'll recall from Chapter 7, the Application component is the main component, and its methods are therefore meant for the main application functions. Some methods are used for debugging purposes when creating messages. There are also methods for setting query variables. Other methods in the Application component enable applications to open new URLs, including other Design Studio applications. All the Application component methods are listed in Table 8.8.

Debug, set query variables

Methods	Descriptions
Alert	Opens a message box.
createErrorMessage	Creates an error message that is visible in the Message view.
createInfoMessage	Creates an info message that is displayed in the Message view.
createWarningMessage	Creates a warning message that is displayed in the Message view.
getInfo	Returns analysis application information.
log	This method creates a message in the error log for analysis. If you have a complex piece of script and it does not work properly, you can use this for debugging purposes.
openPromptDialog	Opens a dialog box.
setVariableValue	Sets query variable values in the internal key format and executes the data source query again.
setVariableValueExt	Sets query variable values in the external key format, then executes the data source query again.
openNewWindow	Opens a new browser window with the specified URL.

Table 8.8 Application Component Methods

8.3.4   Visual Components

Common Methods

Parent class   Just as all visual components have common properties, they also all have common methods. These methods are part of the component class (described in Table 8.9). As a parent class of all the visual components, these components inherit the methods of this class.

The methods in this class are useful for changing the size, the location, and the layout of the objects at runtime.

Method	Description
getBottomMargin	Gives the bottom margin of the component as long as Bottom Margin is set to a number (not Auto).
getCSSClass	Returns the CSS class that is assigned to the component.
getHeight	Returns the height of the component as long as Height is set to a number (not Auto).
getLeftMargin	Returns the left margin of the component as long as Left Margin is set to a number (not Auto).
getRightMargin	Returns the right margin of the component as long as Right Margin is set to a number (not Auto).
getTopMargin	Returns the top margin of the component as long as Top Margin is set to a number (not Auto).
getWidth	Returns the width of the component as long as Width is set to a number (not Auto).
isVisible	Returns whether the component is visible (True) or not (False).
setBottomMargin	Sets the bottom margin as long as Bottom Margin is set to a number (not Auto).
setCSSClass	Sets the CSS class of the component.
setHeight	Sets the height of the component as long as Height is set to a number (not Auto).

Table 8.9 Component Methods

Method	Description
setLeftMargin	Sets the left margin of the component as long as LEFT MARGIN is set to a number (not AUTO).
setRightMargin	Sets the right margin of the component as long as RIGHT MARGIN is set to a number (not AUTO).
setTopMargin	Sets the top margin of the component as long as TOP MARGIN is set to a number (not AUTO).
setVisible	Sets the visibility of the component based on the parameter value (True or False).
setWidth	Sets the width of the component as long as WIDTH is set to a number (not AUTO).

Table 8.9 Component Methods (Cont.)

When you use visual components, you will see that they all have these methods.

Button Component

The methods of the BUTTON component (Table 8.10) allow you to get information about the BUTTON component and change its state. Using a combination of .getEnabled and .setEnabled, for example, allows you to construct an IF THEN ELSE statement that allows the user to toggle the status of a BUTTON component.

Get info and change the state of a button

Method	Description
getText	Gives the text that is displayed on the BUTTON component.
getEnabled	Tells whether the BUTTON component is enabled.
setText	Sets the text that is shown on the BUTTON component.
setEnabled	Sets the BUTTON to enabled or disabled depending on the parameter value.

Table 8.10 Button Component Methods

Chart Component

Manipulate charts

The CHART component methods (Table 8.11) allow you to manipulate the CHART component. You can set the kind of CHART component, the totals, the swapping axis, and perform all kinds of other manipulations. One particularly interesting method is the .getSelectedMember method. With this you can use a data point on the CHART component clicked by a user. For example, when a user clicks on a value in a graph, you can use this interaction to set a filter in a data source. This is helpful when you want to present details about the selected value in a CROSSTAB component.

The script line to do this is:

```
DS_DETAIL.setFilter("0CALYEAR",
  GRAPH.getSelectedMembers("0CALYEAR"));
```

Method	Description
getChartType	Gives the name of the CHART component.
getSelectedMember	Gives you information about the selected data point. With the parameter dimension, you define the dimension value you want to see.
isVisible	Shows the CHART component's visibility status.
setChartType	Changes the CHART component type.
setStyle	Changes the CHART component style.
setVisible	Sets the CHART component's visibility.
showTotals	Shows or hides (sub)totals.
swapAxes	Swaps the axes as they appear in the data source for a different chart perspective.

Table 8.11 Chart Component Methods

Checkbox Component

Status and value of component

The methods for the CHECKBOX component (Table 8.12) return information about the current status of the component as well as the value of the CHECKBOX (selected True or False). The CHECKBOX component script can also be useful to set the value of the CHECKBOX component based on the state of the application.

Let's consider an example where you want to let the user know that the data is up to date. In this case, you can insert a CHECKBOX component that is selected if the data was refreshed the previous night. You use the data source key date, which is set to today, and compare it to the last refresh date. If the dates are the same, then the CHECKBOX is selected, informing the user that everything is up to date. Additionally, you can use a CSS class assignment to create an alert when things are not up to date.

Example to show the state of the data

```
if (DS_THEMEREALESTATE.getInfo().lastDataUpdateMaximum == DS_
PRICEHISTORY.getInfo().keyDate) {
    CHECKBOX_1.setChecked(true);
    CHECKBOX_1.setCSSClass("NoAlert");
} else {
    CHECKBOX_1.setChecked(false);
    CHECKBOX_1.setCSSClass("Alert");
}
```

Method	Description
getText	Returns the text with the CHECKBOX component.
isChecked	Returns True if the CHECKBOX component is selected or False if the CHECKBOX component is not selected.
isEnabled	Returns True if the CHECKBOX component is enabled.
isVisible	Returns True if the CHECKBOX component is visible.
setChecked	Selects the CHECKBOX component when the parameter is set to True. Otherwise, the CHECKBOX component is not selected.
setEnabled	Sets the CHECKBOX component to enabled when the parameter is True. Otherwise, it is disabled.
setText	Sets the CHECKBOX component text.
setVisible	Shows the component when the parameter is True, but not when it is False.

Table 8.12 Checkbox Component Methods

Crosstab Component

As with the CHART component, the CROSSTAB component also has a .get-
SelectedMember method that returns information about the selected value in the CROSSTAB component (Table 8.13). The parameter of this method is the dimension about which you want to receive information. For
example, if your CROSSTAB component has a dimension MONTH, and,
based on the selected cell, you want to filter a data source, you use the
following code:

```
DS_1.setFilter("Month",
  CROSSTAB_1.getSelectedMembers("Month"));
```

Method	Description
removeSelection	If a cell is selected, this method will remove the selection.
getSelectedMember	Provides information about the dimension of a selected cell.

Table 8.13 Crosstab Component Methods

Date Field Component

The DATE FIELD component allows the user to select a date. Methods for
this component deliver or set the date (Table 8.14).

Method	Description
getDate	Returns the date.
isEnabled	Returns True if the component is enabled.
setDate	Sets the date on the component.
setEnabled	Allows you to enable or disable the component.

Table 8.14 Date Field Component Methods

Dimension Filter and Filter Panel Components

The methods in the DIMENSION FILTER and FILTER PANEL components
(Table 8.15) get information about the dimension and the filter, and you
can use this information to apply filters. As the DIMENSION FILTER is a

more generic component, it has a method, `getDimensionName`, to determine the dimension you are working in. This method is not present in the FILTER PANEL component.

Method	Description
Cancel	Removes entered filters that haven't been submitted yet.
getDimensionName	The name of the dimension is returned (only with the DIMENSION FILTER component).
Submit	Applies the filter values that have been entered.

Table 8.15 Dimension Component and Filter Panel Component Methods

Selection Components

The selection components are components where you can select a value from a list of members. These components are:

▶ LIST BOX

▶ RADIO BUTTON GROUP

▶ DROPDOWN BOX

You may recall from Chapter 7 that these components are all part of the *basic components* category. *Selection components* (Table 8.16) are a subset of this category and are grouped together based on the fact that their methods allow you to pick a value from a set of values. In other words, the methods available with these components allow you to determine a number of possible selections and select a value from those selections. One of the main uses for this is to collect the selected value with the `.getSelectedValue` method and use this value as a parameter for other actions.

Determine selections and select values

Method	Description
getSelectedText	Returns the text of the selected item. Each item in the component has a key and an item.
getSelectedValue	Gets the selected value key.

Table 8.16 Selection Component Methods

Method	Description
isEnabled	Allows you to enable or disable the component.
setEnabled	The component can be set to enabled or disabled with this method.
setItems	Assigns a list of items to the components. If there were previous items in the list, these items are removed and replaced with the new items passed in the parameter.
setSelectedValue	Sets the status selected to the item with the specified key.
Sort	Sorts the items in alphabetical order. An optional parameter can be used to set the list in descending order.

Table 8.16 Selection Component Methods (Cont.)

Image Component

Retrieve image paths and set new images

With the methods for the IMAGE component (Table 8.17), you can retrieve the path of the images linked to the IMAGE component and set new images to the component. You can also view or set opacity.

Method	Description
getClickImage	Returns the path of the image file that is shown when clicked.
getHoverImage	Returns the path of the image file that is visible when the mouse hovers over the IMAGE component.
getImage	Returns the path of the image file that is initially visible.
getOpacity	Returns the opacity value. 0 is fully transparent; 100 is fully visible.
setClickImage	Sets the image file to show when the IMAGE component is clicked.

Table 8.17 Image Component Methods

Method	Description
setHoverImage	Sets the image file to show when the mouse hovers over the IMAGE component.
setImage	Sets the main image.
setOpacity	Sets the opacity of the image. 0 is fully transparent; 100 is fully visible.

Table 8.17 Image Component Methods (Cont.)

Input Field Component

In the INPUT FIELD component methods (Table 8.18), the application user can freely write a text. The INPUT FIELD methods can be used to set and retrieve the value and enable or disable the component.

Input free text

Method	Description
getValue	Returns the value that is entered in the INPUT FIELD component.
isEnabled	Returns True if the component is enabled or, otherwise, False.
setEnabled	Sets the component to enabled or disabled.
setValue	Sets the value of the INPUT FIELD component.

Table 8.18 Input Field Component Methods

Pagebook Component

The PAGEBOOK component is a container component that allows you to swipe or drag between pages. The methods in this component (Table 8.19) allow you to retrieve the current page or move to another page based on the name or index number of the page.

Swipe or drag pages

Methods	Description
getSelectedPage	Returns the name of the currently selected page.

Table 8.19 Pagebook Component Methods

Methods	Description
getSelectedPage-Index	Returns the index value of the selected page. If the first page is currently selected, then the index is 0.
setSelectedPage-ByName	Selects the page by passing the name of the page in the parameter.
setSelectedPage-Index	Selects the page by passing the index number of the page in the parameter.

Table 8.19 Pagebook Component Methods (Cont.)

Panel Component

Organize other components

The PANEL component is a basic container that helps you to organize other components. Therefore, the PANEL component has only the .onClick method. A handler method allows you to run the script in a component from another component.

Popup Component

The POPUP component is a screen that shows on top of the application. The methods (Table 8.20) are used for checking if it is visible and showing or hiding the component.

Methods	Description
hide	The POPUP component is not visible anymore.
isShowing	Returns True if the POPUP component is currently visible.
show	The POPUP component is visible.

Table 8.20 Popup Component Methods

Tabstrip Component

Navigate between pages

The TABSTRIP component is a container component that allows you to navigate between pages. The methods (Table 8.21) allow you to retrieve the current page and go to another page.

Method	Description
getSelectedTab	Returns the name of the currently selected tab.
getSelectedTab-Index	Returns the index value of the selected tab. If the first page is currently selected, then the index is 0.
setSelectedTab-ByName	Selects the tab by passing the name of the page in the parameter.
setSelectedTab-Index	Selects the tab by passing the index number of the page in the parameter.

Table 8.21 Tabstrip Component Methods

Text Component

The TEXT component shows text that is visible for the user. The methods (Table 8.22) can set the current text or look at the current text. Combined with the common layout methods described earlier in this section, the TEXT component is very useful for applying layout changes to an application based on interaction with the user.

Set text as visible to user

Method	Description
getText	Returns the text currently in the TEXT component.
setText	Sets the text that is shown in the TEXT component.

Table 8.22 Text Component Methods

8.4   Examples: Building Navigation Items

In this section, we will set up navigation items so the user can move through the application. We will be using different components in combination with scripts and CSS to reflect the choices the user makes in the application.

8.4.1 Menu Navigation

Text
component,
Pagebook
component,
CSS classes
In the first example, we will build a menu navigation. We will use TEXT components in combination with CSS classes to build navigation BUTTON components to navigate through the screens of a PAGEBOOK component in the application. Additionally, we will highlight the last selected BUTTON component so the user can see where he is in the application.

As you can see in Figure 8.18, BUTTON 3 is selected, and the third screen of the PAGEBOOK component is selected.

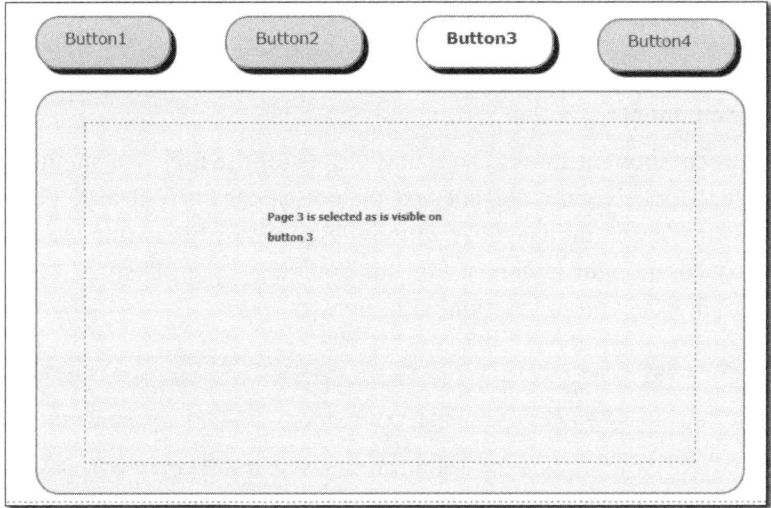

Figure 8.18 Menu Screen

Define the CSS
classes
To create such a menu structure, you first define two CSS classes. For this purpose, we made a CSS file that we have attached to the application's CUSTOM CSS property. In this file, we have defined two CSS classes: one for the standard, unselected button and one for the selected button.

In Notepad create a file with the extension .css and insert the following lines:

```
.button
{
border:2px solid #a1a1a1;
padding:10px 30px;
```

```
background:#dddddd;
border-radius:25px;
font-family:"Verdana", Arial, serif;
color:rgb(128,128,128);
box-shadow: 5px 5px 2px #666666;
font-size:150%;
font-weight:500;
}

.buttonselected
{
border:2px solid #a1a1a1;
padding:10px 30px;
background:#cccccc;
border-radius:25px;
font-family:"Verdana", Arial, serif;
color:rgb(128,128,128);
box-shadow: 5px 5px 2px #666666;
font-size:150%;
font-weight:700;
}
```

In Figure 8.18, you can see that, with this CSS code, we have created rounded buttons with shadows.

Now, for each BUTTON component, we will add a script. The first part of the script is to set all the BUTTON components to the standard style. The second part is to select the PAGEBOOK page. The third and final part is to set the appearance of the BUTTON component to the style of a selected BUTTON component.

Add a script

In the code below, we show the script code that has to be attached to BUTTON 3.

```
//Reset all the buttons to their normal style
TEXT_1.setCSSClass("button");
TEXT_2.setCSSClass("button");
TEXT_3.setCSSClass("button");
TEXT_4.setCSSClass("button");
//Select the right pagebook
PAGEBOOK_1.setSelectedPageIndex(0);
//set the third button to selected status
TEXT_1.setCSSClass("buttonselected");
```

297

You can use this code for each button. The index number of the `PAGEBOOK_1.setSelectedPageIndex(2);` line should be changed to the right number. In addition, the final line should be altered to ensure that the right button receives the `buttonselected` format.

8.4.2 Popup Navigation

Change the behavior of an application

In this section, we will build a popup menu where a user can change the behavior of the application. In the popup menu, the user will be able to select the currency, the unit of measure, and the color settings of the application. In the script, we will use BEx variables to enforce the currency and unit of measure settings for the data sources. For the color settings, we will use CSS classes that we assign based on the user's choice. As an additional technique, we will use an extra component as a placeholder for the script to assign a new CSS class to all the components. This extra component will then be called from other components by using the event handler method.

Put scripting in separate component

As you see in Figure 8.19, the popup screen allows you to set the currency, the measurement unit, and a color scheme for the application. As resetting all the CSS classes is a lot of work, we put all the scripting in a separate component that is added only for holding the script. Additionally, we used a global variable to store the value of the currently selected color scheme so we can reuse that value for any color scheme selected.

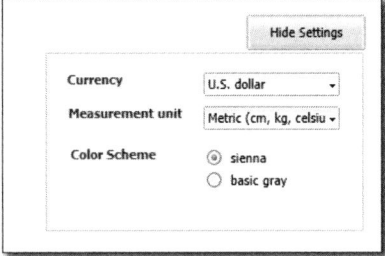

Figure 8.19 Popup Screen

First we want to use a BUTTON component to toggle the POPUP component. If the POPUP is hidden, the BUTTON component should make it visible, and when the POPUP is visible, clicking the BUTTON component should hide the POPUP.

In the script for the BUTTON component add the following code:

```
if (POPUP_1.isShowing()) {
    BUTTON_1.setText("Show Settings");
    POPUP_1.hide();
} else {
    BUTTON_1.setText("Hide Settings");
    POPUP_1.show();
}
```

This code looks at the POPUP component and performs an action based on the its current state.

For the currency and unit of measure setting, we are going to use BEx variables that we will set based on the user's choice. Setting a BEx variable automatically leads to a reload of all the BEx queries that use that variable.

BEx variables

In the first DROPDOWN BOX component, we put the following code in the On Select handler. When the user changes the selected value, the new selected value will be used to change the BEx variable ZCURVAL, which is used for selecting the currency.

```
APPLICATION.setVariableValue("ZCURRVAL", DROPDOWN_1.getSelectedValue());
```

In the second DROPDOWN BOX component, a similar script code will change the BEx variable ZMEASVAL. This will change the unit of measure.

```
APPLICATION.setVariableValue("ZMEASVAL", DROPDOWN_2.getSelectedValue());
```

In the RADIO BUTTON GROUP component, we can select a color scheme for the application. In this example we have two settings: sienna and basic gray.

In the CSS file we have attached to the application property CUSTOM CSS, two classes are defined:

```
.sienna
{
background-color:#A0522D;
border:4px solid #a1a1a1;
border-radius:25px;
}
```

and

```
.basicgray
{
background-color:#D3D3D3;
border:4px solid #a1a1a1;
border-radius:25px;
}
```

In the APPLICATION component we have defined a global variable color-scheme as a string with the initial value sienna.

User controls color scheme
When the application starts, the CSS classes of all components should be set to the initial setting. When the user alters the value of the color scheme in the POPUP component, the CSS classes should be set to reflect that choice.

As setting the CSS class for all components calls for a lot of code, we do not want to write and maintain all those lines in two places. In the application On Startup handler, we see only this code:

```
CODE_COLORSCHEME_SETTER.onClick();
```

When the RADIO BUTTON GROUP component value changes, we only see two lines of code; the first resets the value of the global variable, and the second addresses the colorscheme setter:

```
ColorScheme = RADIOBUTTONGROUP_1.getSelectedValue();
CODE_COLORSCHEME_SETTER.onClick();
```

The component with the name code_colorscheme_setter is a TEXT component that is only used to hold the script for changing the CSS script. It will use the variable value to set all the CSS values.

As there are different CSS classes for buttons, texts, etc., concatenation is used to address the different types of classes.

```
// Sets all the components CSS class to the desired
// color scheme
//Buttons
BUTTON_1.setCSSClass(ColorScheme + "_button");
BUTTON_2.setCSSClass(ColorScheme + "_button");
BUTTON_3.setCSSClass(ColorScheme + "_button");
```

```
BUTTON_4.setCSSClass(ColorScheme + "_button");
BUTTON_5.setCSSClass(ColorScheme + "_button");

//Text boxes
BUTTON_1.setCSSClass(ColorScheme + "_text");
BUTTON_2.setCSSClass(ColorScheme + "_text");
BUTTON_3.setCSSClass(ColorScheme + "_text");
BUTTON_4.setCSSClass(ColorScheme + "_text");
BUTTON_5.setCSSClass(ColorScheme + "_text");
```

By using the variable, we ensure that we only have to put this code in one place. In addition, if there should be a third color scheme choice, this can be easily implemented by adding classes to the CSS file and adding another selection option to the RADIO BUTTON GROUP component.

8.4.3   Navigating between Applications

In this third navigation example, we will move outside the application. Additionally, we will make it possible to pass parameter values from outside the application. These parameters will influence the settings we have chosen in the settings screen in Figure 8.19. We also will look at how to use global variables to make things easier for ourselves.

When you want an application to accept the parameter values from outside the application, you first have to define global variables. As you can see in Figure 8.20, we now have three additional variables in our example, but these are set as URL parameters.

Define global variables

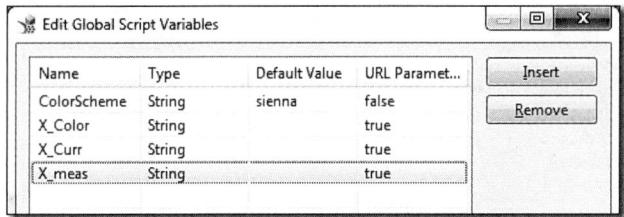

Figure 8.20 Global Variables as URL Parameters

In our On Startup code, we will use these global variables to set the color scheme and our two query variables.

```
APPLICATION.setVariableValue("ZCURRVAL", X_Curr);
APPLICATION.setVariableValue("Z_MEASVAL", X_meas);
ColorScheme = X_Color;

CODE_COLORSCHEME_SETTER.onClick();
```

As you can see, the code uses the parameter values to set the variable values on the application itself. The CSS classes will then be set with the value passed in the parameter. Our application is now able to use the parameters to change the initial settings.

We will now look at what you need to do in another application—let's refer to it as App2—to open our initial application (App1) and pass the parameter values. We will assume that App2 has the same popup screen to specify the setting values.

To start App1, App2 has to open a new window with the URL of App1. This URL consists of three parts: the general server address, the unique CUID of the application, and the parameters.

Link to multiple applications For easier maintenance, we will first set up variables for the server name and for the application CUID in App2. In Figure 8.21, you can see that we store every value in a global variable, because this gives us a lot of flexibility and ease of maintenance. Based on selections in the application, we now can link to several applications. As we will see later, the code to actually open the application is easily readable with the use of these global variables.

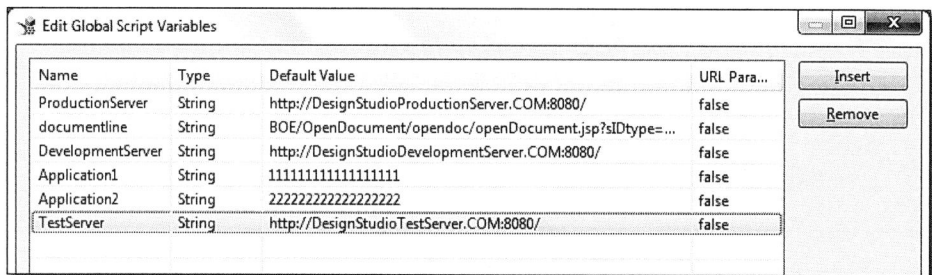

Figure 8.21 URL Values Stored in Global Variables

We can now set up a BUTTON component (or another component) in App2 with the following script in the event handler:

```
APPLICATION.openNewWindow(ProductionServer + documentline
  + Application1 +
    "&X_Curr=" + DROPDOWN_1.getSelectedValue() +
    "&X_meas=" + DROPDOWN_2.getSelectedValue() +
    "&X_color=" + RADIOBUTTONGROUP_1.getSelectedValue()
);
```

This code will result in opening App1 with the settings passed in the parameters.

8.5   Examples: Manipulating Data Output

In this section, we will use scripts to work with the data. We will change the layout of the data, add filters, and change data sources. All this is connected to buttons in the application so the user can perform complex navigations in the data with just one click of a button.

8.5.1   Adding a Filter

In the application (Figure 8.22) we see weather data for over 100 years. On the left is a LIST BOX component with the 12 months of the year. When we click one of these months, the CROSSTAB component on the right will only show the selected month.

Selecting by month

January		precipitation durati ⪰	mean windspeed ⪰	maximum hourly mean ⪰	maximum wind gust ⪰	mean surface air ⪰
February	Decade ▲	H	M/S	M/S	M/S	BIA
March	1900 - 1909	0	4,611	23	0	1.014,952
April	1910 - 1919	0	5,620	30	0	1.013,732
May	1920 - 1929	0	6,496	26	0	1.014,239
June	1930 - 1939	0	6,785	24	0	1.014,027
July	1940 - 1949	0	6,386	30	0	939,512
August	1950 - 1959	1.425	7,056	26	0	1.014,540
September	1960 - 1969	5.565	7,498	27	0	1.013,849
October	1970 - 1979	4.910	6,243	27	38	1.014,607
November	1980 - 1989	5.771	6,037	25	38	1.014,875
	1990 - 1999	6.547	5,915	24	41	1.015,217
	2000 - 2009	766	5,801	19	29	1.012,909

Figure 8.22 Filtering with the List Box Component

We will build this interactivity in two parts. In the first part, at the startup of the application we will fill the LIST BOX component with the

List Box component

selectable items. When we have completed the first part, we will continue by adding a script to use the selected item in the LIST BOX component to filter the data that is presented in the CROSSTAB component.

In the application's On Startup event we will put a script that will populate the LIST BOX component with items based on the data in the data source. If, for example, there are only three months of data available in the data source, the LIST BOX component will only show those three months. The reasoning here is that each of those three months is a valid choice, i.e., resulting in a visible dataset on the right instead of coming up without any data.

The script line at the application's On Startup handler is:

```
LISTBOX_1.setItems(DS_
1.getMemberList("0CALMONTH2", MemberPresentation.INTERNAL_
KEY, MemberDisplay.TEXT, 15));
```

Let's have a closer look at this script: first the method that allows us to fill the LIST BOX component with item values, and then the method that results in a set of items.

```
LISTBOX_1.setItems(ITEMLIST);
```

The LIST BOX component method is used to fill the component with the items. This can be a hard-coded list, but in this case we want to use a data source to populate the component.

```
DS_1.getMemberList("0CALMONTH2", MemberPresentation.INTERNAL_
KEY, MemberDisplay.TEXT, 12)
```

Data source method
The data source method is a bit more complicated, as there are more parameters to fill. First we set the dimension that holds the items to populate our LIST BOX component items. In this case, it is the field holding the calendar months. Next we set the key values. Those are the values that the LIST BOX component will pass to other components when we use the getselectedvalue method. The third parameter determines how we want to show the data to the user—i.e., the text. Finally, we tell the system the maximum number of items we want to show in the LIST BOX component. Because there are 12 months in a year, we set this number to 12.

Now that we have the LIST BOX component filled with the data, the next step is to invoke the script to react to a user click and use the selected value to place a filter on the data source.

```
DS_1.setFilter("0CALMONTH2", LISTBOX_1.getSelectedValue());
```

When we select a value in the LIST BOX component, the script will respond by applying a filter on the data source with the selected value.

Finally, we want the user to be able to reset the filter—in case he has already selected a month but wants to navigate back to the whole year. That reset button has one script line:

```
DS_1.clearFilter("0CALMONTH2");
```

This method clears the filters of the 0CALMONTH2 dimension. It is also possible to clear all the filters on all the dimensions at once. To do so, use the following line:

```
DS_1.clearAllFilters();
```

8.5.2 Adding a Cascading Filter and Drilling Down to a More Detailed Level

In this section we will take the filter option one step further. Instead of months, decades will be shown in the LIST BOX component. In Figure 8.23, you see how this application allows the user to first select a decade, then a year, then the month, and, finally, the day.

Filter by day

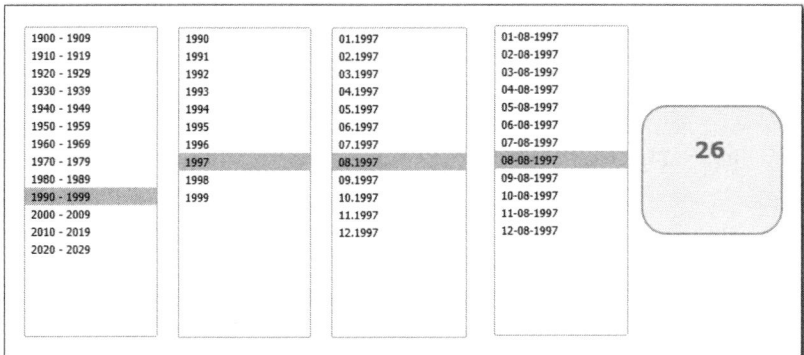

Figure 8.23 Using Cascading Filters to Drill Down

305

When a day is selected, the maximum temperature for that day will become visible. This type of interaction can be very useful to navigate through large dimensions step by step.

As with the previous example, we first have to populate the first LIST BOX component. This is almost the same code as in the application's On Startup handler.

```
LISTBOX_2.setItems(DS_1.getMemberList("ZDS_TDATE__
ZDECADE", MemberPresentation.INTERNAL_
KEY, MemberDisplay.TEXT, 15));
```

However, in these LIST BOX components, more script lines are added. There are a couple of additional tasks that the script now has to perform:

▶ Remove lower-level filters, as they would result in no available data in combination with a new decade.

▶ Set the month and day LIST BOX component to DISABLED, so that, after a decade is selected, the year has to be selected.

▶ Set the new filter on the data source.

▶ Populate the year LIST BOX component.

▶ Make any temperature shown in the LIST BOX component disappear.

```
DS_1.clearFilter("OCALYEAR");
DS_1.clearFilter("OCALMONTH");
DS_1.clearFilter("OCALDAY");

DS_1.setFilter("ZDS_TDATE__ZDECADE", LISTBOX_2.getSelected-
Value());

LISTBOX_3.setItems(DS_
1.getMemberList("OCALYEAR", MemberPresentation.INTERNAL_
KEY, MemberDisplay.TEXT, 10));
LISTBOX_3.setEnabled(true);

// lower level listboxes not available anymore

LISTBOX_4.setEnabled(false);
LISTBOX_5.setEnabled(false);
TEXT_1.setText("");
```

This code will clear the day, month, and year filter. Next it will set a filter on the decade based on the selected value. When the filter is applied, the List Box component for the years will be populated. As there is only one decade left in the dataset, there will be a maximum of 10 years in the List Box component.

After populating the year List Box component, the month and day List Boxes are disabled. (Instead of disabling them, you can also set the visibility to `false` to remove them entirely from sight until they are needed.) Finally, in cases where there is already a temperature shown, the temperature text is cleared.

The code for the next three List Box components is much like the first one. The difference is that other List Box components get populated and fewer have to be disabled. The List Box component for years will populate the month List Box component, while the month List Box component will populate the day List Box component. Finally, the day List Box component will set the last filter and edit the text of the Text Box component.

```
DS_1.setFilter("0CALDAY", LISTBOX_5.getSelectedValue());
TEXT_1.setText(DS_1.getDataAsString("ZA_TX", {}));
```

8.5.3 Moving Dimensions and Measures

After applying filters to the data source, we want to add flexibility to the navigation by allowing the user to change the view on the data. In this example, we will set up an application where you can change dimensions and measures by clicking the appropriate buttons (Figure 8.24). We will move dimensions, select measures, and finally assign a hierarchy. All these actions together provide a very broad set of tools available to help the user to navigate through the data.

Change views on data

In this example, the user can select a dimension and perform an action that will result in a different view on the weather data in a Crosstab component. Furthermore, he can select up to four measures.

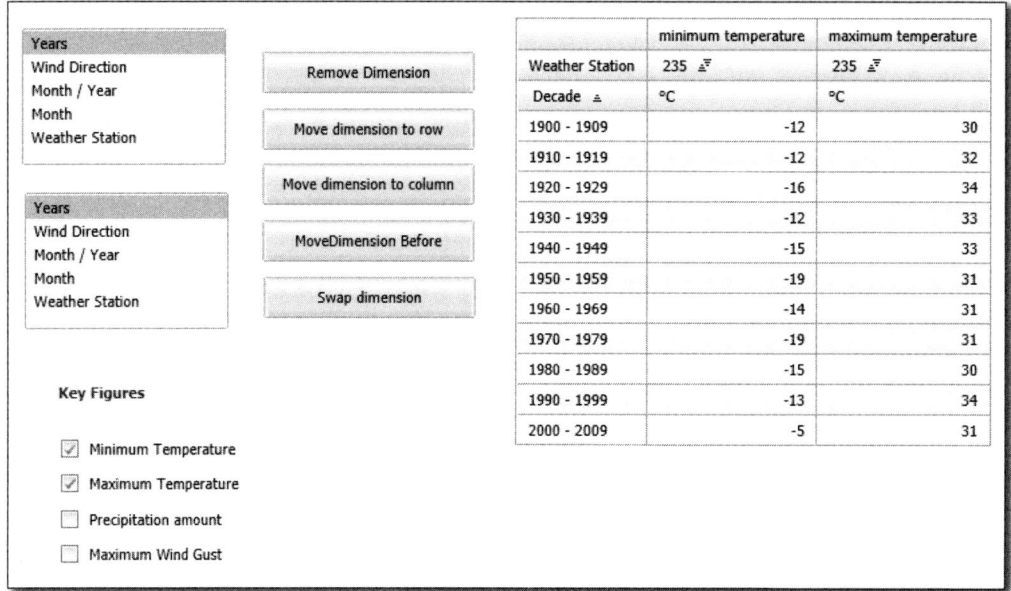

Figure 8.24 OLAP Application

For REMOVE DIMENSION, we take the value of the upper LIST BOX component. In the REMOVE DIMENSION BUTTON component's On Click event handler, we set the following line:

```
DS_WEATHER.removeDimension(LISTBOX_6.getSelectedValue());
```

In each BUTTON component, we will set the appropriate script to perform the action. For the second BUTTON component, MOVE DIMENSION TO ROW, the script is as follows:

```
DS_WEATHER.moveDimensionToRows(LISTBOX_6.getSelectedValue());
```

For the third BUTTON component, MOVE DIMENSION TO COLUMN, the script is as follows:

```
DS_WEATHER.moveDimensionToColumns(LISTBOX_6.getSelected-
Value());
```

For the fourth BUTTON component, MOVE DIMENSION BEFORE, the script is as follows:

```
DS_WEATHER.moveDimensionBefore(LISTBOX_6.getSelectedValue(),
  LISTBOX_7.getSelectedValue());
```

This statement will put a dimension in front of the dimension selected in the lower LIST BOX. If the selected dimension in the LIST BOX is not in the current view of the data source, then the statement is ignored.

Finally, for the fifth BUTTON component, SWAP DIMENSIONS, we also need to select a second value in the lower LIST BOX component. To be able to swap, one of the selected dimensions should be in the row or column of the data set.

```
DS_WEATHER.swapDimensions(LISTBOX_6.getSelectedValue(),
    LISTBOX_7.getSelectedValue());
```

In addition, we want to be able to select one or more measures. The selected measures should be shown in the CROSSTAB component. With four measures, we have a total of 16 possible configurations. We will use global variables, as shown in Figure 8.25. As you can see, only the first measure is already a value. This is also the initial setting of the data source.

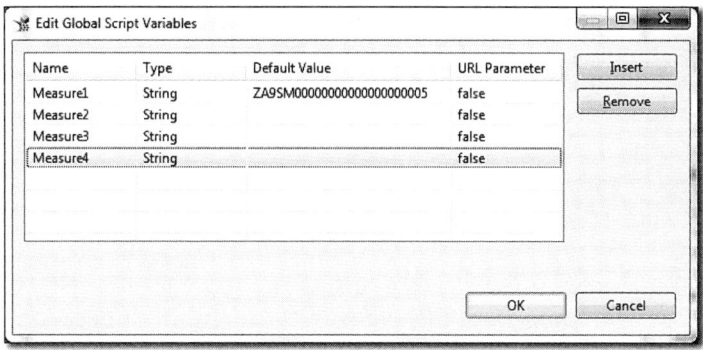

Figure 8.25 Global Variables for Measure Selection

When the user selects one of the CHECKBOX components, the global variable belonging to that component is filled with the appropriate value. When the user deselects one of the CHECKBOX components, the value is removed when deselected.

In the CHECKBOX components, we insert the following code. The listing below is the script attached to the second CHECKBOX component.

```
if (CHECKBOX_2.isChecked()) {
    Measure2 = "ZA9SM00000000000000000005";
```

```
} else {
    Measure2 = "";
}
DS_WEATHER.setFilter("0MEASURES0000000000000009",
  [Measure1, Measure2,Measure3,Measure4]);
```

In the other CHECKBOX components, we insert basically the same code, but we will be using the other variables in those components. As you can see, we also have a complicated value as the first parameter of the method. Luckily, you don't have to enter this yourself—if you press Ctrl+Space, you will be able to select the value via the CONTENT ASSIS-TANCE screen.

It is possible to take the measures selection a step further. Instead of four CHECKBOX components, we now set up four LIST BOX components. The layout is as shown in Figure 8.26. We now have the measures grouped logically so the user can choose one of similar measures. With the choice NONE, we also provide the possibility to limit the number of visible measures.

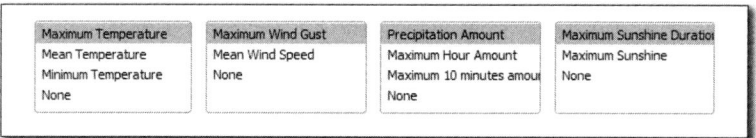

Figure 8.26 More Measure Choices

Instead of the `if then` code we showed earlier, we assign the selected value of a LIST BOX component to a global variable. In the application's `On Startup` handler we will populate the LIST BOX component with a subset of the measures:

```
DS_3.setFilter("0MEASURES0000000000000009", "ZA_T*");
LISTBOX_8.setItems(DS_3.getMemberList("0MEASURES00000000000000
09", MemberPresentation.INTERNAL_KEY, MemberDisplay.TEXT, 5));
```

Note that the filter now has an asterisk (*) in the filter value. The data source will return all the measure names that start with ZA_T.

In the LIST BOX component's `On Select` handler we now set the following code:

```
Keyfigure2 = LISTBOX_8.getSelectedValue();
DS_WEATHER.setFilter("0MEASURES0000000000000009", [Keyfigure1,
  Keyfigure2,Keyfigure3,Keyfigure4]);
```

This setup allows us to give the user a choice from a total of 144 configurations.

8.5.4 Changing Data Sources

Now we will use a script to change the data source properties. With this script, we allow the user to switch from one set of data to another by assigning another query or view to the data source. It is even possible to switch to another system, as long the system is defined on the SAP BusinessObjects BI platform.

In this example (Figure 8.27), the user can again look at weather data. Three backend systems are available: one for the Netherlands, one for Germany, and one for Belgium. There are also three queries to choose from: temperature, precipitation, and wind speed.

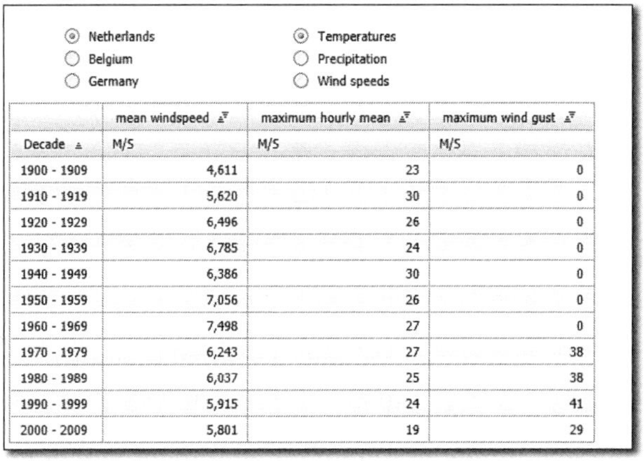

Decade ▲	mean windspeed	maximum hourly mean	maximum wind gust
	M/S	M/S	M/S
1900 - 1909	4,611	23	0
1910 - 1919	5,620	30	0
1920 - 1929	6,496	26	0
1930 - 1939	6,785	24	0
1940 - 1949	6,386	30	0
1950 - 1959	7,056	26	0
1960 - 1969	7,498	27	0
1970 - 1979	6,243	27	38
1980 - 1989	6,037	25	38
1990 - 1999	5,915	24	41
2000 - 2009	5,801	19	29

Figure 8.27 Select System and Query Example

First we change the property Load in script of the data source's Properties view. This is set to True, indicating that we want to load this data source later, instead of immediately at startup.

In Figure 8.28, we manually set up the values and texts for the available systems in a Radio Button Group component. In the Value column,

Load in Script

we see the unique ID of the definition of the system as it is registered on the SAP BusinessObjects BI platform. In the TEXT column the texts are defined as the user will see them.

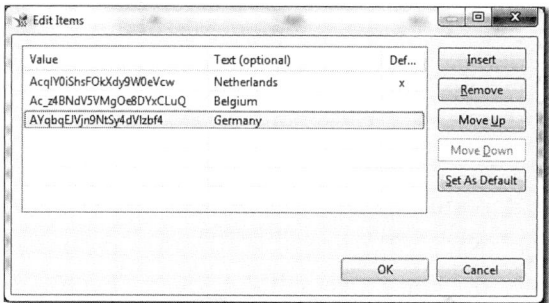

Figure 8.28 System Choices

In the other RADIO BUTTON GROUP component, we create a similar setup. Instead of system CUIDs, we use the query name as a key value and the description as we want the user to see it.

In both RADIO BUTTON GROUP components, we will use the same script.

```
DS_1.assignDataSource("cuid:"+RGB_
SYSTEM.getSelectedValue(), DataSourceType.QUERY, RGB_QUERY.get-
SelectedValue());
DS_1.loadDataSource();
```

By passing the LIST BOX component values as parameters in the assigned data source statement, we connect to the query as defined by the user's choices.

By adding choices in the LIST BOX component, we are able to increase the list of possible queries and/or systems available to the user. We could even use an INPUT FIELD component instead of the LIST BOX and allow the user to access any query that is available in the system.

8.6   Example: Building a Scorecard

Weather scorecard

In this section, we will build a scorecard. In a scorecard, a graphical element indicates whether the value is satisfactory, good, or needs improvement. In Figure 8.29, a weather scorecard has been built with five levels of alerts. In the table, the precipitation amount per day is shown for a week. Based on the amount of rain during the day, an alert level is set and shown in the form of a circle. Black means no rain, while white means a lot of rain, with varying shades of gray in between.

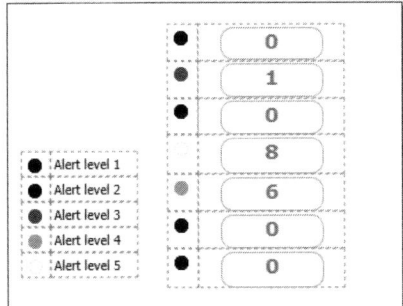

Figure 8.29 Scorecard Application

For this setup, we need a query that has exceptions defined as a data source. In an SAP NetWeaver BW BEx query, you can assign exception values and thus categorize the results. In Figure 8.30, we see the exceptions that have been defined in this example. These are the rules that determine which result leads to which indicator. The layout that is applied based on this outcome is defined in the Design Studio application.

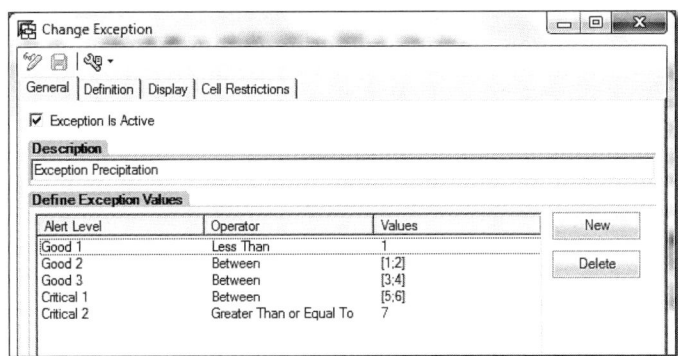

Figure 8.30 BEx Query Exception

In the application's On Startup handler, we will define the code to set the values on the right side of the table in Figure 8.29, and use the exception values that we receive from the data source to apply the appropriate layout to the indicators.

First we set the layout. We have uploaded a CSS file and assigned this to the application's CUSTOM CSS property with five CSS classes. The classes are named `alert1` through `alert5`.

We use the following CSS code:

```
.alert1
{
 border:1px solid;
 border-color:#000000;
 border-radius:25px;
 background-color:#000000;
}
.alert2
{
 border:1px solid;
 border-color:#333333;
 border-radius:25px;
 background-color:#333333;
}
.alert3
{
 border:1px solid;
 border-color:#666666;
 border-radius:25px;
 background-color:#666666;
}

.alert4
{
 border:1px solid;
 border-color:#999999;
 border-radius:25px;
 background-color:#999999;
}
.alert5
{
 border:1px solid;
 border-color:#E6E6E6;
```

```
border-radius:25px;
background-color:#E6E6E6;
}
.alert5
{
border:1px solid;
border-color:#E6E6E6;
border-radius:25px;
background-color:#FFFFFF;
}
```

We use five Text Box components in the application layout, which we will apply to each one of the CSS classes. The size of the Text components is set to 10x10 in the Properties view. Combined with the `border-radius` property, this transforms the Text components into circles. Each class has a different background color, going from white through several shades of gray to black.

In the application's `On Startup` handler, we set the value of the Text component and then set the layout of the indicator. We have seven indicators and seven values. For each set of indicators and values, we apply the same steps.

First we set the value of the Text component using the `.getdata` method from the data source. In this example, we take the precipitation amount of one day. The measure in the code is displayed as a CUID. Use $\boxed{\text{Ctrl}}$ + $\boxed{\text{Space}}$ on the measure parameter, and you will see a list of available measures.

```
VALUE_1.setText(DS_PRECIPITATION.getDataAsString("4SXP85F39
VXDKO4D5EMHYMBPF", {"OCALDAY": "19910316" }));
```

Then we set the CSS class of the indicator Text component using the `get ConditionalFormatValueExt` method. We use a global variable `AlertCSS` to set the first part of the class. The global variable is a string and is assigned the value `alert`. We then concatenate this value with the value returned from the data source.

```
AlertValue = DS_PRECIPITATION.getConditionalFormatValueExt("4S
XP85F39VXDKO4D5EMHYMBPF", {"OCALDAY": "19910316"});
INDICATOR_1.setCSSClass(AlertCSS + AlertValue);
```

Using the global variable gives us a little bit of extra flexibility. In one of our other examples, we showed a way to change a color scheme based on user choices. Using a global variable allows us to offer a similar choice. For example, by adding `alertcolor` classes to the CSS file and setting the global variable to `alertcolor`, you can switch to a different set of alerts.

Variable Usage for Flexibility

By having one variable for the name and another for the number, you can set up lots of layouts that can be applied dynamically. If the variable `Layout-Class` has the value `Class1_`, and the variable `LayoutLevel` has the value 1, you can concatenate these to assign the CSS class `Class1_1` to a component in the application. By altering `LayoutClass` and `LayoutLevel`, you can have as many classes and levels as you like.

8.7   Example: Building a Calculator

Complex calculations

In this section, we will look at how much calculation you can actually do in Design Studio. We are going to build a simple calculator, as shown in Figure 8.31.

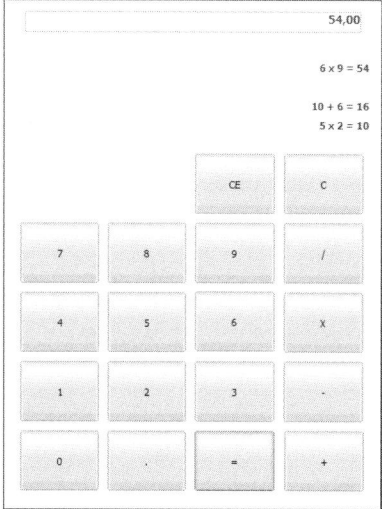

Figure 8.31 Calculator Application in Design Studio

Even though we say "a simple calculator," this is quite a complex example. We will take it step by step and show you how to build this. Once you have mastered this scenario, you'll be able to use the most complex calculations in any scenario you can think of.

8.7.1 Setting up the Layout

Before you start coding, you need to build the layout. First drag a GRID LAYOUT component to the canvas and follow the steps below:

Grid Layout component

1. Set the height to 550.
2. Set the width to 400.
3. Set the number of rows to 2 and the number of columns to 1.
4. Set the row heights, respectively, to 2 and 5.

Now, drag seven TEXT components into the first cell and follow the steps below:

Text components

1. Set the left and right margins of all the TEXT components to 0 and set the width to AUTO.
2. Set the height of the TEXT component to 20.
3. Set the top margin so that all the TEXT components are beneath each other, and set the bottom margin to AUTO.
4. Name the first TEXT component TXT_RESULT and the other TEXT components TEXT_HISTORY1 through TEXT_HISTORY6.
5. Drag another GRID LAYOUT component into the bottom cell.
6. Set all the margins to 0 and the width and height to AUTO.
7. Set the number of rows to 5 and the number of columns to 4.
8. Drag a BUTTON component to the bottom-left cell of this second GRID LAYOUT component. Name this BUTTON component BUTTON_ZERO. Set the text of this BUTTON component to 0. Set all the margins to 5 and set the width and height to AUTO.

9. Copy this BUTTON component to the other cells.

10. Change all the names and texts of the other BUTTON components so that they reflect the number or function they perform.

11. Drag a RADIO BUTTON GROUP component to the left of the main GRID LAYOUT component. Set the items of the RADIO BUTTON GROUP as shown in Figure 8.32.

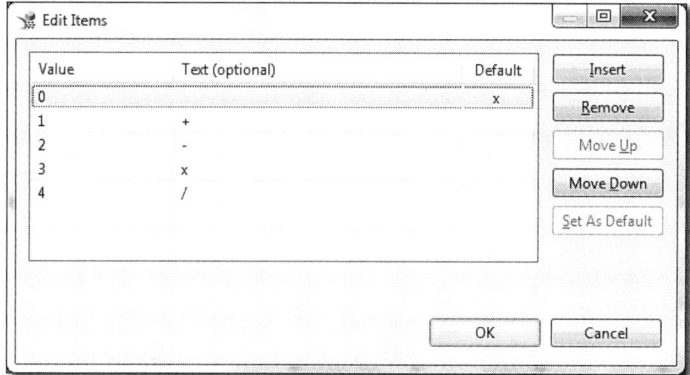

Figure 8.32 Items of the Radio Button Group Component

You have now set up the layout of the calculator. You can enhance the look of the calculator with CSS if you wish. Run the application locally, review the layout, and adjust it to ensure that every component is visible.

8.7.2 Adding the Interactivity

Set up global variables

Before we start building the script itself, we must first set up the global variables. For now we'll just put them in. When we explain the steps to build the script, we will explain how and why the variables are used. Insert the global variables as shown in Figure 8.33.

We will start with the script that runs when the user clicks on one of the number buttons. When you type a number for a new calculation, the result box should be wiped clean and the number should replace the previous content. Otherwise, the new number should be added to the right of the result box.

Name	Type	Default Value	URL Parameter
GV_Operator1	Float	0.0	false
GV_OperatorNumb...	Integer	1	false
GV_Digit	Boolean	false	false
GV_Result	Float	0.0	false
GV_Operator2	Float	0.0	false
GV_Operator	Integer	0	false
GV_CurrentOperator	String	0	false
GV_OperatorReset	Boolean	true	false

Figure 8.33 Global Variables for the Calculator Application

For this script, we will use two global variables. GV_OperatorReset is checked if it is the start of a new number; GV_CurrentOperator holds the value of the number that the user is creating.

```
if (GV_OperatorReset) {
    GV_CurrentOperator = "5";
}
else
{
    GV_CurrentOperator = GV_CurrentOperator + "5";
}
TXT_RESULT.setText(GV_CurrentOperator);
GV_OperatorReset = false;
```

If GV_OperatorReset is True, this means the user is starting a new number. In that case, the value of GV_CurrentOperator is set to the number. If the user already added numbers, the new number is added to the right of the variable GV_CurrentOperator.

The TEXT component will show the current value of GV_CurrentOperator, and the GV_OperatorReset variable will be set to False, indicating for future numbers that there is already a number in GV_OperatorReset.

For the digit sign, we need to check if there is already a digit added. We also have to see if a number is present. Therefore, this code is a little different from the code we used for the numbers. To check for the presence of a digit, we use the global variable GV_Digit. Note that the check in the beginning and the edit in the end is more or less the same as the functionality of GV_OperatorReset.

```
if (GV_Digit) {}
else {
if (GV_OperatorReset) {
    GV_CurrentOperator = "0.";
}
else
{
    GV_CurrentOperator = GV_CurrentOperator + ".";
}
TXT_RESULT.setText(GV_CurrentOperator);
GV_OperatorReset = false;
GV_Digit = true;
}
```

Now let's discuss the main steps involved in adding interactivity to the application.

Starting the Calculation

For the calculation, we use an extra TEXT component for the sole purpose of holding a script that can be used by the +, the −, the ÷, and the × buttons. Name that new component SET_OPERATORS.

Remove
duplication

The BUTTON components only tell the script in the extra TEXT component that they have been clicked. After running the extra script, they set the variable GV_Operator to indicate which calculation is about to take place. This way of coding removes a lot of duplication.

Let's first look at the code in the + button.

```
SET_OPERATORS.onClick();
GV_Operator = 1;
GROUP_OPERATOR.setSelectedValue("1");
```

First we ask the other script to handle the previous formula. Then we set the global variable to 1, indicating that the user now wants to do an addition formula. Finally, we set the RADIO BUTTON GROUP component to + so the user can see what he clicked.

It is possible that the user has already started a formula and this is the second operator. For example, let's say the user already typed "5+4" before again clicking the + button. If this is the case, then the calculator should respond by first calculating 5+4 and then set up the start of the new formula, which consists of the result 9 and the + that the user clicked.

```
if (GV_OperatorNumber == 1) {

    GV_Operator1 = Convert.stringToFloat(GV_CurrentOperator);
    GV_OperatorNumber = 2;
}
else
{
    GV_Operator2 = Convert.stringToFloat(GV_CurrentOperator);
    CALCULATE_RESULT.onClick();
}
GV_OperatorReset = true;
GV_Digit = false;
```

If the formula is still incomplete—for example, it is 4+, and no second number has been entered—then we do not need to calculate. The variable `GV_Operatornumber` is responsible for monitoring the status of the formula in this respect; when the formula is incomplete, the variable will have the value 1 (as you can see in the `IF` statement of the listing above). In this case, no calculation occurs.

In the next part of the code, we raise the value of the variable to 2 because we can do a calculation as soon as we have enough information; for example, if the formula is 4+5+, we want to first calculate the 4+5 part. Setting the `GV_Operatornumber` variable to 2 signals that the formula can be calculated.

If a formula is already set, then we need to calculate the result, put the result in the result TEXT component, and set the history text.

The global variables `GV_OperatorReset` and `GV_digit` are reset to ensure that the user can enter a new number. The calculation itself and updating the history is handled by other components that we will discuss later.

Setting Up the CE and C Buttons

The CE and C buttons perform different functions. The CE button only removes the current number of the formula (clear entry). The C button removes the entire formula and lets the user start with a clean slate.

To build this, the CE script and the C script are a little different. To build the CE function, we only need to remove the current number. The script for this looks like this:

```
GV_CurrentOperator = "0";
TXT_RESULT.setText(GV_CurrentOperator);
GV_OperatorReset = true;
GV_Digit = false;
```

The variables that we have seen in the number and the digit numbers are reset to their original state. The text in the result component is set to 0. If there already was a number and operator before this number, it will remain in place, as there is no script to remove it from the variables.

The C function also looks at an earlier entered number and operator. It resets anything to ensure a clean slate. The RADIO BUTTON GROUP component is also reset, as there is no current operator anymore. The set history function is addressed to input an empty line. That way the user can see that he made a new start.

```
GV_Operator1 = 0.0;
GV_Operator2 = 0.0;
GV_OperatorNumber = 1;
GV_OperatorReset = true;
GV_Digit = false;
GV_Operator = 0;
GROUP_OPERATOR.setSelectedValue("0");
TXT_RESULT.setText("0");
SET_HISTORY.onClick();
```

The last button we will look at is the equals button. This button will show a result like the operator buttons, but then wipe the slate clean so that the user can restart creating formulas. As the C button already performs the clean slate function, we will not retype that script but simply ask the C button to perform its task after we have calculated the result.

```
if (GV_OperatorNumber == 2) {
    GV_Operator2 = Convert.stringToFloat(GV_CurrentOperator);
    CALCULATE_RESULT.onClick();
}
else {
```

```
TEXT_HISTORY1.setText(Convert.floatToStringUsingLocale(GV_
Operator1));
}
BUTTON_C.onClick();
```

First we check to see if there is a formula to calculate. If there isn't a formula to calculate, we simply do not do anything and show the number the user typed in the history. Finally, we use the C button to clear all the variables.

Doing the Calculation and Setting the History

Finally, we will look at performing the calculation. If the calculation handler is called, then the global variables GV_Operator1, GV_Operator2, and GV_Operator have a value. Based on the value of GV_Operator we add, subtract, divide, or multiply. We store the result of the calculation in the global variable GV_Result.

When the calculation is done, we call the SET_HISTORY handler. This handler will move all the previous history one line down to make room for the new result. Then we use all the variables to write the formula plus the result to the top line of the history TEXT components and the result itself into the main result box.

SET_HISTORY handler

Finally, we set up GV_operator2 and GV_Operator1 so the user can continue calculating using the result he just got back from the calculator.

The CALCULATE_RESULT component has the following code:

```
if (GV_Operator == 1){

GV_Result = GV_Operator1 + GV_Operator2;
}
if (GV_Operator == 2){

GV_Result = GV_Operator1 - GV_Operator2;
}
if (GV_Operator == 3){

GV_Result = GV_Operator1 * GV_Operator2;
}
```

```
if (GV_Operator == 4){

GV_Result = GV_Operator1 / GV_Operator2;
}


SET_HISTORY.onClick();
TEXT_HISTORY1.setText(GV_Operator1 + " " + GROUP_
OPERATOR.getSelectedText() + " " + GV_Operator2 + " = " + GV_
Result);
TXT_RESULT.setText(Convert.floatToStringUsingLocale(GV_
Result,2));

GV_Operator2 = 0.0;
GV_Operator1 = GV_Result;
```

The SET_HISTORY handler script is a set of lines where each Text compo-nent text is set to the previous text of its predecessor.

```
TEXT_HISTORY6.setText(TEXT_HISTORY5.getText());
TEXT_HISTORY5.setText(TEXT_HISTORY4.getText());
TEXT_HISTORY4.setText(TEXT_HISTORY3.getText());
TEXT_HISTORY3.setText(TEXT_HISTORY2.getText());
TEXT_HISTORY2.setText(TEXT_HISTORY1.getText());
TEXT_HISTORY1.setText("");
```

This is the setup of the calculator. Even if there are parts that are pretty complicated, there are a couple of things you can take away from this example:

▶ You can do a lot of calculation in Design Studio. If you can build a cal-culator, there are a lot of other possibilities.

▶ Calling event handlers can save you from doing a lot of duplicate scripting.

▶ You can use global variables for checking a status in the application with an IF statement. This way, you can apply lots of logic in the application.

8.8 Summary

In this chapter we looked at several ways to add interactivity to a Design Studio application. In the first half of the chapter, we described the basic information you need in order to script: information about the language syntax, how to use tools like the Script Editor and the New Statement Wizard, and methods. In the second half of the chapter, we walked you through some examples of adding interactivity to Design Studio applications; most notably, we talked about the complex process of building a calculator. After reading this chapter, you should be well on your way to creating interactive Design Studio applications.

In this chapter we will provide you with a number of guidelines to help you build applications with Design Studio.

9 Design Principles and Visualization Options

Building an application using Design Studio is about more than knowing how all the pieces and parts work—it's also about understanding how to put them together in a way that will make sense to users. In this chapter, we'll walk you through some basic design principles to guide you in this process. We'll then describe all the possible visualization options that Design Studio provides, and offer some hints about when which option might be the right visualization method.

9.1 General Design Principles

When building an application, it is very important to remember that you are building it for users. In this section, we will describe some principles that will help you to build an application that has a greater chance of actually being used. Some of these may seem intuitive, but you'd be surprised how often basic, intuitive principles are violated at design time.

9.1.1 Don't Make Users Think

An application should be as obvious and self-explanatory as possible. It is your job as a developer to limit the number of question marks for the user, and make the application navigation as intuitive as possible. If this isn't accomplished, users will not understand how to use the application to find the information they are looking for. Eventually, they will stop looking.

Limit question marks

For example, if a manager asks for a report so he can see how every region performed the day before, you can show him all kinds of comparisons. In the first example in Figure 9.1, we see a table with comparisons to the budget in the month, cumulative year values, last year values, etc. In the second example, shown in the same figure, we see only a percentage. The second one is much easier to grasp because it doesn't require much thinking. Now imagine that this report was about 50 stores instead of just four regions—this has the potential to make a huge difference in user comprehension.

	ACT	BUD	Delta	LYR	Cum	cum Bud	Cum Lyr	Delta
Region A	100	103	-3	101	402	421	413	-19
Region B	96	99	-3	97	391	393	385	-2
Region C	92	94	-2	92	389	430	421	-41
Region D	107	103	4	101	374	371	364	3
Region A	-3%							
Region B	-3%							
Region C	-2%							
Region D	4%							

Figure 9.1 Don't Make Users Think

9.1.2 Don't Make Users Wait

Application performance

When you build an application, always keep performance in mind. How long do users have to wait at the start? How long does it take when they go to page 3 of the PAGEBOOK component? When an application contains many data sources, think of a scenario where some basic information is already visible at startup and the rest will be loaded when needed. Then the user has some instant gratification, as he already sees some results.

It has been found that if a website takes longer than seven seconds to show anything, half the users give up. Another seven seconds and the remaining half gives up too.

9.1.3 Manage User Focus

Use edges, patterns, and motions cautiously

The human eye immediately recognizes edges, patterns, and motions. Think of how often you have reacted to movement you saw out of the corner of your eye. Use those elements for the most important information, and avoid using them for the rest.

In this example, we again show the table with the sales of our four regions. In the bottom table, we highlighted one number that we think is the most important (Figure 9.2). Note that finding this number on the top table is much more difficult.

	ACT	BUD	Delta	LYR	Cum	cum Bud	Cum Lyr	Delta
Region A	100	103	-3	101	402	421	413	-19
Region B	96	99	-3	97	391	393	385	-2
Region C	92	94	-2	92	389	430	421	-41
Region D	107	103	4	101	374	371	364	3

	ACT	BUD	Delta	LYR	Cum	cum Bud	Cum Lyr	Delta
Region A	100	103	-3	101	402	421	413	-19
Region B	96	99	-3	97	391	393	385	-2
Region C	92	94	-2	92	389	430	421	**-41**
Region D	107	103	4	101	374	371	364	3

Figure 9.2 Focus the Eye

9.1.4   Emphasize the Features

Another key principle is to clearly emphasize the important features in your application. Design a clear structure and create buttons that are obvious for the user. At first glance, the user should immediately know where he can click. Letting the user know what is available is one of the fundamental principles of design.

Make buttons obvious

In the example in Figure 9.3, there are three buttons with the same function. The left one is the most obvious. The right one, on the other hand, would give you pause, because it doesn't look like a button.

Figure 9.3 Emphasize Features

9.1.5   Keep It Simple

Users go to an application to get information or perform a particular task. They might be amused by the first look at a fancy design, but in the end they want to get their information or perform their task as easily as possible.

More isn't always better

As you saw in Figure 9.1, the second example was much easier to grasp. One of the reasons for this is that the second table is much simpler and is dedicated to the question "How did we do?" Sometimes, more isn't always better.

9.1.6 Use Conventions

Tradition has its place

Although it is fun to think of new ways to show information, often the basic conventions are the best choice. Users are used to these conventions and therefore do not need much time to get started with a new application. Only deviate from conventions when you have a clear reason why you think that the new option will be an improvement over the convention.

As we saw in Figure 9.3, the left button is the easiest to recognize. This button is easier to grasp than the second one because we are used to this kind of button. Over the years we've clicked thousands of buttons like this. Now when we see a visualization like that, we immediately assume it's a button, without even looking at the text on it.

9.1.7 Get the Most out of the Room on the Screen

Control your screen

The most challenging aspect of application design in this mobile age is that you have to put a lot of information, often very different in theme, into a small amount of real estate: the computer screen, iPad screen, or even the iPhone screen. Inserting all this information mustn't jeopardize the clarity of the application.

The following principles can be applied:

▶ Summarize the information and show the exceptions.

▶ Try to avoid elements that do not present data.

▶ If you cannot avoid nondata elements, try to make them blend in as much as possible.

▶ Highlight the most important information, as it needs to be seen first.

▶ Keep the most important part of the screen for the most important information. The top left and middle are the most important parts.

To help you to do more with less, let's briefly discuss the *data-to-pixel ratio*. The data-to-pixel ratio is derived from the data-ink ratio, which was introduced by Edward R. Tufte. When information is displayed on the screen, some of the pixels show the data, and the other pixels show visual elements that don't represent data. To build a lean dashboard that uses the screen well and avoids overloading the user with a lot of elements, you should try to maximize the ratio. This creates room to put more information in the same amount of space without overwhelming the user with all kinds of signals. In the example in Figure 9.4, we see two tables that show the exact same information. However, notice how the second table provides a lot less distraction.

2013 Year to date

Product Line	Sales	Leads
Product A	39.780,00	424,00
Product B	55.029,00	1.140,00
Product C	27.684,00	1.872,00
Product D	5.258,00	1.229,00
Total	127.751,00	4.665,00

2013 Year to date (1000 $)

Product Line	Sales	Leads
Product A	40	424
Product B	55	1.140
Product C	28	1.872
Product D	5	1.229
Total	128	4.665

Figure 9.4 Tables Redesigned with the Data-to-Pixel Ratio in Mind

The advantage of reducing the number of elements is that you don't have to shout if you want to highlight a particular number. Just emphasizing it slightly is enough, as you can see in Figure 9.5.

Sales per product in ($ 1000)

Product	2008	2009	2010	2011	2012	Total
Product 1	66	64	95	91	43	359
Product 2	18	88	91	77	51	325
Product 3	60	63	73	35	97	328
Product 4	10	36	67	8	51	172
Product 5	30	25	53	36	27	171
Product 6	33	86	89	78	89	375
Product 7	65	44	32	39	27	207
Product 8	93	63	20	24	24	224
Product 9	86	73	84	**22**	81	346
Product 10	62	81	26	93	89	357
Product 11	8	71	80	73	89	321
Product 12	11	16	44	5	65	141
Product 13	72	95	39	14	99	319
Product 14	5	19	37	50	56	167
Product 15	72	17	9	62	76	236
Product 16	26	32	33	17	39	147
Total	717	873	872	730	1.003	4.195

Figure 9.5 Emphasize the Data

Design Studio has a lot of visualization options, which we'll introduce you to next. When choosing your method, make sure to keep the above principles in mind!

9.2 Choosing a Visualization Method

When choosing from among the visualization methods that Design Studio has to offer, it's essential to think about how the user wants to look at the data. Remember to always start by asking yourself these questions:

▶ What is important? Especially, which dimensions and key figures are important?

▶ What is the message that I need to communicate? Do you want to know the trend? The exception? Do you want to compare numbers?

▶ What options do I have in Design Studio to present the data?

▶ Which of the options is best to present the data?

Know your choices In this section we are going to discuss the visualization options in Design Studio.

9.2.1 Single Number

A single number (Figure 9.6) is a very effective way to present data. If the most important metric of the organization is sales, for example, then just one number can convey a lot of information. Single number visualizations are especially useful when you design for mobile devices.

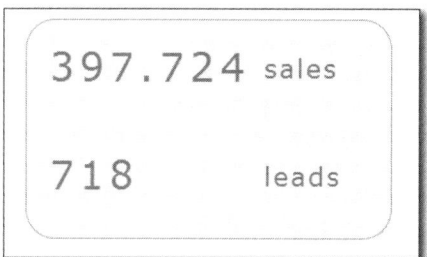

Figure 9.6 Single Number Visualization

For example, if users want to know yesterday's sales, making an application that shows the total number, and perhaps the deviation from target, would be of great benefit.

The disadvantage of a single number visualization is that you do not see any trends. You can add a color to show if a number is good or bad, but you can't give any additional information.

9.2.2 Line Chart

A line chart (Figure 9.7) is a chart where a line flows from left to right. It usually involves time, which is plotted along the x-axis. Because of its format, a line chart is very useful to show trends in data. If you want to emphasize the comparison between values more, then you should think about a column or bar chart instead of a line chart.

Trends in data

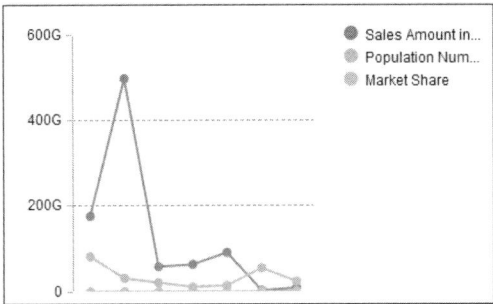

Figure 9.7 Line Chart

There is one variation on a line chart, which we discuss next.

Horizontal Line Chart

A horizontal line chart (Figure 9.8) is similar to a line chart, but instead of showing the data from left to right, this chart goes from top to bottom. If you have a specific need to display labels horizontally, this chart may be useful—but in general, we do not recommend it. It is easier to read trends going from left to right, so the traditional line chart is usually best. (And again, if you want to compare values, we recommend the bar chart.)

Data shown from top to bottom

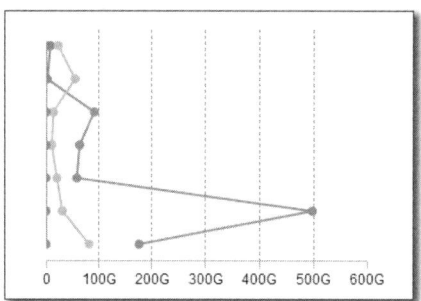

Figure 9.8 Horizontal Line Chart

9.2.3 Bar Chart

Compare values of
multiple entities

A bar chart (Figure 9.9) compares the values of several entities with each other across dimension values that are set below each other. As you can see in the example, it is very easy to see which region has the highest values. An advantage of the bar chart over the column chart is that the labels are horizontal, which makes them easier to read. A bar chart is for comparing values. For trends or exact numbers you are better off using a line graph or crosstab.

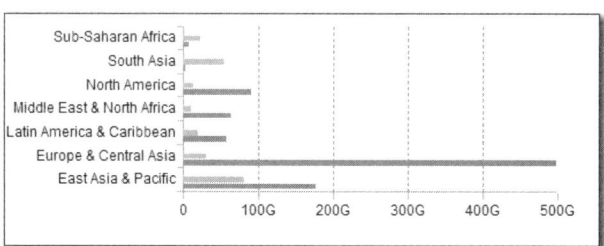

Figure 9.9 Bar Chart

There are several variations on bar charts.

Stacked Bar Chart

Part-to-whole
relationship of
underlying entities

A stacked bar chart (Figure 9.10) is a bar chart where the bar itself is divided into colors based in the part-to-whole relationship of the underlying entities. The chart shows the part-to-whole relationship in the bar, and the bars themselves can be compared to each other. If you have only

334

one bar, a standard bar chart with a bar for each entity is more useful. A stacked bar chart can be used when you have multiple whole values (for example, sales per month) and the whole is divided by region.

Keep in mind, though, that comparing the colored parts across bars is difficult, as the starting points are dependent on values of the entities. For example, suppose you have more than one bar, each divided into five parts. The first part of bar 1 has a value of 10, and the first part of bar 2 is 15. Now, suppose the second part of bar 1 is 8, and the second part of bar 2 is 10. Seeing that the first part of bar 2 is smaller is difficult, because that part of the bar starts at 10 and goes to 18—compared to the second, which goes from 15 to 25. The bottom line is, if you want to compare something easily, you want to have the same base—so you just have to look which bar is the longest.

This type of chart is most useful when you want to compare a value across entities and also want to see something of the part-to-whole relationship with that entity. This chart does not show trends, outliers, or exact values well.

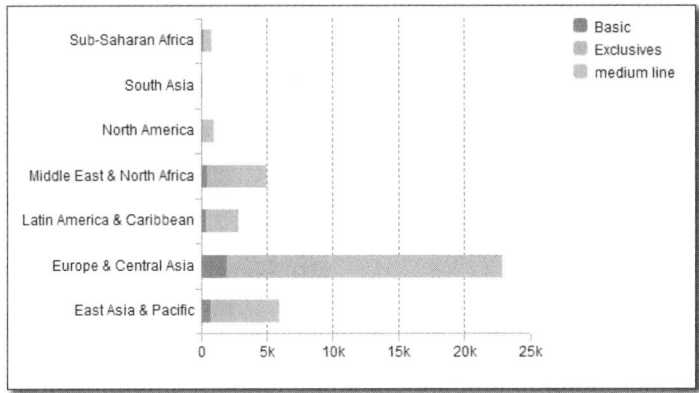

Figure 9.10 Stacked Bar Chart

100% Stacked Bar Chart

A 100% stacked bar chart (Figure 9.11) is a stack of horizontal bars where you show the part-to-whole data. This visualization allows you to show part-to-whole relations across a dimension. The disadvantage is

Part-to-whole data

that you cannot compare the dimension itself, as everything is added to 100%. An alternative that paints a part-to-whole relation more clearly is the bar or column chart, as it is easier to make comparisons with them.

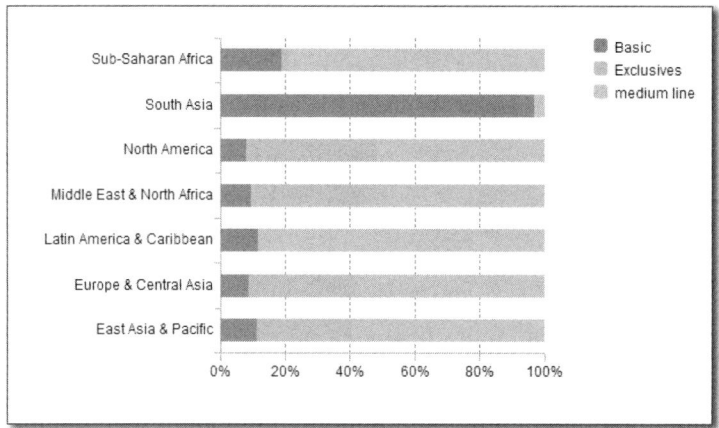

Figure 9.11 100% Stacked Bar Chart

Bar Combination Chart

Two key figures across a dimension

A bar combination chart (Figure 9.12) is a bar chart with a vertical line chart added, allowing you to show two key figures across the dimensions. A bar combination chart is useful for comparing data, like the bar chart, but you can also show a trend, as you also have a line graph at your disposal. For example, if you want to show the profitability per region and want to show the cumulative value as well, a combination chart would be very useful.

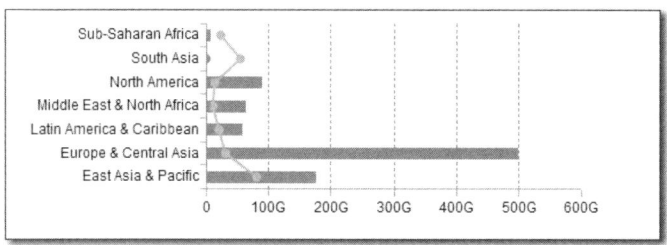

Figure 9.12 Bar Combination Chart

9.2.4 Column Chart

A column chart (Figure 9.13) is a chart that shows columns from left to right, where the height of the column conveys the value for a particular entity. A column chart is used for comparing entities with each other. The size of the bars allows you to compare the values in the chart to each other.

Compare values

We like the bar chart a bit more than the column chart, because the column chart makes it more difficult to place labels—they go beneath the x-axis. A column chart is best suited for comparing values, while it is less useful for showing trends or exact values.

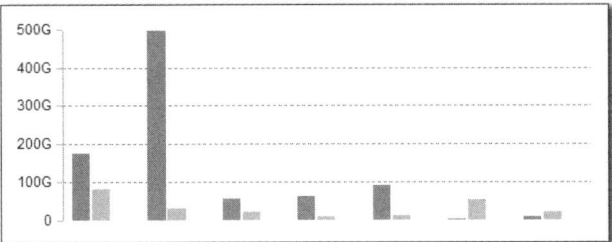

Figure 9.13 Column Chart

As with the line and bar charts, there are several variations of column charts.

Stacked Column Chart

The stacked column chart (Figure 9.14) has the same advantages and disadvantages as the stacked bar chart, but the labels are in vertical alignment.

Vertical alignment

100% Stacked Column Chart

The 100% stacked column chart (Figure 9.15) does the same thing as the 100% stacked bar chart, but it has vertical columns instead of bars. Again, for comparisons of part-to-whole, you're better off with standard bar or column charts.

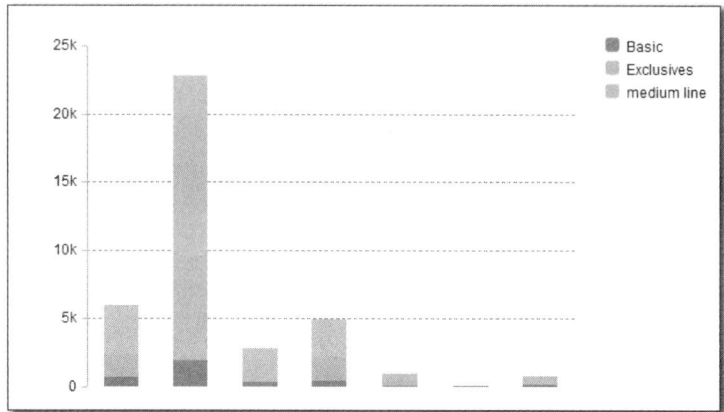

Figure 9.14 Stacked Column Chart

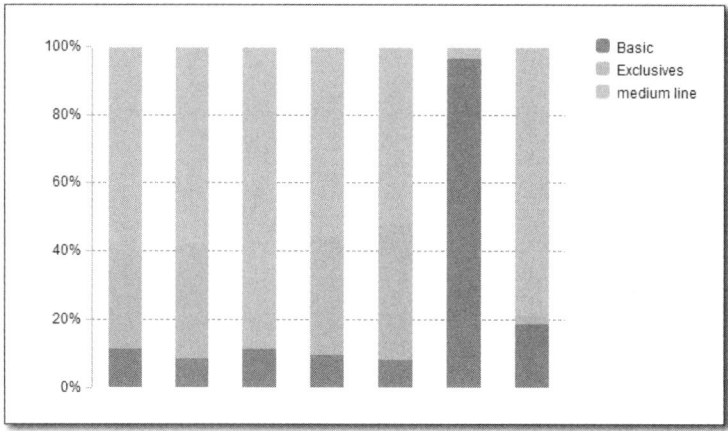

Figure 9.15 100% Stacked Column Chart

Column Combination Chart

Column and line chart

A column combination chart (Figure 9.16) is like a column chart, but with a line chart added so that you can show a second value across the dimension. The column combination chart is best used when data needs to be compared and you also want to show the aggregated part-to-whole relationship. This type of chart is less suitable for exact values and for trend analysis.

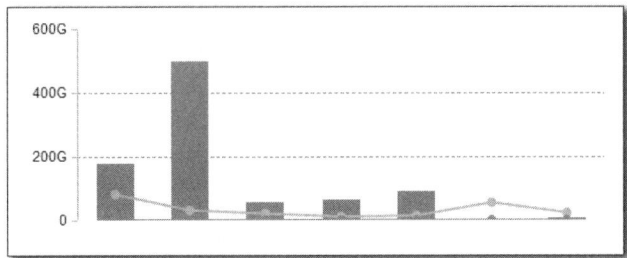

Figure 9.16 Column Combination Chart

9.2.5 Area Chart

An area chart (Figure 9.17) emphasizes trends of data, and allows you to compare the trends of several entities with each other. This visualization type is good for when you need a little bit of both. If you want to emphasize the comparison more, a bar or column chart would be better; for the trend, a line chart would be preferable.

Data trends

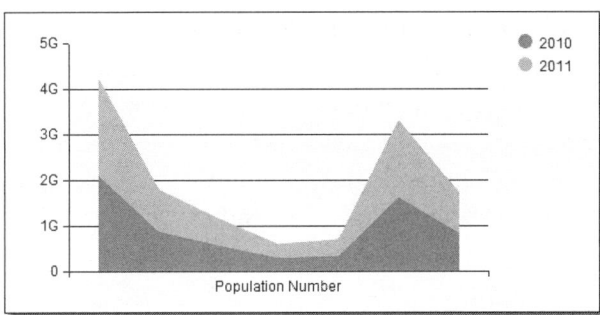

Figure 9.17 Area Chart

There is also one variation of the area chart.

Horizontal Area Chart

A horizontal area chart (Figure 9.18) is a horizontal chart that goes from top to bottom. As with the area chart, it does a bit of comparing and a bit of trending. It does not show exact values.

Does not show exact values

We find horizontal area charts to be a bit less effective than standard area charts, as the trending function is hampered by the fact that you

have to read from top to bottom instead of left to right. As it is quite difficult to compare data using this type of chart, you might want to consider a bar combination chart instead.

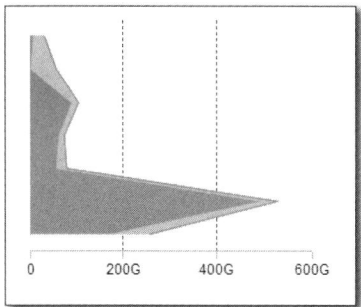

Figure 9.18 Horizontal Area Chart

9.2.6 Crosstab

Look up exact
information

You may recall from our earlier chapters that we often use CROSSTAB
components. A crosstab (Figure 9.19) is a table in which numbers are
presented along rows and columns, which is very useful for displaying
exact information. You can show a lot of data in an efficient way. However, crosstabs are not very useful for identifying trends and other relations between data points. You can highlight outliers by changing the
layout of numbers that are outside of the main trend, but you can't show
how much or *how* good or bad something is.

	Population Number					
	East Asia & Pacific	Europe & Central Asia	Latin America & Caribbean	Middle East & North Africa	North America	South
2000	1,954,678,732.997	861,935,842.630	520,009,692.956	312,830,331.998	312,994,211.000	1,372
2001	1,971,771,540.994	863,464,346.869	527,379,476.040	318,983,494.999	316,113,355.000	1,422
2002	1,988,477,194.997	865,201,391.289	534,600,087.894	325,303,921.999	319,049,993.000	1,446
2003	2,004,430,073.996	867,640,508.691	541,579,345.562	305,545,052.998	321,846,933.000	1,470
2004	2,019,837,879.995	870,316,328.197	548,539,056.997	338,511,776.998	324,863,598.000	1,493
2005	2,034,929,589.997	873,142,178.995	555,383,465.997	345,462,925.998	327,892,199.000	1,517
2006	2,049,659,461.997	876,003,588.996	562,109,274.997	349,321,956.000	331,019,786.000	1,540
2007	2,063,871,996.998	879,407,834.999	568,714,764.998	356,756,318.000	334,222,724.000	1,563
2008	2,077,993,903.999	883,019,381.998	575,242,559.998	364,317,471.999	337,475,828.000	1,586
2009	2,091,610,537.996	886,737,679.998	570,473,965.000	371,868,126.999	340,562,844.000	1,609
2010	2,104,989,546.998	890,744,686.998	576,974,905.999	297,964,006.000	343,540,473.000	1,632
2011	2,118,903,347.998	894,733,567.998	579,782,114.999	281,903,605.000	346,075,892.000	1,656

Figure 9.19 Crosstab Visualization

9.2.7 Bubble Chart

A bubble chart (Figure 9.20) is a chart that shows data in three dimen- **Data in three** sions. You use three values: one shown on the x-axis, one shown on the **dimensions** y-axis, and one shown via the size of the bubble. A well-known example of this is the Boston Consultancy Matrix, where market share and market growth are on the axes, and there are four quadrants for the product life cycle. The size of the bubble is the relative amount of sales.

This type of chart is built for comparison. The position of each bubble allows you to compare the values to each other. The sizes of the bubbles can also be used for comparison, but this is a less exact way of comparing, since you can only tell if a bubble is large or not. You cannot show exact numbers or trends with this chart.

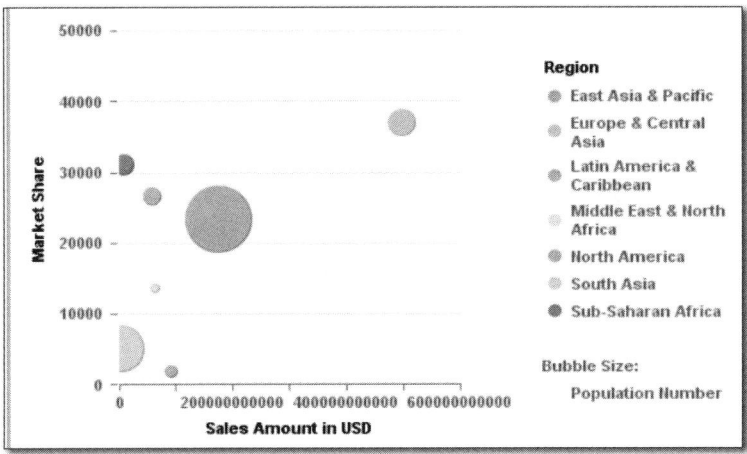

Figure 9.20 Bubble Chart

9.2.8 Waterfall Chart

A waterfall chart (Figure 9.21) emphasizes the cumulative addition to **Present negative** the end result with positive and negative values. A stacked bar chart **values** would have difficulties presenting the negative values, so that is where the waterfall chart comes in handy. If you want to emphasize the comparison between values, a standard bar chart is a better choice.

There are several variations on the standard waterfall chart.

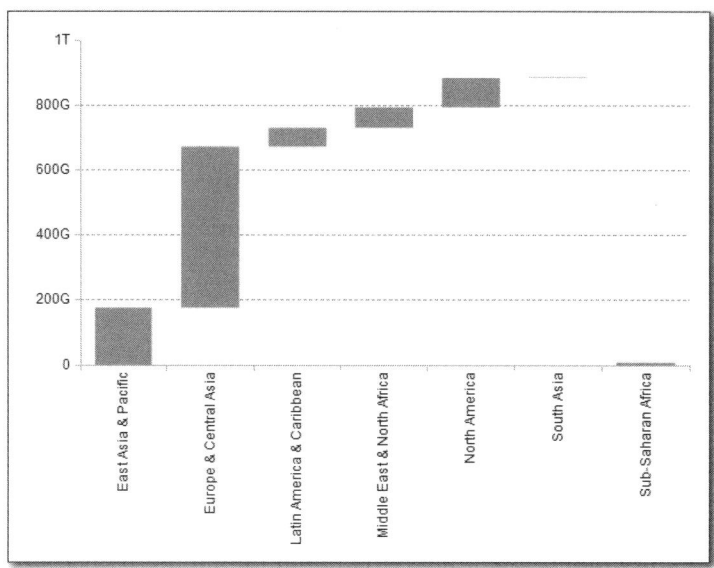

Figure 9.21 Waterfall Chart

Horizontal Waterfall Chart

Cumulative data

A horizontal waterfall chart (Figure 9.22) shows data in a cumulative way, where the starting point of one bar is based on the end point of the previous bar. The endpoint of the final bar is the cumulative result over all the entities. This helps you to see every entity's part of the whole value.

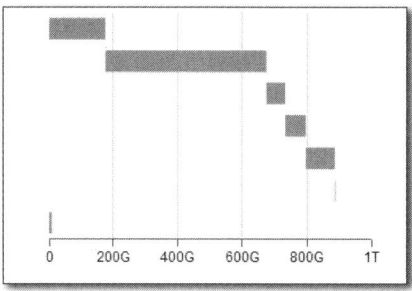

Figure 9.22 Horizontal Waterfall Chart

The advantage of a waterfall chart over a stacked bar chart is that here you are able to see negative values clearly. This is why this chart is often used to show budget over- and under-runs across departments. To make comparisons across entities easier, the entities are often sorted by their value, so the order of entities enables you to compare the contribution of each entity to the whole. This chart is best used when you want to compare results that contain negative values; otherwise, a bar chart will do the job. This chart is not suitable for showing trends or exact values.

Stacked Waterfall Chart

A stacked waterfall chart (Figure 9.23) can put multiple values in each part of the waterfall chart. This makes creating more advanced versions of a waterfall possible. However, these charts are a bit harder to understand—the user has to really concentrate on the chart before he can make sense of all the values, especially when one part of a bar is positive and one is negative.

Enables multiple values

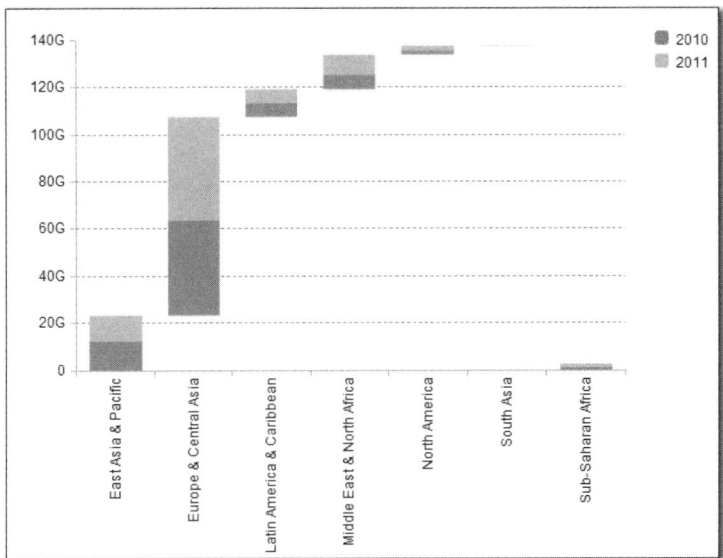

Figure 9.23 Stacked Waterfall Chart

9.2.9 Pie Chart

A pie chart (Figure 9.24) is a chart where values are shown as slices of a circle. A pie chart's strength in that it shows the part-to-whole relation

Not good for trends or exact values

in an easy to understand way. However, as the number of slices grows, it is more difficult to see which entity holds what part—so comparing values gets more difficult. Trends and exact values do not work with this chart.

We generally recommend bar or column charts over pie charts, but they may be effective when you only need to compare two or three values.

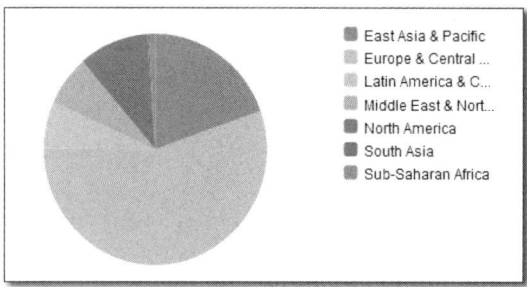

Figure 9.24 Pie Chart

Multiple Pie Chart

Not recommended

A multiple pie chart (Figure 9.25) shows the same pie chart for several key figures, which allows you to show the relative sizes of the entities. However, you could also place three identical bar charts next to each other to accomplish the same goal. The problems we already mentioned for a single pie chart are also valid for this type of chart. We do not recommend using this type of chart.

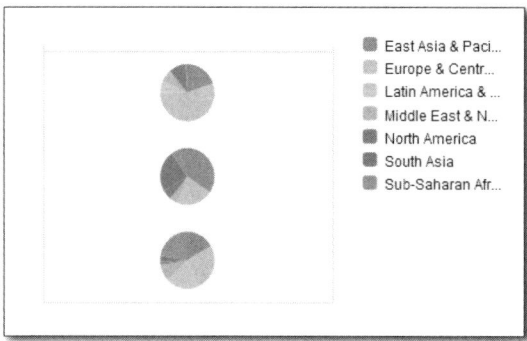

Figure 9.25 Multiple Pie Chart

9.2.10 Radar Chart

A radar chart (Figure 9.26) is basically a line chart in which the x-axis is a circle instead of a line. The result is a circle where a data point's distance from the center shows the value of the key figure. A radar chart can be useful for comparing the shape of properties for several entities in a multiple radar chart or when you want to show data that is naturally ordered in a circular way, like hours on a clock.

Compare shape of properties

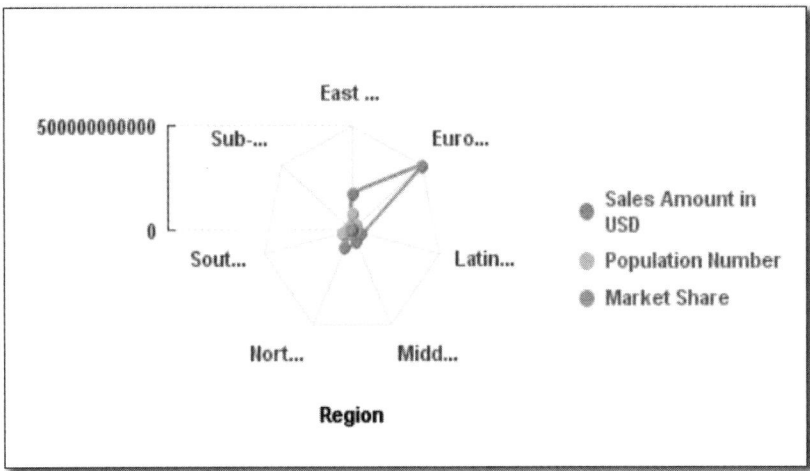

Figure 9.26 Radar Chart

The radar chart has one variation.

Multiple Radar Chart

A multiple radar chart (Figure 9.27) is a multiple version of the radar chart and is useful for comparing several entities with each other for a number of values. Compared to the multiple pie chart, this type of chart emphasizes the shape of the values more than actually comparing the values. This graph is useful when you want to give a rough impression of the properties but not an exact comparison.

Several entities, multiple values

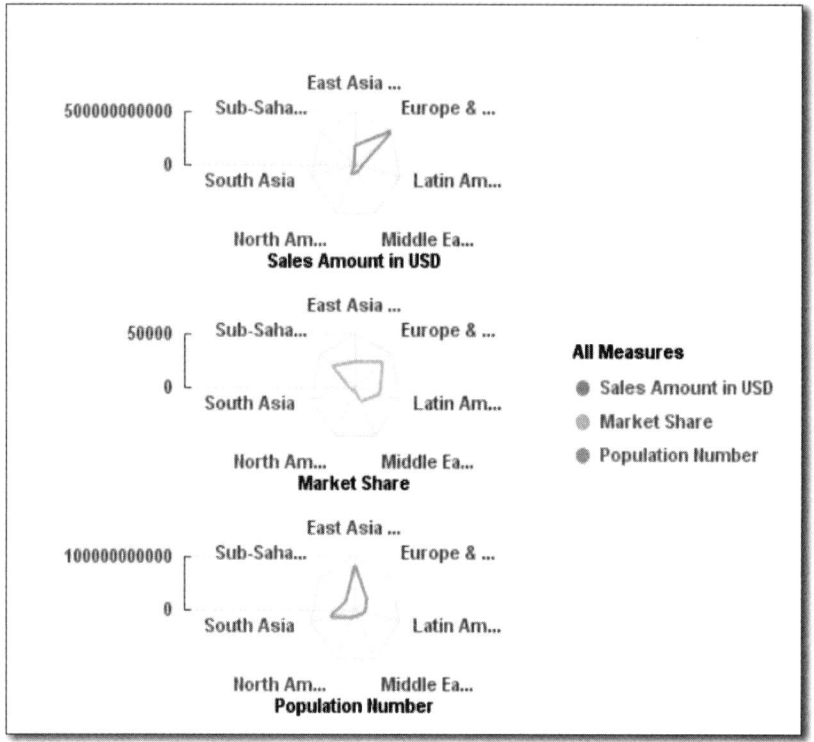

Figure 9.27 Multiple Radar Chart

9.2.11 Scatter Chart

Highlight outliers

A scatter chart (Figure 9.28) is used to show the relationship between two key figures. It is great at showing trends of a relationship as well as highlighting outliers—often you add trend lines to the scatter cloud to identify a trend that you can use for future predictions. Compared to the bubble chart, it lacks one dimension, but in return you get more clarity and you can plot much more data into the chart. This kind of chart is not suitable for showing part-to-whole relationships.

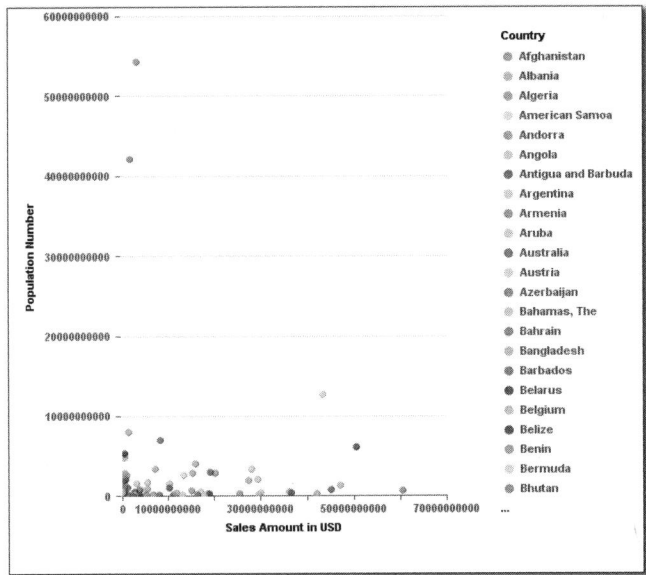

Figure 9.28 Scatter Chart

9.2.12 Chart Comparison

We've covered a lot of charts. For an overview of all the most common charts and their strengths and weaknesses, see Figure 9.29.

	Trend	Compare	Part-to-Whole	Outliers	Relationship	Exact
Number	--	--	--	--	--	++
Crosstab	--	-	-	+	-	++
100% Stacked	--	--	+	-	-	--
Bar/Column Chart	+	++	+	+	--	-
Bar/Column Combination	++	+	+	+	--	-
Bubble	--	+	--	++	+-	--
Line Chart	++	+-	-	+-	--	--
Area Chart	+	+-	-	+-	--	--
Pie Chart	--	+-	+-	+-	--	--
Radar Chart	+-	+-	+	+	--	--
Multiple Pie	--	+	+-	+-	--	--
Multiple Radar	+-	+	+	+	--	--
Scatter	+	+	--	++	++	--
Stacked Bar/Column	--	+	++	+	--	--
Waterfall Chart	--	+	++	+	--	--
Stacked Waterfall Chart	--	+	++	+	--	--

Figure 9.29 Chart Comparison

9.3   Summary

In this chapter, we gave you a crash course in design principles, and also walked you through the various visualization methods available in Design Studio. At this point, you're ready to start building more advanced applications. Read on!

In this chapter we'll take a look at the first of two examples that show you how to build an advanced application using Design Studio.

10 Building a DuPont Analysis Application

In this chapter we are going to use the techniques we described earlier to build a more advanced application with Design Studio: a DuPont analysis model. A DuPont analysis is an in-depth look at the return on equity of a company. Analysts are often not only interested in how profitable a company is compared to its peers, but also how the profit was attained. A company can reach a high return on equity in three ways:

▶ A high net profit margin

▶ Effective use of its assets (high turnover)

▶ High financial leverage (high percentage of loans)

The DuPont analysis breaks the results of a company's activities down into these three points. This shows analysts in which area companies are doing well or where they need to improve compared to their peers. If an analyst wants to compare two or more companies with roughly the same return on equity, this model can help him to make a more thorough analysis.

This chapter is divided into two main parts: an overview of the application and a detailed walk through the steps required to build it.

Three measures of equity

Downloads
The application and CSS files discussed in this chapter are also available for download from the book's website at *www.sap-press.com*.

10.1 Application Overview

Three ways to
input numbers
In the Design Studio application we see the DuPont model in the main screen. (Figure 10.1). At the start of the application the model is empty. The user can input numbers in three different ways.

- ▶ By manual input
- ▶ Using OLAP (online analytical processing) to access a query and insert a number from the query
- ▶ Using the model from an external URL by passing parameters

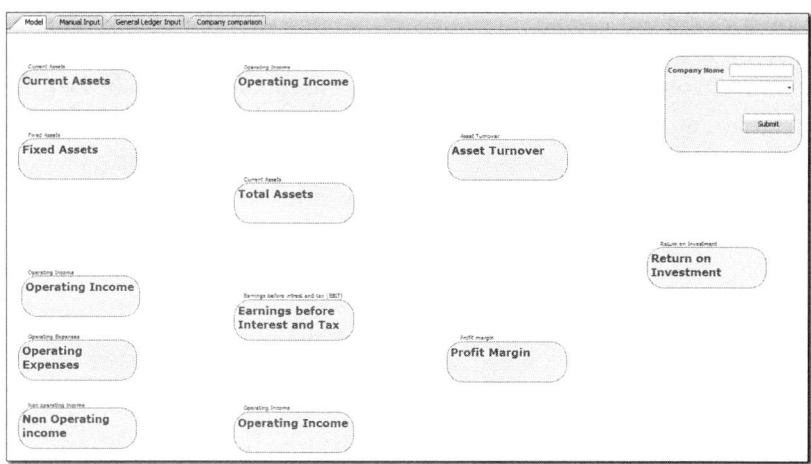

Figure 10.1 Main Screen of the DuPont Analysis Application

If no numbers have been input, the main screen will show the skeleton of the DuPont model. In this model you can see how the return on investment is built up from the combination of asset turnover and profit margin. Asset turnover is built up from operating income divided by the total assets, and profit margin is built up from the earnings before interest and tax, divided by the operating income.

Save the model
When the user has entered numbers into the model and is satisfied with the result, he can save the current model. For this purpose, there is a panel on the top right where he can input the company name and the industry name. When he clicks SUBMIT, he can review the score later in the comparison screen with other saved companies.

> **Note**
>
> To keep the scope of this application manageable, we will focus on the operational performance and thus leave out the financial leverage.

In this section, we'll walk you through the four main functionalities of the application: the three ways of inputting numbers and then the functionality to compare the results.

10.1.1 Inputting Numbers Manually

In the MANUAL INPUT screen, the user can manually input the numbers for all the parameters of the DuPont model (Figure 10.2). Additionally, if there are already numbers inputted by external parameters or OLAP, those numbers will be visible in this screen, and the user can change them manually.

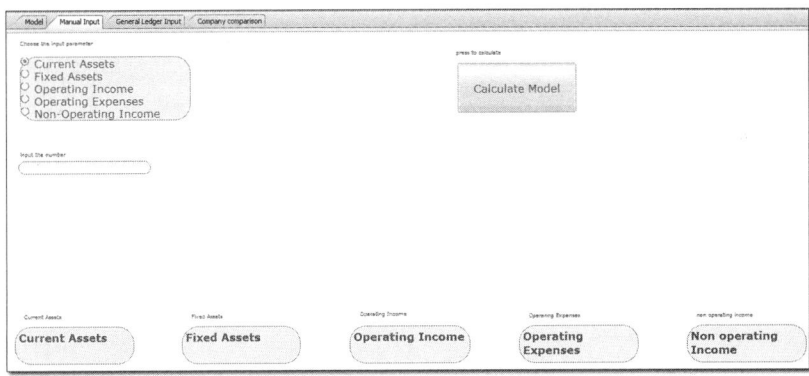

Figure 10.2 Manual Input Screen

On the top left, the user can select the parameter he wants to change manually. After selecting the parameter, he inputs a number in the text box below the parameter choice. After changing the numbers, he will see the inputted numbers appear below. When necessary, he can change the numbers.

In Figure 10.3, we have already entered a couple of numbers as an example. Note how these numbers are visible at the bottom of the screen.

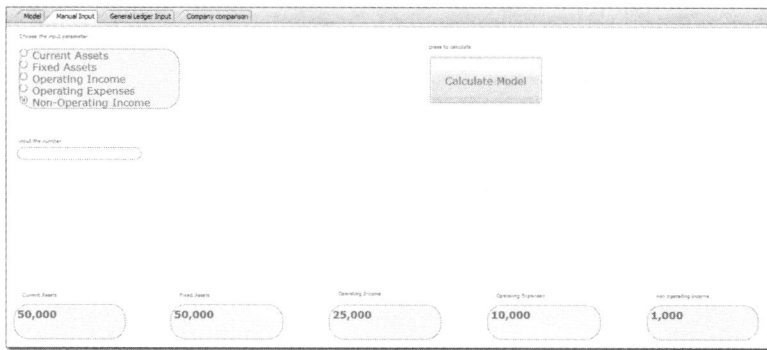

Figure 10.3 Numbers Entered Manually

When all the necessary numbers have been entered, the user can click the CALCULATE MODEL button, and the model will show the model input (Figure 10.4).

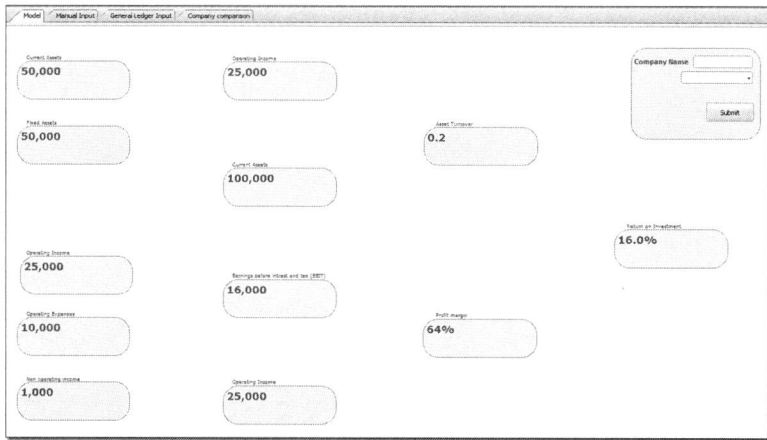

Figure 10.4 DuPont Model with Numbers Input

In this example (Figure 10.4), we see that the company has a return on equity of 16%. The company achieved this result by a high profit margin (64%) and a low turnover (0.2).

10.1.2 Inputting Numbers from an OLAP Connection

In the OLAP input screen, you can use any query or system that is connected to the SAP BusinessObjects BI platform to pick numbers that you want to use for the DuPont model. Instead of manual input here, you can select a query from any defined backend system, look at the data, and select numbers that you want to enter into the DuPont model.

When the user navigates to the GENERAL LEDGER INPUT tab, the first step is to select a backend system and a query that he wants to use for navigation (Figure 10.5).

Select backend system and query

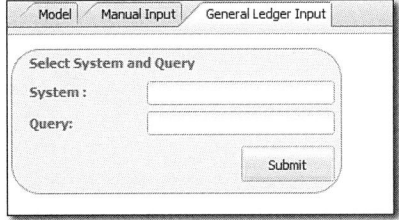

Figure 10.5 Input to Select System and Query

Once the query and system have been selected, the application connects with the selected query. Some new features become available in the screen to allow the user to place filters on the query (Figure 10.6).

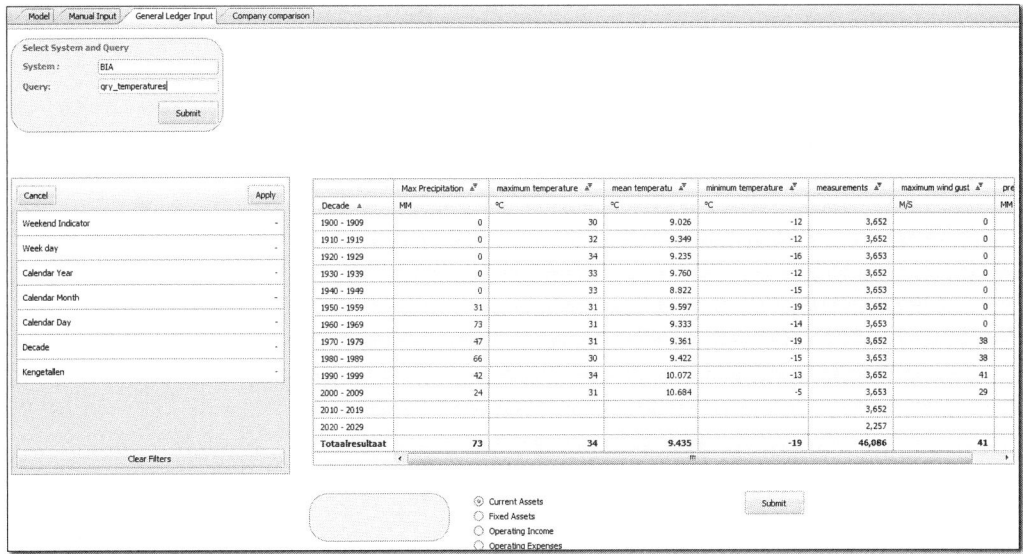

Figure 10.6 Navigate the Query

10.1.3 Calling Numbers from Outside the Application

Insert numbers from outside the application

The third and final way to insert numbers into the model is from outside of the application. When the application is called from somewhere else, numbers can be sent to the application, and they will subsequently be used to fill the model. This option allows web developers to use the DuPont model by calling the application by its URL and parameters. For example, a use case for this application could be to embed it in a website that collects information from financial websites. The application then works as a kind of add-on, where other applications or web pages can use the application to show information enriched in the form of a DuPont model.

10.1.4 Comparing the Results

Scatter chart

In the final tab, the user can use a scatter chart to compare the results of companies. In this chart, the user sees every company as a dot plotted based on the score in asset turnover and profit margin (Figure 10.7).

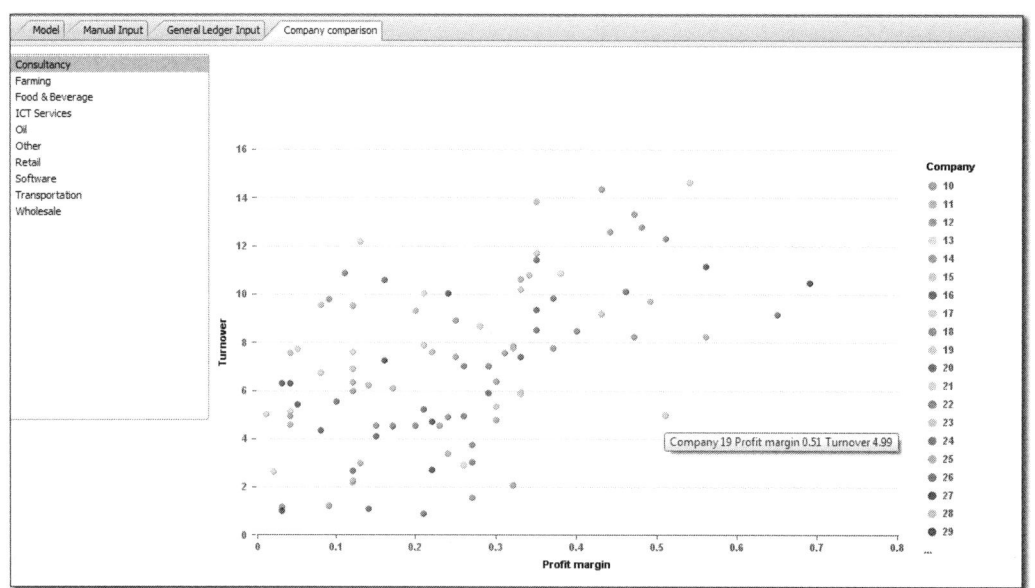

Figure 10.7 Comparison Based on Profit Margin and Asset Turnover

> **Color Images**
>
> Please note that, though the print book shows the application images in gray-scale, full color versions are viewable in the e-book. The full application is also available for download from the book's website at *www.sap-press.com*.

The scatter chart shows a cloud of dots in which outliers are easily identifiable. When an interesting outlier is spotted, the user can hover the mouse cursor over the value and see which company is the outlier.

10.2 Building the Application

In this section, we are going to show step by step how to build the application. First we'll explain how to lay out the components by dragging them onto the canvas and setting the properties. Then we will build the actual functionality of the application, including working with the data sources and showing the script code that was added to each component.

10.2.1 Setting Up the Layout

In this section we are going to set up the layout of the application. First we will set up the basic layout, then we will add the CSS classes for additional formatting, and finally we will set up the necessary components.

Structure

First you set up the basic structure for the application:

1. Drag a TABSTRIP component onto the canvas.
2. Set the top margin, left margin, right margin, and bottom margin to 0 and the height and width to AUTO.
3. Name the first tab "Model".
4. Create three additional tabs. Give these additional tabs the names "Manual Input", "General Ledger Input", and "Company Comparison".

Model tab   Now go to the first tab, MODEL. You will add several GRID LAYOUT components to the tab page so that you can place the TEXT components in a fixed environment, as each component is limited by the cell boundaries. When you are done with the grids, the MODEL tab should look like Figure 10.8.

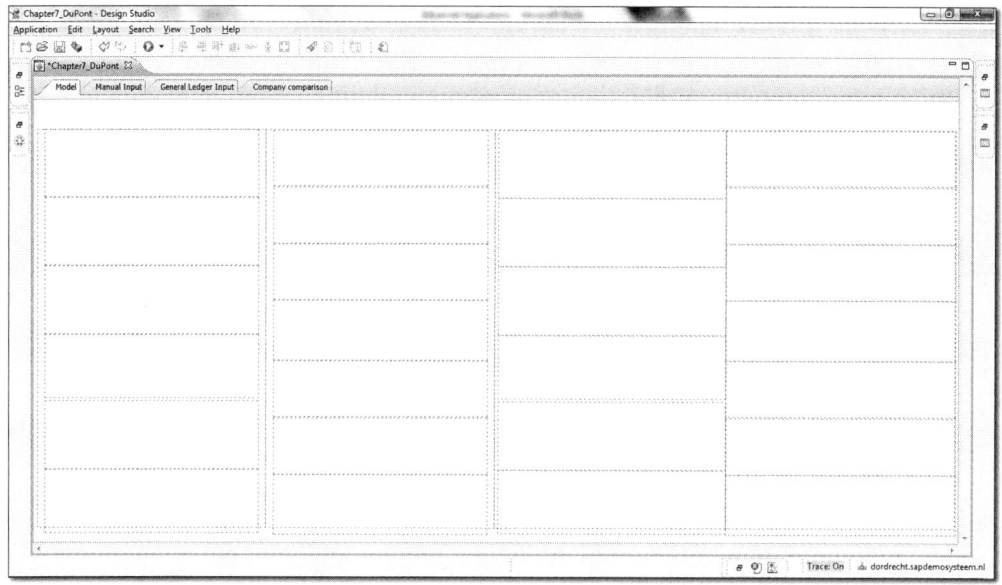

Figure 10.8 Basic Layout for the DuPont Model

Five Grid Layout components   To build this structure, you will need five GRID LAYOUT components:

1. Drag a GRID LAYOUT component onto the canvas and name this component GRID_LAYOUT_TOP.

2. Set the top margin to 40, the left and right margin to 5, and the bottom margin to 20. The width and height are AUTO.

3. The number of rows is 1, and the number of columns is 4. Column widths are evenly distributed, and they all have the value 1.

4. Create a GRID LAYOUT component in cell 0,0 of grid GRID_LAYOUT_TOP.

5. Name the new component GRID_LEVEL1 and set all the margins to 0.

6. The number of rows is 6, and they are evenly distributed (all value 1).

7. Create a GRID LAYOUT component in cell 0,1 of grid GRID_LAYOUT_TOP.

8. Name the new component GRID_LEVEL2 and set the left and right margins to 5 and the top and bottom margins to 0. The height and width are Auto.

9. Set the number of rows to 7, evenly distributed.

10. Create a Grid Layout component in cell 0,2 of grid GRID_LAYOUT_TOP.

11. Set the margins identical to GRID_LEVEL2, and set the number of rows to 6.

12. Create a Grid Layout component in cell 0,3 of grid GRID_LAYOUT_TOP.

13. Set the margins identical to GRID_LEVEL2, and set the number of rows to 7.

You now have set up the initial structure that will help you to place the components into the model. With the structure in place, you can continue with the components that will show the numbers. But before you start adding these components, you must set up the custom CSS file so you can assign the right layout classes immediately to the components.

Set Up the Custom CSS File

Before you can insert the CSS code, you need to upload a CSS file. Use Notepad or a similar program to create a file with the extension .css.

Upload CSS file

The following classes are defined in the CSS file:

```
.header
{
letter-spacing:5px;
font-family:"Verdana", Arial, serif;
font-size:300%;
color:rgb(128,128,128);
}
.button
{
border:2px solid #a1a1a1;
padding:10px 30px;
background:#dddddd;
border-radius:25px;
font-family:"Verdana", Arial, serif;
```

```
color:rgb(128,128,128);
box-shadow: 5px 5px 2px #666666;
font-size:150%;
font-weight:500;
}

.buttonselected
{
border:2px solid #a1a1a1;
padding:10px 30px;
background:#cccccccc;
border-radius:25px;
font-family:"Verdana", Arial, serif;
color:rgb(128,128,128);
box-shadow: 5px 5px 2px #666666;
font-size:150%;
font-weight:700;
}

.panel
{
background-color:#F5F5F5;
border:4px solid #a1a1a1;
border-radius:25px;
}

.listbox
{
border:2px solid #a1a1a1;
padding:10px 30px;
background:#dddddd;
border-radius:25px;
font-family:"Verdana", Arial, serif;
color:rgb(128,128,128);
box-shadow: 5px 5px 2px #666666;
font-size:110%;
font-weight:400;
}

.textbox
{
border:1px solid #a1a1a1;
background:#eeeeee;
```

```
border-radius:25px;
font-family:"Verdana", Arial, serif;
color:rgb(128,128,128);
font-size:150%;
font-weight:700;
text-align:center;
padding: 5px 5px 5px 5px;

}
.textbox2
{
border:1px solid #a1a1a1;
background:#eeeeee;
border-radius:25px;
font-family:"Verdana", Arial, serif;
color:rgb(128,128,128);
font-size:150%;
font-weight:500;
position:absolute;
top:50%;
}
.smalltext
{
font-family:"Verdana", Arial, serif;
color:rgb(128,128,128);
font-size:70%;
text-align:center;
}
```

Listing 10.1 Classes Defined in the CSS File

Use this code to build a CSS file and assign the CSS file to the CUSTOM CSS property of the APPLICATION component.

Set Up Components

You can now set up the first two TEXT components. The first is the box with the name of the measurement; the second is the small label on top of the box. Once you have set them up completely, you will copy these two objects into the other GRID LAYOUT components' cells. You want the text box to look like Figure 10.9.

Set up Text components

359

1. Drag a Text component to cell 0,0 of Grid Layout component GRID_ LEVEL1.

2. Set the CSS class to `textbox`.

3. Set the text to "Current Assets".

4. Rename the Text component TXT_1CURRENTASSETS.

5. Set the top margin to 15, left margin to 5, width to 175, and height to 50. The right margin and bottom margin should be set to Auto.

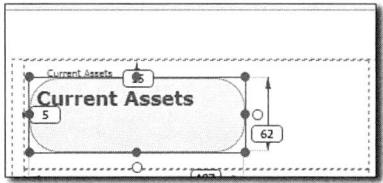

Figure 10.9 First Text Box

These steps result in a gray panel Text component. The next step is to add a description label above the Text component. This ensures that the user can always see what the name of each key figure is.

1. Create a new Text component in the same grid cell.

2. Set the CSS class to `smalltext`.

3. Set the top margin to 0, left margin to 20, width to 80, and height to 30. The right margin and bottom margin should be set to Auto.

4. Set the text to "Current Assets".

5. Rename the object TXT_LBLCURRENTASSETS.

Use components as templates

You now have set up the first two components. Now you can use these two components as templates for the Text components that will be placed in the other cells. To do so, copy the two Text components until you have all the components that you need for the entire model. The process for each step is to copy the components, paste them in other cells, and alter the text and name properties of the newly pasted components.

1. Copy the two text components that you previously made.

2. Right-click on cells 1,0; 3,0; 4,0; and 5,0 and paste the Text components.

3. Rename the larger Text component in cell 1,0 TXT_1FIXEDASSETS and the label TXT_LBLFIXEDASSETS, and set the text for these components to "Fixed Assets".

4. Rename the panel in cell 3,0 TXT_1OPERATINGINCOME1 and the label TXT_LBLOPERATINGINCOME1. Set the text to "Operating Income".

5. Rename the panel in cell 4,0 TXT_1OPERATINGEXPENSES and the label TXT_LBLOPERATINGEXPENSES. Set the text to "Operating Expenses".

6. Rename the panel in cell 5,0 TXT_1NONOPERATINGINCOME and the label TXT_LBLNONOPERATINGINCOME. Set the text to "Non Operating Income".

You have set up the first column of the model. Let's move on to the second column.

1. Copy the two Text components from cell 0,0 in the Grid Layout component GRID_LEVEL1.

2. Go to Grid Layout component GRID_LEVEL2.

3. Paste the components into cells 0,0; 2,0; 4,0; and 6,0.

4. Rename the panel in cell 0,0 TXT_2OPERATINGINCOME3 and the label TXT_LBLOPERATINGINCOME3. Set the texts to "Operating Income".

5. Rename the larger Text component in cell 2,0 TXT_2ASSETS, and rename the label TXT_LBLASSETS. Set the texts in both components to "Assets".

6. Rename the larger Text component in cell 4,0 TXT_2EBIT, and rename the label TXT_LBLEBIT. Set the texts to "Earnings before interest and tax".

7. Rename the panel text component in cell 6,0 TXT_2OPERATINGINCOME2 and the label TXT_LBLOPERATINGINCOME2. Set the texts to "Operating Income".

Now for the third column:

1. Go to Grid Layout component GRID_LEVEL3.

2. Paste the components in cells 1,0 and 5,0 of GRID_LEVEL3.

3. Rename the panel TEXT component in cell 1,0 TXT_3ASSETTURNOVER and the label TXT_LBLASSETTURNOVER. Set the texts of both to "Asset Turnover".

4. Rename the larger TEXT component in cell 5,0 TXT_3PROFITMARGIN and the label TXT_LBLPROFITMARGIN. Set the texts of both components to "Profit Margin".

And, finally, the last column:

1. Copy the two components again from cell 0,0 in GRID LAYOUT component GRID_LEVEL1.

2. Go to GRID LAYOUT component GRID_LEVEL4.

3. Paste the components into cell 4,0.

4. Rename the larger TEXT component TXT_4ROI and the label TXT_LBLROI. Set the text to "Return on Investment".

Insert a Panel component

That's all the objects. Now when you run the application it should look roughly like the example in Figure 10.1. The next step is to insert a PANEL component that allows the user to insert a name and submit the results.

1. Insert a PANEL component into cell 0,0 of GRID_LEVEL4.

2. Set the top margin to 20 and the left margin to 25.

3. Set the width to 200 and the height to 135.

4. Add a TEXT component in the PANEL component. Set the top margin to 10, left margin to 1, width to 95, height to 30, and right margin and bottom margin to AUTO.

5. Add an INPUT FIELD component. Set the top margin to 10; left margin and width to 100; and the height, right margin, and bottom margin to AUTO.

6. Add a DROPDOWN BOX component. Rename the component DROPDOWN_INDUSTRY. Set the top margin to 35, left margin to 80, width to 120, and the rest to AUTO.

7. Add a BUTTON component. Rename the button BTN_SUBMITCOMPANY.

8. Set the top margin to 72, left margin to 108, width to 80, height to 30, and the rest to AUTO.

You have now created the MODEL tab. The result should look like Figure 10.10.

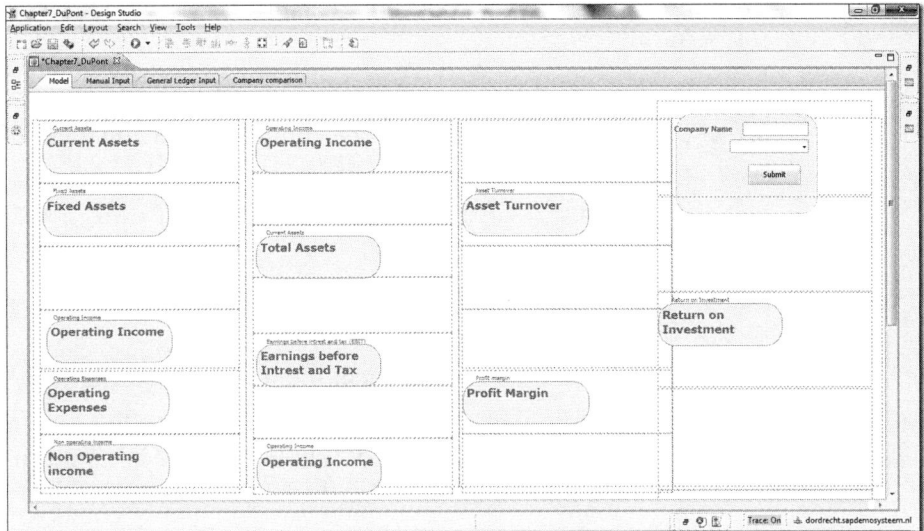

Figure 10.10 First Tab Layout

The layout for the MANUAL INPUT tab looks like Figure 10.11.

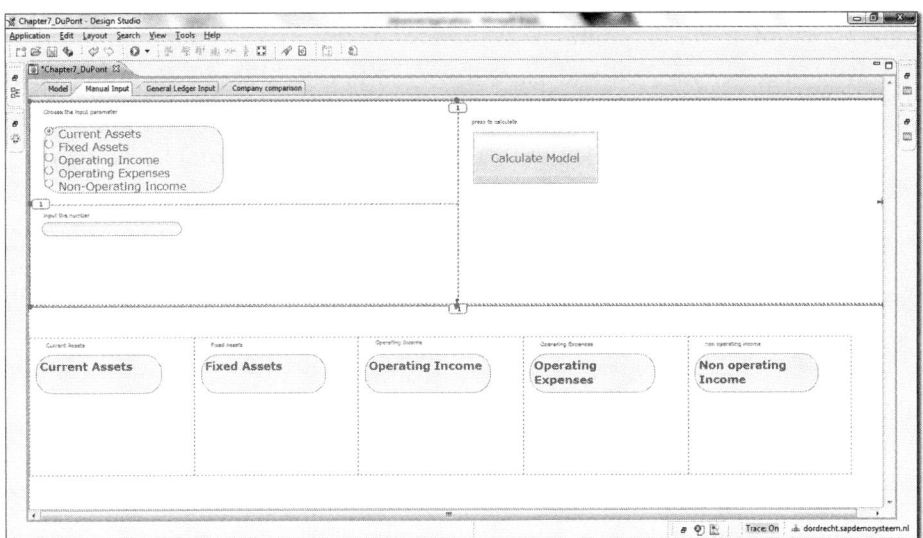

Figure 10.11 Second Tab Layout

Grid Layout
components First you again will use GRID LAYOUT components to build a screen structure before you insert the objects:

1. Go to the second tab of the TABSTRIP component. This is the MANUAL INPUT tab.

2. Insert a GRID LAYOUT component and rename it GRID_TAB2.

3. Set all the margins to 0, width and height to 0, and the number of rows to 2.

4. Insert a new GRID LAYOUT component in cell 0,0 of GRID_TAB2. Rename the component GRID_TOP.

5. Set all the margins to 0, width and height to 0, and the number of rows to 2.

6. Insert a new GRID LAYOUT component into cell 1,0 of GRID_TAB2. Rename the component GRID_INPUTRESULTS.

7. Set the left and top margins to AUTO. Set the right and bottom margins to 50. Set the width to AUTO and the height to 200.

8. Set the number of columns to 5.

9. Set all the margins to 0, width and height to 0, and the number of rows to 2.

10. Insert a new GRID LAYOUT component into cell 0,0 of GRID_TOP. Rename the component GRID_TOPLEFT.

11. Copy the text and label from cell 0,0 in GRID_LEVEL1 and paste them into each of the cells of GRID_INPUTRESULTS.

12. Name the gray TEXT components, respectively, from left to right:
    ▶ TXT_INPCURRENTASSETS
    ▶ TXT_INPFIXEDASSETS
    ▶ TXT_INPOPERATINGINCOME
    ▶ TXT_INPOPERATINGEXPENSES
    ▶ TXT_INPNONOPERATINGINCOME

13. Adjust the layout parameters, margins, etc. to your own taste.

14. Insert a RADIO BUTTON GROUP component into cell 0,0 of GRID_ TOPLEFT.

15. Rename the component RB_GROUP_PARCHOICE.

16. Set the items as shown in Figure 10.12.

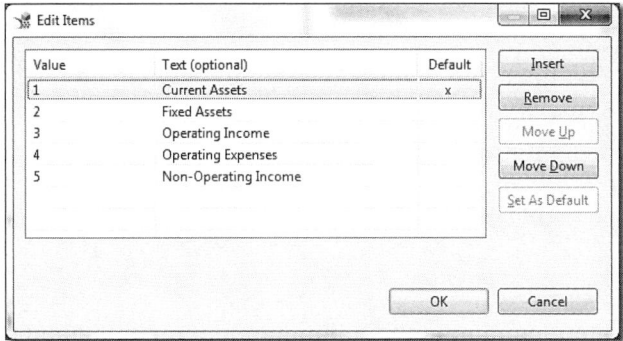

Figure 10.12 Items in the Radio Button Group

17. Set the CSS class to TEXTBOX2.

18. Add a label and adjust the components within the cell.

19. Add an INPUT FIELD component into cell 1,0 of GRID_TOPLEFT.

20. Set the CSS class to TEXTBOX2.

21. Rename the component INPUT_PARNUMBER.

22. Add a label and adjust the layout.

23. Add a BUTTON to cell 0,1 of GRID_TOP.

24. Rename the BUTTON component BUTTON_CALCULATEMODEL.

25. Set the CSS class to `button`.

26. Add a label and resize to your own taste.

You now have added all the components of the MANUAL INPUT tab.

In the third tab, COMPANY COMPARISON, you add a CHART component and a LIST BOX component. The CHART component will compare companies according to their scores in the profit margin and turnover category.

Company Comparison tab

1. Go to the COMPANY COMPARISON tab.

2. Add a CHART component to the canvas.

3. Set the top margin to 90, bottom margin to AUTO, left margin to 225, right margin to AUTO, height to 450, and width to 830.

4. Set the chart type to SCATTER.

5. Rename the CHART CHART_COMPCOMP. Later you will connect the chart to a data source.

6. Add a LIST BOX component to the canvas.

7. Set the top margin to 10, left margin to 5, bottom margin and right margin to AUTO, width to 215, and height to 380.

The result for now will look like Figure 10.13.

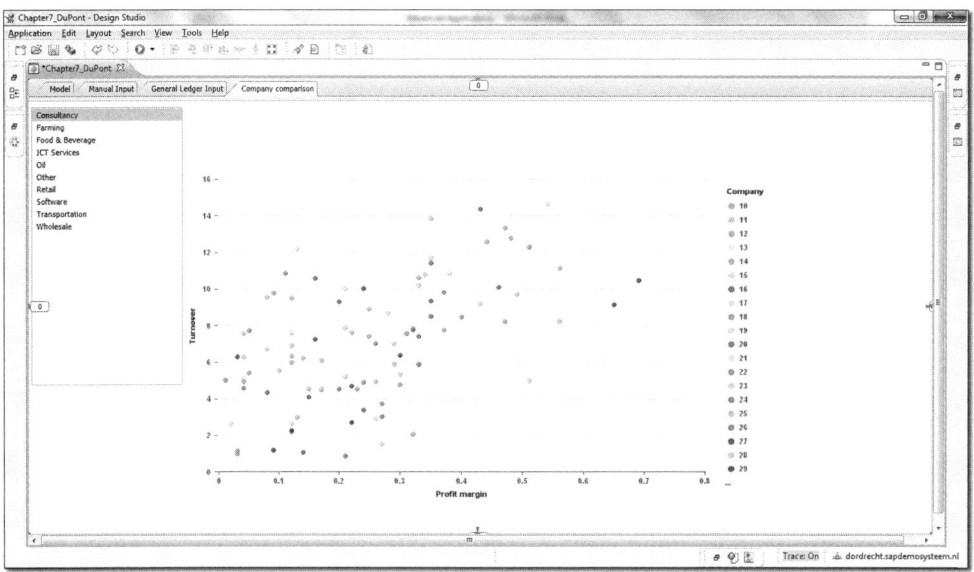

Figure 10.13 Company Comparison Screen

Note that your preliminary result will not look exactly like the example in the figure. You still need to populate the LIST BOX component and attach the CHART component to a data source.

For now we have set up all the components we need for the application structure. We will now go on and build the scripts to make the application work.

10.2.2   Defining Global Variables

Before you insert the script, you must first define the global variables you need in the script code. Add the global variables as they are listed in Figure 10.14.

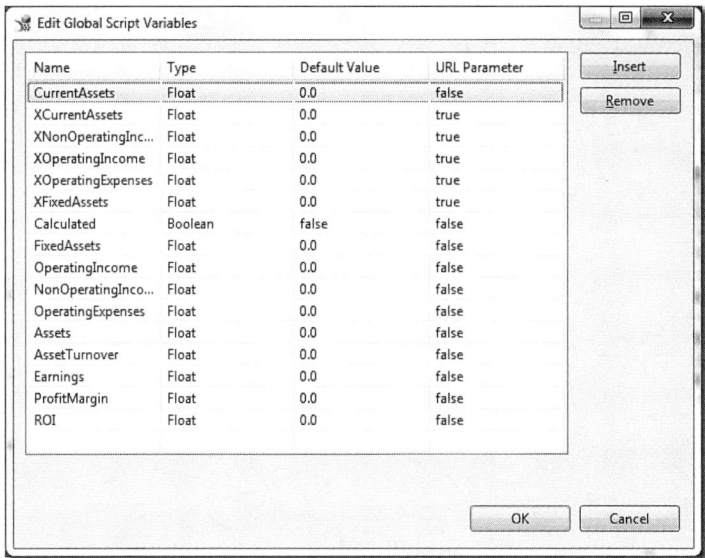

Figure 10.14 Variables for the DuPont Application

All these global variables are used to store the model values or pass parameters. Note the `Calculated` global variable. When this variable is set to `True`, this will alter the behavior of the application such that each change in the input numbers will immediately result in a recalculation of the model. The normal behavior of the application is to wait until the user clicks the CALCULATE button.

Calculated global variable

10.2.3 Setting Up the Data Sources

This application uses two data sources: one to enable OLAP input into the model and the other for the company comparison chart.

Two data sources

For the first data source, it doesn't matter which query you connect it to. The tab page for OLAP input will use an INPUT FIELD component to define the system and query where we will look at the numbers for our model. Once the user enters values in these components, the initial query will be replaced with the one the user selected.

Set the LOAD IN SCRIPT property for this data source to TRUE. You only want to load the data source when the user selects a query to view. Loading data at startup is a waste of time.

Load in Script property

367

The second data source is an SAP NetWeaver BW query, with the initial layout as shown in Figure 10.15.

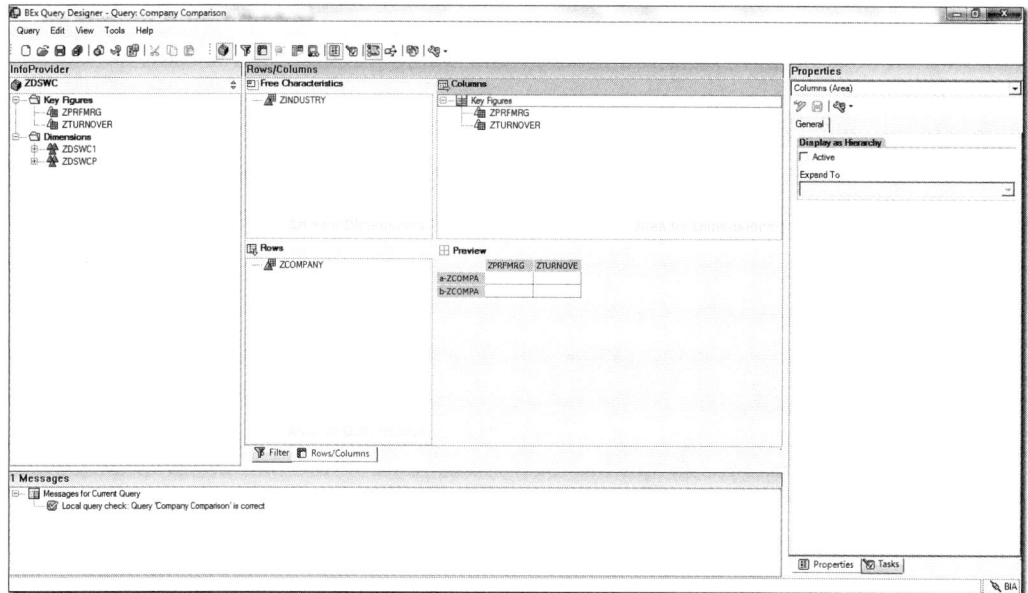

Figure 10.15 BEx Query for Company Comparison Data Source

Create a second data source, connect it to your own version of this query, and name the data source DS_COMPANYCOMPARISON.

10.2.4 Scripting for the On Startup Handler

Populate the
List Box

In the APPLICATION component's On Startup handler, we will add a script to fill the items in the company comparison LIST BOX component. We will also add script code to check if external parameters are passed that can be used for the calculation. If there are any values, they will be assigned to the components and internal variables.

```
//Populate the List Box in the company comparison tab.

LISTBOX_SELECTINDUSTRY.setItems(DS_
COMPANYCOMPARISON.getMemberList("ZINDUSTRY", MemberPresentation
.INTERNAL_KEY, MemberDisplay.TEXT, 10));
```

```
//Pass the parameter values to the variables used
//in calculation.

CurrentAssets = XCurrentAssets;
FixedAssets = XFixedAssets;
NonOperatingIncome = XNonOperatingIncome;
OperatingExpenses = XOperatingExpenses;
OperatingIncome = XOperatingIncome;

if (CurrentAssets != 0.0) {
    BUTTON_CALCULATEMODEL.onClick();

}
```

Listing 10.2 Populating the List Box Component and Passing Parameter Values

We will use the script that is already entered in the BUTTON_CALCULA-TEMODEL BUTTON component by calling the handler of the component. Writing code this way avoids inserting the script for the calculation of the model twice.

Call the handler of the component

10.2.5 Writing Data to the Backend System

In this section we will show some advanced coding in ABAP to circumvent the fact that there is currently (at the time of this writing) no standard way to write data back to the backend system. We will show the script code in the BUTTON component BTN_SUBMITCOMPANY and the ABAP code that is used to work with the BEx variable values that are passed to SAP NetWeaver BW with the data source.

> **Fair Warning**
>
> This section will go into some ABAP coding in SAP NetWeaver BW. If this is a step too far for you to follow, just skip the part about inserting the values of the companies. We added this part to show how to store values in the backend system, but, in later versions of Design Studio, we expect that there will be more standard ways to achieve this goal—via SAP NetWeaver Integrated Planning.

For inserting the values from the model into SAP NetWeaver BW, we have to do some custom coding, as SAP NetWeaver BW Integrated

Integrated Planning

Planning isn't available in Design Studio yet. For this we will build an ABAP variable in SAP NetWeaver BW.

The BUTTON component BTN_SUBMITCOMPANY script will set values to BEx variables and then run a BEx query. The ABAP in the BEx query will then use these variable values to write them into a table. This table then can be used as a data source for SAP NetWeaver BW to make the values available for reporting in the COMPANY COMPARISON tab.

In the BUTTON component BTN_SUBMITCOMPANY we have the following script:

```
// Set the variable values so they can be passed to BW

APPLICATION.setVariableValue("ZCOMPANY",
  INPUT_COMPANY.getValue());
APPLICATION.setVariableValue("ZINDUSTRY",
  DROPDOWN_INDUSTRY.getSelectedValue());
APPLICATION.setVariableValue("ZTURNOVER",
  Convert.floatToString(AssetTurnover));
APPLICATION.setVariableValue("ZPROFITMARGIN",
  Convert.floatToString(ProfitMargin));

DS_INPUTDS.loadDataSource();
```

Avoid Loading Multiple Times

By setting the Load In script property to True, we make sure the application will not automatically load the query at startup. If the query loaded automatically at startup, this would cause it to load each time a variable is set. In the example below, it would run five times. We only want the query to run if we want to store values to the back end system.

Four manual variables

In SAP NetWeaver BW, we have a query with four manual variables (ZCOMPANY, ZINDUSTRY, ZTURNOVER, and ZPROFITMARGIN) that will be populated with the variable values as stated above.

One ABAP variable

In the BEx query, we also have a fifth ABAP variable that will use these four variables to populate a table in SAP NetWeaver BW.

In CMOD, we will add the following code:

```
WHEN 'ZDS_EXITVAR'.
   BREAK-POINT.
   IF i_step = 2.
      TABLES ZDS_COMPANIES.
      DATA wa TYPE ZDS_COMPANIES.
      DATA wa2 TYPE ZDS_COMPANIES.

      READ TABLE i_t_var_range INTO LS_T_VAR_RANGE
      WITH KEY vnam = ZCOMPANY'.
      wa-ZCOMPANY = LS_T_VAR_RANGE-low.
      READ TABLE i_t_var_range INTO LS_T_VAR_RANGE
      WITH KEY vnam = 'ZINDUSTRY.
      wa-ZINDUSTRY = LS_T_VAR_RANGE-low.

      READ TABLE i_t_var_range INTO LS_T_VAR_RANGE
      WITH KEY vnam = 'ZTURNOVER'.
      wa-zturnover = LS_T_VAR_RANGE-low.
      READ TABLE i_t_var_range INTO LS_T_VAR_RANGE
      WITH KEY vnam = 'ZPROFITMARGIN'.
      wa-zprofitmargin = LS_T_VAR_RANGE-low.

   SELECT ZCOMPANY FROM ZDS_COMPANIES
INTO CORRESPONDING FIELDS OF wa2
      WHERE ZCOMPANY = wa-ZCOMPANY.
      ENDSELECT.

   IF SY-SUBRC NE 0.

         INSERT INTO ZDS_COMPANIES VALUES wa.
   ELSE.
UPDATE ZDS_COMPANIES
zindustry = wa_zindustry
zturnover = wa-zturnover
zprofitmargin = wa-zprofitmargin
WHERE zcompany = wa-zcompany.
      ENDIF.
```

Listing 10.3 ABAP Code to Write Back to the Table

This ABAP code will look in the ZDS_COMPANIES table to see if there is already an entry for that company. If there is already a value present, the ABAP code will update the values in the table. If there are no values present, the ABAP code will add a new row to the table.

After the loads in SAP NetWeaver BW, where the data is transferred from the table into an InfoCube, the results will be shown in the COMPANY COMPARISON tab. However, you need to set up the transformation and InfoCube/MultiProvider before you can replicate the result.

10.2.6 Scripting for Manual Input

Script for the model calculation

In the MANUAL INPUT tab, we add script code for the calculation of the model. We also insert script code to transfer the inputted values to the boxes on the bottom of the MANUAL INPUT screen. In this section, we will show you the script code that we have inserted in the INPUT FIELD component INPUT_PARNUMBER and the BUTTON component BUTTON_CALCULATEMODEL.

INPUT_PARNUMBER on change

In the INPUT FIELD component INPUT_PARNUMBER, we set the following script code:

```
if (RB_GROUP_PARCHOICE.getSelectedValue() == "1") {
    CurrentAssets = Convert.stringToFloat(INPUT_
PARNUMBER.getValue());
    TXT_
INPCURRENTASSETS.setText(Convert.floatToStringUsingLocale(Cur
rentAssets));
}
if (RB_GROUP_PARCHOICE.getSelectedValue() == "2") {
    FixedAssets = Convert.stringToFloat(INPUT_
PARNUMBER.getValue());
    TXT_
INPUTFIXEDASSETS.setText(Convert.floatToStringUsingLocale(Fix
edAssets));
}
if (RB_GROUP_PARCHOICE.getSelectedValue() == "3") {
    OperatingIncome = Convert.stringToFloat(INPUT_
PARNUMBER.getValue());
    TXT_
INPUTOPERATINGINCOME.setText(Convert.floatToStringUsingLocale
(OperatingIncome));
}
if (RB_GROUP_PARCHOICE.getSelectedValue() == "4") {
```

```
    OperatingExpenses = Convert.stringToFloat(INPUT_
PARNUMBER.getValue());
    TXT_
INPOPERATINGEXPENSE.setText(Convert.floatToStringUsingLocale(
OperatingExpenses));
}
if (RB_GROUP_PARCHOICE.getSelectedValue() == "5") {
    NonOperatingIncome = Convert.stringToFloat(INPUT_
PARNUMBER.getValue());
    TXT_
INPUTNONOPERINCOME.setText(Convert.floatToStringUsingLocale(N
onOperatingIncome));
}

INPUT_PARNUMBER.setValue("");

if (Calculated) {
    BUTTON_CALCULATEMODEL.onClick();
}
```

Listing 10.4 Using the Inputted Numbers

When the user inputs a number, the script will check which number from the model is selected in the LIST BOX component. The TEXT component that corresponds with the selected number will be updated.

After this, the script will check if the global variable Calculated has the value True. If the value is indeed True, then the model will be recalculated immediately; otherwise, the model will not be recalculated until the CALCULATE button has been clicked.

BUTTON_CALCULATEMODEL on click

This button will perform the actual calculation and will fill all the TEXT components in the model. Once the calculation button is clicked, the calculated variable will be set to True, resulting in each change of number immediately leading to a recalculation of the model instead of waiting for a new click of the button.

```
TXT_
1OPERATINGINCOME1.setText(Convert.floatToStringUsingLocale(Op
eratingIncome));
```

```
TXT_
1FIXEDASSETS.setText(Convert.floatToStringUsingLocale(FixedAs
sets));
TXT_
1CURRENTASSETS.setText(Convert.floatToStringUsingLocale(Curre
ntAssets));
TXT_1OPERATING_
EXPENSES.setText(Convert.floatToStringUsingLocale(OperatingEx
penses));
TXT_
1NONOPERATINGINCOME.setText(Convert.floatToStringUsingLocale(
NonOperatingIncome));

TXT_
2OPERATINGINCOME2.setText(Convert.floatToStringUsingLocale(Op
eratingIncome));
TXT_
2OPERATINGINCOME3.setText(Convert.floatToStringUsingLocale(Op
eratingIncome));

Assets = CurrentAssets + FixedAssets;
Earnings = OperatingIncome + NonOperatingIncome -
 OperatingExpenses;

TXT_
2ASSETS.setText(Convert.floatToStringUsingLocale(Assets));
TXT_
2EBIT.setText(Convert.floatToStringUsingLocale(Earnings));

AssetTurnover = OperatingIncome / Assets;
ProfitMargin = Earnings / OperatingIncome * 100;

TXT_
3ASSETTURNOVER.setText(Convert.floatToStringUsingLocale(Asset
Turnover,1));
TXT_
3PROFITMARGIN.setText(Convert.floatToStringUsingLocale(Profit
Margin)+ "%");

ROI = AssetTurnover * ProfitMargin;
```

```
TXT_
ROI.setText(Convert.floatToStringUsingLocale(ROI, 1)+ "%");

Calculated = true;
```

Listing 10.5 Recalculating the Model

10.2.7 Scripting for OLAP Input

On the OLAP INPUT tab, the script code is used to allow the user to input his own query for selecting numbers for the model. Before navigating through data, the user first will see a submit panel where he can select a backend system and a query.

Select backend system and query

Using the selected system and query, the script will assign the query to the data source. The query panel and the CROSSTAB component that will be used for navigation are connected to that data source.

BTN_QUERYSUBMIT on click

```
DS_FREEHAND.assignDataSource(INPUT_
QUERY.getValue(), DataSourceType.QUERY, INPUT_
SYSTEM.getValue());
DS_FREEHAND.loadDataSource();
PNL_QUERYNAVIGATION.setVisible(true);
PNL_ASSIGNQUERYRESULT.setVisible(true);
```

Listing 10.6 Using Your Own Query from Any Connected System

When you select a value in the CROSSTAB component, you can insert the selected value into the model by clicking the SUBMIT button. In this example, we limited the script to just add numbers to the input. An extra option was to build a complete SUBMIT tab like the one we already built in the MANUAL INPUT tab. The SUBMIT button takes the value and the model item in the LIST BOX component, and uses this to update the number in the model.

Submit button

In this example, you can use the model to add filters until you reach the value you want for the model. Then click the button to actually add it to the DuPont model.

BUTTON_QUERYINPUT on click

```
if (QUERYINPUT_NUMBERTYPE.getSelectedValue() == "1") {
    CurrentAssets = Convert.stringToFloat(DS_
FREEHAND.getDataAsString("4SXI09YNYC75HX1Y41Z7X8XXF", {}));
    TXT_
INPCURRENTASSETS.setText(Convert.floatToStringUsingLocale(Cur
rentAssets));
}
if (QUERYINPUT_NUMBERTYPE.getSelectedValue() == "2") {
    FixedAssets = Convert.stringToFloat(DS_
FREEHAND.getDataAsString("4SXI09YNYC75HX1Y41Z7X8XXF", {}));
    TXT_
INPUTFIXEDASSETS.setText(Convert.floatToStringUsingLocale(Fix
edAssets));
}
if (QUERYINPUT_NUMBERTYPE.getSelectedValue() == "3") {
    OperatingIncome = Convert.stringToFloat(DS_
FREEHAND.getDataAsString("4SXI09YNYC75HX1Y41Z7X8XXF", {}));
    TXT_
INPUTOPERATINGINCOME.setText(Convert.floatToStringUsingLocale
(OperatingIncome));
}
if (QUERYINPUT_NUMBERTYPE.getSelectedValue() == "4") {
    OperatingExpenses = Convert.stringToFloat(DS_
FREEHAND.getDataAsString("4SXI09YNYC75HX1Y41Z7X8XXF", {}));
    TXT_
INPOPERATINGEXPENSE.setText(Convert.floatToStringUsingLocale(
OperatingExpenses));
}
if (QUERYINPUT_NUMBERTYPE.getSelectedValue() == "5") {
    NonOperatingIncome = Convert.stringToFloat(DS_
FREEHAND.getDataAsString("4SXI09YNYC75HX1Y41Z7X8XXF", {}));
    TXT_
INPUTNONOPERINCOME.setText(Convert.floatToStringUsingLocale(N
onOperatingIncome));
}

INPUT_PARNUMBER.setValue("");

if (Calculated) {
```

```
    BUTTON_CALCULATEMODEL.onClick();
}
```

Listing 10.7 Adding a Value from the Query

Fixed Value for Key Figure

Note that this script is not fully flexible. The code has complex values hard-coded to select the right key figure. A way to make this script more flexible is storing these key figure IDs in variables or storing those values in InfoCubes/tables, enabling you to look them up with data sources.

10.2.8 Scripting for Numbers from Outside the Application

Now let's insert the script for calling numbers from outside the application. To open the application, you have to know the URL. After the general URL of the SAP BusinessObjects BI platform, enter the CUID of the application. Then add the parameters that you want to pass to the DuPont application.

For example, the URL below would open the application and pass the value 10,000 to the current assets.

http://192.168.0.1:8080//BOE/Opendocument/opendoc/
openDocument.jsp?sIDType=CUID&iDocID=1111111111111&
xCurrentAssets=10000

Using Variables to Store Parts of the URL

When you want to open applications from within your applications, the easiest way to handle the complex URLs is to store the parts into variables. For example, the URL above can be divided into several parts.

```
ServerAddress = http://192.168.0.1:8080
ServerDirectory = "//BOE/Opendocument/opendoc/openDocument.
jsp?sIDType=CUID&iDocID"
Application1 = "1111111111"
```

With these three variables in place, opening the application would look like this:

```
APPLICATION.openNewWindow(ServerAddress+ServerDirectory+
Application1);
```

When you want to link to outside applications often, it is much easier to maintain the code using variables than by repeating the URL in the application's components.

To be able to work with these parameters in the URL, we first need to define global variables with the property `URL Parameter` set to `True`. As you can see in Figure 10.16, we defined a global variable for each number in the application.

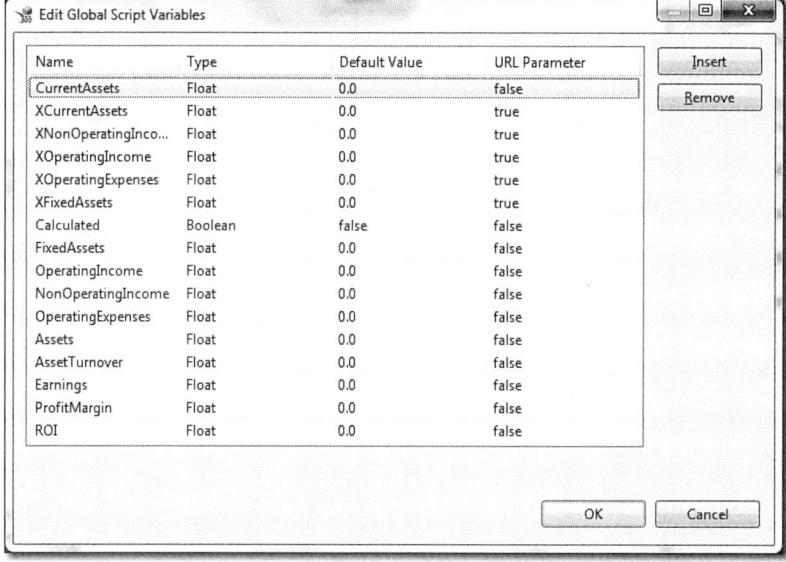

Figure 10.16 Global Variables Set as URL Parameters

After setting these variables, we will add a script in the application `On Startup` handler that assigns the values of the external URL parameters to the variables we use in the application.

```
//
pass the parameter values to the variables used in calculation

CurrentAssets = XCurrentAssets;
FixedAssets = XFixedAssets;
NonOperatingIncome = XNonOperatingIncome;
OperatingExpenses = XOperatingExpenses;
OperatingIncome = XOperatingIncome;
```

Everything works the same way in the application—but now some values are already filled because the application was opened with parameters.

10.2.9 Scripting for Comparing the Results

Finally, in the COMPANY COMPARISON tab, we will add a little script to be able to refresh the graph based on the selection in the LIST BOX component. If the user selects an industry, the graph will show only the companies within that industry.

Refresh the graph

LISTBOX_SELECTINDUSTRY on click

```
DS_COMPANYCOMPARISON.setFilter("ZINDUSTRY", LISTBOX_
SELECTINDUSTRY.getSelectedValue());
```

Listing 10.8 Selecting a Company

10.3 Summary

In this chapter we showed you how to build a complex model using the scripting in Design Studio. We also used several features for a standard layout. As you can see, the complexity can rapidly increase once you start adding features to the model. The main point of this example is to show how you can select values from different sources and use them in calculations.

In this chapter, we'll take a look at the second of two examples that show you how to build an advanced application using Design Studio.

11   Building a Sales Dashboard Application

In this chapter, we will show a sales dashboard application that reports on worldwide sales. In this world wide sales scenario, we will track the sales data of seven global companies and the local market. We are mostly interested in those countries where the market for their product is the largest, so we always look at the top countries in terms of expected sales.

This chapter is divided into two main parts: an overview of the application and a detailed walk through the steps required to build it.

Downloads

The application and CSS files discussed in this chapter are also available for download from the book's website at *www.sap-press.com*.

11.1   Application Overview

In this sales dashboard application, we have two pages where we can look at the sales data from all over the world. In the first page, the start screen, we have an overview of the all the countries. The second page is more focused on analyzing the data of one company.

Look at countries of a particular continent

The start screen of the application is shown in Figure 11.1. From here, the user can apply a filter to the application to look only at the countries of a particular continent.

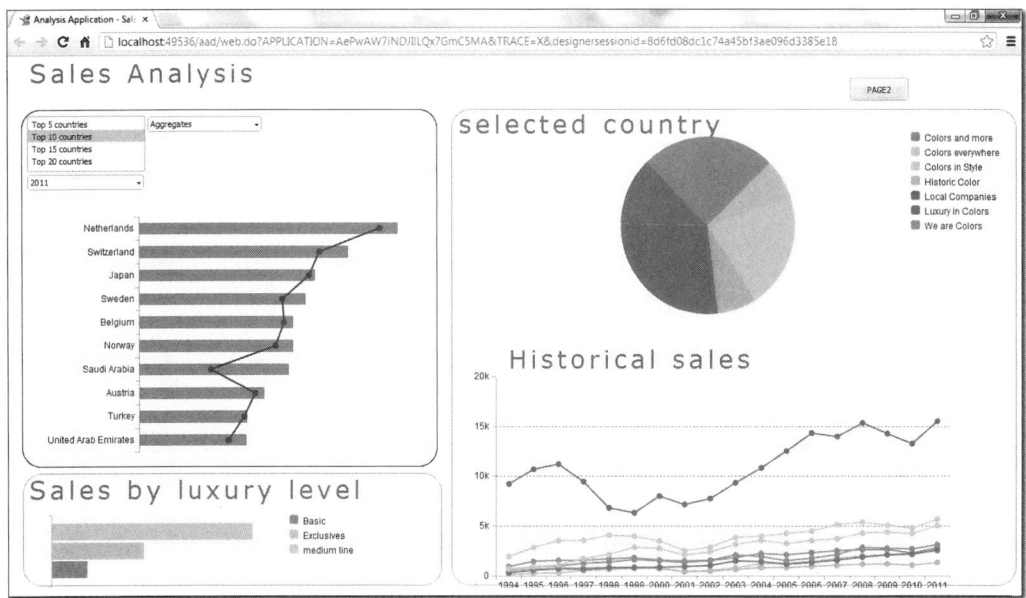

Figure 11.1 World-Wide Sales Dashboard Application Start Screen

Actual sales vs. sales targets

Color Images

Please note that, though the print book shows the application images in gray-scale, full color versions are viewable in the e-book. The full application is also available for download from the book's website at *www.sap-press.com*.

When we look in Figure 11.1 at the total sales without any filter, the largest country in terms of sales is the Netherlands. On the left we see the actual sales per country as bars and the sales target as the line. One quick scan across the bar chart tells us that all the top countries are beating their targets. Saudi Arabia, in particular, seems to do exceptionally well, as their sales are much better than the sales target.

Top N countries

If we want to see the top 15 or top 20 countries, we can change the top *n* value by selecting another item in the LIST BOX component on the top left. When we set it to the top 20, the list of countries in the sales versus target chart grows to 20 countries. We now see the United Kingdom appear as the 20th country in the graph (Figure 11.2).

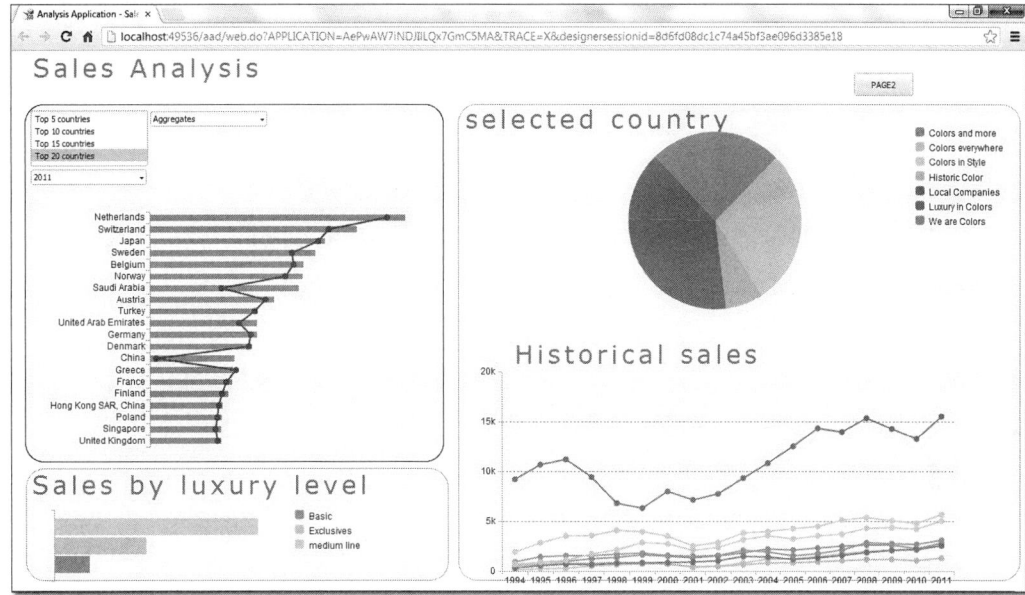

Figure 11.2 Top 20 Countries in the Start Screen

We can apply additional filters to the list. For example, if you want to analyze the top 15 countries of 2006, you can set the year filter, and the chart will show the countries with the highest budgeted sales for 2006. You could also set a filter for region.

Apply additional filters

In the example in Figure 11.3, we see the top eight countries. Although the setting for top *n* is still 15, there are only eight countries we can report on.

In this example we selected India, as this country is the largest in the region. On the right you see in the pie chart that there were no global companies selling products in India in 2006; the whole market was being served by local companies. Below the pie chart is the line chart visualizing sales development over the years. A first impression is that 2007 must have been a very bad year for the local market, as there is a steep dive in sales for that year. Since that year there has been a slow recovery, but the sales level until 2011 is nowhere near the level of 2006.

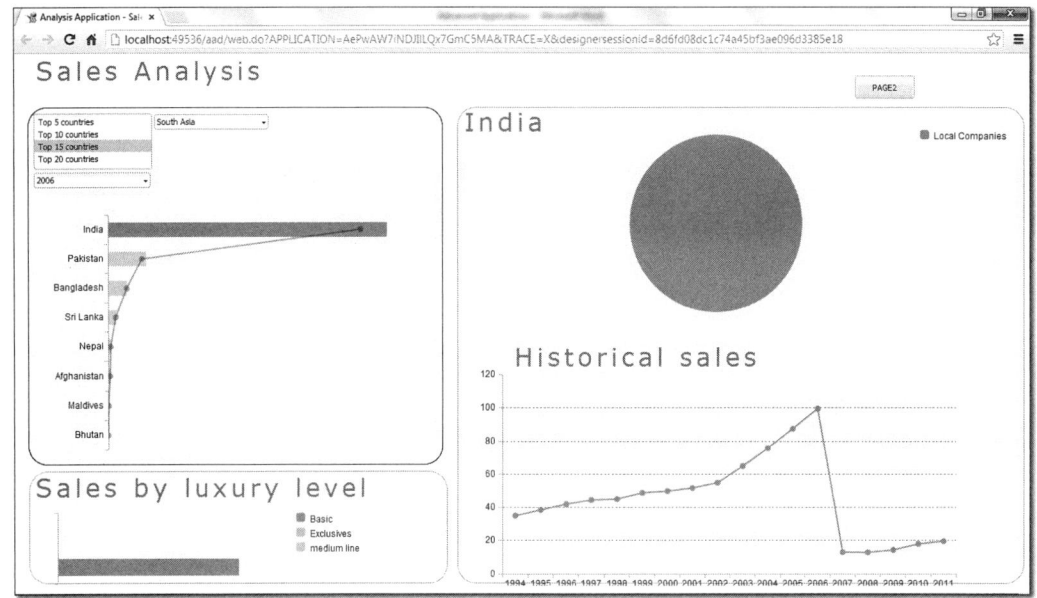

Figure 11.3 Top Countries for South Asia in 2006

On the bottom left, you see the sales divided by luxury level. By looking at the graph, we can conclude that there is not a market for medium or luxury products; there is only a market for basic products in India.

India vs. Switzerland

Let's compare the data from India to another country. If we now filter on Europe and Central Asia, we again see a list of top countries. We select Switzerland, which is in second place in the top *n* list (Figure 11.4).

Our first impression is that the detailed graphs on the right and the bottom left are very different from what we saw for India. In the pie chart, we see that there are six global companies in Switzerland, competing with the local market. When we hover over the pie chart, we can get a closer look at the market shares of each company. As you can see in Figure 11.5, the market share for colors in style is about 20%, with sales of $464 million.

On the historical line chart on the bottom right, we see that some of the global companies only recently entered the Swiss market. The company We are Colors entered the market in 2002. The company Colors Everywhere entered the market in 2004.

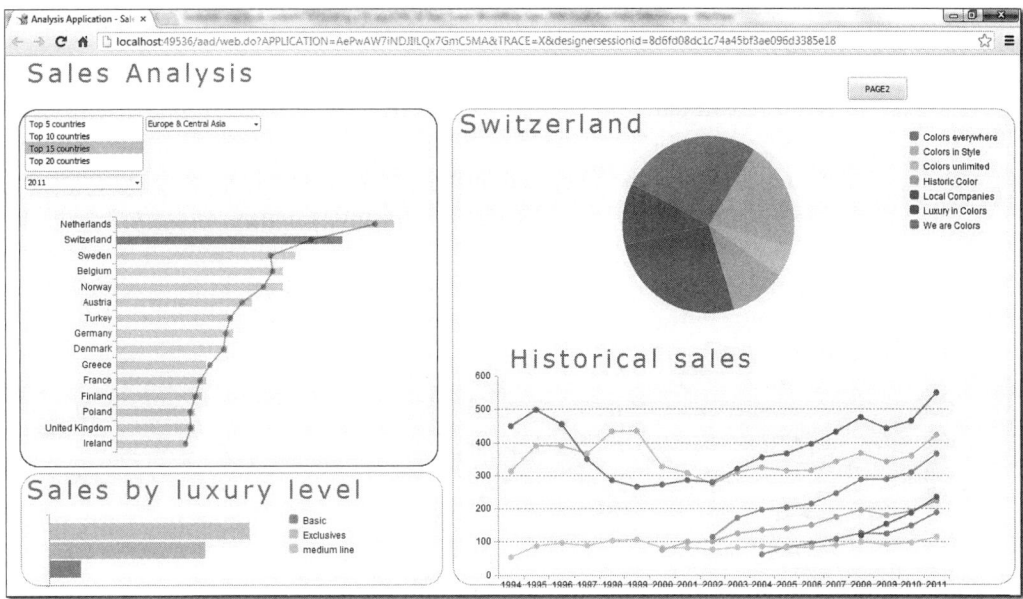

Figure 11.4 More Information about Swiss Sales

On the bottom left of the dashboard, we see that the division by luxury level is very different from the Indian market. Here the basic lines are only a small part of the total market in Switzerland. The luxury line is a large part of the total market, almost as large as the medium line.

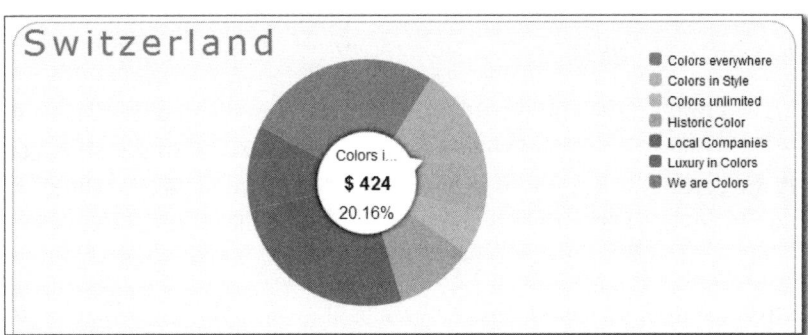

Figure 11.5 Market Share for Colors in Style in Switzerland

If we want to know more exact numbers of the market shares of the companies in Switzerland, we can either click a segment of the pie chart or click on a company in the legend. For the example, we wanted to know more about Colors in Style. Their sales are a bit over 20% of the total market, totaling roughly $424 million.

In the company detail view of the worldwide sales dashboard application, we can look at the data in more detail (Figure 11.6). We now can navigate through the top countries list for individual companies. On the left you can apply filters, select a company, a region, or the year. On the bottom is a waterfall chart. This chart shows the cumulative contribution of every country to the deviation from the sales target.

Figure 11.6 Sales per Country Filtered by Company and Year

This example shows the top 10 countries in Europe and Central Asia in terms of sales for the company Historic Color for 2011. In the table you see the country, the amount of sales in millions of dollars, and the deviation from the sales target.

If you want to go to the next 10 countries, you can click the appropriate button on the bottom right. Countries 11 through 20 will then be shown, and a button will appear at the top right, enabling you to go back to the top 10 countries. The NEXT 10 COUNTRIES button will send you to countries 21 through 30. When there are no countries left, the table will remain empty.

11.2 Building the Application

In this section, we will go step by step through the process of building the application. First we will set up the layout of the application (Section 11.2.1). In the rest of the section, we will perform the various steps required to add interactivity to the application. We will look at the filters, the top *n* variables, and how to build all this in the script and in the SAP NetWeaver BW queries. We will also set up a data source that will be filtered using BEx variables that are set up in the script. (Remember, you can download the application and CSS files from the book's website at *www.sap-press.com*.)

11.2.1 Setting Up the Layout

Let's start by building the main structure of the application (Figure 11.7). As described earlier, there are two pages in the application. In the two pages are some basic elements and a grid component. The GRID LAYOUT components hold most of the other components.

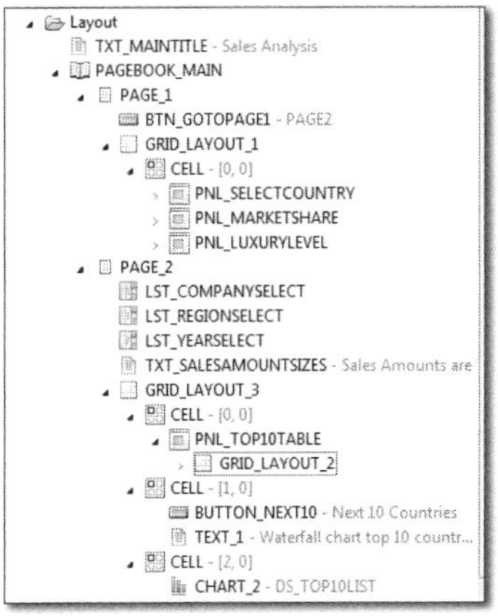

Build the main structure

Figure 11.7 Outline View of the Sales Dashboard Application

CSS Classes

First upload a CSS file to the application with the following CSS classes:

```
.header
{
```

387

```
letter-spacing:5px;
font-family:"Verdana", Arial, serif;
font-size:300%;
color:rgb(128,128,128);
}
.header2
{
letter-spacing:2px;
font-family:"Verdana", Arial, serif;
font-size:200%;
color:rgb(128,128,128);
border:1px solid #ffffff;
}

.messageclass1
{
letter-spacing:2px;
font-family:"Verdana", Arial, serif;
font-size:200%;
color:rgb(60,153,41);
border:1px solid #ffffff;
}

.messageclass2
{
letter-spacing:2px;
font-family:"Verdana", Arial, serif;
font-size:200%;
color:rgb(139,204,126);
border:1px solid #ffffff;
}

.messageclass3
{
letter-spacing:2px;
font-family:"Verdana", Arial, serif;
font-size:200%;
color:rgb(128,128,128);
border:1px solid #ffffff;
}
.messageclass4
{
```

```
letter-spacing:2px;
font-family:"Verdana", Arial, serif;
font-size:200%;
color:rgb(235,150,150);
border:1px solid #ffffff;
}

.messageclass5
{
letter-spacing:2px;
font-family:"Verdana", Arial, serif;
font-size:200%;
color:rgb(242,27,27);
border:1px solid #ffffff;
}
.button
{
border:2px solid #a1a1a1;
padding:10px 30px;
background:#dddddd;
border-radius:25px;
font-family:"Verdana", Arial, serif;
color:rgb(128,128,128);
box-shadow: 5px 5px 2px #666666;
font-size:150%;
font-weight:500;
}

.buttonselected
{
border:2px solid #a1a1a1;
padding:10px 30px;
background:#cccccc;
border-radius:25px;
font-family:"Verdana", Arial, serif;
color:rgb(128,128,128);
box-shadow: 5px 5px 2px #666666;
font-size:150%;
font-weight:700;
}

.panel
{
```

```
background-color:#F5F5F5;
border:1px solid #a1a1a1;
border-radius:25px;
}

.listbox
{
border:1px solid #a1a1a1;
padding:10px 30px;
background:#F5F5F5;
border-radius:25px;
font-family:"Verdana", Arial, serif;
color:rgb(128,128,128);
font-size:100%;
font-weight:400;
}

.textbox
{
border:1px solid #a1a1a1;
background:#eeeeee;
border-radius:25px;
font-family:"Verdana", Arial, serif;
color:rgb(128,128,128);
font-size:150%;
font-weight:700;
text-align:center;
padding: 5px 5px 5px 5px;

}
.textbox2
{
border:1px solid #a1a1a1;
background:#eeeeee;
border-radius:25px;
font-family:"Verdana", Arial, serif;
color:rgb(128,128,128);
font-size:150%;
font-weight:500;
position:absolute;
top:50%;
}
```

```
.smalltext
{
font-family:"Verdana", Arial, serif;
color:rgb(128,128,128);
font-size:70%;
text-align:center;
}
```

Listing 11.1 CSS Classes

Building Components

Next let's start building the components. Follow the steps below:

1. Add a PAGEBOOK component on the canvas.

2. Set the margins to top: 15, bottom: 0, left: 0, and right: 0. Width and height are AUTO.

3. Add a TEXT component to the canvas (not in the PAGEBOOK component).

4. Set the text to "Sales Analysis" and the name to TXT_MAINTITLE.

5. Set the margins to top: 10, left: 20, right: AUTO, width: 350, height: 45, and bottom: AUTO.

6. Set the CSS class to `header`.

7. Add a GRID LAYOUT component to page 1 of the PAGEBOOK component.

8. Set the name to GRID_LAYOUT_1.

9. Set the margins to top: 30; bottom, right, and left: 0; and height and width: AUTO.

10. Set the number of rows: 1 and number of columns: 1.

11. Insert three PANEL components in GRID_LAYOUT_1.

12. Panel 1:

    ▶ Name: PNL_SELECTCOUNTRY

    ▶ CSS class: `panel`

    ▶ Margins: top: 25, bottom and right: AUTO, width: 560, height: 465

    ▶ Added CSS style: `border:1px solid; border-radius:25px`

13. Panel 2:

   ▸ Name: PNL_LUXURYLEVEL

   ▸ CSS class: panel

   ▸ Margins: top: 500, left: 20, bottom: 5, right: Auto, width: 565, height: Auto

14. Panel 3:

   ▸ Name: PNL_MARKETSHARE

   ▸ CSS class: panel

   ▸ Margins: top: 25, left: 600, bottom: 5, right: 10, height and width: Auto

The result of these steps is the basic skeleton of page 1, as shown in Figure 11.8.

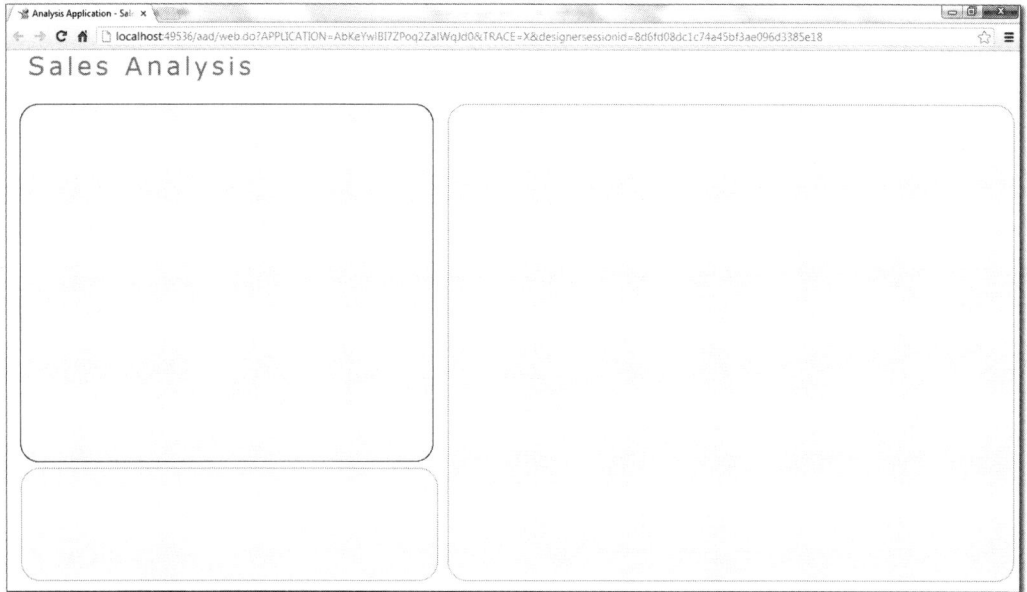

Figure 11.8 Skeleton Page 1 of Worldwide Sales

Page 2 of the Pagebook component We now move on to page 2 of the PAGEBOOK component. In this page we are going to build the structure as shown in Figure 11.8. For an overview of the components that we are going to add, see Figure 11.9.

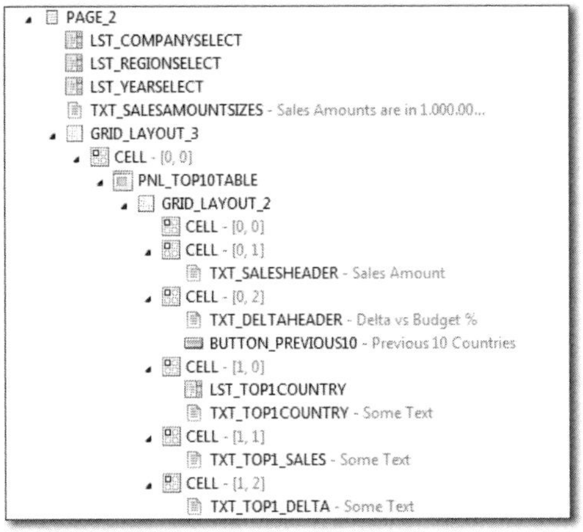

Figure 11.9 Outline View of Page 2 of the Sales Application

1. Add a LIST BOX component to page 2 of the PAGEBOOK component.

   ▹ Name: LST_COMPANYSELECT

   ▹ CSS class: listbox

   ▹ Margins: top: 40, left: 20, bottom: AUTO, right: AUTO, width: 200, height: 200

2. Add another LIST BOX to page 2 of the PAGEBOOK component.

   ▹ Name: LST_REGIONSELECT

   ▹ CSS class: listbox

   ▹ Margins: top: 260, left: 20, bottom: AUTO, right: AUTO, width: 200, height: 205

3. Add a DROPDOWN BOX component to page 2 of the PAGEBOOK component.

   ▹ Name: LST_YEARSELECT

   ▹ CSS class: listbox

   ▹ Margins: top: 475, left: 25, bottom: AUTO, right: AUTO, width: 200, height: 50

4. Add a GRID LAYOUT component to page 2 of the PAGEBOOK component.

   ▹ Name: GRID_LAYOUT_3

   ▹ Number of rows: 3, number of columns: 1

5. In cell 0,0 of GRID_LAYOUT_3 add a PANEL component.

    ▶ Name: PNL_TOP10TABLE

    ▶ CSS class: `Panel`

    ▶ Margins: top, bottom, left, right: 0; width, height: 0.

6. In cell 1,0 of GRID_LAYOUT_3 add a BUTTON component.

    ▶ Name: BUTTON_NEXT10

    ▶ CSS class: `listbox`

    ▶ Margins: top: 8, left 900, right: AUTO, bottom: AUTO, width: 125, height: 30

    ▶ Text: Next 10 Countries

7. Add a TEXT component.

    ▶ Name: TXT_WATERFALLLABEL

    ▶ Text: Waterfall chart top 10 countries

    ▶ Margins: top: 5, left: 5, bottom: AUTO, right: AUTO, height: 30, width: 465

The result of these components is shown in Figure 11.10. There is still something missing, however. In the figure there is a table with multiple TEXT components. That table is a GRID LAYOUT component inside the PANEL component PNL_TOP10TABLE.

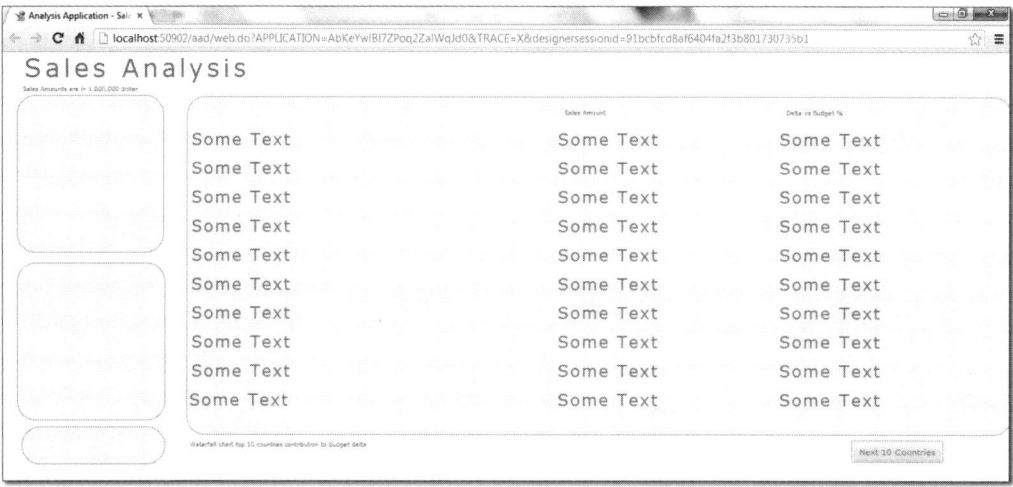

Figure 11.10 Skeleton of Page 2

We will now add the table. As you can see, there are temporary texts inserted in the TEXT components for the time being. Later in Section 11.2.3 we will walk through the steps to fill all the TEXT components with the countries and numbers data.

Add the table

For now go to the PANEL component PNL_TOP10TABLE.

1. Add a GRID LAYOUT component to the table.
   - ▸ Name: GRID_LAYOUT_2
   - ▸ Number of rows: 11, number of columns: 3
   - ▸ Margins: left, right, top, bottom: 5; height, width: AUTO
2. Add a TEXT component to cell 0,1 of GRID_LAYOUT_2.
   - ▸ Name: TXT_SALESHEADER
   - ▸ CSS class: `smalltext`
   - ▸ `Text`: Sales Amount
   - ▸ Margins: top: 5; left: 10; bottom: 0; right: 10; width, height: AUTO
3. Add a TEXT component to cell 0,2.
   - ▸ Name: TXT_DELTAHEADER.
   - ▸ CSS class: `smalltext`
   - ▸ Text: Delta versus Budget %
   - ▸ Margins: top: 5; left: 10; bottom: 0; right: 10; width, height: AUTO
4. Add a BUTTON component to cell 0,2.
   - ▸ Name: BUTTON_PREVIOUS10
   - ▸ CSS class: `listbox`
   - ▸ Text: Previous 10 Countries
   - ▸ Margins: top: 5; left: 160; bottom, right: AUTO; width: 125; height: 30

We will now add components in the next 10 rows. We will describe the steps to build the first row. The following nine rows are identical except for the names. We will copy all the components from the first row to the next nine rows.

Add components

1. Add a LIST BOX component to cell 1,0.
   - ► Name: LST_TOP1COUNTRY
   - ► Visible: `false`

2. Add a TEXT component to cell 1,0.
   - ► Name: TXT_TOP1COUNTRY
   - ► CSS class: `header2`
   - ► Margins: top, bottom, left, right: 0; width, height: AUTO

3. Add a TEXT component to cell 1,1.
   - ► Name: TXT_TOP1_SALES
   - ► CSS class: `header2`
   - ► Margins: top, bottom, left, right: 0; width, height: AUTO

4. Add a TEXT component to cell 1,2.
   - ► Name: TXT_TOP1_DELTA
   - ► CSS class: `header2`
   - ► Margins: top, bottom, left, right: 0; width, height: AUTO

5. Copy the TXT_TOP1COUNTRY component to cells 2,0 through 10,0. Name the new components TXT_TOP2COUNTRY through TXT_TOP10COUNTRY.

6. Copy the component TXT_TOP1_SALES to cells 2,1 through 10,1. Name the new components TXT_TOP2_SALES through TXT_TOP10_SALES.

7. Copy the component TXT_OP1_DELTA to cells 2,2 through 10,2. Name the new components TXT_TOP2_SALES through TXT_TOP10_SALES.

The result is the layout we showed in Figure 11.10.

Customize the CSS code This would be a nice moment to play around with the CSS code. Change some colors, backgrounds, or fonts to your liking. With a layout like this, you can learn a lot by just trying things and seeing what happens.

Reference for CSS Code

If you need a reference for CSS code, a great place to start is:

http://w3schools.com/css/default.asp

This site has hundreds of examples of CSS code, as well as a built-in editor where you can try things yourself.

11.2.2 Setting Up the Filters and Countries

Now, let's set up the filters to enable the user to select the top *n* countries in terms of sales and enable filtering on regions. Then we will build the functionality that shows detailed information when the user selects a particular country.

In order to create the option for the user to select the top countries, first we set up the LIST BOX component to show the top *n* countries. Create a LIST BOX component in page 1 and name the component LISTBOX_TOPN. Then manually fill in the items in the properties as shown in Figure 11.11.

List Box component

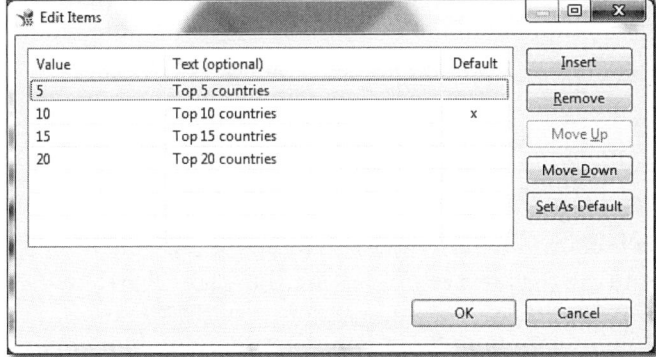

Figure 11.11 Items in the List Box Component for Number of Countries

In the On Select handler of the LIST BOX component, add the following code:

```
APPLICATION.setVariableValueExt("TOPN", LISTBOX_TOPN.getSelect-
edValue());
```

When the variable value is reset, all the data sources that depend on that variable will automatically refresh. The chart that is linked to the data source will then automatically change to the selected number of countries.

Add a LIST BOX component. Name the component DRPDWN_SELECT-YEAR. In the application, set the following code to fill the items of the components:

```
DRPDWN_SELECTYEAR.setItems(DS_
TOPNCOUNTRIES.getMemberList("0CALYEAR", MemberPresentation.INTE
RNAL_KEY, MemberDisplay.TEXT, 20));
APPLICATION.setVariableValueExt("SELJR", DRPDWN_SELECTYEAR.get-
SelectedValue());
```

Dropdown Box component

Add another DROPDOWN BOX component. Name this component DRPDWN_REGION. In the application `On Startup` handler, add the following script code to fill the items in the DROPDOWN BOX component.

```
DRPDWN_REGION.setItems(DS_TOPNCOUNTRIES.getMember-
List("ZCOUNTRY__ZREGRION", MemberPresentation.INTERNAL_
KEY, MemberDisplay.TEXT, 20));
```

In the `On Select` handler of the DROPDOWN BOX component, add the following script code:

```
APPLICATION.setVariableValue("ZREGION", DRPDWN_REGION.getSe-
lectedValue());
```

The result of the script code is that the top countries chart on the top left is refreshed when the component values are changed.

Add script code

The next step in building interactivity is to add script code that will use the selected country in the top n chart to change the other charts, so they will show the data of that selected country.

Why We Use Variables Instead of Filters

Instead of the `setfilter` method of the data source component, we use the `setvariable` method of the APPLICATION component. The reason for this choice is that we want the top countries within the scope of the filters. If we set the filter to 2011 and EUROPE & CENTRAL ASIA, we want to see the top 10 countries within these filters. Using the `setfilter` method would only give us the countries in a region within the scope of the initial 10 countries.

To show the users the market share of each company in a country, we will use a pie chart that shows the relative size of each company for a selected country. Add a CHART component to panel PNL_SELECTCOUNTRY. Use a data source with the layout as shown in Figure 11.12.

Country ⩲	Actuals Sales Amount ⩲ * 1.000.000 $	Budget Amount ⩲ * 1.000.000 $
United Arab Emirates	1.087	904
Turkey	1.092	1.061
Austria	1.260	1.171
Saudi Arabia	1.506	727
Norway	1.549	1.371
Belgium	1.550	1.456
Sweden	1.672	1.439
Japan	1.770	1.706
Switzerland	2.101	1.812
Netherlands	2.589	2.408
Total	**38.545**	**33.583**

Figure 11.12 Data Source Layout

Change the CHART TYPE property in the CHART component to BAR COMBINATION. In the On select handler of the CHART component, we set the following code:

Chart Type property

```
DS_MARKETSHARES.setFilter("ZCOUNTRY", CHRT_TOPNCOUNTRIES.getSe-
lectedMember("ZCOUNTRY"));
DS_HISTORY.setFilter("ZCOUNTRY", CHRT_TOPNCOUNTRIES.getSelect-
edMember("ZCOUNTRY"));
DS_LUXURYLEVELS.setFilter("ZCOUNTRY", CHRT_TOPNCOUNTRIES.getSe-
lectedMember("ZCOUNTRY"));
TXT_SELECTEDCOUNTRYLABEL.setText(DS_MARKETSHARES.getFilter-
Text("ZCOUNTRY"));
```

Three data sources are being filtered on the selected country. A TEXT component will show the selected country.

Three data sources

In the PANEL component PNL_MARKETSHARE, add a CHART component. Name the CHART component CHRT_MARKETSHARE. For the CHART component, we need a data source with a layout with the sales amount in the column and companies in the rows. Set the CHART type to PIE.

Add a TEXT component to PNL_MARKETSHARE. Name the component TXT_SELECTEDCOUNTRYLABEL. Set the CSS class to `header`.

Add last two charts Also add the last two CHART components for the history and the luxury level. The history chart is chart type LINE and the luxury level chart is chart type BAR.

To be able to link these charts to the code in the first chart, the data sources must have the same name as the data sources in the script code of the first chart.

11.2.3 Setting the Top 10 Countries

Values for Text components Next, let's focus on filling the TEXT components in page 2 with values. We'll also look at how the layouts of the delta figures are altered based on their values.

The LIST BOX components are filled like the examples we showed in the previous section. They also use script code to change the variable values in their On Select handlers.

Script code for each Text component We need to write a lot of script code. Each TEXT component requires a script line. Extra script line is needed for applying the layout. To avoid duplicate coding, we use the PAGEBOOK component's On Select handler to fill the values. We also chose this place because this part will only be executed when the page is actually accessed.

In the PAGEBOOK component On Select handler, we have the following code. (For brevity's sake we won't write the code for all 10 rows. We will use the third row as an example; the other rows are almost identical.)

```
if (PAGEBOOK_MAIN.getSelectedPageIndex() == 1)
{
//2nd page setup top 10 companies.

LST_TOP3COUNTRY.setItems(DS_
TOP03.getMemberList("ZCOUNTRY", MemberPresentation.INTERNAL_
KEY, MemberDisplay.TEXT, 1));
```

```
TXT_TOP3COUNTRY.setText(LST_TOP3COUNTRY.getSelectedText());
TXT_TOP3_SALES.setText(DS_
TOP03.getDataAsString("4UI2Y4WGS336B7BRTKB18T1VN", {}));
TXT_TOP3_DELTA.setText(DS_
TOP03.getDataAsString("4UI2XJZP5VZPLUDRXPXLVGJPF", {}));
//Apply layout based on delta %
TXT_TOP3_DELTA.setCSSClass(messageclass +
    DS_
TOP03.getConditionalFormatValueExt("4UI2XJZP5VZPLUDRXPXLVGJPF
", {}));
```

In the example code, we see that there is a separate data source for this row in the table. A data source is defined for each row. We have to take an extra step to get the country from the rows, which is to fill a List Box component with the one item. Using the item, we transfer the country value to the Text component.

We get the sales amount and the delta amount by using the get-DataAsString method from the data source.

For the layout we use the getConditionalFormat method. Using the exceptions in the BEx queries, we get a value from 1 to 5. We use that to define the CSS class for each delta value.

Define the CSS class

Advancing to the Next 10 Countries

To be able to go to the next 10 countries, we use a variable in the underlying BEx queries. When clicked, this button will set the number 10 positions higher and the query variable will be changed. The queries will then produce the new list of countries based on the new variable value.

Variable in BEx queries

```
APPLICATION.setVariableValueExt("TOPN", LISTBOX_TOPN.getSelect-
edValue());
BUTTON_PREVIOUS10.setVisible(true);
```

We know that once this button is clicked, the countries that are visible for the user are at least number 11 to 20 or higher. Knowing this, we can set the visibility of the button to go back up the list to true.

11.2.4 Creating a Top N Query

Ten data sources The application works with top *n* lists in the first page. In the second page, there are 10 data sources: one data source for each row in the list. Now let's learn how to use variables to build a flexible top *n* query and how to set up a query to show single countries in the top 10 list.

In the top *n* query, we used a query variable. The value for this variable was set using the LIST BOX component in the application. When you build a BEx query, you can set up conditions. A condition is a filter on the key figure, and one of the condition operators is the TOP N condition, where we define N as a manual variable. This is the variable that we change at runtime by selecting a value in the LIST BOX component.

In Figure 11.13 you see how the condition in the BEx query was set up.

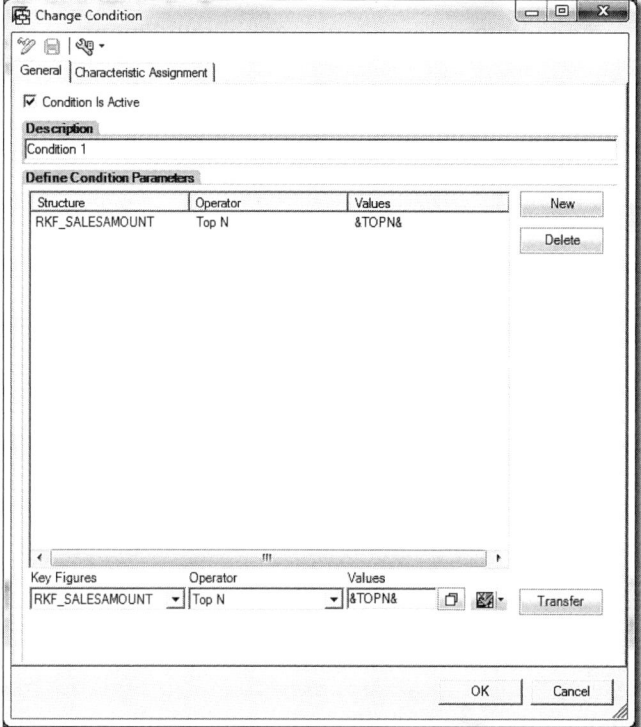

Figure 11.13 Top N Variable in BEx Query Condition

Creating a BEx Query to Get the Company in Third Place

To give you a general idea of how to view a single company that has a particular position in a ranking order, we are going to show you how to combine conditions in a BEx query to achieve this.

First we make a combination of a TOP N condition and a BOTTOM N condition like the example in Figure 11.14.

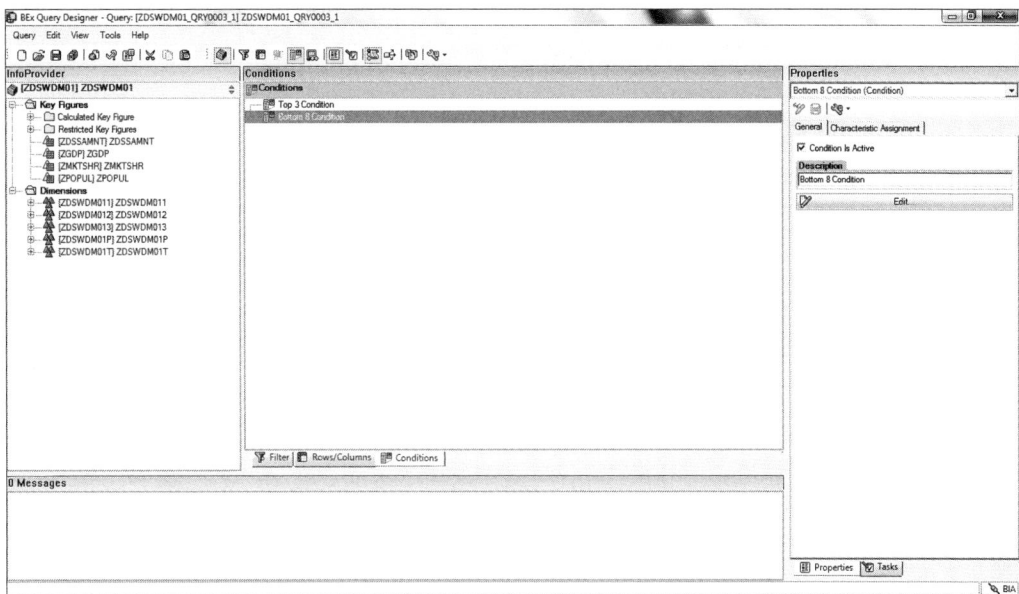

Figure 11.14 Top N and Bottom N Conditions

Again, the TOP N condition is defined as already shown in Figure 11.13. For the BOTTOM N condition we use another variable (Figure 11.15).

The combination of these two conditions can set the query up to give us one country. For example, if we want the third position from a list of ten countries, we need to combine the top three country condition with the bottom eight condition. As you can see in Figure 11.16, there is only one rank that fulfills both conditions.

Figure 11.15 Bottom N condition with Variable ZIV_BOTN

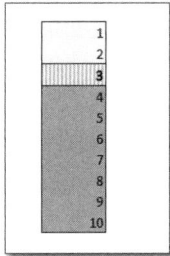

Figure 11.16 Combination of Top Three and Bottom Eight Conditions

Set variables to view rankings

By setting variables in the application, you can use this query to get any rank you wish. For example, in our list of countries we have a total of 216 countries. If we want the 32nd country, we combine the top 32 with the bottom 183.

Defining BEx Query Exceptions

To get the layout for the target deltas, we used BEx query exceptions. We got values ranging from 1 to 5 back from the data source based on the rules in the query. We defined the exception in the query as shown in Figure 11.17.

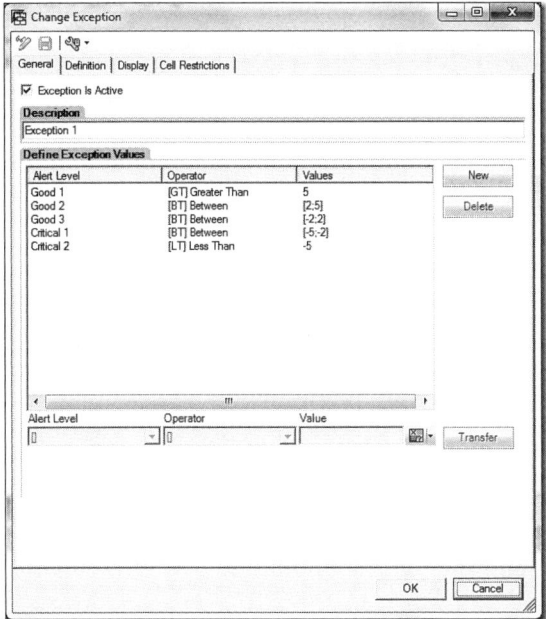

Figure 11.17 Query Exception

The maximum number of exception levels you can define is nine. We used the top five numbers so we could concatenate the exception number to a CSS class named `alertlevel`. When the exception level is five, then the CSS class `alertlevel5` will be assigned to the relevant component.

Maximum amount of exception levels

11.3   Summary

In this chapter, you saw another example of an advanced application built using Design Studio. We discussed the way it worked, how it was set up, and the techniques we used to give the application its necessary functionality.

The future of Design Studio has a lot to offer. Let's take a look at it in this last chapter of the book.

12   Outlook for SAP BusinessObjects Design Studio

As you may know, SAP has spent the last few years focusing on their mobile strategy. Their goal is to enable the mobilization of information, and to give users the possibility to get instant answers and turn these new possibilities into strategic use cases for increased productivity (Figure 12.1).

Mobility at SAP

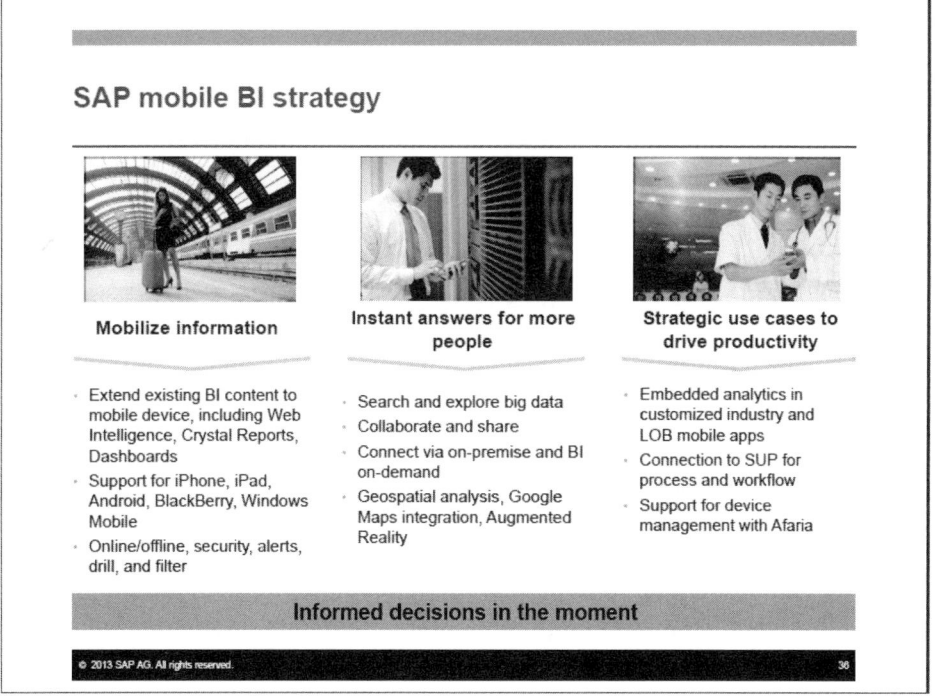

Figure 12.1 SAP Mobile BI Strategy

Design Studio fits well into this strategy, as it is designed to work with tablets and smart phones but also works directly on the backend systems of SAP NetWeaver BW and SAP HANA. With the added functionality of SAP mobile technologies, users are able to share and communicate information to other people from their devices.

Because of its importance to mobility and to SAP in general, this chapter will take a look at the roadmap for Design Studio. As you can see in Figure 12.2, the main focus of the Design Studio roadmap is on expanding functionality for the next release.

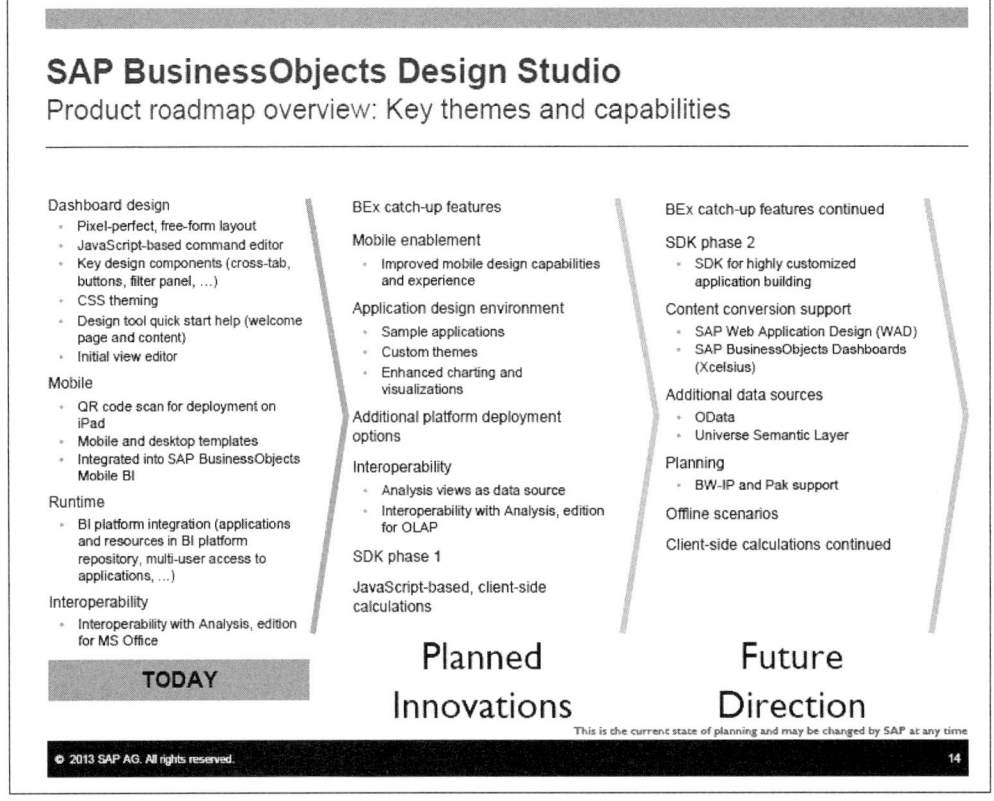

Figure 12.2 Design Studio Roadmap

More BEx functionalities will be incorporated, the SDK program will be introduced and further expanded, additional data sources will be made available, offline scenarios will be possible, and the number of ways that you can insert calculations in applications will be increased. Additionally, content conversion support will be available from BEx Web Application Designer applications and dashboards made with SAP BusinessObjects Dashboards.

> **Design Studio and SAP BusinessObjects Dashboards**
>
> Although this chapter is about the outlook for Design Studio, it's worth briefly addressing how Design Studio affects other products in the SAP Business-Objects BI portfolio—specifically, SAP BusinessObjects Dashboards. The official SAP statement is that both products will continue to be developed over the next few years—but Design Studio will be the main application for the long run.
>
> What their exact roles will be is still not clear. In the roadmap, content conversion from SAP BusinessObjects Dashboards to Design Studio is planned. Also, once Design Studio has access to universes and OData connections, most of the connectivity reasons to use SAP BusinessObjects Dashboards instead of Design Studio will disappear. On the other hand, you might use Design Studio for a more centralized view of dashboards, and SAP Business-Objects Dashboards for more local freedom.

12.1 Software Development Kit (SDK)

The Software Development Kit (SDK) is planned for version 1.2 of Design Studio. The Component SDK beta program targets SAP customers and partners who want to create new visualizations in Design Studio. The Component SDK allows developers to create new web components for data visualization based on the same data sources that can be used in native components (SAP NetWeaver BW and SAP HANA). | Component SDK beta program

Some of the partners who already offer SDK add-ons for SAP Business-Objects Dashboards are developing add-ons for Design Studio. For example, Graphomate, a company that delivers visualizations for SAP BusinessObjects Dashboards, has posted a YouTube movie in which they show their progress with the SDK add-on for Design Studio (Figure 12.3):

http://www.youtube.com/watch?v=knsojJJq904 | Graphomate

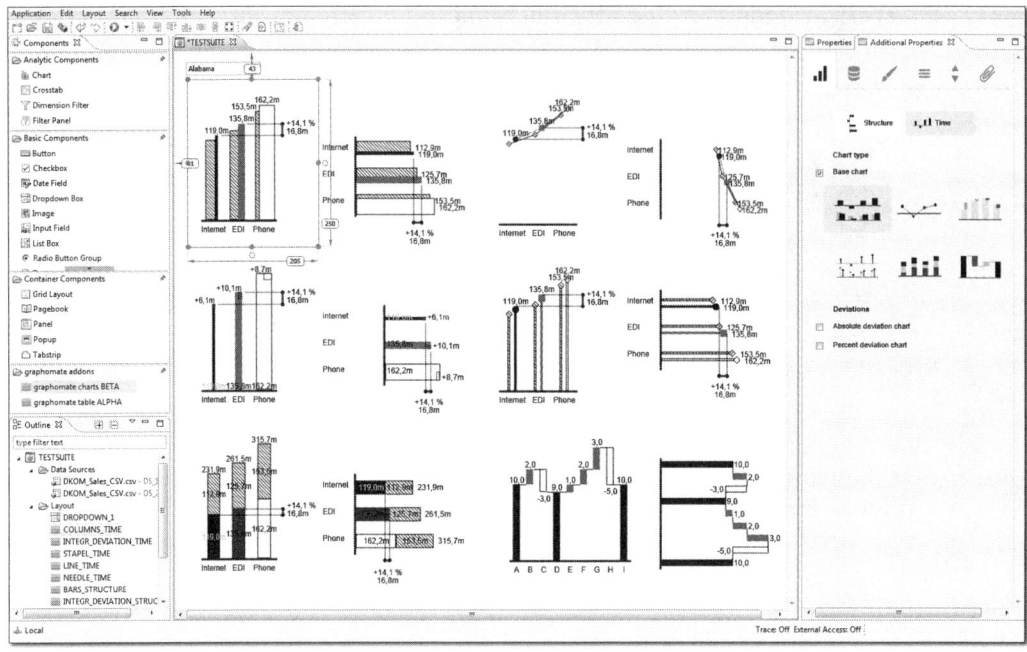

Figure 12.3 Graphomate Component Screenshot

12.2 Integrated Planning and Planning Application Kit Support

Writing data to the backend

In future releases of Design Studio, SAP NetWeaver BW Integrated Planning (BW-IP) and the Planning Application Kit (PAK) are planned. This is an important addition to Design Studio, as it would enable users to input values to the backend in a secure way. Currently, users are using workarounds to enter values into the backend system from a Design Studio application, so this should have a big impact on user acceptance. Since Design Studio is explicitly designed with remote scenarios in mind, we expect that this will have some priority for the SAP development team.

> **Note**
>
> For some tips on how to work around the issue of writing data to the backend, refer back to Section 10.2.5 of Chapter 10, where we cover a little ABAP.

12.3 Universes and OData

In future releases you will be able to connect to additional types of data sources. Specifically, you will be able to connect to SAP BusinessObjects BI universes and external data sources using the OData protocol. OData is a standardized protocol for creating and consuming data APIs. It builds on core protocols like HTTP and commonly accepted methodologies like REST. The result is a uniform way to expose full-featured data APIs, which can then be transferred in either ATOM or JSON. As there is already a variable type JSON in the current version of Design Studio, we foresee that OData will provide a way to either load as a data source or to load data into a variable. In Figure 12.4, you see how OData is a protocol between producers and consumers of data.

Universes, external data sources

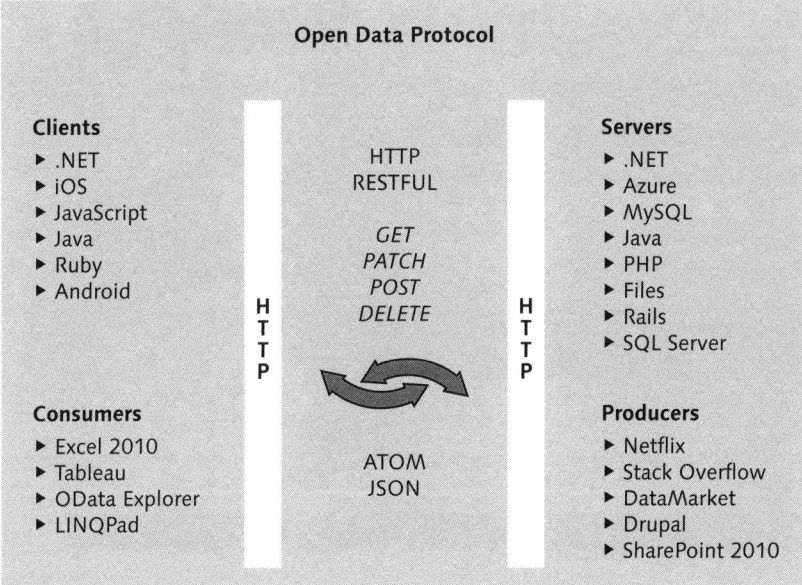

Figure 12.4 OData Overview

More on OData

For more on OData, refer to *OData and SAP NetWeaver Gateway* by Carsten Bönnen et al. (SAP PRESS, 2014).

411

12.4   Mobilize, Visualize, and Unify

SAP
BusinessObjects
Dashboards
Mobilize

To sum it all up, the future direction of Design Studio is built on the themes *mobilize* (Figure 12.5), *visualize* (Figure 12.6), and *unify* (Figure 12.7). For the mobilize theme, the goal is to have applications for mobile devices. These dashboards and applications need to be deployed easily and securely.

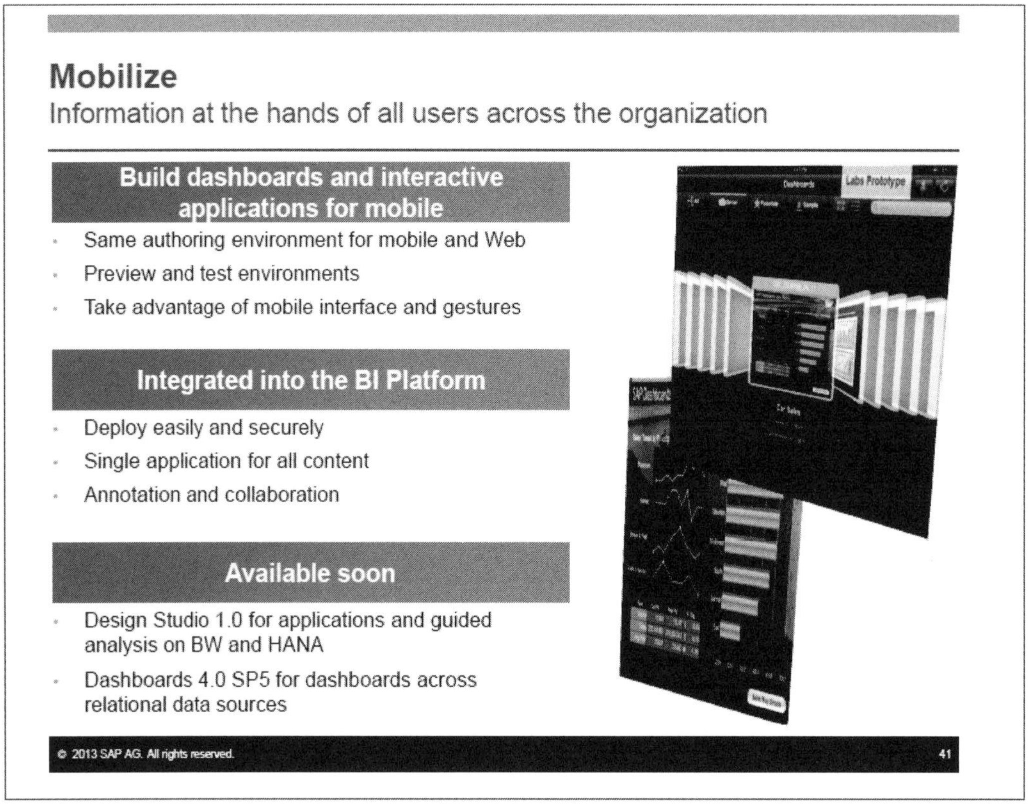

Figure 12.5 Mobilize

Visualize   To achieve the visualize theme, work is being done to build a common visualization engine that will be used across multiple applications. In the future, each tool will have access to the same visualizations. Furthermore, an SDK will be available for parties to build their own custom visualizations on top of the standard library.

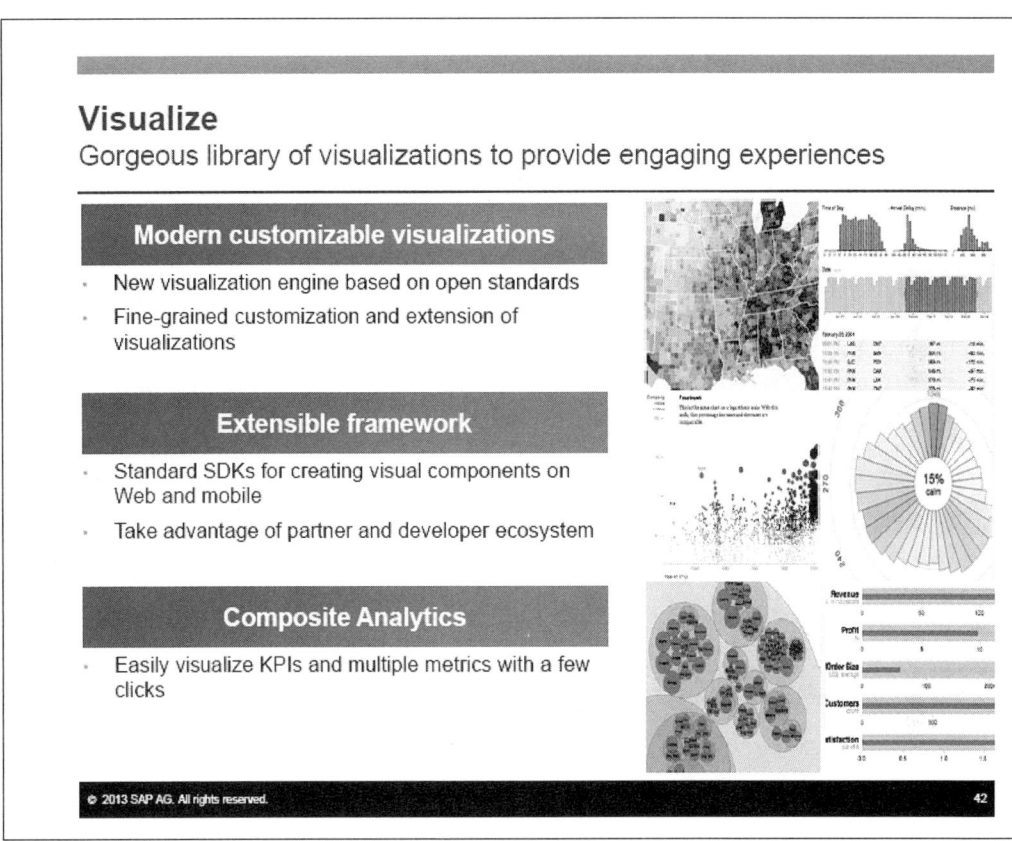

Figure 12.6 Visualize

For the unify theme, Design Studio shows that one tool can build all kinds of applications. We see in the roadmap that other data sources, such as universes and the OData protocol, are planned, which will further accomplish this goal. And, as Design Studio applications are based on HTML5, a single runtime for web and mobile is also guaranteed.

Unify

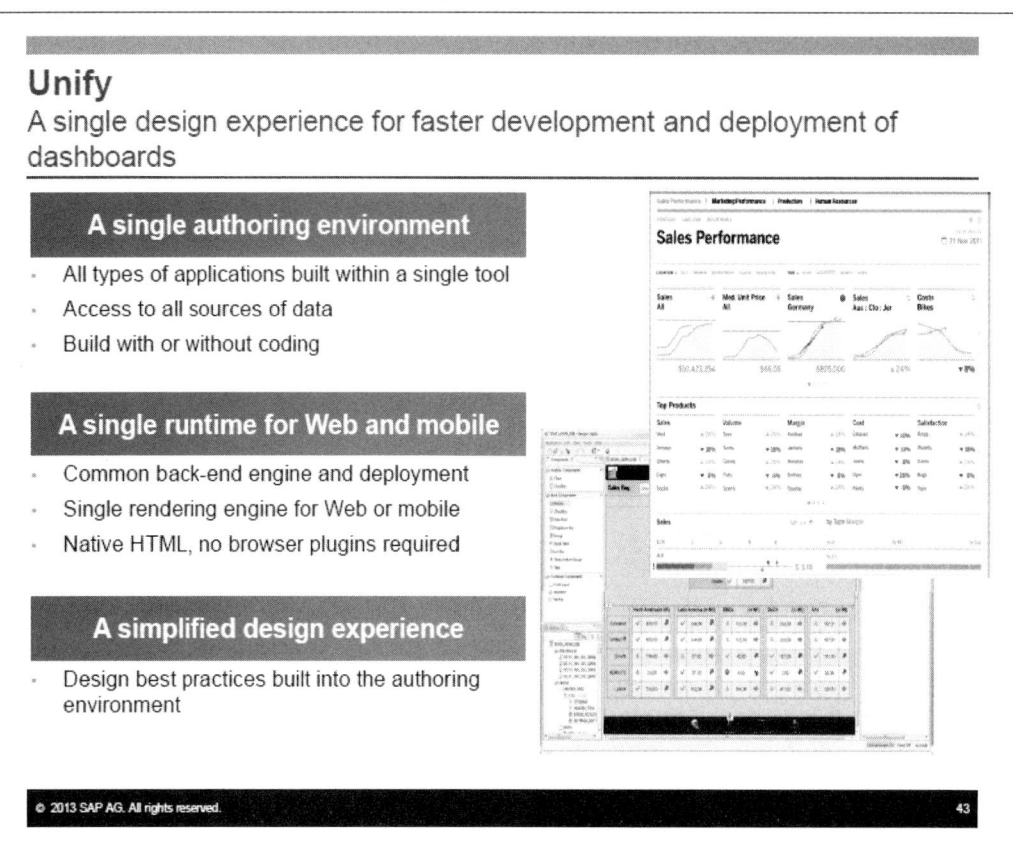

Figure 12.7 Unify

12.5   Summary

In this chapter we described the outlook of Design Studio, including its future functionality and direction.

Appendices

A   Using CSS

CSS plays a very important role in the layout settings of a Design Studio application. CSS is first applied by the standard theme, then by the custom CSS class, which you can add to the application, and—finally—by editing the CSS style of individual components. For faster development, it is very important to have a standard set of classes available. The developer then only has to assign classes to components to use the predefined style.

Before you create applications, it is advisable to think about how you want to deal with custom CSS files. Basically, there are three strategies that you can apply:

▶ **Centralized**
In this scenario, there is a single CSS file on the SAP BI platform that will be used by every application. The advantage is that every application will have the same look and feel, as they all will be using the same CSS file and thus the same colors and fonts. The disadvantage is that there is only limited freedom for applications to apply their own format. The only way is to use the CSS STYLE property in components.

▶ **Federated**
In this scenario, you have a central CSS file—but when you start the development of an application, you copy the central CSS file to the repository of the application. You can then alter the CSS of this copied file. The advantage here is that everyone has the same starting point and still has some flexibility. The disadvantage is that when the central CSS file changes, you have a rollout scenario to deal with.

▶ **Local**
In this scenario, everyone can build his own CSS file. The advantages and disadvantages are exactly the opposite of the centralized scenario. Now there is a lot of freedom, but every application will look different and different standards will be applied.

In this appendix, we'll give you some basic information about working with CSS files.

A.1   The Structure of a CSS File

You can define classes in a CSS file. You define a class by starting with a point and the class name. After this you set up all the properties between brackets: { }.

```
.mycssclass {
property1: value;
property2: value;
property3: value;
}
```

When you assign mycssclass to a component, the component will use these properties. Let's look at the following example that we used earlier in the book:

```
.alert1
{
 border:1px solid;
 border-color:#000000;
 border-radius:25px;
 background-color:#000000;
}
```

The class alert1 adds a border, sets the color property of the border, rounds the angles, and sets the background color of the component.

You can also define subclasses. For example, let's say you have a component and you only want to alter its layout when it is assigned to a specific class. To define a subclass, you add another class selector in front of the class you already defined:

```
.AlternateClass.alert1 {property: value; property: value; }
```

(In Section A.3, we will explain how you can use this defining of subclasses to change the inner layout of components.)

CSS Reference

Rather than listing all the possible CSS codes here, we advise you to go to *http://www.W3schools.com*, where all available CSS codes are explained with examples, and an online editor is available to try it out for yourself.

A.2   Tips for Building CSS Files

In this section we are going to share a couple of common guidelines for writing CSS files. These guidelines will help you in building and maintaining custom CSS files. It is especially important to follow these rules when you build a master CSS file that is to be used by many applications.

A.2.1   Give the Classes Appropriate Names

Do not name a class for the style it performs; name it for its function. For example,

```
.redmessage { background-color: yellow }
```

could also be named

```
.alertmessage { background-color: yellow }
```

In addition, when assigning a class to a TEXT component that is supposed to give an alert message, the latter naming method is much more logical and easier to understand.

A.2.2   Try to Keep the Declarations in One Line

Although keeping your code on multiple lines may look nicer, it doesn't help you to find the class you're looking for. If you know that each line starts with a new class, you only have to scan the first word of each line.

A.2.3   Use Shorthand Code

Shorthand code is a lot easier to write than the full code. Furthermore, having fewer characters in the CSS file increases the speed of the application (although, admittedly, not very much).

For example, if you want to set the background settings with CSS, the full code would be:

```
.mycustomclass
{
background-image:url('img_tree.png');
```

```
background-repeat:no-repeat;
background-position:right top;
}
```

In shorthand, the code is:

```
.myclass {background:#ffffff url('img_tree.png') no-
repeat right top;}
```

Shorthand Guide

For those who want to learn about shorthand code, we recommend this site:

http://www.dustindiaz.com/css-shorthand/

It is an old site, but one of the few that gives an overview of all the shorthand codes. All the shorthand codes are also mentioned at W3Schools.

A.2.4   Know the Browsers

If you build CSS code, you'll want to know which browsers are being used and if your application will be run on an iPhone or iPad. Do not try to build in support for all the browser versions—just maintain it for the browser types that are actually being used.

A.2.5   Group Your Classes

If you have more classes with the same properties, group them. This will save you a lot of double entries. If you want to define more classes, but those classes will have the same layout for the time being, it saves a lot of time.

Without grouping:

```
.class1
{ font-family:Arial,Helvetica,Lucida,Sans-
Serif; color:#000; margin:1em 0;}
.class2
{ font-family:Arial,Helvetica,Lucida,Sans-
Serif; color:#000; margin:1em 0;}
.class3
```

```
{ font-family:Arial,Helvetica,Lucida,Sans-
Serif; color:#000; margin:1em 0;}
```

With grouping:

```
.class1 .class2 .class3
{ font-family:Arial,Helvetica,Lucida,Sans-
Serif; color:#000; margin:1em 0;}
```

A.3   Changing the Inner Style of Components with CSS

For really fine-tuning the layout, you can alter the inner style of the standard components. To be able to do this, you need to know the CSS classes that SAP assigned to the components. By using these classes within a class of your own, you can assign a class to a component, which results in a changed layout.

First you need to know how to look for the CSS classes that are defined for the components:

1. Create a new application and put one CROSSTAB component on the canvas. For the rest leave the application empty. Set the application theme to MOBILE IPAD.

2. Within Google Chrome (or another browser), you can choose the option INSPECT ELEMENT. You will see the code underlying the application as shown in Figure A.1. Double-clicking LIBRARY.CSS in the CROSSTAB directory opens the CSS file (Figure A.2) that holds the classes that build the layout of the CROSSTAB component.

Now you can apply this knowledge in your own custom CSS file. There are two ways.

You can force the application to always apply your standard. In your CSS file apply the following code:

```
.sapzencrosstab-DataCellTotal { property: value;
  property: value}
```

Figure A.1 Finding CSS Code in the Application

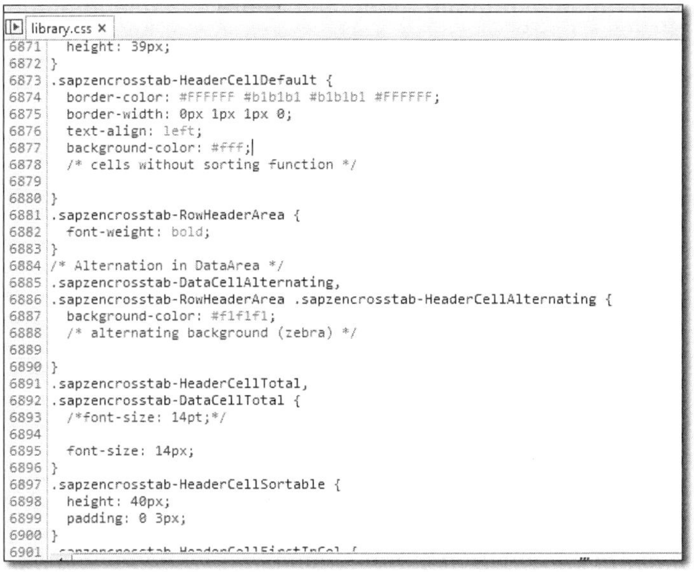

Figure A.2 CSS Code

Alternatively, you can change the layout of the CROSSTAB component when there is a CSS class assigned to that component. In your CSS file, apply the following code:

```
YourCSSClass.sapzencrosstab-
DataCellTotal { property: value; property: value}
```

The first option has the advantage that you can apply your company's style without having to assign classes. The second option has the advantage that you keep the SAP standard CSS themes in place.

B Tips for Using SAP BusinessObjects Design Studio and SAP BusinessObjects Analysis, Edition for Microsoft Office

SAP BusinessObjects Analysis, edition for Microsoft Office, is part of the SAP BusinessObjects BI portfolio, and it allows advanced multidimensional analysis of OLAP sources. It is the successor to the BEx Analyzer and it runs, just like the BEx Analyzer, as a plugin within Microsoft Excel. It is also possible to use SAP BusinessObjects Analysis from within Microsoft PowerPoint. Besides the Microsoft Office version of SAP BusinessObjects Analysis, there is also an online web version available, called SAP BusinessObjects Analysis, edition for OLAP. This application is integrated into the SAP BusinessObjects BI platform and can be accessed from the BI Launch Pad.

> **Note**
>
> This appendix is devoted specifically to the Microsoft Office edition of SAP BusinessObjects Analysis. We will refer to the product as simply SAP BusinessObjects Analysis, but know that we specifically mean the Microsoft Office, not the OLAP, edition.

There are two hidden features in SAP BusinessObjects Analysis that can be useful when you want to develop a Design Studio application:

- Creating a Design Studio application
- Smart copying data sources

SAP BusinessObjects Analysis also has a few features that are not available in Design Studio yet. You can, for example, add calculations, conditional formatting, and exceptions—all features that we can make use of in Design Studio. In this appendix we will show you how.

B.1 Creating a Design Studio Application

It is possible to transfer the components of an SAP BusinessObjects Analysis workbook to a new Design Studio application. The following components are supported:

▶ CROSSTAB components

▶ CHART components (pie, line, column, bar, surface, radar, bubble, and scatter charts)

▶ FILTER components

To transfer components, follow the steps below:

1. Open SAP BusinessObjects Analysis.

2. Open an existing workbook or create a new one (Figure B.1).

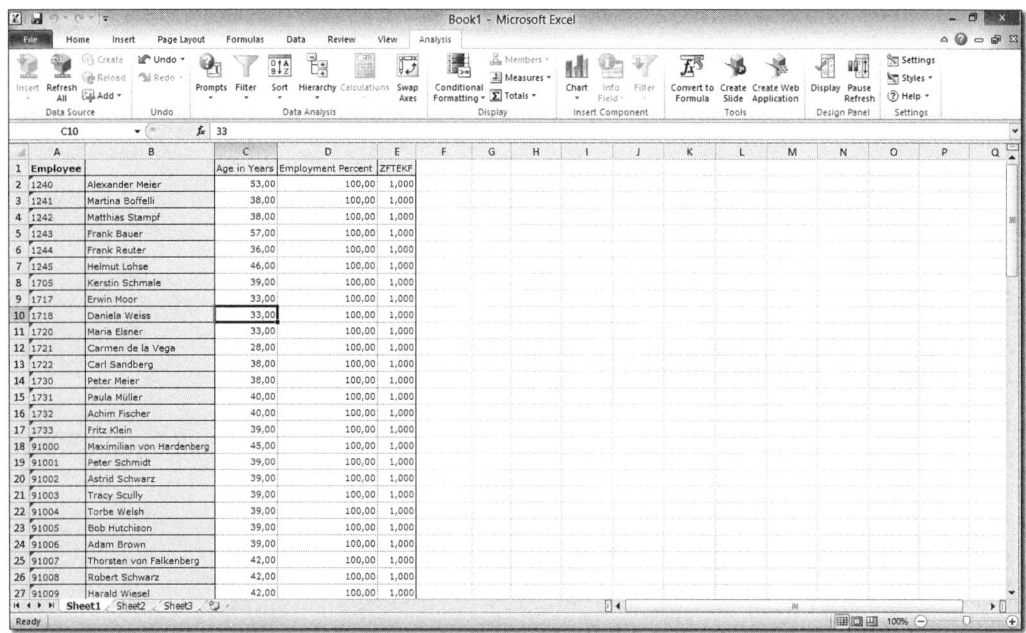

Figure B.1 SAP BusinessObjects Analysis

3. Check whether the CREATE WEB APPLICATION icon is present in the ANALYSIS ribbon (Figure B.2).

Figure B.2 Create Web Application Icon

4. If this icon is not available, go to SETTINGS • ADVANCED SETTINGS and select the option for SHOW "CREATE WEB APPLICATION" IN TOOLS GROUP (Figure B.3). Click OK.

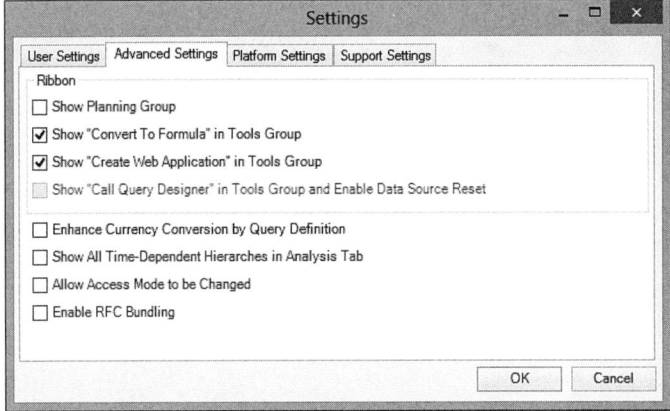

Figure B.3 SAP BusinessObjects Analysis Settings

5. Make sure that Design Studio is not currently running. If it is, save your work and close Design Studio.

6. Select the workbook sheet you want to transfer to Design Studio.

7. Click the CREATE WEB APPLICATION button in the ANALYSIS ribbon (Figure B.2).

8. Design Studio starts now. Enter your credentials and click OK to log on to Design Studio.

9. You will now see a new Design Studio application based on the Analysis workbook, including the components and data sources (Figure B.4). You can continue working on this application from here.

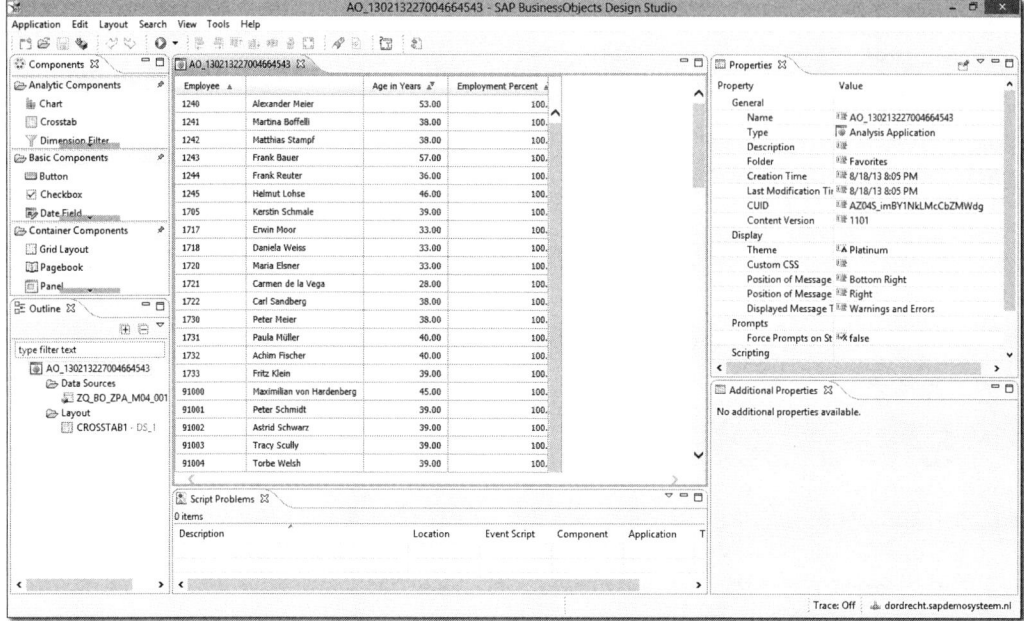

Figure B.4 New Design Studio Application Based on SAP BusinessObjects Analysis

B.2 Smart Copying Data Sources

Instead of transferring a whole workbook from SAP BusinessObjects Analysis, we can also copy only the data source from the workbook.

1. Open SAP BusinessObjects Analysis.

2. Open an existing workbook or create a new one.

3. Now right-click the result table and select SMART COPY from the context menu (Figure B.5).

4. In Design Studio, right-click the DATA SOURCES folder in the OUTLINE view (Figure B.6). Select SMART PASTE. The data source is now added to the Design Studio application.

Another option is to right-click the LAYOUT folder in the OUTLINE view and select SMART PASTE. In this case, not only the data source is added to the Design Studio application, but also a new CROSSTAB component is added and already assigned to the new data source.

Figure B.5 Smart Copy Option in SAP BusinessObjects Analysis

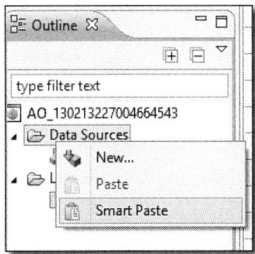

Figure B.6 Smart Paste Feature in Design Studio

C   SAP BusinessObjects Mobile and SAP BusinessObjects Design Studio

In this appendix, we will introduce SAP BusinessObjects Mobile (Figure C.1). With the SAP BusinessObjects Mobile application, users of mobile devices can get access to several content types of the SAP Business-Objects BI platform from a single mobile application. Besides Design Studio applications, this includes content from SAP Crystal Reports, SAP BusinessObjects Web Intelligence, and SAP BusinessObjects Dashboards. Additionally, you can access SAP BusinessObjects Explorer information spaces and the SAP Lumira Cloud.

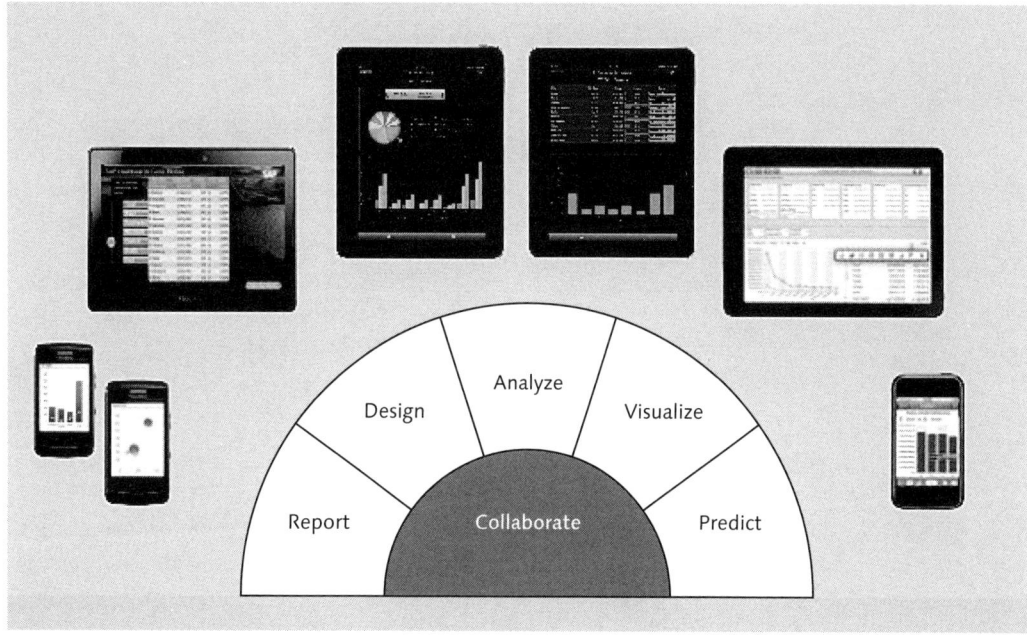

Figure C.1 Mobilizing the SAP BusinessObjects BI Suite

In this appendix we will take a quick look at the features of this mobile application. We use version 5.0.5.

C.1   Supported Platforms

The SAP BusinessObjects Mobile application is currently available for iOS devices (iPhone and iPad) and Android smartphones and tablets. The applications can be downloaded for free from the Apple App Store in iTunes and the Google Play Store.

▶ **SAP BusinessObjects Mobile 5 for iOS**
   https://itunes.apple.com/us/app/sap-businessobjects-mobile/ id441208302?mt=8

▶ **SAP BusinessObjects Mobile 5 for Android**
   https://play.google.com/store/apps/details?id=com.sap.mobi&hl=en

Support for Design Studio Applications

Unfortunately, only the SAP BusinessObjects Mobile application for iOS currently supports Design Studio applications.

Mobile Server on the SAP BusinessObjects BI Platform

To be able to connect to an SAP BusinessObjects BI platform and use its content on the mobile applications, the SAP BusinessObjects Mobile Server needs to be installed and configured on the SAP BusinessObjects BI platform. More information about the Mobile Server can be found at *http:// help.sap.com/bomobile40*.

C.2   Connectivity

Connecting the SAP BusinessObjects Mobile application to an SAP BusinessObjects BI platform requires that you have set up a connection in the application. This can be done via BROWSE • SETTINGS (the gear icon) • APPLICATION SETTINGS • CREATE NEW CONNECTION. In this screen, you can enter the connection name, provide the server URL and CMS name, and set the authentication mode. You also have to enter your user credentials (Figure C.2).

Figure C.2 Connection Setup

C.3 Using Content

Before you can use content from the SAP BusinessObjects BI platform, you have to make that content available for mobile usage. This should be done by filing the content documents—for example, a Design Studio application—in the MOBILE category. This is explained in Section 4.4.4 of Chapter 4.

C.3.1 Browsing the Application

After connecting to the SAP BusinessObjects BI platform, the available content shows up on the home screen of the application (Figure C.3). Here you can open a report, dashboard, or application and refresh it. You can also view information about a document by tapping the information icon (i) and assign it to a custom category (Figure C.4). By tapping the plus icon (+), the content will be downloaded and can be used offline.

433

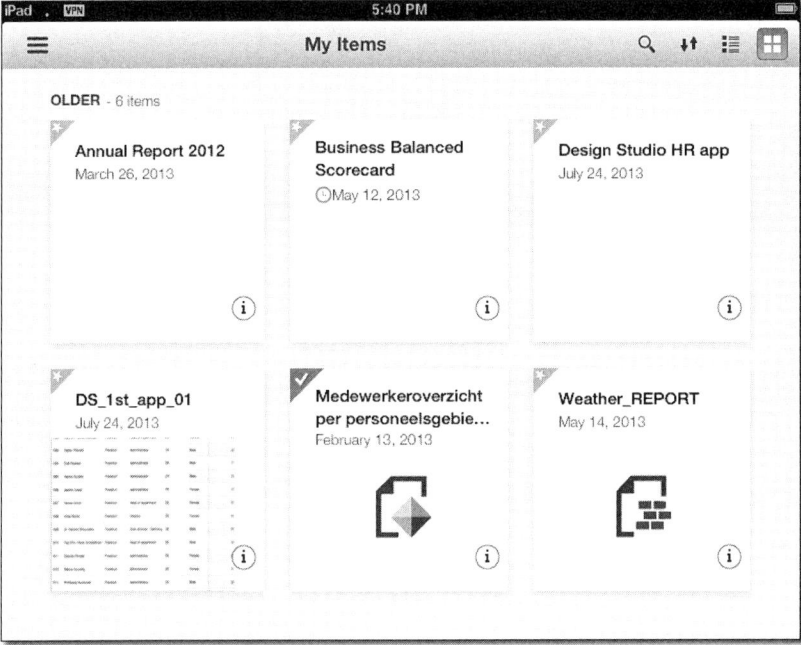

Figure C.3 Browsing through Mobile BI Content

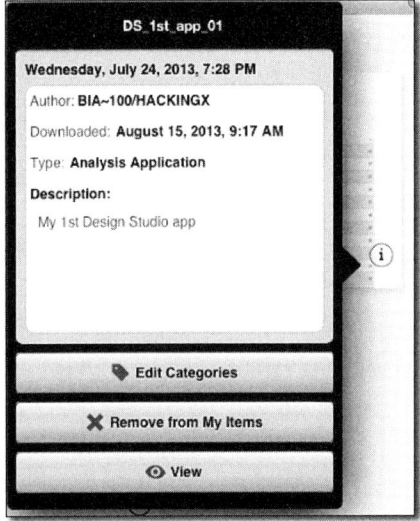

Figure C.4 Information Screen

C.3.2 Running SAP BusinessObjects BI Content

When running a Design Studio application in SAP BusinessObjects Mobile, the exact same functionality is available as when you execute the same application in a browser. The only difference is that now you use your fingers instead of the mouse to interact with the components.

In Figure C.5, you can see the first tab of the Design Studio application that we created back in Chapter 6, displayed in full-screen mode. We selected the HEADCOUNT measure and tapped a data point on the chart. This action resulted in a detail box giving the exact value of the tapped data point.

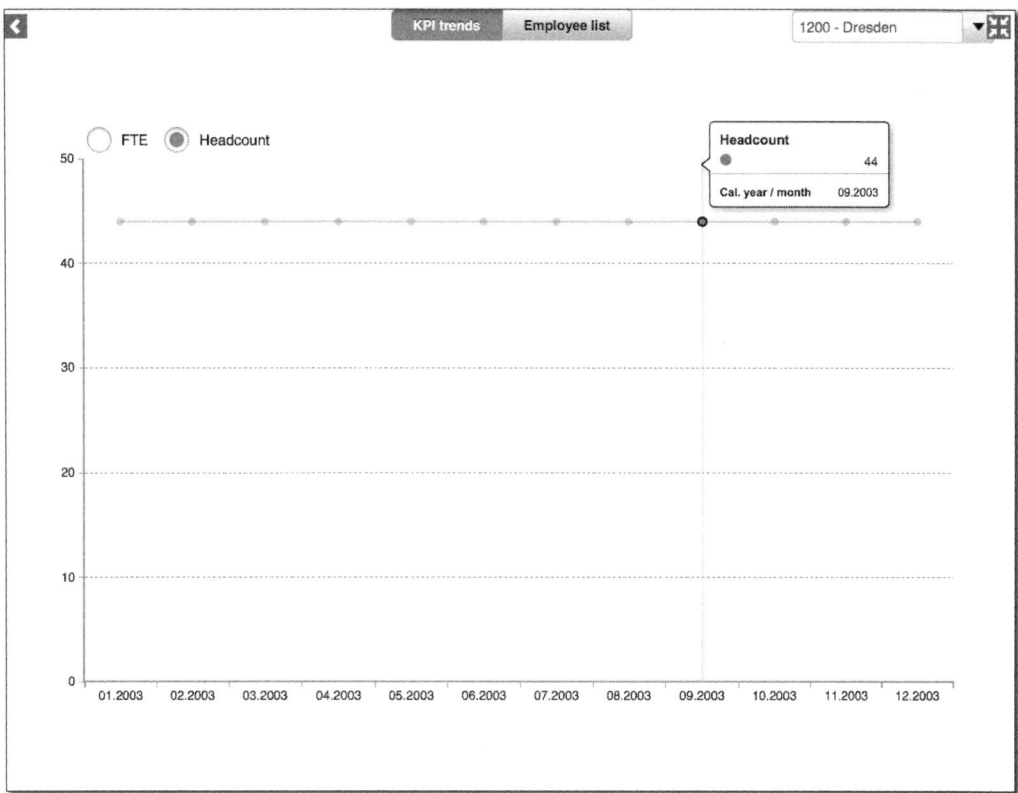

Figure C.5 Design Studio Application in SAP BusinessObjects Mobile: Part 1

Figure C.6 shows the second tab of the application, which appears after you tap the EMPLOYEE LIST tab. Here the DROPDOWN BOX component is

435

selected, and a selection is made for department 1300 – FRANKFURT. The filtered data is shown in the CROSSTAB component.

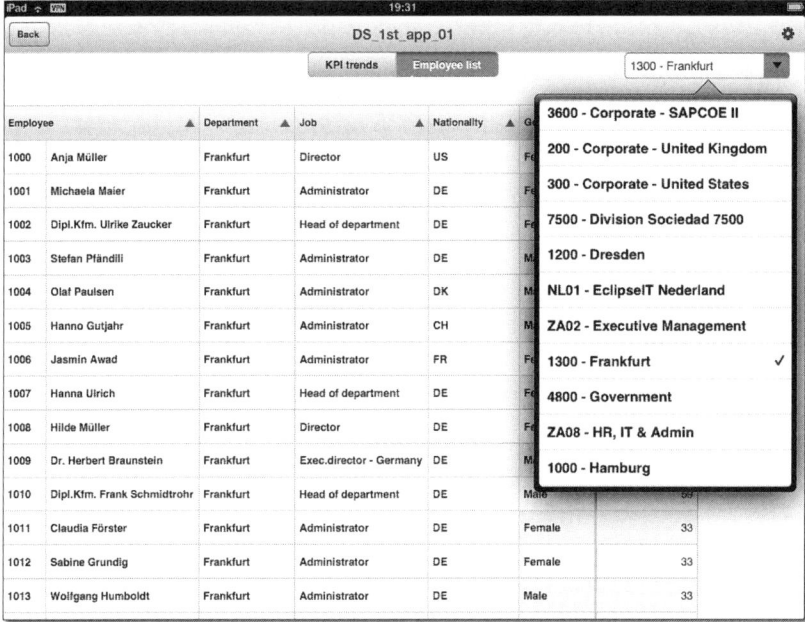

Figure C.6 Design Studio Application in SAP BusinessObjects Mobile: Part 2

C.3.3 Collaboration Features

When a report, dashboard, or application is running, a settings toolbar can be made visible by tapping the settings button in the upper-right corner of the screen (Figure C.7). This gives you access to some interesting collaboration features.

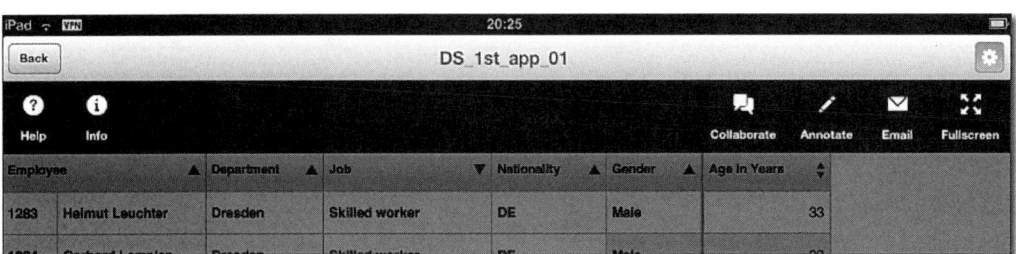

Figure C.7 Settings Toolbar

The content can be shared and discussed with colleagues over the SAP
Jam collaboration platform. If you want to add some texts, lines, or
boxes; blur parts of the content; or crop the output of the content, you
can use the ANNOTATION option (Figure C.8). You can even record a
voice memo as an annotation (Figure C.9). Finally, you can send an
email that contains a screenshot of the content (annotations included),
with links to the content (Figure C.10).

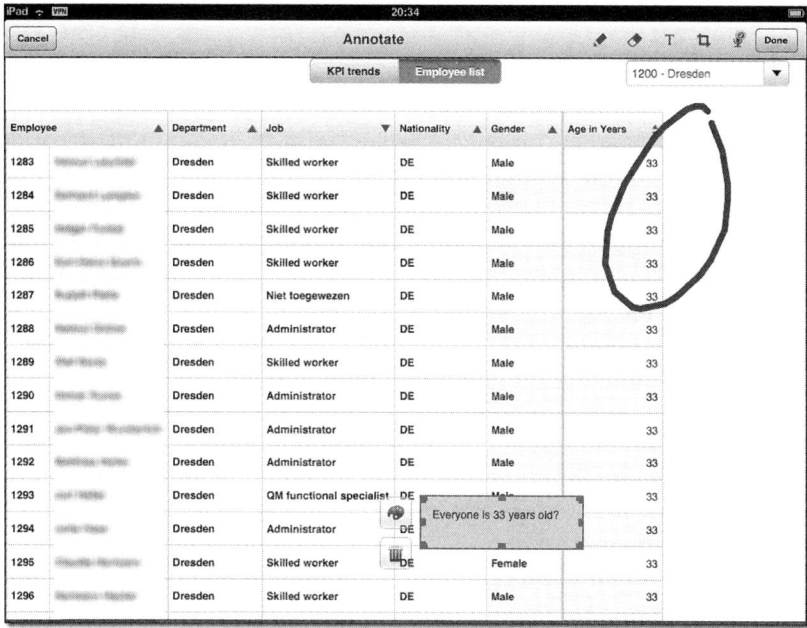

Figure C.8 Annotation Options

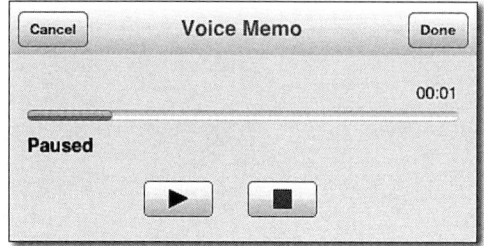

Figure C.9 Recording a Voice Memo

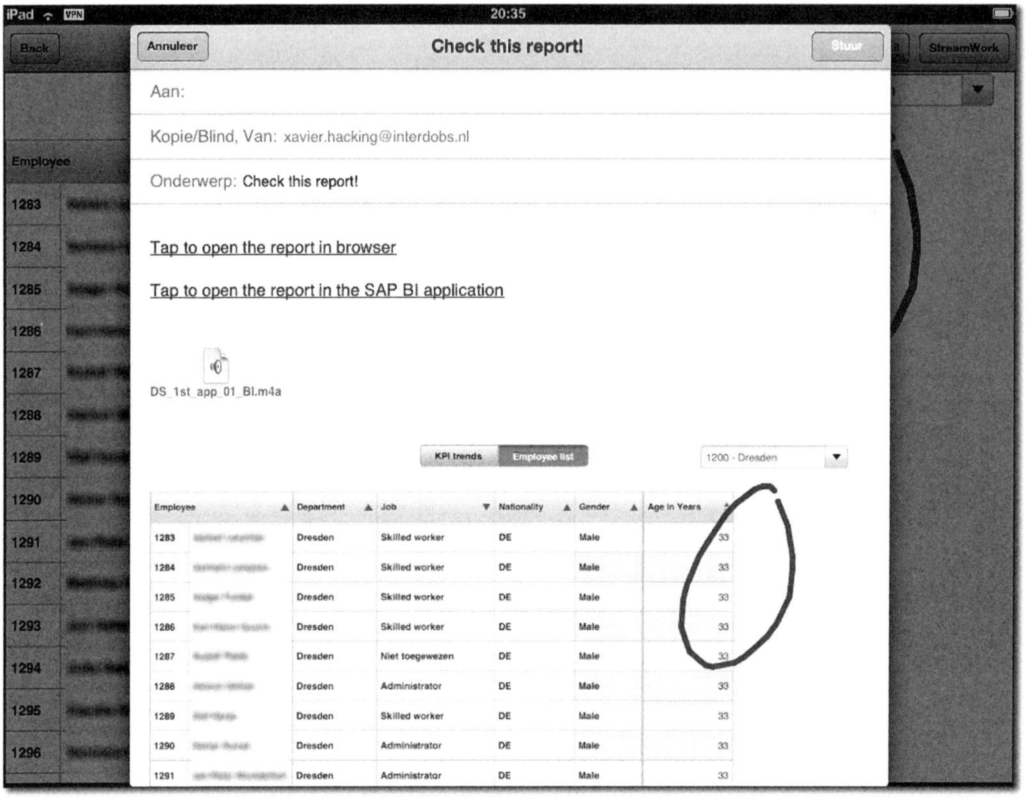

Figure C.10 Sending an Email

D Comprehensive List of Methods and Parameters

D.1 Application Component

Methods	Descriptions
Alert	Opens a message box. **Parameter** ▶ Message type string: message text
createErrorMessage	Creates an error message that is visible in the MESSAGE view. **Parameter** ▶ Message type string: message text
createInfoMessage	Creates an info message that is displayed in the MESSAGE view. **Parameter** ▶ Message type string: message text
createWarningMessage	Creates a warning message that is displayed in the MESSAGE view. **Parameter** ▶ Message type string: message text
getInfo	Returns analysis application information.
log	This method creates a message in the error log for analysis. If you have a complex piece of script and it does not work properly, you can use this for debugging purposes. **Parameter** ▶ Message type string: message text
openNewWindow	Opens a new browser window with the specified URL. **Parameter** ▶ newURL type string: URL

Methods	Descriptions
openPromptDialog	Opens a dialog box. **Parameters** ▸ Width type integer: width of the dialog box ▸ Height type integer: height of the dialog box
setVariableValue	Sets query variable values in the internal key format and executes the data source query again. **Parameters** ▸ Variable type variable: query variable to change ▸ Value type string: value to set in internal key format
setVariableValueExt	Sets query variable values in the external key format, then executes the data source query again. **Parameters** ▸ Variable type variable: query variable to change ▸ Value type inputstring: value to set in external key format
openNewWindow	Opens a new browser window with the specified URL.

D.2　Button Component

Method	Description
getText	Gives the text that is displayed on the BUTTON component.
getEnabled	Tells whether the BUTTON component is enabled.
setText	Sets the text that is shown on the BUTTON component. **Parameter** ▸ Text type string: message text

Method	Description
setEnabled	Sets the BUTTON to enabled or disabled depending on the parameter value. **Parameter** ▶ Enabled type Boolean: specifies whether to enable or disable the button

D.3　Chart Component

Method	Description
getChartType	Gives the name of the CHART component.
getSelectedMember	Gives you information about the selected data point. With the parameter dimension, you define the dimension value you want to see. **Parameter** ▶ Dimension type Dimension: dimension of the selected members
getStyle	Shows the name of the CHART component style.
isVisible	Shows the CHART component's visibility status.
setChartType	Changes the CHART component type. **Parameter** ▶ chartType type ChartType: chart type to set
setStyle	Changes the CHART component style. **Parameter** ▶ Style type ChartStyle: chart style to set
setVisible	Sets the CHART component's visibility. **Parameter** ▶ Visible type Boolean: specifies whether to show or hide the component
showTotals	Shows or hides (sub)totals. **Parameter** ▶ Visible type Boolean: specifies whether to show or hide the subtotals

Method	Description
swapAxes	Swaps the axes as they appear in the data source for a different chart perspective. **Parameter** ▶ swapAxes type Boolean: specifies whether to swap axes

D.4   Checkbox Component

Method	Description
getText	Returns the text with the CHECKBOX component.
isChecked	Returns True if the CHECKBOX component is selected or False if the CHECKBOX component is not selected.
isEnabled	Returns True if the CHECKBOX component is enabled.
isVisible	Returns True if the CHECKBOX component is visible.
setChecked	Selects the CHECKBOX component when the parameter is set to True. Otherwise, the CHECKBOX component is not selected. **Parameter** ▶ Checked type Boolean: specifies whether the CHECKBOX component should be checked or unchecked
setEnabled	Sets the CHECKBOX component to enabled when the parameter is True. Otherwise, it is disabled. **Parameter** ▶ Checked type Boolean: specifies whether the CHECKBOX component should be enabled or disabled
setText	Sets the CHECKBOX component text. **Parameter** ▶ Text type String: CHECKBOX component text

Method	Description
setVisible	Shows the component when the parameter is True, but not when it is False. **Parameter** ▶ Visible type Boolean: specifies whether to show or hide the component

D.5 Convert Component

Method	Description
floatToString	Converts a float number type value to a string and applies a formatting pattern. English local is standard, but you can apply your own formatting in a parameter.
floatToString-UsingLocale	Converts a float number type to a string and applies the local formatting pattern. You can set the number of decimals.
stringLength	Returns the length of the string type value given in the parameter.
stringToFloat	Converts a string type to a float number.
stringToFloat-UsingLocale	Converts a string type to a float number using the local formatting pattern.
stringToInt	Converts a string type to an integer.
Substring	Returns a substring of the original string based on the start and end positions set in the parameters.

D.6 Crosstab Component

Method	Description
removeSelection	If a cell is selected, this method will remove the selection.

Method	Description
getSelectedMember	Provides information about the dimension of a selected cell. **Parameter** ▶ Dimension type Dimension: dimension of the selected member

D.7 Data Source Alias Component

Method	Description
assignDataSource	Assigns a new data source to the alias. You can select a system, a query, and whether it has to load immediately. **Parameters** ▶ Datasourceconnection type Datasourceconnection: connection alias ▶ Datasourcetype type datasourcetype: type of data source ▶ Datasourcename type datasourcename: name of data source ▶ Optional loadnow type Boolean: specifies if the data source is loaded after assignment
assignHierarchy	Assigns a hierarchy to a dimension. **Parameters** ▶ Dimension type dimension: dimension to be displayed as hierarchy ▶ Hierarchy type hierarchy: hierarchy to be displayed
clearAllFilters	Removes all filters on all dimensions.
clearFilter	Removes filter for dimension. **Parameter** ▶ Dimension type dimension: dimension where filters need to be removed

Method	Description
getConditional-FormatValue	Gives the conditional format applied. 0 is no format. 1-9 is the priority. **Parameters** ▸ Measure type measure: measure corresponding to returned value ▸ Selection type multidimfilter: combination of dimension members in internal key format that specifies the data cell selection
getConditional-FormatValueExt	Gives the conditional format with the use of external format keys. **Parameters** ▸ Measure type measure: measure corresponding to returned value ▸ Selection type multidimfilter: combination of dimension members in internal key format that specify the data cell selection
getData	This results in the value of a single data cell from the dataset. A data cell holds information about the value, formatted value, scaling factor, and unit of measure. A DATA CELL is a component in itself; we will describe it in the next subsection. **Parameters** ▸ Measure type measure: measure corresponding to returned value ▸ Selection type multidimfilter: combination of dimension members in internal key format that specify the data cell selection
getDataAsString	This results in the return of a single data cell from the dataset with external member keys. **Parameters** ▸ Measure type measure: measure corresponding to returned value ▸ Selection type multidimfilter: combination of dimension members in internal key format that specify the data cell selection

Method	Description
getFilterText	This method results in the filter value of the filter in the dimension passed in the parameter. **Parameter** ▶ Dimension type Dimension: dimension of the data source
getFilterText	Returns the filter value of a dimension. As this method returns the text of the value, you use this for displaying the filter. **Parameter** ▶ Dimension type Dimension: dimension of the data source
getInfo	Returns data source information, for example, the key date or the technical name.
getMemberList	Returns a list of dimension members. **Parameters** ▶ Dimension type dimension: dimension of the data source ▶ memberPresentation type memberPresentation: presentation of the member keys ▶ memberDisplay type Memberdisplay: textual display of members ▶ Maxnumber type integer: maximum number of members to be returned ▶ Optional allmembertext type String: text of the item that represents all members
getStaticFilter-Ext	Returns the static filter value of a dimension. **Parameter** ▶ Dimension type dimension: dimension of the data source
getStaticFilter-Text	Returns the static filter value of a dimension. As this method returns the text of the value, you use it for displaying the filter. **Parameter** ▶ Dimension type dimension: dimension of the data source

Method	Description
getVariableValue-Ext	Returns the value of the variable in the external key format. **Parameter** ▶ Variable type variable: data source variable
getVariableValue-Text	Returns the value of the variable. Use this method to display the value of the variable. **Parameter** ▶ Variable type variable: data source variable
loadDataSource	Loads the assigned data source.
moveDimensionAfter	Adds the dimension after another dimension in the data source. **Parameters** ▶ Dimension type dimension: dimension to be added to the axis ▶ Otherdimension type dimension: dimension where the above dimension is placed after
moveDimensionBefore	Adds the dimension before another dimension in the data source. **Parameters** ▶ Dimension type dimension: dimension to be added to the axis ▶ Otherdimension type dimension: dimension where the above dimension is placed before
moveDimensionToColumns	Moves the dimension to a selected column in the data source. **Parameters** ▶ Dimension type dimension: dimension to be moved to a column ▶ Optional pos as integer: position on the axis
moveDimensionToRows	Moves the dimension to a selected row in the data source. **Parameters** ▶ Dimension type dimension: dimension to be moved to a row ▶ Optional pos as integer: position on the axis

Method	Description
reloadData	Reloads the data from the source. When the source data changes, this is a useful method.
removeDimension	Removes the dimension from the row or column. **Parameter** ▶ Dimension type dimension: dimension to be removed
setFilter	Sets a filter for a dimension in the internal key format. If there is already a filter on the dimension, that filter is removed. **Parameter** ▶ Dimension type dimension: dimension to be filtered ▶ Filter type array of filter: filter to be set
setFilterExt	Sets a filter for a dimension in the external key format. If there is already a filter on the dimension, that filter is removed. **Parameter** ▶ Dimension type dimension: dimension to be filtered ▶ Filter type array of filter: filter to be set
setMemberDisplay	Changes the member display for a data source dimension. Options are KEY, TEXT, KEY + TEXT, or TEXT + KEY. **Parameters** ▶ Dimension type dimension: dimension for which a member display is set ▶ Memberdisplay type memberdisplay: display mode of members
swapDimensions	Two dimensions change place. This only works when at least one of the dimensions is placed in the row or column. **Parameters** ▶ Dimension1 type dimension: first dimension to be swapped with dimension2 ▶ Dimension2 type dimension: second dimension to be swapped with dimension1

Method	Description
unassignHierarchy	Unassigns a hierarchy from the dimension. **Parameter** ▶ Dimension type dimension: dimension that should not be displayed as a dimension anymore

D.7.1 Data Cell Component

A DATA CELL component is an object providing information about a data cell or result set. This component is a result that is derived from methods such as datasource.getdata.

Method	Description
formattedvalue	The formatted value of this cell. The scaling factor has already been applied to this value. This value also reflects the user locale and number settings of the BEx Query Designer.
scalingFactor	Scaling factor in powers of 10 that has been applied to the value of this cell.
unitOfMeasure	Unit of measure of the value of this cell.
Value	Raw data value of this cell.

D.8 Date Field Component

Method	Description
getDate	Returns the date.
isEnabled	Returns True if the component is enabled.
setDate	Sets the date on the component. **Parameter** ▶ Date type string: date to be set in YYMMDD

449

Method	Description
setEnabled	Allows you to enable or disable the component. **Parameter** ▸ Enabled type Boolean: specifies whether the component should be enabled or disabled

D.9   Dimension Filter and Filter Panel Components

Method	Description
Cancel	Removes entered filters that haven't been submitted yet.
getDimensionName	The name of the dimension is returned (only with the DIMENSION FILTER component).
Submit	Applies the filter values that have been entered.

D.10   Image Component

Method	Description
getClickImage	Returns the path of the image file that is shown when clicked.
getHoverImage	Returns the path of the image file that is visible when the mouse hovers over the IMAGE component.
getImage	Returns the path of the image file that is initially visible.
getOpacity	Returns the opacity value. 0 is fully transparent; 100 is fully visible.
setClickImage	Sets the image file to show when the IMAGE component is clicked. **Parameter** ▸ Imageurl type String: path of image file

Method	Description
setHoverImage	Sets the image file to show when the mouse hovers over the IMAGE component. **Parameter** ▶ Imageurl type String: path of image file
setImage	Sets the main image. **Parameter** ▶ Imageurl type String: path of image file
setOpacity	Sets the opacity of the image. 0 is fully transparent; 100 is fully visible. **Parameter** ▶ Opacity type integer: sets opacity for image

D.11   Input Field Component

Method	Description
getValue	Returns the value that is entered in the INPUT FIELD component.
isEnabled	Returns True if the component is enabled or, otherwise, False.
setEnabled	Sets the component to enabled or disabled. **Parameter** ▶ Enabled type Boolean: specifies whether the component should be enabled or disabled
setValue	Sets the value of the INPUT FIELD component. **Parameter** ▶ Value type string: input value

D.12　Pagebook Component

Methods	Description
getSelectedPage	Returns the name of the currently selected page.
getSelectedPage-Index	Returns the index value of the selected page. If the first page is currently selected, then the index is 0.
setSelectedPage-ByName	Selects the page by passing the name of the page in the parameter. **Parameter** ▸ Name type string: name of the page to select
setSelectedPage-Index	Selects the page by passing the index number of the page in the parameter. **Parameter** ▸ Index type integer: index of the page to select

D.13　Panel Component

The PANEL component is a basic container that helps you to organize other components. Therefore, the PANEL component has only the .onClick method. A handler method allows you to run the script in a component from another component.

D.14　Popup Component

Methods	Description
hide	The POPUP component is not visible anymore.
isShowing	Returns True if the POPUP component is currently visible.
show	The POPUP component is visible.

D.15 Selection Components

The selection components are components where you can select a value from a list of members. These components are:

► LIST BOX

► RADIO BUTTON GROUP

► DROPDOWN BOX

Method	Description
getSelectedText	Returns the text of the selected item. Each item in the component has a key and an item.
getSelectedValue	Gets the selected value key.
isEnabled	Allows you to enable or disable the component.
setEnabled	The component can be set to enabled or disabled with this method. **Parameter** ► Enabled type Boolean: specifies whether the component should be enabled or disabled
setItems	Assigns a list of items to the components. If there were previous items in the list, these items are removed and replaced with the new items passed in the parameter. **Parameter** ► Value type valuetextlist: list of value-text pairs
setSelectedValue	Sets the status selected to the item with the specified key. **Parameter** ► Value type listvalue: value of the item to be selected
Sort	Sorts the items in alphabetical order. An optional parameter can be used to set the list in descending order. **Parameter** ► Optional asc type Boolean: specifies if the sortorder is ascending or descending

453

D.16 Tabstrip Component

Method	Description
getSelectedTab	Returns the name of the currently selected tab.
getSelectedTabIn-dex	Returns the index value of the selected tab. If the first page is currently selected, then the index is 0.
setSelectedTab-ByName	Selects the tab by passing the name of the page in the parameter. **Parameter** ▸ Name type string: name of the tab to be selected
setSelectedTabIn-dex	Selects the tab by passing the index number of the page in the parameter. **Parameter** ▸ Index type integer: tab to be selected

D.17 Text Component

Method	Description
getText	Returns the text currently in the TEXT component.
setText	Sets the text that is shown in the TEXT component. **Parameter** ▸ Text type string: text to set in the component

D.18 Visual Components: Common Methods

Method	Description
getBottomMargin	Gives the bottom margin of the component as long as BOTTOM MARGIN is set to a number (not AUTO).
getCSSClass	Returns the CSS class that is assigned to the component.
getHeight	Returns the height of the component as long as HEIGHT is set to a number (not AUTO).

Method	Description
getLeftMargin	Returns the left margin of the component as long as LEFT MARGIN is set to a number (not AUTO).
getRightMargin	Returns the right margin of the component as long as RIGHT MARGIN is set to a number (not AUTO).
getTopMargin	Returns the top margin of the component as long as TOP MARGIN is set to a number (not AUTO).
getWidth	Returns the width of the component as long as WIDTH is set to a number (not AUTO).
isVisible	Returns whether the component is visible (True) or not (False).
setBottomMargin	Sets the bottom margin as long as BOTTOM MARGIN is set to a number (not AUTO).
setCSSClass	Sets the CSS class of the component.
setHeight	Sets the height of the component as long as HEIGHT is set to a number (not AUTO).
setLeftMargin	Sets the left margin of the component as long as LEFT MARGIN is set to a number (not AUTO).
setRightMargin	Sets the right margin of the component as long as RIGHT MARGIN is set to a number (not AUTO).
setTopMargin	Sets the top margin of the component as long as TOP MARGIN is set to a number (not AUTO).
setVisible	Sets the visibility of the component based on the parameter value (True or False). **Parameter** ▶ Visible type Boolean: specifies whether to show or hide the component
setWidth	Sets the width of the component as long as WIDTH is set to a number (not AUTO).

E   The Authors

Xavier Hacking is an SAP BI specialist from Eindhoven, the Netherlands, and works as a consultant for Interdobs. He has a master's degree in Industrial Engineering and Management Science from the Eindhoven University of Technology. He has worked with a wide range of products from the current SAP NetWeaver BW and SAP BusinessObjects BI toolset, with a focus on dashboard development within SAP environments.

Xavier co-authored *SAP BusinessObjects Dashboards 4.0 Cookbook* and is a writer for *SAP BusinessObjects Expert* magazine. He is also part of the Dutch BI Podcast, and blogs on all sorts of business-intelligence-related topics at *http://www.hackingsap.com*. You can follow him on Twitter at *@xjhacking*.

Jeroen van der A is a passionate SAP BI consultant from the Netherlands working for Interdobs. He has over 15 years of experience with business intelligence and started using SAP products in 2005. Jeroen is focused on finding innovative ways to use BI products to create added value, and uses a broad range of products to achieve this goal.

Jeroen is a writer for the Dutch SAP user magazine *VNSG* and is part of the Dutch BI Podcast. He writes regular blogs on *http://scn.sap.com* and on *http://www.interdobs.nl*. You can follow him on Twitter at *@hyronimous*.

Index

E

F

- Create interactive dashboards with the tool also known as Xcelsius

- Understand how to use SAP BusinessObjects Dashboards in an SAP environment

- 2nd Edition Updated for release 4.0

Ray Li, Evan DeLodder

Creating Dashboards with SAP BusinessObjects
The Comprehensive Guide

With this comprehensive guide to SAP BusinessObjects Dashboards, your job just got easier. Learn how to use the tool formerly known as Xcelsius to build effective, visually appealing dashboards that display crucial information in an easy-to-digest format. This is the reference both SAP and non-SAP users need to learn about all the features of SAP BusinessObjects Dashboards 4.0 and 4.1. With its fully illustrated content and detailed instructions, this one-stop guide is your ticket to becoming a Dashboards expert.

679 pp., 2. edition 2012, 59,95 Euro / US$ 59.95
ISBN 978-1-59229-410-7
www.sap-press.com

Galileo Press

■ Your one-stop reference for all things WebI: queries, reporting, and analysis

■ Integrate Web Intelligence with multiple data sources and platforms

■ Learn about mobility analytics for Web Intelligence

■ 2nd edition updated and expanded for release 4.0

Jim Brogden, Heather Sinkwitz, Mac Holden, Dallas Marks, Gabriel Orthous

SAP BusinessObjects Web Intelligence
The Comprehensive Guide

Revolutionize your company's data presentation with SAP BusinessObjects Web Intelligence 4.0 with new flexibility and functionalities. This comprehensive guide will help you build a foundational understanding of WebI by beginning with the fundamentals; or you can jump straight into the advanced discussions that are new to the latest release, including advanced charting, advanced formula writing, and report scheduling and distribution.

591 pp., 2. edition 2012, 79,95 Euro / US$ 79.95
ISBN 978-1-59229-430-5
www.sap-press.com

■ Understand the specifics of running SAP BusinessObjects BI products on top of SAP NetWeaver BW and SAP ERP data

■ Learn how to set up your SAP NetWeaver system for SAP Crystal Reports, SAP BusinessObjects Dashboards, and more

Ingo Hilgefort

Integrating SAP BusinessObjects BI Platform 4.x with SAP NetWeaver

Take full advantage of the benefits offered by SAP BusinessObjects XI by learning how best to integrate it with SAP NetWeaver. With this book, you'll learn about the integration process for each of the XI tools. If you are a BI administrator, consultant, or developer involved in the integration of SAP BusinessObjects XI and SAP NetWeaver, this is the resource you need to answer your questions.

437 pp., 2. edition 2012, 79,95 Euro / US$ 79.95
ISBN 978-1-59229-395-7
www.sap-press.com

■ Learn about the capabilities of the different reporting and analysis tools from SAP BusinessObjects

■ Determine which tool is the right choice for your business intelligence needs

■ Build your first report with each of the SAP BusinessObjects products

Ingo Hilgefort

Reporting and Analysis with SAP BusinessObjects

Get started with SAP BusinessObjects business intelligence tools! This book will teach you about all the features and functionalities offered in the SAP BusinessObjects XI 4.x toolset. Take advantage of the reporting and analytics capabilities of SAP BusinessObjects, and learn how they can be used to satisfy specific business reporting requirements. This book tells you everything you need to know, and then shows how it can be applied via practical, real-life examples.

501 pp., 2. edition 2012, 79,95 Euro / US$ 79.95
ISBN 978-1-59229-387-2
www.sap-press.com

Interested in reading more?

Please visit our website for all new
book and e-book releases from SAP PRESS.

www.sap-press.com